Two Loves:

The Story of a Baseball Polygamist

By Joey Buchholz

ISBN   978-0-615-26879-8

Cover Design by Sheena Luckett
Cover Photo by Heather Nelson
Back Cover Photo by Amber Kavelaris
Printing by Ikon Office Solutions
Binding by City Press, Inc.
2009

This book is dedicated to my daughter, Grace Naomi Buchholz, and my niece, Gina Grace Conigliaro, my two loves.

You each remind me everyday that life is beautiful.

ii

Very special thanks to…

My mom, Nina Conigliaro (you are my idol, and I thank you for all of your support), my dad, James Buchholz (thank you so much for making this book a reality), my sister, Jill Buchholz (the biggest Brewers fan I know), and my Grandma, who is with me every day.

Amber Kavelaris, Sheena Luckett, Mike Schwingle, Heather Nelson, the Prude family, Jed Hanson, Tracy and Kathy Norrell, Brian Hancock, Jesus Maldonado-Reyes, Alberto Maldonado, Demond Stewart, Steven Forst, Danny Forst, Randy Goree, Bob Buege, Neal Pease, Jamie Armata, Susan O'Connor, Nate Wolf, Kelly Bell, Andy Gilson, Hope Sterken, Sue D'Amato, Todd Kemper, Michael Weber, Lisa Hare, Joe Dahms, Matt Sathoff, John Koloske, Diane DeLeon, Matt Weiss, Dave Reinholdt, Matt Schewe, John Paly, Addy and Carmen Bonnetti, Star Watson, Tiffany Herrera, Kate Adametz-Jenkins, Rob and Frank Crivello, Jeff Martinkoski, Pat Kacmarynski, the Hohlweck family, the Fefer family, the Moser family, William Horstman, Karen and William Dredge, Erik Hemming, the great folks at Tomaso's in Mequon, Mark Mollenhauer and the gang at Leonardo's in Mequon, my coworkers at UW Credit Union and the many employees and students of the University of Wisconsin-Milwaukee.

Also to Linda Levenhagen, who showed me how exciting it is to experience life's "firsts".

And finally, to James Redding, who asks me each day, "Do you want to be right, or do you want to be happy?" I want to be happy, James. I want to be happy.

Table of Contents

Introduction

Before the 1998 season, the Brewers and Mets had never played each other, not even in a Spring Training game. I never once had to choose between the two on any given night. Of course, this all changed when the Brewers moved to the National League. Since then, I've had a personal policy to cheer for the home team when the two teams compete against each other. I made an exception to this policy on July 31, 2007. For this was the night that Tom Glavine would go for win #300 at Miller Park. I made the decision to buy a ticket down the 3rd base line, and I would be wearing my Mets cap and road jersey, for the first time ever, openly rooting for the opponent of the Brewers in their own park. I wasn't rooting *against* the Brewers that night. Never have, never will. But I did want to see history made. I would have done the same if Ben Sheets were going for #300 in New York. OK, #200. This just in : Sheets has 73 big league victories in his first seven seasons...I would have done the same if Ben Sheets were going for his (gulp) 100th win in New York (but don't quote me on that).

As it turns out, my buddy Andy also had a ticket to that game, in the same section, none the less. We talked about the upcoming game all day at work. I reminded him several times that I'm not rooting against the Brewers, but rather *for* the Mets, and Glavine's pursuit of history. He respects my stance, but naturally, wanted to see the Brewers hold on to, or even extend their lead in the National League Central. Coming into the night, the Brewers were hanging on to a one game lead over the Cubs, and the Mets had a 3 game cushion on the Phillies.

I decided when I got to the ballpark that I would score the game, with the idea of one day getting Glavine to sign my scorecard, and I could one day hang it on my Mets wall. Shortly after I sat down, Andy arrived with a couple of friends, and we chatted for a bit. We both commented on the number of Mets fans that were sitting in our section. It looked like it was pretty close to 50/50 Brewers/Mets fans. His seats were directly behind mine, about six rows back, so it was going to be easy to talk to each other non-verbally during the game through a series of gentlemanly fist pumps, mouthed "wow's", and even a few Jordan-esque "I just made my sixth 3 pointer in the first half of Game 1 of the NBA Finals vs Portland" shoulder shrugs when something great happened. The Brewers carried a 1-0 lead in the 6th inning, with Jeff Suppan on the hill for the crew. Suppan surprised the baseball world by leaving the World Champion St Louis Cardinals, and signing a four year contract with the Brewers on Christmas Eve, 2006. He looked great tonight, but the Mets got to him for two runs in the top half of the sixth. Glavine had a 2-1 lead going into the bottom of the 7th. Coming into the inning, he had only given up one base hit, but he had walked five, and his pitch count was hovering around 95. The first Milwaukee hitter in the 7th was Damien Miller, and he promptly singled to center. Mets manager Willie Randolph came calling, signaling for Aaron Heilman to hold this one, and Glavine's night was done. He was greeted to a standing ovation by Mets and Brewers fans alike. Glavine tipped his cap to the capacity crowd of 41,790, and I shed a tear and clapped for a guy I openly rooted against from 1991 to 2002, while an Atlanta Brave. If Heilman could hold on in the 7th, the stage would be set for Glavine to win #300. And that he did, getting Tony Graffanino to ground into a 3-6-3 double play, and retiring Corey Hart after a Craig Counsell bunt single.   The Mets were six outs away from securing the win for old number 47. But it wasn't meant to be, as Bill Hall hit a ground rule double in the bottom of the 8th to tie the game, ruining any chance of Glavine getting #300 tonight. I had mixed emotions. I was upset that I wouldn't witness history tonight, but inside, I was really proud of Bill Hall, and the way he stepped up for the crew. I was really hard on Hall after he came up to the big leagues, but always believed in him. It's great to see him coming around as a well rounded ball player, who quite frankly, has done everything the Brewers have asked of him, and I hope he's around for a long, long time. At this time, I stopped scoring the game, looked back at Andy and gave him a wink, and took a moment to think to myself just how much fun I was having this evening. The fun was just getting started…

The Brewers held serve in the top of the 9th, setting up some serious drama in the bottom half. Geoff Jenkins, who doesn't hit lefties well, did not get the start tonight, but was asked to pinch hit for Francisco Cordero to lead off the inning. He was walked. We then witnessed something that I don't think I've seen in the Yost era. Corey Hart sacrificed Jenkins to 2nd, and reached safely on a Carlos Delgado error. J.J. Hardy then sacrificed himself to set up 2nd and 3rd with one out. Two consecutive sacrifices!! We ARE in the National League after all! The stage was set for Ryan Braun, who in just over 2 months in the bigs, is already turning heads, and I'll have you know, has had quite an effect on my little sister, Jill. I haven't seen her this smitten since Donnie Wahlberg. The Mets decide to take their chances with Braun, rather than walk him to set up a bases loaded and one out situation vs Prince Fielder, the NL leader in home runs. The crowd is electric, and you can tell Braun is locked in on the Mets pitcher, Jorge Sosa. He gets in some monster cuts, but goes down swinging. Naturally, the Mets walk Fielder intentionally, while boos are flooding the ballpark. Bill Hall steps up with the bases juiced, two outs, and the game on the line. Hall proceeds to rip a liner to center, and it looks like he's done it again, however, Lastings Milledge makes an incredible diving catch to strand the bases loaded, and we're heading to extra frames. I look back at Andy, and we're both amazed at what we've just seen. It's at this point that I realize that Michael Weber, a colleague of ours who works in Madison, is standing in between us, and to our right. He notices me, and is visibly upset that I'm draped in orange and blue.

In the top of the 10th, Matt Wise walked the first two Mets batters he faced, David Wright and Carlos Delgado. Yost scurried out, visibly upset, and yanked his struggling righty in favor of Brian Shouse. Wise clearly hasn't been the same since he hit Pedro Lopez six days ago in Cincinnati. Shouse comes through, getting Moises Alou to hit into a 6-4-3 double play, leaving Wright at 3rd with 2 out. Chris Spurling relieved Shouse and got Damien Easley swinging to the end the Mets half of the 10th. The Brewers went down 1-2-3 in the 10th, and would strand runners in scoring position in the 11th and 12th innings, leaving Andy and I to wonder how long we could stay, for we had a 7:30 am meeting the following morning. I decided that I'm here for the long haul. I can't come this far, and leave, after all that's happened. In the top of the 13th, Yost called upon Dave Bush, who was to start for the Brewers the following night. Bush allowed an infield hit to lead off the inning, but set the next three down in order. With Aaron Sele now entering his 3rd inning of work for the Mets in the 13th, Tony Graffanino led off the inning with a towering double to deep left. The Mets decided to pitch to Geoff Jenkins, instead of walking him to set up the double play.   Jenkins responded by promptly depositing a 1-2 fastball into the right field bleachers (barely clearing the right field fence) to beat the Mets on a walk off HR. The crowd was going nuts, I looked back at Andy and Michael, they were ecstatic, and while I was "the enemy" tonight, I couldn't help but pump the little fist in my head when I saw Jenkins embraced at home by his teammates. As I stood there, I forgot about standings, records, milestones and alliances and came to the realization that I had never had more fun at a game. And though I was always thought it would be hard to watch a Mets/Brewers playoff series, because of the eventual heartbreak for one team, I was hoping for just that.

Walking back to my car the night of the Glavine game, I couldn't help but wonder what a joy it would be to have the Mets and Brewers play each other in the N.L.C.S. later that year. It really felt like that was a possibility. At one point, each team had an 8 game lead in their respective divisions. But things would slowly fall apart, as each teams' lead would dwindle. My thinking started to lean toward, "just having them each make the playoffs in the same year would be really cool", and after the Brewers fell out of contention with 3 days left in the season, I thought, "we just need the Mets to hold on, and we're going to the Series". The Mets ended up blowing a seven game lead with seventeen to play, and their season came down to a Sunday afternoon game vs the Marlins. If they win, they would force a one game playoff. Lose, and their done. They got killed. I was numb for about a week. It wasn't the same feeling I had when Beltran left the bat on his shoulder vs Wainwright, but it was also along the lines of, "What the hell??"

Shortly after the season, a season that ended with the Boston Red Sox sweeping the World Series for the 2nd time in four years, there were rumblings about the Sox being the favorite to land Johan Santana in a trade with the Minnesota Twins. The rich get richer. The Yankees were also in the mix, and the Mets were considered in the running, but a long shot. The Sox were offering Jon Lester or Jacoby Ellsbury, but not both, and they fell out of the running. The Yankees were offering Phillip Hughes and Melky Cabrera, but soon pulled out of the sweepstakes. This opened the door for the Mets to steal Santana away, and they offered the Twins Carlos Gomez and three young pitching prospects, including Phil Humber, the Mets 1st round draft pick in 2004. After agreeing to the trade, the Mets were given 72 hours to finalize an extension, and used every second of those hours, plus an extension of two hours, to offer Santana a 6 year, $137 million contract, with an option for 2014. After passing his physical, Santana was introduced as the newest Met on February 2nd, 2008. Santana will join Pedro Martinez, John Maine, Oliver Perez and Orlando Hernandez in the starting rotation this year, replacing…Tom Glavine. Guys like Jose Reyes, David Wright and Carlos Beltran should have no problem scoring runs for the staff, and Ryan Church and Brian Schneider, both acquired in a trade with the Washington Nationals, should add much needed veteran leadership to a very talented Mets team.

After the Brewers collapse, many wondered if Ned Yost would return to the helm as Brewers skipper. Yost would get an extension, and the Brewers turned there focus to improving their team defense, their bullpen, and adding key role players to a great young lineup that lead the National League in home runs in 2007. For a team that finished two games out of their division, improving their defense was priority #1 for the crew. NL Rookie of the Year, Ryan Braun, welcomed a possible move to LF, to allow the Brewers to move Bill Hall back to the infield to play 3rd base. The signing of Mike Cameron to play center field instantly improved the defense at two positions, and now puts Ryan Braun at a position where we won't feel compelled to replace him defensively late in games. After losing out to the Reds in the Francisco Cordero sweepstakes, the Brewers set their sights on former NL Cy Young, Eric Gagne. Gagne accepted a 1 year deal, worth $10 million, and would assume the role as closer for the upcoming season. The crew also brought in a number of other fresh arms, namely David Riske, Solomon Torres and Guillermo Moto to join Derrick Turnbow, Brian Shouse and Seth McClung in a vastly improved bullpen from 2007, even with the loss of CoCo. Prince Fielder, the reigning NL Home Run King, anchors one of the great young infields in the majors, which includes Rickie Weeks, J.J. Hardy and Hall. Add Jason Kendall's veteran leadership and patience at the plate, not to mention how he will handle the staff of Ben Sheets, Jeff Suppan, Dave Bush, Yovani Gallardo and Carlos Villaneuva, and you have the makings of a team that could do some great things in the National League Central in 2008.

Both the Mets and the Brewers represent pieces of me that are linked to the past, present and future, but more importantly, are the reasons that I embrace America's past time. It is impossible for me to place one team ahead of the other, and with the 2008 season drawing near, I plan to follow both with equal passion. If I have one wish, the Mets and Brewers will face each other in the National League Championship Series in October of 2008. For those of you that secretly pledge allegiance to two teams, and can sympathize with my undying love for this game, and cannot live without it, this is as much your story as it is mine. I hope you enjoy following the season with me, as you get inside the mind of a man who has, and will always have...

Two Loves

1. The Promise of a New Season

March 29th

  This very well may be my favorite weekend of the entire year. The NCAA Tournament is in full swing, and by tomorrow evening, we will have our Final Four in tact. WrestleMania XXIV is tomorrow night, and of course, the major league baseball season kicks off on Sunday night, with the Braves visiting Nationals Park, the brand new home of the Washington Nationals. Yes, the Sox and A's "officially" kicked the season off in Japan this past Tuesday, but the games started at 5:00 am my time, and as it turns out, I couldn't get the games on directv for whatever reason. I did see about six innings of the Tuesday game while at the gym, but it just didn't "feel" like Opening Day. They split their two games, flew 18 hours back to the states, and still had to play a handful of spring training games before their seasons resumed. I am currently watching the Mets and White Sox play in the 2nd annual Civil Rights Game on ESPN. It's appropriate that they chose these two teams, as the Mets have a Hispanic general manager and African-American manager, and the Chi-Sox have an African-American general manager and a Hispanic manager. I've been looking forward to this game for a few months. It looks like Memphis got a lot of rain today, and there aren't as many people in attendance as I would have guessed.

  With the start of the Mets and Brewers seasons just two days away, I'm getting those butterflies I get each and every spring. I am very excited for this season to start for many reasons. 2008 is the last year at Shea Stadium for the Mets. There have been so many great moments at Shea.....none greater than Game Six. I got to see my first game at Shea last year. I flew out there on a Friday morning, ate lunch at the ESPN Zone in Manhattan, took the 7 to Shea and met my friend Jesus for the Mets game against the Reds. How appropriate that the first game I see in person at Shea pits the same two teams that played the very first time I saw a Mets game on TV. Before I could find my seat, however, the Mets were down 4-0, as Brandon Phillips was hitting a grand slam off of John Maine. We ended up losing, but I loved the experience and I really took everything in. I was in awe of the stadium's history, but I was not in awe of the building. But I used to think County Stadium was dungy and dirty, and now I miss it a ton. At the same time, I love Miller Park, and can't wait to see Citi Field in 2009. I'm sure when Shea is torn down, I'll get emotional. I will be back one last time this July, as I will be attending the Last Play at Shea on July 16th. I've seen Billy Joel a number of times, but this will be the first time seeing him in New York. I cannot wait!

This is also the season the Brewers had targeted as being a serious contender when hiring Ned Yost before the 2003 season. Since that time, we've put together one of the most potent lineups in the majors, and we've started to spend the money necessary to build a winner. I purchased a full season ticket package for this season. We have four tickets for every game, up in the Terrace Reserve. It won't be possible to see all the games, so I have sold a number of the games to various friends and co-workers. One day, when money allows me to, I'll keep all the games, and have a draft much like Jimmy Fallon in Fever Pitch. I want to see Schwingle dance for those Giants games.

My dream this season is too see the Mets and Brewers win their respective divisions and culminate with a meeting in the National League Championship Series, wait, hold the phone....Brady Clark is a Met? Brady Clark just lined out to short. I guess Brady Clark is a Met.   He signed a minor league contract on Feb 15th, and may make the team. We'll keep an eye on that. Moving on… I'm going to spend the next six (hopefully seven) months documenting their seasons….Beltran just went yard, and the Mets lead 2-0 in the 4th.   I've purchased the Extra Innings package on directv to follow the Mets last season at Shea, and I've got Bob Uecker in my ear all season to tell the Brewers story.

I always tell people that I was born into the Brewers, but I married the Mets. The Brewers are my brother, and the Mets are my lover. The Brewers hold my head over the toilet after a night of drinking and sex with the Mets. Metaphors, people. These are metaphors!! What I'm trying to say is that I love both teams, but the relationships I have with each team are different. I'd love to see them face each other for the chance to represent the Senior Circuit in the Fall Classic.

The Mets held on to win today, 3-2. They are the 2008 Civil Rights Champions of the World!

March 30th

I was up late last night, watching the WWE Hall of Fame Ceremony. We miss you, Rock, and Naitch; you are and always will be The Man. We have a full slate of fun scheduled for today. The final two Regional Final games are tipping off shortly. I need Texas and Davidson to win to have any chance at coin this year. WrestleMania starts around 5:30, and the Braves and Nationals will christen Nationals Park at 7:00. Pizza will be consumed, cokes will wash down said pizza and good times will be had.

In between reading up about tomorrow's pitching matchups, I'm chasing my daughter around. She likes to pull DVD's off of the entertainment center, and I'm very particular about my media, so I warn her to not play with daddy's DVD's. She proceeds to pull *Funny Farm* off the shelf. *Funny Farm*? You own *Funny Farm*, Heather? Did you make a special trip, seeking this out, asking for this by name? Were they sold out of copies of *Vacation*? Did you mean to grab *Fletch*, and were too embarrassed to bring back *Funny Farm*? Walk me through the thought process. Certainly, you didn't wake up that morning, and after a shower and breakfast, create a to-do list that included the phrase, "pick up copy of *Funny Farm* on digital video disc". Really, Heather? Really?

The Mets will kick off the Johan Santana era on the road vs the Florida Marlins and Mark Hendrickson. The two questions on the mind of every Mets fan are, 1) Does Brady Clark make this team and 2) Will he wear #93 if he does. Expectations are high with the Santana acquisition, especially after the way the Mets seasons ended the past two seasons. The Phillies look to be the other great team coming out of this division, and it'll be great to see these two teams go at it eighteen times over the next six months.

The Brewers open up the 2008 Season vs the hated Cubs at Wrigley Field. It'll be Ben Sheets, making his sixth opening day start for the crew, vs Carlos Zambrano. They are expecting rain tomorrow, but hopefully they can get it in. I'll be leaving shortly to get the pizzas for tonight. Opening day is less than 24 hours away, but tonight, Ric Flair walks that aisle, one more time. Wooo!

March 31st

Opening Day! Nothing like it....It's the promise of a new season, everyone is in first place (well, actually, the Mets are a ½ game behind the Nationals after Ryan Zimmerman's bomb last night), and tons of fans are making their last minute "sick" calls to work. I decided to come to work today. I wanted to listen to Opening Day with my boys, Andy and Joe. Andy and I were supposed to present to some students today on campus, but nobody showed up, so we went down to the Gasthaus and got to see the top of the 1st inning. They always say the season's first batter will indicate how the season will go, and Rickie Weeks went down on three pitches. Ouch.....off to a bad start. We shared some nachos and the pizza that I bought for the students, talked baseball for a bit, and headed back upstairs after a scoreless 1st. The game experienced a couple of rain delays, and was scoreless until the top of the 9th. When Ryan Braun drove in the game's first run, many fists were pumping in our office. When Corey Hart drove in two on a long triple, it looked as if the crew would pull off an Opening Day coup. Gagne came on to close in the 9th as I was leaving the office, and before I got to Capitol Drive.......single, walk, 3-run homer, we're tied. He eventually got out of the inning, but this was certainly not the way you want to start out with a new team. Craig Counsell pinch-hit for Gagne in the 10th, and promptly doubled to lead off the inning. Jason Kendall, hitting in the 9 hole (and this is why), sacrificed Counsell to 3rd, setting up a Tony Gwynn sacrifice fly to take the lead, as I'm pulling into the parking lot. When I got home, I was able to see David Riske shut the door to give the Brewers a 4-3 Opening Day win over the Cubs. Despite Gagne's choke job, a great win for the Brewers.

The Mets started the season in Florida, and put up a six spot in the 4th inning, led by David Wright's 3 run double. I joked with Joe at the office on Johan Santana sitting down the first 9 men he faced, but begged that he not say those words you don't say when a guy is perfect. In hindsight, maybe the 4th inning is too early to jinx anything, but sure enough, Josh Willingham would homer moments later. The Mets would go on to win, 7-2, and all is well in the world.

I had my last of five fantasy drafts tonight. I ended up with 4 Mets (Reyes, Beltran, Maine and Martinez). I drafted John Maine in all five of my drafts; so naturally, I'm thinking this year he goes 27-3 with a 1.31 ERA. I promise not to saturate this book with a ton of wrestling references, but while I was drafting, I watched the Ric Flair farewell on RAW, and it was the coolest thing that the WWE has done in a long time. It was great to see the Four Horsemen, and everyone on the roster came out to pay their respect.

It was a great day. The Brewers and Mets each start their seasons with big road victories. I got to share lunch and some laughs with a good friend, drafted a competitive team and bawled my eyes out with Flair. Valvano was right. If you laugh, you think and you cry - that *is* a heck of a day. I'll even forgive my sister for FORGETTING THAT OPENING DAY WAS TODAY! You just heard what I said.....

April 1st

The Brewers have today off, and resume their series with the Cubs tomorrow afternoon, as Jeff Suppan takes on Ted Lilly. Tonight, the Mets are playing game two at Florida, as Pedro

Martinez takes the hill. I had planned to watch this game, but as I walked in the door, my wife surprised me by having a steak dinner ready, with all the fixings (baked potato, mushrooms, salad). What a great surprise! And as I was about to sit down to dinner, my mom knocked on the door to pick up Gracie. She was asked if she'd like to watch her tonight, so we can have a nice dinner for two. Although the baseball season is barely a day old, I'm not going to pass up steaks! We enjoyed a wonderful dinner, had a lot to talk about, we made each other laugh....it really felt like old times. I was lost in her beauty, and I leaned over to kiss her. She kissed me back, and this led to a night of sweet love making. I didn't see an inning of the game. (april fools !!!)

Got home, dropped a deuce, made a sandwich, had the game on as I played basketball with Gracie. We came back from 4-0 down to tie it, only to drop it in extras when Matt Wise allowed a walk off to some guy I've never heard of. Oh, and Pedro is lost for a month to a pulled hammy...time for bed.

April 2nd

I promised myself when I committed to writing this book that I would limit the number of, "woke up, took a shit, checked my e-mail" references to a minimum. Kevin Smith already wrote that book, and for the record, I loved every word of it. But, this will be consecutive days that I do just that (hopefully, we're all set until at least mid-May). Today, I'm deucin' it on my lunch break, and I notice that someone has spray painted, "God is not real" on the back of the bathroom stall, in hot pink, none the less. Three thoughts came to me. 1) People get really opinionated after eating taco bell, 2) What ever happened to word of mouth? Did the guy buy the pink spray paint specifically for this poignant message?, and 3) He must have been a Cubs fan.

It's been exactly 100 years since the Cubs last won the World Series. To offer some perspective, in 1908, a first class stamp was 2 cents, the first Model T automobile sold for $850, and it would still be twelve years before the NFL was founded.

The Cubs have been pegged as the favorites to take the NL Central this year by many publications, and today, Ted Lilly takes the hill in an attempt to bounce back from Monday's extra innings loss to the crew. Jeff Suppan is going for the Brewers. It's another day game, which means we'll have it on the radio while we enable financial dreams. Joe admits to me that he's getting excited about baseball. We each have DIRECTV extra innings free this week, and we both caught a couple of innings of Scully calling the Giants/Dodgers game last night. Honestly, I could listen to Scully argue with his neighbors, and it would sound beautiful to me. While Jim Powell is giving us the staring lineups, Joe says that he can't wait to hear the first home run call of the year by Uecker. He left for a minute, and on the very first pitch of the game, Rickie Weeks took Lilly deep. As the ball is flying out of Wrigley, I'm motioning for Joe to hurry back from the other side. He knew right away. This would be the start of something big, as the Brewers went on to pound out 14 hits in an 8-2 win over the Cubs. Ryan Braun and Jason Kendall would combine for 6 of those hits, and 4 RBI. Jeff Suppan went 6 1/3, gave up 2 earned, for the Brewers second consecutive quality start. I told Joe that the starting pitching has been "lights out", and we argued for a bit as to what "lights out" meant. I'd consider a 1.38 ERA on the road vs the Cubs lights out, wouldn't you? The bullpen has also looked great, with the exception of Gagne, whose appearance on Monday afternoon was "lights on". I have to give Joe full credit for that line. The brooms will be out tomorrow as we go for the sweep!

The Mets bounced back tonight in a huge way to trounce the Fish, 13-0. Ryan Church hit the first Mets homer of the year, and David Wright added a 3-run bomb in the 6th. Oliver Perez pitched six shutout innings, striking out eight, and walking only one batter. The Mets announcing team is doing something this year where they are taking calls during select games, and someone called to ask Keith Hernandez which hat he'd wear, the Cardinals or Mets, if he ever made the Hall of Fame. In 2004, Hernandez received less than 5% of the votes needed to stay eligible, but may be considered for induction by the Veterans Committee in 2011. He said it was a tough question, and reminded "John" from Long Island that MLB decides what hat you wear, and he has no say in it. He eventually said, "I like the color blue, so I'll say Mets", but he really seemed torn between the two franchises. See, I'm not alone, world.

April 3rd

Walks. Walks! Too many walks!! Dave Bush walked five today, and hit another, including a bases loaded free pass to give the Cubs the lead for good, as the Brewers lost to the Cubs, 6-3. The game got off to a great start as two runs scored on a Prince Fielder sacrifice fly in the 1st. Rickie Weeks barreled over Cubs catcher Geovany Soto, forcing the ball to pop away, and allowing Tony Gwynn's son to score as well. The Cubs would get 2 back in the 2nd, took the lead in the 4th, and never looked back. The Brewers will now head back to Milwaukee for the home opener, which I will now be attending. Originally, my sister was going to use the tickets, but fate determined that I would hit for the "sausage cycle" tomorrow. For those of you wondering, the sausage cycle is when you have a dog, brat, Polish, Italian and chorizo during one game. I have been challenged to accomplish this feat once this year. It probably won't happen, on a count that I'm trying to lose some of the weight. I've actually lost nine pounds since March 10th, but I very may well gain seven back tomorrow. I'll be meeting Jamie at 11:00, and walking to the park from his house.

The Mets are off tonight, and will open a three game series with Atlanta tomorrow night. All is quiet on the home front. I left for an hour to workout, and when I got home, my daughter asked for music, and fell asleep on my chest three songs into Glass Houses. She's sleeping now. Not much going on in the majors tonight. Think I'm gonna watch some Curb Your Enthusiasm, and maybe make a Ted Danson sandwich.....

April 4th

I woke up this morning equally excited and sore. I'm excited, naturally, for today's home opener, and sore from my workout last night. Some days, I miss the love affair I had with a lady named, "Laying Around While Shoveling French Onion Dip In My Mouth". Yes, that was her full name. The plan this morning is to leave the house around 9:45, grab some snacks for the tailgate, and get to Jamie's house around 11:00. I arrive at Jamie's place a little late, due to some much expected Opening Day traffic. Before we leave, Jamie has to make sure that the DVR properly recorded the New Kids on the Block on the Today Show for his wife. Once this is confirmed, I grab the Spicy Chili Doritos and Dill Pickle Lays, and we start walking to the park.

Once we get there, we decide to skip the tailgate, and head right in. We notice immediately that there is a new Brewers Team Store located at the home plate entrance. I was thinking an impulse buy was in the works, but as quickly as I saw the $130 price tag on the hooded sweatshirt I was looking at, those thoughts escaped me faster than Clarke putting his wallet away as Eddie asked for $52,000. We walked around for a bit, and when we realized that Gorman wasn't at Gorman's Corner, we decided to go up to our seats. We took a moment to see what kind of view we'd have for the season, and I'm happy with the seats. We are behind the plate, about a section or two over towards third base, with no obstructions and a great view of the scoreboard. After soaking in the beauty, we decide it's time for the season's first dogs. There's nothing like the first dog of the season. I knew coming into today that the concession prices were increasing, what I didn't know was that the item "hot dog" would not be on the menu. For a second, it felt like Wally World was closed. For those of you scoring at home, that is 3 *Vacation* references thus far, and the first pitch of the home opener hasn't been thrown yet. It may be a long book if you're not a Chase fan. I was used to seeing "hot dog" and "kosher dog", and this year, I see "kiddie dog" and "jumbo dog". I initially thought they scrapped the kosher dog, and made much larger and much smaller versions of what I've grown to love. It turns out, they just changed the names. The kosher dog is now the jumbo dog, and the hot dog is now the kiddie dog. I will now have to say, "Two kiddie dogs" when ordering for myself. I can't wait for the day when my daughter asks why I eat the kiddie dogs. I chased two dogs with a brat, and washed it down with a tasty Miller Lite, and was now officially ready for baseball!

As the starting lineups were being announced, I mentioned to Jamie how little I knew about the San Francisco Giants, and that it looked like Carlos Villanueva would only have to record nine major league outs to throw a perfect game.

"Nine, maybe twelve if you count Jose Castillo", said Jamie. Despite being a Brewer killer while with the Pirates, he failed to beat out Jorge Cantu and Alfredo Amezaga for the Marlins 3rd base job this Spring.

"Why isn't Ray Durham playing?" I asked Jamie. "Was he still with the Giants? Was he hurt?"

"Durham has been nursing a shoulder injury lately, and missed the last few Spring Training games to a tweaked hammy. Oh, and he's terrible." Jamie commented. Durham did hit .218 last year, but I figured he'd break into a lineup that is featuring names the likes of Eugenio Velez and Brian Bocock.

After Villanueva set the Giants down in order, the Crew wasted no time getting on the board. Rickie Weeks singled to left, stole second, and scored on a seeing-eye Prince Fielder single. Weeks not only set a Brewers record, scoring in his 17th straight game, he is one shy of the modern day major league record, most recently set in 2000 by Cleveland's Kenny Lofton. After Ryan Braun struck out, Bill Hall hit a towering home run to left, to give the Brewers a 3-0 lead. In the 2nd inning, we decided to do a little gambling, as Andy now applauds. Basically, we start passing a cup around, and the four of us take turns putting $1 in the cup. While you have the cup, if the player that is hitting singles, you get your dollar back, if he doubles, you get $2, a triple gets you $3 and a home run wins you the entire cup. If your player strikes out or hits into a double play, you put an additional $1 in the cup. It's fun, because with four players and nine batters, you don't end up with the same players all game, it gives incentive to follow every at-bat closely, and…it's gambling! By the time the cup reached me in the 5th inning, the Brewers had tacked on two more runs, to make it 5-0, and Bill Hall was stepping up to the plate with two on and one out. While I was asking Lisa and Jamie if onions were vegetables, I heard a thunderous roar, turned my head, and realized I had just won $18 on Bill Hall's 2nd HR of the day. That $18 will go for either two weeks of my gym membership, or three nights of "fourthmeal" at Taco Bell.

Going into the 6th inning, Villanueva had a shutout going, and had 6 strikeouts. Not bad for a 24 year old who spent most of last year as our long reliever. The fantasy owner in me wanted him to finish the 6th, so I could get the quality start that Jamie couldn't get out of Jonathan Sanchez (4 IP, 7 ER), but he had just went over 100 pitches after allowing back to back run scoring hits to Castillo and Aurilia. Yost called for Shouse, and the veteran got out of the jam. The Brewers would put up another 5 spot in the 6th, to go up 13-2. Salomon Torres would work the final three innings to get the rare three inning save, in a 13-4 final. Six Brewers had multiple hits, including 3 each for Prince Fielder, Bill Hall and Gabe Kapler (who Robb Edwards referred to as Gabe Kaplan up until his 3rd at bat of the game). It was an incredible day at the ballpark. My only question is, if the guy who was laying down on his back, covered in his own blood in the parking lot is reading this……..what exactly did you say to warrant that beat down?

When I got home, I was excited to sit down to the Mets and Braves from Turner Field, only to find out the game was called due to rain. So I spent the night going back and forth between coloring with Gracie, and watching the Red Sox/Blue Jays game. The Jays were wearing their throw backs blues at home. This MLB Extra Innings has won my heart.

April 5th

It's a noon start today for the Crew, and four Brewers are starting for the first time this year. Gabe Gross is starting in center, Craig Counsell is playing today at short, Mike Rivera is catching, and Manny Parra is making his first start of the year, his 3rd start ever in the bigs. The Giants still have a lineup that resembles a Double A All Star team. My sister is joining me for the game today, and we both have chosen Ryan Braun in mlb.com's "Beat the Streak". This is the daily fantasy league they offer where you pick a hitter each day that you think is going to get a base hit. If you do this successfully for 57 straight days, you win a million dollars. In four years, the highest I've ever gone is 21 days.

I'm learning today that the mlb extra innings package is great for weeknights, but not so hot on the weekends. Due to the national coverage provided by Fox on Saturdays and TBS on Sundays, I am limited to the number of games available on directv. This means no Mets game on my TV today. In fact, nothing is available until Mariners/Orioles at 6:00. No Felix Hernandez? No thanks. So the plan today is to enjoy the Brewers game, get some biking in before the Final Four, watch said Final Four, and tonight, Walken will host SNL like no one else can.

The first two RBI's today belonged to.......Mike Rivera? Rivera would get credit for an RBI on a slowly hit grounder to 3rd, with Corey Hart scoring from 2nd on the throw to first. Great hustle by Hart, and an indication of the way the Brewers are playing to start the season. They seem to be running more often. I see more of a hop to their collective step. Rivera would then double home Hart in the bottom of the 5th. Going into the 6th inning, the Brewers were up 3-0, and Manny Parra held the Giants hitless. Jill and I honored the unwritten rule of not mentioning the no-hitter aloud, but Brian Anderson did not. The very first hitter in the 6th inning tripled, and the Giants would get two back. Ryan Braun, who wasted little time in the first getting Jill and I our base hit, came up in the 6th with nobody on, and proceeded to hit his first bomb of the season, which prompted me to go into a medley of wrestling taunts, Jill to do some sort of arms only dancing, and my daughter Gracie to sneak a couple of pretzels while we were celebrating. Each team trades runs in the 7th, with the Brewers coming off of a pinch-hit HR by new female family favorite, Gabe Kapler. Ray Durham would touch Guillermo Mota for a solo shot in the 8th, to bring the score to 5-4 Brewers. It would be up to Eric Gagne to redeem himself from opening day. He hasn't pitched since then, but he looked pretty good to me today, setting the

Giants down in order to notch his first save in a Brewers uniform. The Brewers now have saves from three different pitchers (Riske, Torres and Gagne).

It looks like the Fox game we get today is White Sox at Tigers. The Tigers would end up dropping their 5th straight home game to start the season. The story here is the big bats that haven't done much, no starting pitching behind Verlander, and a terrible pen. The game ends early, so Fox gives up bonus coverage of the Mets at Atlanta, just in time for me to see Kelly Johnson hit a pinch-hit grand slam off Jorge Sosa to extend the Braves lead to 9-3. The Mets would go on to lose this one, 11-5.

Memphis beat UCLA, ending any chance of a respectable finish in the NCAA pool for myself, and as I type this Kansas is up 33-10 on North Carolina. It looks like a typo, but they are indeed up 33-10. Billy Packer is saying this game is over with 9:00 left in the first half. Way to keep those viewers, BP. Ya just lost me.

April 6th

Last night was not the best SNL that Walken has done, but some good stuff. I loved the Walken family reunion sketch, and the surprise party sketch was funny. I like that Wiig. I like her a lot.

The Brewers go for the sweep today against the Giants. Ben Sheets will toe the rubber for the crew, and the Giants will go with Barry Zito. And it looks like I'm getting a lot more games today on extra innings than I did yesterday. Santana is going for the Mets, who will try to split with the Braves, and he is opposed by John Smoltz. We'll be flipping between the two games, while keeping an eye on young Ian Snell of the Pittsburgh Pirates, who I have going in two leagues today.

Sheets looked unhittable in the 1st, striking out the side on 11 pitches. When he's on, he's the definition of an ace. Sheets' problem has been injuries. I still think he's capable of a 20 win, Cy Young type season, and hopefully 2008 is the season he could put it all together. Meanwhile, Santana looks just as good through

2 innings in Atlanta. What a treat it will be to see these two men pitch this season.

Jill brought over one of those Home Run pizzas, and damn, it's tasty. As I help myself two a couple of slices, I notice that J.J. Hardy has broken out of his slump to give the Brewers a 1-0 lead. The way Sheets is throwing, that may be all he needs today. The Brewers would add single tallies in the 3rd and 4th to make it 3-0, and in the 5th, Gabe Kapler and Ryan Braun would once again go deep, and much like yesterday, Jill is swooning while I am DXing oncoming traffic. The Brewers now lead 5-0, and Sheets is rolling.

In Atlanta, Johan Santana is pitching wonderfully, giving up a run in the 2nd, but nothing since, however, the Mets bats have gone cold, as the Braves carry a 1-0 lead into 7th. Santana would go one more inning, before giving way to Aaron Heilman in the 8th. Heilman would get touched up for a 2 run homer by Mark Teixeira. I quick check to see what league I have Teixeira in, only to find out that I did not draft him in any of them. When you're in 5 leagues, it gets hard to keep track. I did have him targeted in the 3rd round for a few of the drafts, but he either was taken right before my pick, or someone else fell that I thought added more value to my roster. The Mets would score in the 9th, but fall short to the Braves, 3-1, to fall to 2-3. They are only a half a game back, in a very competitive NL East thus far.

The Brewers added runs in the 7th and 8th, giving Sheets a 7-0 lead heading into the 9th. He looked as good in the final inning as he did in the first, getting the Giants in order to cinch his first complete game shutout since May of 2001, his rookie year. It also gives the Brewers a clean sweep of the Giants in their first home series of the season. These guys are playing with a lot of confidence, getting great starting pitching (Sheets alone has gone 15 1/3 innings, and has yet to allow a run), and the bullpen has also looked great (with the exception of Gagne on Opening Day). Five guys are hitting above .300 (Kendall .467, Kapler .438, Fielder .364, Braun .321 and Hart .304), and the team has only made two errors in six games, in route to a 5-1 record, which is the best record in baseball thus far.

The Brewers and Mets are the only two National League teams that do not play tomorrow, so I plan to tell you how I became a baseball fan as a young man.

April 7th (The Beginning)

My earliest baseball memories are of my dad playing slow pitch softball on Friday nights, and me thinking he was the best player in the world. It seems like every time I went to see him play, he went 4-5 with 2 dingers, and I got lost in the sounds of chatter, the *ding" of the bat (which of course, would be replaced by the "crack" of the bat), the hustle, the enthusiasm of the spectators, everything. Shortly after my parents separated, we moved to a town called Mauston in South Central Wisconsin. I no longer got to see my dad play, but I still loved baseball. One afternoon, my cousin Lisa found a glove at the local park, and gave it to me. My first glove, and I remember it like it was yesterday. When we got home, she wrote the word "OUCH" in the middle of the glove, and showed me that night where to catch the ball. I've been glove in hand ever since, whether I have a ball or not, and regardless of whether I'm outdoors or inside lying on the couch. I have very fond memories of my mom and I playing catch, and I remember getting so upset when our catch was interrupted by a phone call, or a neighbor coming over to chat. How dare these neighbors cut in on a mother/son catch. To this day, it's one of the purest things in my life. Whether it was with mom when I was 6, tossing it around with Andy or Joe on our lunch break at work, or taking my sister and my niece out to the soccer fields in summer for a quick throw around. There is a certain bond that is formed when you're playing catch. Sometimes I think my job would be really easy if I could have a catch with each member I serve at the credit union for 5 minutes before we talk about their finances, and I very much look forward to having my first catch with my daughter.

It would be easy for me to say that I fell in love with the Milwaukee Brewers in the summer of 1982, which was the year we moved back to Milwaukee, to live with my Grandma, but that simply wasn't the case. Although I still loved baseball, I knew it as a game I played in the backyard with my mom and cousin, a game I observed my dad play on hot, summer nights and a game I daydreamed about at night while clutching my glove and gripping a ball. I didn't know from the Brewers at the age of six. I guess I knew of them. I remember my mom listening to games on the radio while reading or doing a crossword puzzle, I'd be in my room playing with my Star Wars action figures, or as I called them back then, my "friend toys", and occasionally I'd hear something like, "GET OUT BABY" or "GO GO GO........WOO-HOO" from the top of my mom's lungs, and just didn't get what the fuss was about. As a matter of fact, when the Brewers beat the Angels to win the ALCS, my mom erupted in tears and received several phone calls from friends and relatives about the game, and I couldn't understand why my mom was crying so hard. My grandma tried to explain it, she also in tears, and I just remember being confused as to what was happening. When the Brewers lost the World Series, I was in another room when the final out was made. I walked in to see my mom crying, and I assumed we won, based on this new found idea of crying when happy. She explained that they lost, and I remember not caring either way, but thinking this is causing too much unwanted tears.

I saw my first Brewers game in April of 1983. My dad got four tickets right behind the Brewers dugout. While a bunch of kids were screaming to the various players for a ball and an autograph, my sister and I just sat their quietly, again, not understanding what the big deal was, and this "strategy" was rewarded, as I was handed a ball by Ben Oglivie, and my sister was handed a ball by Don Sutton. Man, did she have a crush on Sutton for a year or so after that day. I recently showed her a picture of Sutton from 1983, and she laughed for about an hour. It was later that year I started to know the players, and quickly had a new favorite player, Gorman Thomas. Initially, I think I liked him because he kind of looked like my dad, but just like a lot of seven year olds, I was drawn to the long ball, and Thomas hit a ton of them. And it would not be long for me to shed my first baseball tear, as we would read in our evening edition of the Milwaukee Journal the day after it happened that Gorman Thomas was traded to the Cleveland Indians. Who the heck are the Cleveland Indians? And what in the blue hell does "traded" mean? My mom explained that Gorman was traded because he wasn't doing that well, and the team was struggling, and had to do this to get better. You're speaking Spanish to me mom! How can Gorman Thomas not be a Brewer anymore? We don't *live* in Cleveland, so how can Gorman play *there?* Traded? Just as easily as I trade flavors of gum with my sister, my new hero is traded to another team?? To a seven year old, it felt at the time that anything was in play. Would I come home from school one day to find out my Grandma was now contractually obligated to make pancakes for the Hunt family down the block, or Santa will somehow be dealt to the Jewish kids, and there goes Christmas.

The Brewers ended up in 5th place in 1983, and ended up being the worst team in baseball in 1984. It was April of 1984 that my Grandma got cable. As the cable guy was installing it, Grandma was telling me that we would get a lot more baseball games on TV than what I was used to. She was leafing through the TV guide, and I asked if any games were on today. She told me there was a game on at 12:15 and a game at 1:00 tomorrow. I just assumed these were Brewers games, and she told me the game today was Reds/Mets, and the game tomorrow was Phillies/Cubs. What the phuck? Ya damn near knocked my head off when you said Gorman was an Indian, but who in the hell are the Reds, Mets and Cubs? I knew of the Phillies from the 1983 World Series (watched about six innings of Game One, couldn't get into it). No Brewers, what do you want from me? Apparently, there was a whole other league I wasn't aware of. We watched the Reds/Mets, and it was the first time I had watched a day game on TV. The next day, I watched the Phillies/Cubs, and was really entertained by this old man announcing for the Cubs. That summer, my Grandma and I watched Cubs games during the day, and I would watch the Mets games at night, and on weekends. I was drawn to both of these teams, if not for the fact that they were on all the time. My Grandma would get into the Cubs games with me, and it was during this time, I was introduced to her famous phrase, "Miss it, you PIG" as a lazy fly ball was hit to an opposing center fielder. This was the first year I was conscious of such things as pennant chases and playoff runs, and that summer, the

Cubs ended up winning the NL East, and would play the Padres in the NLCS. They eventually would lose, and my heart was broken. Not so much because I considered myself a Cubs fan, but that now meant the end of watching Cubs games with my Grandma, at least for the next six months. To this date, I still find myself rooting for the Cubs on occasion, because of the memories I have spending summer afternoons with my Grandma, watching Ryno, the Bull, Sarge, the Penquin, not to mention Larry Bowa, Jody Davis, Keith Moreland, Rick Sutcliffe and Lee Smith. Having Harry Carey tell me about it certainly added to the fun. The Brewers move to the NL Central in 1998 makes it hard to cheer for them these days, but the baseball fan in me would love to see the Cubs win it all.....maybe a year when I'm not writing a book about the Brewers and Mets, and their road to the NLCS.

April 8th

Steven Forst is good people. He's a professor at UW Milwaukee, and just happens to be a huge Mets fan. He also follows the Brewers, and occasionally will surprise me with some baseball goodies. Today, he brought me a Prince Fielder bobble head for Gracie, and a Mets pin commemorating the last year at Shea Stadium, which reminded me that the Mets home opener was at noon, the last in the 45 year history of Shea. Today's opponent is the Philadelphia Phillies, the team that came back from a 7 game deficit with 17 to play to pass up the Mets, and take the NL East last year. The Phillies have also won their last 8 meetings with the Mets. I have another speaking engagement on campus today, which will keep me away from following them for the majority of the game. Just before I am scheduled to present, I peek at the score to see that Carlos Delgado has gone yard to give the Mets an early 1-0 lead. Things continued to look good, as the Mets carried a 2-0 lead into the 7th, but things became unglued in the top of the 7th (it's no coincidence that I use the word unglued on the day I find out that Stone Temple Pilots is doing a reunion show at Summerfest on July 4th). A throwing error by Delgado allows two unearned runs to score, and Aaron Heilman gave up two hits and walked three in his inning of work, to give the Phillies a 5-2 win. The Mets have fallen to 2-4, but are now 0-3 vs the Braves and Phillies (our main competition). Oliver Perez looked great for a second consecutive start, and has yet to allow a run in 11 2/3 innings pitched this season, and the Mets have six regulars hitting above .300 (Delgado, Beltran, Church, Schneider, Pagan and Wright). What we are lacking is bullpen depth and hitting in the clutch. We'll beat you 13-0 like nobody's business, but we need to win the close ones, too.

The Brewers welcome the Cincinnati Reds to town tonight, in what will be the return of Francisco Cordero to Milwaukee. Cordero signed with Cincinnati as a free agent after a year and a half as Milwaukee's closer. No hard feelings. I'm sure the extra $4,000,000 was worth going from a contender to a 5th place team. I'm sure he'll do smashingly, saving his 22 games for the Reds. Good for him. Jason Kendall continues to rip the cover off the ball, driving in J.J. Hardy in the 3rd inning, raising his NL leading batting average to .500. The starting pitching is once again solid, as Jeff Suppan has a shutout going through six. Cincinnati rookie Johnny Cueto has looked equally impressive, allowing only one run on four hits through his first six.

I left the game for a bit to tuck my daughter in and put in a Winnie the Pooh movie for her. She loves her Pooh. She was calling for it during her bath earlier tonight......"Come on dada......watch it, pooh?" This is two minutes into a bath I thought she was really enjoying. There's nothing like seeing your child happy. I love her to pieces.

I came back to find that the Reds scored in the top of the 7th. The game is now tied 1-1, going into the bottom half of the 7th. Cueto is still going for the Reds...HALL TO LEFT! GET UP, BALL! **The...space...goes...down, down baby, down, down the roller coaster. Sweet, sweet baby, sweet, sweet don't let me go. Shimmy, Shimmy Cocoa Pop. Shimmy, Shimmy Rock. Shimmy, Shimmy Cocoa Pop. Shimmy, Shimmy Rock. I met a girlfriend, a triscuit. She said a triscuit - a biscuit. Ice cream, soda pop, vanilla on the top....Ooh, Shelly's out, walking down the street, ten times a week. I read it. I said it. I stole my momma's credit. I'm cool. I'm hot. Sock you in the stomach three more times...What, you guys don't sing that song from "Big" when your team hits a go-ahead homer in the 7th against a division rival? You think you're better than me?

Eric Gagne is coming on to save this one. He gets the first two easily, and the Reds are down to Corey Patterson. Gagne gets two strikes on him, and it looks like he gets Patterson to fly out to right to end it, but the ball kept sailing back, Hart made a valiant effort to keep it in, and Gagne has now blown his second save in three chances with the Brewers. This is a guy who blew 11 saves for his career coming into the season, the best save percentage ever, and now he's blown two out of three. The Brewers fail to score in the 9th off David Weathers, and Salomon Torres holds the Reds scoreless in the 10th.

In the bottom of the 10th, with David Weathers still in the game, and Francisco Cordero warming up in the bullpen, the Brewers lead off the inning with a J.J. Hardy single, his third hit of the night. Ned calls on Joe Dillon to bunt Hardy over, and does just that. Jason Kendall then singles to right, with a drawn in outfield, and Hardy is unable to score. Weeks has to be aggressive in this situation, men on the corners with one out, and he delivers, with a single to left, to give the Brewers the win, and bring them to 6-1. The team is off to a great start, but you have to be concerned about Gagne. Just not looking like the Gagne of old.

A couple of notes from the Dodgers/D-Backs game from Arizona......First, Doug Davis is pitching for the D-Backs tonight, two days before he is scheduled to undergo thyroid cancer surgery. We all wish Doug a speedy recovery....a Class A guy. I'll never forget when we were in Vegas for Phil's bachelor party, and Davis went 8 1/3 innings in a 2-0 win over the Cubs at Wrigley in a late August game in 2003. If I'm not mistaken, his first start with the Brewers was five days earlier, a 7-1 win over the Reds where he went the distance. Second, and this is completely true.....My niece used to call me Unjigo, because when she was really young, she couldn't say, Uncle Joe, and it came out Unjigo. I just noticed that the current Dodgers pitcher is named Hong-Chih Kuo. I've been laughing for ten minutes.

It's time for me to hit the sack. One last observation...Matt Vasgersian is doing ads for San Diego County Credit Union. He claims they gave him a great rate on his auto loan. C'mon, Matt. After those XFL games you did, you're telling me you didn't pay cash? We miss you, man. I'm glad I get a chance to hear you do games this year. Hey, Daron.....hit me up when you have a minute. We're all still curious why *you* left. My celly is 262-339...eh, I'm not that curious. Brian Anderson's doing a great job.

April 9th

We have tickets for tonight's game vs the Reds. I will be joined by Jamie once again, and Joe. We're gonna use the fourth seat for our jackets and the what not. The Mets are playing on ESPN tonight, but missing it is not a big deal this year, since I'll get plenty of chances to see the Mets with the extra innings package.

I finally got the courage to call Bob Buege and Neal Pease today. Both of these men teach at UWM, and have written about baseball in the past. Bob wrote a book about the history of the Milwaukee Braves and Neal teaches a Baseball in American History class. They both came highly recommended as people that may be able to give me some pointers about the process. I was a little nervous calling them...some schmuck banker writing a silly book about loving two teams. But Neal and I had a good conversation, he told me that he, too, as two teams he follows, the Brewers and the Red Sox, and told me about a column that Bill Simmons wrote that specifically states that you CANNOT truly love two teams. Bill is the "Sports Guy", and has been campaigning to be the next General Manager of the Milwaukee Bucks. I'll make sure to send him a copy.

Before the Brewers game got under way, the Mets already had a 7-1 lead on the Phillies, with the help of four Philadelphia errors in the first three innings. The Mets would go on to finally beat the Phillies, 8-2, despite only five hits. Mike Pelfrey looked good in his first start of the year, and the bullpen held the Phillies scoreless for four innings.

The Brewers game was great for the first five innings. They took a 3-2 lead in the 5th when it appeared that Rickie Weeks would ground out to end the inning, but the ball went through the legs of Brandon Phillips, and two runs scored. The crowd went crazy, but there was little more to cheer for the rest of the way. The Reds would go on to score ten runs in the next four innings, and the Crew was down 12-3 going into the last half of the ninth. It was at that moment that I was hit on for the first time in ages. A young lady sitting behind us, who was making Joe and I blush for about two innings, with her tales of lesbian curiosity, tapped me on the shoulder and asked how old I was. She figured I was much too young to be married. I took it as a compliment, but wasn't ready for what I was about to hear. She asked me if the Brewers would come back tomorrow and win, and I said, "Young lady, the Brewers are gonna win….tonight!" She asked if I knew what the score was, and before I could answer, her older friend said she'd, and I quote, "sit on my face" if they came back. I didn't want to hurt her feelings, but if she wasn't 50, she was 65, and I proceeded to make the sick face you make when milk turns. At this point, I could tell that Joe never wanted to be seen with me at a game again. Back to baseball…..The Brewers are 6-0 when Dave Bush doesn't pitch, and 0-2 when he does. It looks like he may be the odd man out when Yovani Gallardo comes back. He's scheduled to come back next Tuesday at St Louis. And I think it's too early to worry that I have as many home runs as Prince Fielder does at this point. I predict he'll snap out of it soon.

April 10th

I shared my experience last night with Andy before we opened, and I think I've also scared off another friend from ever seeing a game with me. More games for Jamie, I suppose. The Brewers played at noon today, but we were pretty busy at work, so we couldn't really follow it too closely. Carlos Villanueva had a no-hitter through four innings, but the bats never woke up today. Jason Kendall went 2-3, and leads the planet with a .538 batting average. He could go 0 for his next 16, and still be hitting .333. The Reds would eventually get to Villanueva, and had a 4-1 lead going into the 9th. Francisco Cordero came on in the 9th, and was booed wildly. He retired his old teammates in order, and the Reds took the series.

The Mets took the field tonight with a chance to take the series from the Phillies, and John Maine took the hill. He walked five through 6+ innings, and but left with a 3-1 lead after allowing a solo shot to Pedro Feliz. The bullpen (Heilman) cost him the win by giving up 2 runs in the 8th. Both teams combined to use 13 pitchers tonight, and the Mets would end up taking this one in the bottom of the 12th, as Angel Pagan singled home Jose Reyes (who looked like he was out.....but sorry, no replay). We are now 4-4, and I've just read that help may be on its way, as the Mets have signed Claudio Vargas to a minor league contract.

April 11th

The Brewers open a three game series at Shea Stadium against the Mets tonight, and everyone has been asking me who I'm rooting for. The answer I've been giving is the Mets.......and the Brewers. As I've stated before, I can't root against either team. I watch these games the same way I would observe an Elton John/Billy Joel concert. Just sit back and enjoy hit after hit (or out after out, if you like pitching). When these rare Mets/Brewers games occur (usually six of them a year), I tend to lean towards the home team (and yes, I am rocking my home Mets jersey tonight), but really, I just want to see well played, close baseball games. What I don't want to see on either side is a sweep. This is the Brewers very last trip to Shea Stadium, and I'd like for them to get a win this weekend. Manny Parra is pitching for the Brewers, coming off of a great start vs the Giants last week. The Mets will send Nelson Figueroa to the mound today. Figueroa finds himself in the rotation with Pedro and El Duque on the disabled list. He was a Brewer in 2002, posting a 1-7 record, with an ERA well over 5.00. His last big league win came with Pittsburgh in 2003.

I'm also keeping an eye on a couple of other series around the bigs. The Phillies are hosting the Cubs, and the Red Sox are hosting the Yankees. Clay Buchholz gets his first taste of the Sox/Yankees rivalry tonight. I remember feeling a sense of pride when Taylor Buchholz got his first major league win as a member of the Astros and 2006, and when Clay threw a no-hitter in his 2nd major league start last year, I couldn't help but get emotional. The headline, "Buchholz tosses gem" is one that has been dancing in my head my whole life. Am I over the fact that I didn't realize my dream to pitch in the big leagues? No. But I don't dwell on it on a daily basis. I live through the Clay and Taylor Buchholz's of the world, and will root for them, regardless of which team they may pitch for.

Nelson Figueroa was perfect through four innings tonight, and Parra looked good in his first three innings. The Mets got to Parra for 3 runs in the 4th, and surprisingly, would only go four innings tonight, despite only walking one batter, and having a pitch count around 70. I figure with Parra coming up in the 5th, that Yost wanted to maximize his team's chances at scoring, with Figueroa pitching the way he is. After Corey Hart walked, J.J. Hardy erased the no-hitter and shutout by doubling home Hart. The Brewers would add another run in the sixth, and Figueroa would leave after six with a 3-2 lead. The Mets added some insurance in the 7th to make it 4-2, and the Mets bullpen would go on to shut down the Brewers to take the first game of the series.

This was a close game to the end, but not necessarily a well played game by the Brewers. They managed only two hits all night, and made two costly errors in the 4th inning. The bats have been really quiet as of late, and it won't get any easier tomorrow, as Johan Santana makes his 2008 home debut for the Mets. The Mets will be carrying a three game winning streak into tomorrow afternoon's game, and will face Ben Sheets, who comes into the game with a 0.00 ERA through 15+ innings pitched. It should be a wonderful game.

April 12th

A lot of stuff going on today, so here's a brief summary of today's game.....Quality start by Sheets, bats light up Santana for three dingers (Hall, Weeks and Kapler), and Gagne shuts the door for a 5-3 Brewers win. If you feel ripped off, don't worry. You'll be getting full play by play for the series finale. I've been spending the day getting the house ready for tonight. The plan is to see Jamie's boy, Jonathan Rundman, do an intimate acoustic set at Christ the King Lutheran Church here in Port Washington, then head back to my place for some wings, some pies and a little SNL, with Ashton Kutcher. Phil and Erika are bringing Lincoln, so it should be a fun night.

April 13th

Well, the Brewers and Mets have split the first two games of their series at Shea, and the rubber game is scheduled for noon today. It'll be Jeff Suppan vs Oliver Perez, and just like Sheets yesterday, Perez comes into the game with a perfect 0.00 ERA. Since this is the last Brewers/Mets game until early September, I will make my best attempt to give you, the reader, some play by play AND color commentary of today's game. I will try to do this periodically throughout the season, most likely on Sundays. So, as Vin Scully would say, "Pull up a chair, and join me for a while".....

(Top of 1st) As Perez takes the hill, there is a noticeable change in the Brewers batting order. Braun is hitting 3rd, and Prince is in the cleanup spot. With Bill Hall raking lately, this will hopefully give Prince an opportunity to see some better pitches. I notice that Brian Anderson said that this is the final regular season game at Shea Stadium between the Brewers and Mets this year, and I like the emphasis he put on "regular season". Rickie Weeks leads off, and looks patient up there, looking at the first 3 pitches

Perez delivers, getting a feel for what he's got today. After fouling the next pitch off, Weeks reached base after being hit on the back foot by Perez. So Gabe Kapler steps up to the plate with one on, and ARE YOU KIDDING ME, HE JUST WENT YARD! Kapler took the 2nd pitch he saw deep to left to give the Brewers a 2-0 lead. That's 4 on the year for Kapler. Braun grounds the first pitch he sees to short, and there's one down for Fielder. Prince looks at a called strike, than hits a lazy fly to center for the second out. Bill Hall is now up, and like Weeks, looks very patient, looking at 3 straight without lifting the bat off of his shoulder. He would eventually strikeout swinging, but the Brewers do what no one has done so far in 2008, get to Perez, and give Suppan an early 2-0 lead heading to the bottom half.

(Bottom of 1st) Pagan leads off for the Mets, with Jose Reyes sitting out a second straight game with the tweaked hammy. Pagan rips one down the line, just foul, but Suppan gets him swinging on four pitches. Luis Castilllo attempts to bunt for a base hit, but Suppan fields his position well, and gets Castillo by a step. With two outs, David Wright is the batter. Wright has struggled this year, but has worked a 3-1 count on Suppan. After fouling off a couple of pitches to bring the count to 3-2, Wright shows his opposite field muscle by homering to right field, to make it 2-1. That's two dingers in the series for Wright, and it's good to see him snap out of his drought. Beltran grounds out to Weeks to end the first. As we go to the second, it's the Brewers 2, Mets 1.

(Top of 2nd) Corey Hart leads off the 2nd with a base hit to center. It looks like the Brewers are getting good looks at Perez. J.J. Hardy steps in, with Hart at 1st, always a threat to steal. Hardy promptly deposits a single to left, and the Brewers are in business again as Suppan steps up. He's looking to bunt, but the first pitch gets away from Schneider, and now the Crew have men on 2nd and 3rd, and Suppan will now swing away, and try to help himself out with a couple of ribbies. Perez gets him swinging, and now he'll have to contend with the NL's leading hitter, Jason Kendall. On a 2-0 pitch, Kendall popped up to Delgado, and now it will take a two out hit to score a run. Weeks, who reached base on a HBP in the first inning, steps in with ducks on the pond. He's still showing great patience at the plate, waiting for his pitch. He's spoiled a couple of breaking balls from Perez, and now with the count 1-2, Weeks looks at a couple of fastballs up and in. The 3-2 pitch is low and away, and now Kapler comes to the plate with the sacks full. It should be noted that the Brewers lead the NL in hitting with RISP, at .341, but with a chance to give the Brewers a huge lead, Kapler strikes out swinging to end the inning. A golden opportunity flushed down the drain.

(Bottom of 2nd) Carlos Delgado leads off the Mets 2nd by walking on five pitches. Ryan Church is the next batter, and looks to build on his .300 batting average. He takes the first pitch for a strike, and Gracie has just handed me a crayon. So I'll be coloring Sponge Bob dark blue between at-bats. Church doubles to right, and the Mets are in the same situation that the Brewers were at the top of this inning. 2nd and 3rd, nobody out, and the batter will be Damion Easley, starting at short for Reyes. Easley has struggled in limited service thus far, hitting .167, but does his job this at bat, grounding out to Weeks to score a run and tie the game at 2. The Mets now have a man at third with one out for Brian Schneider. Schneider works the count to 3-0, and swings at 3-0, grounding to Weeks, but the ball goes right under his glove, and the Mets take the lead, 3-2. Put the glove down, son! Perez sacrifices Schnieder to 2nd, and Pagan steps in with a chance to add to their lead. He would ground to Hardy to end the inning, but the Mets add two, and now head to the 3rd up 3-2.

(Top of 3rd) I'm trying to sell the extra pair of tickets I purchased to the Billy Joel show in New York this summer, and I asked my friend Amber what she thought of him on a scale of 1-10. She said 4. That's not high enough to warrant the Last Play at Shea follow up question I had in mind. I was looking for an 8 or higher. Oh, well, looks like these tickets will remain unsold for awhile....Braun steps in, with the Brewers now trailing 3-2, and hits a short fly ball to right, and Church catches it for the first out. Fielder hits a drive to left, but playable for Pagan, and it's two up, two down, as Billy Hall steps in. Hall struck out in the 1st, and hits a lazy fly ball to right, and Perez gets out of the inning, 1-2-3.

(Bottom of 3rd) Luis Castillo leads off the Mets 3rd with a broken bat double down the left field line. David Wright, who hit his third HR of the year in the first, has a chance to build on the

Mets lead. He hits a bullet past Suppan, but Weeks is there, and
retires Wright, while Castillo advances to 3rd. The batter is Carlos
Beltran, and on the first pitch he sees, he singles to right to give
the Mets a 4-2 lead. Carlos Delgado, who walked in the 2nd, is
taking some huge cuts here in the 3rd. He proceeds to ground into
a super-rare 3-4-1, as the ball bounced off of Fielder's glove, went
right to Weeks, with Suppan covering. Beltran advanced to 2nd,
and Yost has decided to walk Church to set up a force with Easley
coming up. Easley, who tied the game in the 2nd on a groundout,
reaches base on an infield single, giving the Mets six hits already,
and loading the bases for Schneider. Schneider wastes no time
singling to right-center, and two runs cross the plate, giving the
Mets a 6-2 lead. Suppan would get Perez looking to end the 3rd,
but the damage has been done, and the Mets head to the 4th with
a commanding 6-2 lead.

(Top of 4th) Corey Hart, who led off the 2nd with a single,
does the same in the 4th, lining a screamer past Luis Castillo.
Perez seems to be pitching around Hardy, and J.J. has worked
the count to 3-0. Perez comes in with a couple of fastballs to
bring Hardy to a full count, as Brian Anderson reminds us that
there is a lot of day baseball in the big leagues today. Really? On
a Sunday? Hardy draws ball four, and Suppan comes up with the
same mind set he had in the 2nd. He lays down an excellent bunt,
and Wright's throw is in the dirt, but Delgado scoops it to retire
Suppan. Kendall again comes up with men on 2nd and 3rd with
one out. This time, Kendall comes through, singling to center,
Hart and Hardy score, and it's now a 6-4 game. Weeks steps up
for the 3rd time in 4 innings. He has reached twice, and looks
aggressive here in the 4th. On an 0-2 pitch, Weeks was clearly
looking for a breaking pitch, and looked at strike three, a fastball
right down the middle. Gabe Kapler, who homered in the 1st,
stayed hot by doubling down the left field line. It'll be interesting to
see how Perez pitches to Braun with first base open, and the
struggling Prince Fielder on deck. He comes in with an off-speed
pitch for strike one. Braun knocks the next pitch to left, and with
Kapler getting an early lead off second, two runs score to tie the
game! Braun advanced to second on the throw home. What a
game thus far! Each team has six runs on seven hits. Fielder

steps in, still looking for that first dinger of the year. Perez is going right after him, and Fielder is getting some good swings in. Fielder would ground out to 2nd to end a huge inning for the Brewers. After 3 ½ innings, the Brewers and Mets are tied at 6.

(Bottom of 4th) Pagan leads off the 4th, 0-2 thus far, but he's been hot, and extends his hitting streak to six games with a double to right. Castillo fights off a few pitches, then singles to center, and here we go again. The Mets have men on 1st and 3rd with nobody out, and the heart of the order coming up. Suppan gets Wright to pop up to shallow right, and the runners are not able to advance. The batter is Carlos Beltran, who is 1-2 with an RBI single. Suppan doesn't look like he's giving Beltran anything "meaty", but on a 3-1 pitch, Beltran hits a bullet, but snagged by Fielder, and in the process, doubles off Castillo to end the inning. Now we head to the 5th inning, it's the Brewers 6, Mets 6.

(Top of 5th) Bill Hall leads off the 5th hitting a fly ball to center, but Beltran retires him easily. Corey Hart then singles to center, to give him three hits on the day thus far. This brings up J.J. Hardy, who has also reached base twice with a single and a walk. Perez is approaching 100 pitches, and is really laboring at this point. Hardy has worked Perez to a full count, and checks his swing on ball four. Yost is calling for Joe Dillon to pinch hit for Suppan, and Willie Randolph counters by going to his bullpen. Because Suppan only went four innings, he can not win this one, but leaves with the game tied, so he cannot lose it either. The new pitcher for the Mets is Jorge Sosa, who has struggled this year. He comes in with a 5.13 ERA, and inherits two base runners. He looks like he's having a hard time locating the plate, with the last three pitches all low and away. Dillon pops up a 3-1 pitch to Delgado, and the piping hot Jason Kendall will get a chance to deliver again. It was Kendall's single last inning that brought the Brewers to within two. He's fought off a couple of 1-2 pitches vs Sosa, and lays off a good 1-2 breaking pitch, just off the plate. Kendall flies out to center to end any threat of taking the lead. As we head to the bottom of the 5th, the Brewers and Mets are still tied at 6.

(Bottom of 5th) Salomon Torres comes on to work for the Brewers in the 5th. Torres has looked great thus far in 2008, after almost retiring from baseball after being traded to Milwaukee from Pittsburgh. He walks Delgado on four straight pitches. After missing the plate with his first delivery to Ryan Church, Kendall visits Torres to have a word. Church fouls off the next two pitches before grounding into a bang-bang 4-6-3 double play. Whatever Kendall was selling, Torres was buying. Suddenly, there are two outs for Damion Easley. Easley would fly to Braun to end the inning, and the devil has worked his way into the story today. 6-6, heading to the 6th. Get it?

(Top of 6th) OK, Amber, I'll give you Mary J Blige, but Kid Rock and Don Henley? Tens?? To each their own...Rickie Weeks has just gone yard off Sosa to give the Brewers a 7-6 lead. That's consecutive days going deep for Weeks. The Brewers have hit 15 homers thus far in 2008, and all of them have been hit by just four men. Hall leads the team with 5, Kapler has 4, and Braun and Weeks each have 3. Kapler draws a walk, and the boo-birds have come out at Shea, with Ryan Braun coming up. Braun tied the game in the 4th with a two run single. The first pitch to Braun gets by Schneider, and Kapler advances to 2nd. The 1-1 to Braun is also a wild pitch, Kapler is now at third, and it is now officially raining boos in Flushing, New York. Sosa battles back to get Braun swinging. Naturally, the Mets are going to give Prince Fielder a free pass to set up the opportunity at an inning-ending double play. I will take this break in the action to make some lunch for Gracie. She loves her green beans and corn, and that just happens to be today's special at Casa de Fugazzi. Bill Hall steps in with two on and one out. He's 0-3 on the day, but has a chance here to extend the lead. He drops his shoulder, and pops to short. Corey Hart now looks to add to his already big day, and does just that, singling to left, scoring Kapler, and Hart is now 4-4 with an RBI and a run scored. It is now 8-6 Brewers, with Hardy coming up. Hardy is 1-1 with two walks, and had a great at-bat vs Sosa, but ended up flying out to left after seven pitches. The Crew puts two up on the Mets, and now lead 8-6 going to the bottom of the sixth.

(Bottom of 6th) Torres starts his second inning of work, facing Brian Schneider. Schneider's two run single in the 3rd gave the Mets a 6-2 lead, and since that base hit, the Brewers have scored 6 unanswered. Schneider hits a single to right, and he's now 3-3. Did they give him a single in the 2nd? Wow! Endy Chavez is on to pinch-hit for Sosa, and promptly grounds into a 1-6-3 double play. A great play by Torres, and a great throw by Hardy to get the speedy Chavez. Angel Pagan shows bunt, but looks at strike one. The next four pitches aren't close, and Luis Castillo will face Torres with a man on first and two out. You want to get Castillo, and not have to deal with Wright if you're the Brewers. But Torres walks Castillo on five pitches, and now it gets interesting. Surprisingly, after throwing eight balls in his last nine pitches, Wright swings at the first pitch, and hits a weak grounder to Bill Hall at third to end the inning. You're a better hitter than that, David. Make him throw you a strike before you do that. At the end of six, it's 8-6 Crew.

(Top of 7th) Scott Schoeneweis is coming on to pitch for the Mets in the 7th. The first batter for the Brewers is Hernan Iribarren, who collected his first big league hit on the first pitch he ever saw in the bigs in yesterday's game. He's pinch hitting for Torres. He rips a 1-1 pitch, but right at Easley for the first out. Randolph will go right back to the bullpen, and get a righty to face Kendall. As this is happening, Gracie goes into an impromptu rendition of the ABC's. Joe Smith is the new pitcher, and gets Kendall to ground to third. Two down for Rickie Weeks, who homered in the sixth. He hits a chopper to Wright, who throws to Delgado, but can't hang on to it. E-3, and now a man on first for Kapler. Weeks steals second uncontested on a 1-0 pitch. He got out to a great jump, and Schneider never had a chance to get him. Kapler works the count to 3-2, and proceeds to double down the right field line to add to the Brewers lead. That's three hits for Kapler, a homer and two doubles, 3 RBI and three runs scored. Braun would go down swinging to end the 7th, but the Brewers now carry a 9-6 lead into the bottom half.

(Bottom of 7th) Brian Shouse will come on in the 7th to try to hold the lead for Torres, who is the pitcher of record for the Brewers. Carlos Beltran will turn around to hit from the right side against Shouse. He's a better hitter from the left side, but has more pop from the right. I'm currently watching the game on a half hour delay. I wanted to play with Gracie, so the game could very well be over as I'm typing this. I'll try not to peek at my fantasy teams to ruin the outcome. But you're reading this a year later, so depending on how fondly you remember this series, you may already know the outcome. Beltran walked, and Delgado hit into a fielder's choice, erasing Beltran from the base paths. Ryan Church quickly singles to left, and the Mets are rallying in the seventh, with two on, and one out. Damion Easley, who is 1-3, steps up, and the Brewers stick with Shouse. It's unusual to see Shouse face four batters in an inning. J.J. Hardy is unable to knock down a grounder to left, and Delgado scores to bring the Mets to within two, at 9-7. Brian Schneider digs in to face Shouse, already with three hits today (although one was a gift). He hits one into the hole, Weeks comes up with it, spins and throws to Hardy for one, and on to Fielder for another Brewers double play, their fourth of the game. The inning is over, and after seven, it's 9-7 Brewers.

(Top of 8th) Pedro Feliciano comes on to face Prince Fielder in the 8th. Fielder is hitting .227 on the year, and looked pretty bad vs Feliciano. He was unable to check his swing twice in the at-bat. Randolph will now make a double switch, bringing in Aaron Heilman to face Bill Hall, and Brady Clark will come on to play right field and hit in the 9 spot. Hall is 0-4 today. He's able to work the count to 3-1, then looks at a called strike two, before fouling off a couple of pitches. Hall would go down swinging, and has had a rough day at the plate. Corey Hart comes to the plate, looking for his fifth hit of the day, but pops up to Castillo on the first pitch, a 1-2-3 inning for the Mets. Still 9-7.

(Bottom of 8th) Guillermo Mota is now pitching for the Brewers, and is greeted to a ton of boos. Mota is a former Met, coming to Milwaukee in the off-season. The first batter he faces is a former Brewer, Brady Clark. Clark singles to center, and the crowd begins to chant, "Let's Go Mets". Angel Pagan steps in, but immediately falls into an 0-2 hole vs Mota. Clark takes off, and the throw isn't close, and he's able to steal second. The Mets now have a man in scoring position for Pagan. He drops a blooper past Hardy, but Clark is unable to score. There are men on the corners with nobody out for Luis Castillo. The tension builds! Castillo takes a ball, and the crowd is really into this one now, and Derrick

Turnbow begins to work in the Brewer's bullpen. I'm showing a lot of discipline by not fast forwarding or checking mlb.com. Castillo grounds to first, Fielder steps on the bag, and fires to Kendall to cut down Clark! A tailor made 3-2 double play, their fifth of the game, and you can hear a pin drop in Shea. That double play by the Brewers ties a National League record for double plays turned in a 9 inning game. David Wright still represents the tying run at the plate, with Pagan at second. A wild pitch advances Pagan to third, but with 2 outs, the focus is on Wright. Wright works the count, and draws a walk, bringing up Carlos Beltran, who will turn around once again, and hit from the left side of the plate. The first pitch is up and in for ball one. Mota drops a fastball for strike one. The 1-1 is low, setting up a hitter's count for Beltran. The change up on 2-1 is low and Mota can't locate a 3-1 fastball. The bases are now loaded for Carlos Delgado. I'm exhausted, but I'm having a great time watching these two teams battle. It looks like Mota is going to get out of it, as Delgado pops up to Hart. Calling. Waiting. Grabbing. Inning over. Still 9-7 Brewers as we go to the 9th.

(Top of 9th) J.J. Hardy leads off the 9th with a weak pop up to Easley. Craig Counsell pinch hits for Mota, and flies out to center. It looks like Eric Gagne will get another chance to save one for the Brewers vs the Mets. Heilman hits Kendall to extend the inning for Rickie Weeks. Kendall is the active career leader in HBP, with Craig Biggio now retired. Weeks grounds to Wright to end the inning, and on comes Gagne to try to shut the door. 9-7 Brewers.

(Bottom of 9th) Marlon Anderson is asked to pinch hit for the Mets to start the ninth. Anderson works the count, and on a 3-2 pitch from Gagne, Anderson swings and misses at a 94 MPH fastball for the first out. It's the first time since the 1st that the Mets do not reach base to start the inning. Damion Easley battles as well, but grounds out to Weeks for the second out. FSN is already naming Gabe Kapler today's MVP, and I hate when they do that before the game is over. As I say that, Brian Schneider lines to short to end it. If you ask me, I think Gabe Kapler was today's MVP.

So, the Brewers take two of three from the Mets, and will next face each other in early September at Miller Park. Both teams have off tomorrow, before returning to action on Tuesday night. The Brewers head to St Louis, a half a game behind the Cardinals in the NL Central, and the Mets will host the Washington Nationals, a game and a half behind the surprise Marlins in the NL Central. It has yet to be determined if Jose Reyes will be back for the Mets. While my teams take the day off, let me tell you about 1985, which may be one of the most important years of my baseball life.

April 14th (Brewers, Mets and....Falcons??)

In 1985, I made a decision to devote myself to two teams, the Brewers and the Mets. Since the Cubs and Mets were in the same division, I found it hard at the time to cheer for both teams equally, and the fact that Wrigley Field had no lights made it hard for me to follow them at night. My days were spent playing baseball in summer, and spending time indoors trying to catch up on the Cubs was not the priority at this time of my life. 1985 was also the year that I started to play Little League Baseball in Brown Deer. Brown Deer Little League was split into two levels. The 3rd, 4th and 5th graders played in the Bird League, and the 6th, 7th and 8th graders played in the animal league. I was chosen to play my Bird League ball with the Falcons. At my very first practice, my coach, Mr. Kettlehohn, asked he what position I wanted to play. I told him I wanted to pitch. I didn't know this at the time, but the 3rd graders didn't really get a chance to pitch too much. That was left to the 5th graders, and a select few of the 4th graders. But the first time Mr. Kettlehohn saw me pitch, he was impressed. I still remember to this day, the way he looked at the other coaches, as if to say, "This kid is in 3rd grade"? I wasn't the hardest thrower they'd ever seen, but what they liked was my control. Strike after strike after strike. He'd even instruct me to throw a few up, a few in, just to see if I could, and I did. He wanted someone who had a history of working with pitchers to work with me. He asked my mom if I could come up the school for a special practice on Saturday morning, just me, coach and the instructor. I threw for about ten minutes. These two guys just kept looking at each other. I was only 9 years old at the time, but I knew the look. I knew I had something.

Mr. Kettlehohn told me that I would get the chance to pitch this year in a game. I was thrilled. My first chance to pitch in a game came in the second to last game of the year, against the Eagles. In a game we were winning 11-8 going into the last inning, I was playing 2nd base, and our pitcher started the inning by giving up a single and walking the next batter. Coach came out, and motioned for me to come to the mound, and to this date (two marriages, birth of a child, Yount's 3000th hit, etc...), it was the most nervous I'd ever been, but equally excited. I inherited two runners, with nobody out, a chance to shut the door on the Eagles, and gain ground on the Orioles. Coach told me to not think too much, just throw strikes like he knows I can, and you'll be fine. The nerves got to me, and I walked the first batter I faced on five pitches. Now they've got the bases loaded with nobody out, but Coach believed in me, and nodded to me, letting me know I could do it. I struck out the next two batters on six pitches, and the electricity is running through my body. Just as quickly as I experienced the highest high of my young life, I experienced the lowest low. The next batter hit a towering three run double to left field to tie the game. The Eagles were going crazy, and I'm sure my guys were wondering why Kettlehohn went to the 3rd grader. I got the next guy to ground out, and to my surprise, I had about five or six teammates pat me on the head, and told me they'd pick me up, and get me the win. I just blew the lead, and they were congratulating me. Sure enough, we did it, and I was credited with a win in my first outing. I pitched again in the season finale, and knew at the very young age of 9 what I wanted to do when I grew up.

Meanwhile, the end of the little league season did not mean the end of baseball for me in 1985. The Brewers had a rookie pitcher by the name of Teddy Higuera, and despite a career that was cut short by injuries, Higuera would end up being one of the best left handed starting pitchers in Milwaukee Brewers history, and one of my personal favorites. The Mets also had a fine young pitcher in 1985. Dwight Gooden, who won the Rookie of the Year the previous year, went on to win the Cy Young in 1985, posting an incredible 24-4 record.   This was the first summer that baseball truly consumed my life. Naturally, all of my friends were huge Brewers fans, but I will have you know, that two of them were also Mets fans, Todd Asmondy and Rob Crivello. See what being on a SuperStation does for a fan base? Are they Mets fans today? I have no idea, but they were then. The Mets were in a tight pennant race with the Cardinals that summer, but eventually the Cardinals took the East, and went on to the World Series to face the Royals. By fall of 1985, I understood the history of the Cardinals beating the Brewers in the '82 series, and they just edged out my Mets for this year's pennant, so guess what, I'm rooting for the Royals.   God Bless Bret Saberhagen, and can we finally get off Don Denkinger's back already??

April 15th

Everyone file their taxes? Quick, Brewers fans.....what happened 21 years ago tonight? Ya damn right. Juan Nieves threw the first no-hitter in Brewers history against the Baltimore Orioles.   It's still one of the most memorable nights in Brewers history, for a couple of reasons. Yount's catch to seal the deal was amazing, and people forget that Jim Paciorek had an even better catch in the 2nd inning. This was also the Brewers' 9th win in a row to start the season. They would of course go on to win 13 straight to start the 1987 season.

April 15th is also important in baseball history because Jackie Robinson broke the color barrier on this date in 1947. Major League Baseball has since proclaimed April 15th "Jackie Robinson Day", and every year on this date, the league allows any player who wants to wear #42 to do so for that day's games.

The Mets are honoring Jackie Robinson in a number of ways. Not only is every member of the team donning number 42 tonight, but the main gate to Citi Field will be a tribute to Robinson. The Jackie Robinson Rotunda will pay homage to this brave man and his values, and will open in April of 2009. The Mets are coming off back to back losses to the Brewers, but got Jose Reyes back in the lineup tonight. All he did was go 4-5 in a 6-0 win over the Nationals. David Wright looks like he's cracking out of his slump, hitting a booming home run, and raising his average up to .311. Mike Pelfrey looked great, dare I say, amazin', going seven scoreless, and lowering his ERA to 1.50.

The Brewers did not look so good, making Braden Looper look like a Hall of Famer. The Cardinals scattered three hits in a 6-1 over the Crew. I'm a Yost supporter, don't get me wrong, but sitting Braun in this game puzzles me. I'm not a huge believer in the day off after a day off. Look, Brauny is struggling, I understand that. But this is the first game against the Cardinals this season, it's on the road, and I think we should have our best nine out there. I'm all about getting Joe Dillon his swings, but I would have played Braun in this one. But, that's why Yost is the manager, and I wear the "bank clothes". He's paid to make tough decisions, and like I said, I'm a Yost guy. I want to see him succeed in getting the Brewers back on Wisconsin Avenue for a late October parade. Dave Bush pitched ok, but I don't think he pitched well enough to keep his spot in the rotation. Yovani Gallardo will be back this weekend, and I think the Brewers will make Bush the long reliever for now. We'll see what happens. We've also signed Jeff Weaver today. Not a bad move. They're gonna send him to Nashville for extended Spring training. Weaver's a wily veteran who pitches well in late in the season. He's basically here if one of our arms goes down, and a viable option if that happens.

During the Brewers game, I got a call at home from Bob Buege, who wrote "The Milwaukee Braves : A Baseball Eulogy" in 1988. A colleague of Bob's saw me reading his book about a year ago, and when I told him that I was writing a baseball book, he told me to give Bob a call. I left a message for him about a week ago, and when I answered the phone, I was amazed it was him. We talked for about ten minutes, and we'll be meeting on Monday to discuss my idea. I'll also be meeting with Neal Pease later that day. Neal teaches European history at UW Milwaukee, and also teaches a course called "Baseball in American History". Jamie referred me to Neal, and took his baseball course. Neal has written several baseball essays, and I look forward to gaining any knowledge he can lend me regarding this baseball project of mine.

A couple of non-baseball related notes from today. I had somewhat of a big brother moment this morning, as a good friend of mine asked me what a MILF was. I nearly fell over, but as I gained the feeling back in my legs, I explained it to him, and we had a laugh. Apparently, he heard it on 30 Rock last week. For those of you who don't know, of course, MILF is an acronym for "Mets I'd Like to Forget"...George Foster, Anthony Young, Victor Zambrano, Kenny Rogers, etc. Also, Jamie and Alisa will be joining us at Shea for the Billy Joel show in July. Yay! But, I found out today that Amber is moving to Chicago at the end of this month. Boo! Henley sucks....

April 16th

Let me tell you about Keith Hernandez. That's a cool cucumber, I tell ya. Mex always has that look on his face like he's thinking of a sexist joke, but he knows he's on the TV, and he'll save it for Gary Cohen on the flight to Philly. I loved Hernandez as a kid. I don't wanna get all Robby Gordon on you, but my desert island top five favorite Mets ever are Howard Johnson, Lenny Dykstra, Mike Piazza, John Franco and Keith Hernandez. Hernandez makes the top five on the sole fact that he hit Elaine Benes on Seinfeld. Did they make the sex? I forget, and I don't want to ruin the spontaneity by "googling" it......Let's just say they did, and move on to tonight's games.

John Maine took the hill for the Mets tonight, and pitched well enough to keep the Mets in the game. Trailing 2-1 in the 5th, Jose Reyes and Carlos Beltran each homered, to give Maine a 5-2 lead to work with. Maine went 6 2/3, walked four, but held the Nats to two earned runs. The bullpen was unhittable tonight, and Billy Wagner notched his second save of the season. David Wright singled in the 3rd, to extend my Beat the Streak to nine games. If I continue to guess correctly for the next 48 days, I become a millionaire on June 3rd...if you're reading this book, and it has solid gold binding, that means I either won the million, or I'm a vain asshole....or both.

The Brewers continued to struggle in St Louis, losing tonight 5-4. Villanueva gave up two costly dingers to Adam Wainwright and Skip Schumaker. They did get to Jason Isringhausen in the ninth, plating two runs to bring it to within one, but Rickie Weeks bounced back to the mound to end it. The Brewers bullpen looked great, keeping the Crew in the game, but clutch hitting was at a minimum tonight. Game three is a day game tomorrow, and I will be presenting on campus, so I won't have a chance to follow it. Holy shizz! It's 12:50, I have to get to bed.

April 17th

I eat my candy with the pork and beans.....excuse my manners if I make a scene. Rivers, I love the stache, and I love the new single. Yeah, like Rivers Cuomo is reading this shit....

When I got back to the office today, the Brewers were down 3-0 after seven. I could tell by the look on Joe's face that they weren't doing well. From what I read, Manny Parra let ten men reach base in four innings before he was lifted. As soon as I settled down to listen, we began to rally. Hernan Iribarren doubled home Craig Counsell, who played third today for the struggling Bill Hall. A few batters later, Ryan Braun hit a sac fly to bring the Brewers to within one, and Prince Fielder doubled to score Weeks to tie the game. We all look at each other as if to say, "Did you hear, we're tied!" The next time Fielder stepped up, he hit a 2-run homer off of Brad Thompson to give the Brewers a 5-3 lead. Eric Gagne scared the crap out of us again in the bottom of the 10th, allowing a double and a walk before retiring the next three batters to secure his 4th save of the year, and 3rd of the current road trip. I know it's only April 17th, but this is a huge early season win, to avoid the sweep in St Louis, and to stay within a game and a half of the Cards. The bullpen pitched six shutout innings, and the team never gave up at the plate. It's good to see Prince finally go yard. Ryan Braun added a couple of hits and Craig Counsell collected three hits on the afternoon. Tomorrow night, the Brewers start a three game series in Cincinnati, with Ben Sheets taking the hill vs Bronson Arroya. A couple of roster notes...Hernan Iribarren was sent down immediately after the game, and the Crew recalled Mitch Stetter to add another lefty arm in the bullpen. Shouse has pitched great this year, but I imagine the Brewers don't want to overuse him. Also, it looks like Yovani Gallardo will pitch on Sunday, as the Brewers are listed TBD as their starter for Sunday. We'll see what happens with Dave Bush, who is scheduled to go that day.

The Mets were looking for the sweep tonight vs the Nationals. Nelson Figueroa looked great again, going seven innings, striking out 7, and only allowing three hits. Despite his performance, the Mets bats were quiet, and trailed 2-1 going into the 8th inning. I forgot to pause the game on TiVo as I was taking out the garbage, and as I was walking in, Carlos Delgado was driving in the tying run in the bottom of the 8th. This would be the last run scored in the game for a couple of hours. In the bottom of the 14th (moments after the 14th inning stretch at Shea), Damion Easley led off with a single. Frustrated that Reyes couldn't bunt him over, Easley stole 2nd, and advanced to 3rd on a pickoff attempt gone wrong moments later. Ryan Church struck out swinging, setting up David Wright with a man on 3rd and two outs. With Delgado and the pitcher's spot due up after Wright, the Nats decide to walk Wright and Delgado intentionally to load the bases for Jorge Sosa. The Mets then go to the only position player they have left, Brian Schneider, to pinch hit for Sosa. So now, we're looking at the sacks full with two outs, and the former Washington catcher, Brian Schneider trying to be the hero. He never got a chance to be the hero, however, because the first pitch traveled about 54 feet, and scurried past the Nationals catcher for a wild pitch, scoring Easley, and securing the sweep. The story here, just like with the Brewers earlier today, was the bullpen. The Mets bullpen combined for seven innings pitched, three hits allowed and no runs scored. That's 13 innings scoreless between the

Brewers and Mets today. That is sexy, folks. No matter how you slice it....

I guess the sweep was worth missing Jake Peavy's performance tonight. I was looking forward to seeing him pitch vs Colorado, and he ended up going eight innings, striking out eleven, and leaving the game in a scoreless tie. The game is still scoreless in the 11th inning, and I think I'm gonna turn off this computer and see how it turns out. After all, tomorrow's Friday, I've got some adrenaline pumping from the two extra inning wins today, why not enjoy some more extra inning baseball.

April 18th

Last night, I feel asleep while watching the Padres/Rockies game, and was amazed when I woke up three hours later to see the game entering the 22nd inning. Thought I was dreaming for a second. When I realized I wasn't, I decided to finish the game. The Rockies scored in the top of the 22nd, and the Padres were unable to score in their bottom half, ending one of the longest games in major league history.

The Brewers begin a three game set in Cincinnati tonight. Rickie Weeks is getting the night off, J.J. Hardy has been moved to the #2 hole, and Hart and Hall have swapped spots in the order, with Hart now hitting sixth. The Mets are in Philadelphia tonight, and it is Johan Santana vs Cole Hamels. I love Hamels, but not tonight. Here's to the Mets winning a well pitched, 1-0 game. I'll be bouncing back and forth between the two.

And wouldn't you know it, before I can even settle down with a beverage and a sammy, the Brewers are already up 2-0 in the first, and the Mets are leading the Phillies, 1-0. Gracie could care less, holding five crayons in her right hand, and trying to grab ten more with her left. The Mets game is not on SNY tonight, so I'll be listening to another legend, Harry Kalas. Much like Vin Scully, Kalas has one of those voices that I could listen to forever. Not only is he the voice of the Phillies, he is also the voice of NFL

Films. If this book is ever released as a book on tape, I'd ask Kalas to do it, just so I can hear him say phrases like "deucin' it" and "holy shizz".

Bill Hall just hit a monster home run to left, into the upper tank at Great American Ballpark. The Brewers are now up 4-0, and have been knocking Bronson Arroya around thus far. That homer gives Hall six on the year, and now ties him for the NL league lead. David Wright, who doubled home the first run for the Mets in the 1st inning, just tripled to make it 2-0 Mets. Do we have a cycle in the works tonight?

Ben Sheets is simply coasting through 4 innings in Cincinnati. He's faced one over the minimum, and has only allowed two hits. And as good as he's looked, Johan Santana has looked even better. Through five innings, he's allowed one hit, and has struck out eight Phillies. David Wright just singled, and the cycle watch is officially on. He needs the HR.

The Mets will be featured on national television the next three days, as their game with Philadelphia will be the game that most of America will get as the Fox Game of the Week tomorrow. Game three with Philly will be the Sunday night ESPN game, then game one of their series with the Cubs at Wrigley Field will be the Monday night ESPN game. The next time I work is Tuesday, so you can bet I'll be watching these games, to get the national perspective of the '08 Amazins. Meanwhile, Johan Santana continues to roll, pitching as well as he has all year. The Mets still lead 2-0 going into the seventh inning. David Wright will have at least one more at-bat tonight, and hopefully he's blatantly swinging for the fences. In the sixth inning of the Brewers game, Rickie Weeks is pinch hitting for Sheets. This is puzzling, because Sheets is mowing down Red after Red, and he's only at 60 pitches. With his history of injuries, one has to wonder if something happened in the fifth. As we sweat the Sheets situation, Jason Kendall has singled to give the Brewers a 5-0 lead. Gracie is starting to do headstands on the floor, not a care in the world, not concerned about the reports I'm now hearing that Sheets was experiencing tightness in his right triceps muscle, or the fact that Chase Utley has gone yard off Santana to cut the Mets lead to 2-1. Ah, the innocence of youth….

David Wright has just ripped a single to left, and is now 4-4, still a HR shy of the cycle. With it being the 8th inning, I doubt he'll hit again, but if he does, you will hear about it here first, approximately a year after it happened. Just act surprised, fellow Mets fans....don't ruin it for the people who don't know. His average is now .333. What a dirty, sexy boy....MAN CRUSH!! Now it looks like he could hit again, as the Mets have strung together four straight hits to extend the lead to 5-1.

I think tomorrow will be a good day to have the first catch of the year. April 19th is an important day in Brewers history, as that was the day in 1987 that the Brewers extended their winning streak to 12 games on the strength of the Rob Deer and Dale Sveum Easter Sunday home runs. Let's celebrate that history by breaking out the gloves for the first time this season. Texting Schwingle right now....

Johan got into some trouble to start the 8th, and after 106 pitches, his night is done. Hopefully Aaron Heilman can hold the.....there it goes, damnit, damnit, damnit, three run homer by Greg Dobbs. This is what I know about Greg Dobbs. He's on the Phillies, per mlb.com. That's all I can tell you about him. Now it's 5-4. Mitch Stetter also dug himself a hole in the 8th, walking two and allowing a single, but he struck out the next two batters, and David Riske retired Corey Patterson to strand the bases loaded for the Reds. Boy, the Jeff Weaver signing could not have come at a better time, now they're talking about Sheets maybe missing a start. We all saw it coming. We love the guy, but we all saw it coming.

The Mets have just added an insurance run, and head to the bottom of the 9th up 6-4. Billy Wagner will attempt to shut the door on the Phillies, his former team. He has yet to allow a run this year, and has a strikeout/walk ratio of 5 to 1 on the young season. It is power vs. power as Wagner faces Ryan Howard. Howard taps back to Wagner for out number one. He looks like he's throwing hard tonight, as he just hit 96 on the radar gun against Pat Burrell. Slider looks good as well. If the Mets can hold on to win, and the Nationals hang on to their 6-4 lead on the Marlins, we will take over first place in the NL East. Burrell just popped up to Ryan Church for the second out. Pedro Feliz is the last chance for Philly, and looks silly chasing a hard slider.

Another slider is fouled off, as Wagner is clearly setting him up for a fastball up and in. He misses with the high heat, but Feliz grounds weekly to Wright on the next pitch, to give the Mets the win. That is four straight heading into this weekend's games.

As I switch back to the Brewers game, I notice that the Reds have put up two in the ninth, and have the tying run at the plate in Javier Valentin. Both runs were charged to David Riske, and now it's in the hands of Eric Gagne, trying to notch his fourth save in the first seven games of this road trip. Valentin has been battling Gagne, but Gagne pulls the string on a 3-2 change up to get him swinging, and now Paul Bako (yes, thee Paul Bako) will try to keep the Reds alive. On a side note, has Gagne always looked like Seth Rogen? Hopefully Bako doesn't knock…him…up. Folks, try the veal, and stick around, the 11:00 show is completely different from the 9:00 show. Gagne got Bako looking to end it, and the former Brewers third string catcher looked, dare I say, "superbad" in that at-bat…I'll shut up.

April 19th

Last year, the fellas and I took some time to rank all thirty major league teams from favorite to least favorite. I think you know who my top two were, and if you haven't figured that out yet, this book is probably boring the heck out of you. I remember the Reds being high on that list, maybe 5 or 6. Pete Rose is one of my all time favorites, and in 1990, I was a huge fan of "The Nasty Boys" (Dibble, Myers and Charlton). The Reds AA team plays in Chattanooga, so I've seen a number of their games since 2004, and it's always fun to see someone I've seen in Chatty come up to the parent team Reds. Joey Votto was one of those players I remember seeing with the Lookouts, and he is now the starting first basemen with the Reds.   He's battling Jeff Suppan here in the 2nd inning, with the Brewers up 1-0 on a solo HR by Corey Hart, his first. I'm not sure if we'll see a Lookouts game this year. We'll be heading down to Chatty in May, and we've committed to seeing a Mets/Braves game at Turner Field, so we may not have the time to see the Lookouts. I'm sure as we get closer to that time, we'll *make* the time to see a Lookouts game. Votto struck out to end the inning. Tracy and I are taking a baseball trip at the end of July, and I'm looking for hotels between innings. All the tickets are bought and paid for, but I haven't booked a single hotel room yet. The Brewers are up 3-1 going into the fifth inning. It looks really nice out, and Schwingle's on his way here, so we're gonna have that catch.

After about 20 minutes of catch, and a controversial end to our championship game of HORSE, we sit down to catch the end of the Brewers game. Suppan left with a 3-1 lead, but Brian Shouse allowed a two run homer to Joey Votto (the irony) to tie it in the 7th inning. Guillermo Mota was asked to pitch the 8th and 9th, and held the Reds scoreless, sending this one to extras. The Brewers are 3-0 in extra innings thus far, and they've all been 10 inning wins vs. division opponents. After pitching the 9th, Francisco Cordero gives way to David Weathers. This supports my argument about most closers. Cordero only goes one inning, and leaves a 2-2 game that the Reds clearly need, and hands the ball to David Weathers, who the Brewers have already beaten this season. That's a $44 million dollar player? Weathers walked two, and allowed two hits, including a 2 run double by Bill Hall to give the Brewers a 5-3 lead. Bill Hall has been a Cincinnati Reds killer his entire career. Gagne set down the Reds in order for his sixth save (fifth on this road trip), and the Crew is now 11-6.

Howard Johnson is announcing the Mets starting lineup for the Fox television audience. He is the current hitting coach for the Mets, and as I mentioned a couple days back, one of my all time favorite Mets. Johnson was a switch hitting, 30/30 type player for the Mets in the mid to late 80's and early 90's. He looks pretty much the same as he did as a player, complete with the signature moustache that defined the 80's.

I haven't seen Mike in a while, so we spent most of the Mets game catching up, talking about the NFL Schedule that just came about, and loosely committing to hitting a BW3's or Chili's in the near future. We have tickets for Wednesday night's game vs Philadelphia, and it looks like Mike will be joining us for the action.

David Wright wasted no time getting the Mets on the board, with a two run double in the first. Oliver Perez gave up no earned runs for the third time in four starts, but left the game after only 5 and 2/3 innings, because the walks were up. Perez lowered his ERA to 2.49 (it's only that high due to the rough outing vs the Brewers last Sunday), and he will be an important part of the Mets run for the pennant this season. Jose Reyes jacked a long dinger in the seventh to give the Mets a 4-0 lead. The bullpen got touched for single tallies in the 7th and 8th, but Billy Wagner slammed the door in the 9th, giving the Mets their fifth straight win, and a 10-6 record.

Nothing is grabbing my attention tonight in the bigs, so I decided to watch a movie I recently purchased, *Walk Hard: The Dewey Cox Story*. I thought it was pretty good, despite being a box office bomb. The scene where Cox finds his band smoking pot is extremely funny. Timmy Meadows steals the scene, telling Reilly, "You don't want no part of this shit". Reilly concurs, stating reasons not to do drugs, and Meadows commands, "It doesn't give you a hangover, it's not habit-forming, you can't OD on it, it makes sex better, it's the cheapest drug there is!" Then concludes again with, "YOU DON'T WANT IT!!"

It's time for bed. Big day tomorrow, as the Brewers and Mets each go for series sweeps tomorrow. Yovani Gallardo is making his first start tomorrow, and Mike Pelfrey gets the nod for the Mets.

April 20th

It's my party (book), and I'll cry (bitch) if I want to.....the bullpen blew a golden opportunity at a sweep today. Yovani Gallardo and Aaron Harang had a good old fashioned pitching duel this afternoon, each only giving up four hits through seven and eight innings respectively. The score was 1-1 going into extra frames, the 5th such game for the Brewers thus far in 2008, and third vs the Reds. Each teams' only run came on a solo HR. J.J. Hardy went deep for his first in the 4th, and Edwin Encarnacion hit one out in the 5th. In the top of the tenth inning, Encarnacion kicked a couple of grounders around, enabling the Brewers to score two runs. Eric Gagne was called upon to finish for the fourth straight game, and gave up back to back HR's to Encarnacion and Paul Bako, yes, thee Paul Bako, to tie the game. After walking the next batter, Yost had enough of Gagne, and called upon Salomon Torres to stop the bleeding. He struck out Corey Patterson on four pitches, and battled Brandon Phillips, before he reached on an infield single. That left men on first and second with one down for Ken Griffey, Jr. Junior got a fastball he liked, and ripped it over Corey Hart's head to plate the winning run. Gagne is now 6/9 converting saves. That is not a great percentage, in fact, it's terrible. Remember, this guy blew eleven saves in his career coming into the season, and has now blown three by April 20. I do worry about the back end of this bullpen. The games are only going to get tougher.

It was another wonderful day today. We almost hit 70 degrees up here in Port Washington. Played some catch with Jill while my mom and daughter played on the swings. Gracie is sleeping right now, and I think I want to come back to that list I mentioned yesterday. I don't have the one I created two years ago, but I'm sure it's changed a little since then. With that being said, here is my current list of all 30 major league teams, ranked from least favorite to favorite, and how's about I sprinkle in some Mets/Phillies ESPN Sunday Night Baseball observations for you....let's get those brooms out !!

(30, Yankees) Every movie needs a villain, and the Yankees are the Darth Vader of major league baseball. Being a Mets fan, it's easy to root against the Yankees, and I've always taken the side of the Red Sox in the great Yankees/Red Sox rivalry. They are, after all, the evil empire. I think it was Adam Morrow who once said, "Rooting for the Yankees is like rooting for the house in black jack". That's no fun! The Yankees are at #30 because somebody has to be. I don't hate the Yankees. I have a great respect for their history, the 26 championships. I loved Don Mattingly growing up, I would have loved to seen Joe DiMaggio

play, and I admire the way Derek Jeter plays today. Now if you want to hear about sports teams I hate, ask me about the Baltimore Ravens or Minnesota Vikings. But don't expect to ever see me donning a Yankees cap.

(29, Braves) They left Milwaukee in the 60's, and they spent a good portion of the past 17 years dominating the National League. Although I will never root for this team, Turner Field is a great place to watch a game (we'll be there May 22nd to see the Mets). I remember in 1999, the Mets came back from 9 to beat the Braves at Shea. When Piazza homered to tie it, Moser called to see if I was watching, and I told him, "I'm gonna loot town! Daddy needs a VCR!" They ended up beating the Mets in the NLCS that year, forever etching their place at 29 on this list.

Checking in on the Mets game, the wind is blowing in at Citizens Bank Park, and Greg Dobbs thought he just went yard, but Ryan Church corralled it at the wall to retire him, but Chase Utley's fly ball could not be contained by mere wind. Utley's homer makes it 1-0 Phillies.

(28, Cardinals) The Cards beat the Brewers in the 1982 World Series, and I've rooted against the Cardinals in every other World Series they've played in since then. They have won more world championships than any other National League club, which kind of makes them the Yankees of the National League. I do remember being a huge John Tudor fan in the 80's, and I did get caught up in the McGwire/Sosa HR race of 1998, but this is another team I don't see myself cheering for under any circumstances. I will see my first game at Busch Stadium as the first game of my baseball trip with Tracy this summer, and it will be against the Brewers.

(27, Blue Jays) It just seemed like the Brewers were always chasing the Blue Jays when I was a kid. When Paul Molitor bolted for Toronto, it felt like I was punched in the stomach. The Blue Jays are another team I've always rooted against. I wanted to see the Phillies beat them in 1993, so that Molitor wouldn't get his ring in Toronto, and I wanted to see Lenny

Dykstra win another one. I have no ambition to ever see the Sky Dome, or whatever they are calling it these days.

(26, Twins) Some of this may lie deeper than baseball. I spent a half a year in St Paul in 2002, and am not real fond of the time I spent there. The Metrodome is easily the worst venue I've ever seen a game at. Rats run the building, the food was horrible, and they can't sell out playoff games. I did root for the Twins in the World Series in 1987 and 1991, but only because they were against the Cardinals and Braves respectively. In every other scenario, I'd root against the Twins. With that being said, Game Seven of the 1991 Series may still be the best game I've ever seen. Morris going 10 scoreless....incredible.

(25, Astros) The Astrodome didn't seem like anything special, and from what I see on TV, I'm not a huge fan of Minute Maid Park. Game six of the 1986 NLCS is one of the most memorable games I've ever seen. The Mets won in 16 innings to advance to the World Series. With other teams in the NL Central ranking much higher, it probably explains why the Astros find themselves at 25.

(24, Rangers) With the Rangers, we're starting to get into the teams that I don't really have any strong feelings about either way. I would love to see a game at Rangers Ballpark in Arlington. I remember when that park was built, I thought it was the best of the new wave of ballparks in the early 90's. My fondest Rangers memory is Greg Harris yielding the tying and winning HR's to Deer and Sveum on Easter Sunday, 1987.

(23, Giants) I've gone on record saying the best player of all time was Willie Mays. I'm certainly not qualified to make a statement like this, after all, Mays retired two years before I was born. But if I had to choose one player that I wish I could have seen play, it's Mays. I had plenty of chances to see Barry Bonds play, and he's one of the reasons that the Giants are lower on this list than they probably should be. Their park looks amazing (don't ask me who owns the naming rights today), and they have a great

history (especially in New York). Will Clark is another favorite of mine. Damn, what a sweet swing…

(22, Diamondbacks) The order of these teams could change on a daily basis, if asked to provide a daily list. One reason the Diamondbacks are towards the lower end today is that they are…….really good! And they pose a threat to the Brewers and Mets in the National League. I also don't want Daron Sutton being a part of a winner. Not until he gives me that reason. Daron? E-mail me! My address is joe…….eh, nevermind. I'm sure you'll write a "tell all" one day. And yes, I'll write the forward.

(21, Rays) Have the Rays ever NOT taken last place? It's hard to place this team too low on this list, because they've never been a winner. There is little to no history to speak of, and they play at Tropicana Field. Unfortunately, they are not higher than 21 for the exact same reasons. I want to like the Rays. Changing the team name isn't enough. Build a new stadium, and create an identity. And beat those Yankees!!

The Mets are still down 1-0 in the 5th inning. The Phillies are rallying with 2 on and nobody out, with Utley, Howard and Burrell coming up. Every Phillie but Adam Eaton has one hit, and the Mets have but two hits thus far. Chase Utley just ripped one…..get foul, GET FOUL…….shit. Chase Utley 4, Mets 0.

(20, Rockies) How could you not enjoy the run the Rockies went on at the end of the 2007 season. I don't remember the specifics, but they won something like 13 of 14 games at the end of the season to force a tie with the Padres. They beat Trevor Hoffman in the tiebreaker game to advance to the NL playoffs, then swept the Phillies and Diamondbacks to get to the World Series. Still, not much of a history, the Rockies should be an AL team.

Gracie, you just saw the most exciting play in baseball……the lead off triple. And even better, a Jose Reyes lead off triple. The triple is much more exciting than a home run. The triple sits on your lap, seduces you, and you never know how it's gonna end. The home run is over as soon as it starts. Chase the Reyes triple with a Castillo single, a Wright double, a Beltran single and a Church single, and we are tied at 4! Game on!

(19, Nationals) The former Expos climb this list just by not playing in Olympic Stadium or old RFK. From what I've heard, Nationals Park is a gem. I will definitely make it out there one of these years.

(18, Marlins) This is another team that will benefit by building a new stadium, and probably would like them more if they weren't in the NL East. The Marlins have kind of a weird history. They've won two titles since they entered the league in 1993, but each time, they've disbanded the team in the off-season immediately after winning the Series. Must be frustrating, but ask yourself this....Is winning a World Series worth losing your entire roster and being terrible for the next four years?

(17, Mariners) Have you noticed I'm basing a lot of this list on the parks the teams play in? Safeco looks incredible, and that certainly increases the stock of the Mariners. When Gorman Thomas was a Mariner in 1984, I rooted for them, and I love Felix Hernandez now.

(16, Angels) After the heartbreak that Angels fans suffered in 1982 and 1986, it was good to see the Angels win it all in 2002. They played the Giants in the World Series the year I was living in St Paul, and I remember this being a pretty compelling series. The Angels play in another beautiful park. Just stop renaming the team already. You'll always be the California Angels to me.

(15, White Sox) There was a brief stint in the early 90's when I considered myself somewhat of a White Sox fan. I was a big fan of Jack McDowell and Bobby Thigpen back then, and this was also around the time that Frank Thomas was becoming the most dangerous hitter in the game. Not a huge fan of U.S. Cellular, though. The thing I miss most about the Brewers move to the National League is the rivalry we had with the White Sox. The Sox played a portion of their games at County Stadium in the

late 60's, and for a while, it looked like they might move to Milwaukee. It never happened, but the Sox did finally win their first World Championship since 1917, when they beat the Astros in the 2005 World Series.

Pedro Feliz just led off the home half of the 7th with a solo HR, to give the Phillies a 5-4 lead. It looks like that's all the Phillies will manage, and the game will now move to the 8th inning. Let's go Mets! Let's go Mets! Let's go Mets!

(14, Royals) These days, the Royals are considered the poster child for small market clubs, but when I was a kid, it seemed like NBC always had the Royals on their game of the week. Brett, Saberhagen, Quisenberry, the list goes on and on. The 1985 World Series was the first Series I ever saw in it's entirety. I'd love to see a game in Kansas City. I've always been drawn to the way it looks. I hope to see the Royals turn it around. It would be good for baseball to see them be a player again in the American League.

(13, Orioles) Camden Yards is another park I have to see. The Orioles have a great history, and they won the first World Series I really paid attention to. Much like the Royals, having the Orioles contend late in the season is great for the game. This June, I'll be seeing my first Orioles game in over a decade as they visit Miller Park for an interleague series.

(12, Athletics) I was drawn to the A's teams of the late 80's for a couple of reasons. First, what a cast of characters! The Hendu Bros, Canseco, McGwire, Eckersley, Stewart, Welch. They were simply a fun team to watch. I also had this idea that I'd one day be drafted by the A's, since their Class A team was in Madison at the time. I'm also fascinated with the early 70's team that won three straight championships. Mandatory moustaches? I love it!

(11, Phillies) As I type, the Phillies are #30, as they are beating my Mets, 5-4 in the 8th inning. But I have historically liked the Phillies. Pete Rose was a Phillie when I started following

baseball. *Always loved Schmidt. The 1993 team was a fun bunch of guys.....Dykstra, Kruk, Mitch Williams, Darren Daulton. They have a fun team now, too, with Ryan Howard, Chase Utley, Jimmy Rollins, and one of my favorite pitchers, Cole Hamels. Citizens Bank Park is another ballpark that is a must see, from what I've read.*

(10, Dodgers) Great history, classy organization, and Alyssa Milano. What more do you need? The Dodgers did break my heart in 1988, upsetting the Mets in the NLCS, but this is another team that baseball is better off for having. Tons of greats have worn Dodger Blue.....Koufax, Robinson, Valenzuela, Piazza. I haven't even scratched the surface.

(9, Pirates) This one is a mystery. I have no solid reason why the Pirates are 9. I can't think of too many Pirates that I've thought of as a favorite, they haven't played in a World Series since I've been following this great sport, and they play in Pittsburgh! But, PNC Park is the best park I've seen on paper, and they've been losing forever, and I want to see them turn it around (just not this year).

(8, Cubs) The Cubs had a solid hold on #3 for years, but it's just hard to root for them these days, for they are the number one rival of the Brewers. The reason they are this high is that I cannot ignore history. I loved the Cubs in 1984. I wanted them to win it all in 2003, and there is nothing like an afternoon game at Wrigley Field. Look, it may seem hypocritical, but if the Cubs get to the playoffs in a year when the Mets and Brewers fall out early, I'm hopping on board. I want to see the Cubs win it all, again, just not in 2008. I could not bring myself to cheer for the Cubs in the playoffs last year, after the Mets and Brewers choked away their leads. I had to watch last year's playoffs subjectively for that reason.

OK, it's the top of the ninth. Brad Lidge is on to save it for the Phillies. We are off to a good start, as Damion Easley has drawn a walk, and Jose Reyes has reached on an infield single. Come on, baby! Two on, nobody out for Luis Castillo. Look for him to bunt.....damn, I love this game! Castillo is still squaring to bunt with two strikes, I'm not sure if I like that. He swings away, fouling one back. The next pitch is a slider, down and in, and Castillo swings and misses for strike three. David Wright, who is hotter than two hells (thanks, Tracy), will come to the plate with two on, and one out. It looks like the wind has kept a Wright foul ball in play, and Ryan Howard secures it for the second out. It's up to Carlos Beltran. He's just hit a smash to short, Bruntlett dives, and gets Beltran by half a step, and that's the game. Great game, off to Wrigley Field for a short two game series. Back on ESPN tomorrow night......enjoy the rest of the list.

(7, Padres) The current roster is the reason the Padres are ranking this high. Jake Peavy may be my favorite pitcher to watch these days, and I also enjoy Chris Young. What can you say about Greg Maddux, he's always been a joy to watch pitch, and Mark Prior may crack the rotation this season. Hey, I don't care what my business cards say, I'm a pitcher, and I love good pitching, of which the Padres have a ton. Petco Park is probably the number one reason I'd ever visit California. It just looks phenomenal.

(6, Reds) A lot of this has to do with all the Chattanooga Lookouts games I've seen in the last four years. As I mentioned earlier, the Lookouts are the AA team of the Reds, and it's kind of neat to see the kids you've seen in the minors have success in the bigs. We were gonna see Great American Ballpark this summer, but decided to see a minor league game in Indianapolis instead. Cincinnati will be added to the to-do list for future games.

(5, Red Sox) You would think the Red Sox would be really low, since they were the opponents of the Mets in the '86 Series. But, because of the way Game Six ended, I've always had compassion for the Red Sox fans. They seem like the best fans in the world. I was really happy to see them win in 2004. Good for those fans, and good for Bill Buckner. Buckner was a solid player, compiling over 2700 hits and a lifetime batting average of .289, but he'll always be remembered for game six. It's not fair what he had to go through since then, and when I saw him throw out the

first pitch at the Sox home opener a couple of weeks back, I couldn't help but cry. I simply have to get to Fenway for a game. I have to. I have some "family" ties to the Sox as well. Tony Conigliaro was a cousin of my Grandfather's, and Clay Buchholz, although not related to me, is making good of the Buchholz name, and living the dream I could not. When he no-hit the Orioles last year, my mom and I choked back tears of joy. And I would not be writing this book had I not first read "Faithful", the 2004 chronicle of the 2004 Boston Red Sox, written by Stewart O'Nan and Stephen King.

(4, Tigers) One of my all time favorite teams was the 1991 Detroit Tigers. The team was stacked with a bunch of long ball hitters, such as AL Home Run King, Cecil Fielder, Mickey Tettleton, Pete Incaviglia, and Lou Whitaker. And they added another one in the off-season. Rob Deer. This is not the last time you'll hear about Deer in this book. He was a Brewer from 1986-1990, and along with Gorman Thomas and Robin Yount, among my favorite Brewers of all time. I wish I would have seen a game at Tigers Stadium, and I will get a chance to see Comerica Park this July.

(3, Indians) Yeah, this is probably because I'm a Browns fan, so what. The Browns fans are great fans, and that means the Indians fans are great as well. When Gorman was traded, I didn't understand it at first, I was too young, but soon after, I started following the Indians. Major League was filmed in Milwaukee, and the Indians played a three game series here at Miller Park in 2007, due to a huge snow storm in Cleveland. It was neat to see the Milwaukee fans cheer the Indians as if they were their own. Proof positive that Milwaukee is a great baseball town. The Jake, I'm sorry, Progressive Field, is a fantastic place to watch a game. We'll be back this summer. I would love to see the Indians make it out of the AL if the Mets or Brewers were to represent the NL. I truly couldn't be upset with the outcome if this were to happen. Cleveland is like a second home to me.

(2, Brewers) and (1, Mets) I flipped a fucking coin.

April 21st

Today I spent the day talking to a couple of gentlemen who have done some baseball writing, and they each gave me some good information that I will use in the next couple of months. What I forgot to do was call Pizza Shuttle to reserve a table for their $500, 28 inch pizza challenge. They are challenging any two people to finish a 28 inch pizza in one hour, and Joe and I have agreed to do it. Our respective families aren't happy with us, but for five hundo, I'll eat some serious pie! I'll get on that later in the week. Another thing I didn't do tonight is watch baseball. Amber starts her job in Chicago on May 1st, and tonight we all met at BW3's to send her off. I got to see Timmy Vertz for the first time in a while, and we ate well. The Brewers game was on a couple of the TV's, and I took a peek occasionally. What I did see was Derrick Turnbow giving up the winning run to the Cardinals in the 9th, the final score was 4-3. I also learned that Ben Sheets will miss his scheduled start on Wednesday night. Dave Bush will start in his place.

I called Mike to get a Mets score, and it looks like they lost 7-1. I'm reading now that they were in the game entering the 8th inning, but the Cubs scored 5 runs in the 8th, 4 of them unearned. John Maine pitched pretty well over six innings, but the bats were dead tonight.

It's been five days since I've worked out at all, as I've had a lot on my mind. Hopefully the Mets and Brewers can turn it around tomorrow afternoon, and tomorrow night, I gotta get back on that bike. The writing may be light over the next few days, for I also have to prepare for a financial presentation I'll be making to anywhere from 40-200 students on Saturday afternoon. I'll make up for it throughout the season.

April 22

The Brewers played a rare Tuesday afternoon game at home to cap a short two game series with St Louis. Work was busy, and the game was on in the background, but I don't recall much about the game. I was the only one in the room that was unaware that Rickie Weeks hit a bases loaded triple in the sixth inning to make it 8-3 Brewers. As a matter of fact, when Joe said that it was 8-3, I was upset, assuming the Cards were up. The Cardinals scored 4 in the seventh to make it 8-7, and Eric Gagne blew another save, his fourth blown save in ten chances, to send the Brewers to their sixth extra innings game already in 2008. This one was not entirely Gagne's fault, as Rickie Weeks threw in the dirt at the backend of a 5-4-3 double play, allowing the tying run to score. The game should have ended right there. Uecker implied that Weeks rushed the throw, and he would have had Pujols by a good four feet with a good throw. The game would end up going 12 innings, with Gabe Kapler driving in Gabe Gross on an RBI single in the 12th. Ironically, the Brewers traded Gabe Gross to Tampa Bay shortly after the game. This move doesn't shock me. Mike Cameron will be joining the roster on the 29th, Tony Gwynn is ready to come off the DL, and Gabe Kapler has had an amazing start to the season. Best of luck to you, Gabe Gross.

The Mets apparently forgot to bring their bats to Chicago, as they dropped game two by a score of 8-1. The Mets were outscored 15-2 in the two game series, and they have now lost three in a row. Ronny Cedeno hit a grand slam in the eighth to seal the deal. The Mets travel to Washington tomorrow to visit Nationals Park for the first time. Hopefully, they can turn it around against the same team they swept at Shea last week.

April 23

Tonight marks the return of Geoff Jenkins to Milwaukee. Jenkins signed with Philadelphia in the off-season, when the

Brewers made it clear that they would not shell out $9 million to keep him around as a fourth outfielder. Look, I like Jenkins, but it was the right move. And I wish Jenkins all the success in the world with Philadelphia. We took in the game tonight, and Heather and I each brought someone to talk to. Heather's friend, Maureen, said I looked nice for date night, and I corrected her immediately, saying this was no date night. I don't think I've ever downed three tubular meats on a date. I'm here to see the Brewers win, and one of my favorite pitchers is going for the Phillies, Cole Hamels. By the way, on a side note, I learned tonight that it's not cool to ask a woman if she's had a nose job. Sorry 'bout that, Maureen. The Brewers gave Jenkins a video montage before the lineups were announced, and Jenkins acknowledged the crowd with a tip of the cap. Neat moment.

Dave Bush, who lost his rotation spot to Yovani Gallardo last week, found himself starting tonight, with Ben Sheets scratched due to last week's injury. But he would be facing a Philadelphia lineup without it's normal 1 and 2 hitters, with Jimmy Rollins and Shane Victorino on the DL. 3 and 4 will hurt you, however, with Chase Utley, who came into tonight's game with a major league leading 9 HR, and Ryan Howard, who was the 2006 NL MVP, while hitting 58 dingers, and knocking in 149 runs.

The Phillies were unable to score in the 1st, and the lefty Cole Hamels took the hill against a lineup of eight righties and Prince Fielder. The Brewers hit lefties well, and got to Hamels early tonight. Weeks led off with a double, and Gabe Kapler singled to center to score Weeks. Kapler ended up on third after a couple of errant Phillie throws. Ryan Braun popped up to 2nd base to kill the buzz. I know it's early, but Braun doesn't look himself up there. He seems to be trying to pull everything, and I don't see that swagger I saw last year. Gee, those sophomore slumps are for real, aren't they? As Prince Fielder stepped to the place, I noticed the shift the Phillies were putting on him. Greg Dobbs, the 3B tonight, was standing near shortstop. With Kapler on 3rd, and one out, I turned to Mike and started to sell the idea of Fiedler laying one down the 3rd base line to score Kapler. I figured that getting two runs right out of the box against Hamels would be huge, but before Mike could buy what I was selling, Fiedler hit a rope over the right field wall for a two run shot. I quietly asked

Mike never to mention that crazy idea to anyone we knew. This was Fielder's first HR at Miller Park this season. 3-0 Brewers after the 1st.

I want to take a moment to amend something I reported the day of the home opener. It turns out that the "kiddie dog" is only named as such at the concession stand near the Kids Zone in the upper deck. This was confirmed as we were walking to our seats, and we noticed "hot dog" on the menu. Also, I had a bite of the "jumbo" hot dog, and it really *is* just a bigger version of what I love. It did not taste "kosher", and I think I will indulge in a "jumbo" on Saturday night. Also, I had an Italian dipped in marinara, and it was, as Erik Ferrar would say, "OUTSTANDING".

Chase Utley hit a HR to the deepest part of the ballpark in the 3rd inning, his league leading 10th of year, prompting me to text "Chase Utley is good at baseball" to Jamie, who drafted him in the first round of our Rotisserie League. Greg Dobbs, yes, thee Greg Dobbs, hit a two run bomb in the 5th to tie the game. Dave Bush is not feeling the love tonight from the 30,000 plus fans. Pat Burrell added a knock in the sixth, and the fans really let Bush have it. I was out taking a walk as Burrell was taking Bush deep (these damn knees!). Hey, Beavis....I said, taking Bush deep....

Entering the bottom of the 8th, Cole Hamels was still on for the Phillies, despite being at 110 pitches. Ryan Braun led off the inning with a long double to right center, and Hamels would stay in to face Fielder. He went right after him, and Fielder did not wait long to hit his 2nd home dinger of the year, depositing a 1-1 fastball in the same general area he hit his first inning homer. 5-4 Brewers! I thought that homer warranted a curtain call, but we didn't get one. I notice Derrick Turnbow warming up in the pen, and it looks like he'll be called on to save this one tonight. Eric Gagne has pitched in five of the last six games, and he has four blown saves already this season. Turnbow was greeted with a nice ovation, keep in mind, only two years removed from being an All Star. He would face 8-9-1 in the order to start the inning. He got Eric Bruntlett on strikes, as the crowd roared. Maybe not a roar, but......nah, we'll just say we roared. So Taguchi walked, stole second, and advanced to third on a throwing error by Jason Kendall. Now the Phillies have a man on third with one out. The next batter was Jayson Werth, who looked at a couple of pitches, then battled Turnbow deep into the count. Werth would strike out swinging, and now everybody is up. Pedro Feliz now stands between the Brewers and a 13-8 record. From section 426, I'm pleading with Turnbow to just throw strikes, take your chances with Feliz, and not throw anything in the dirt. I don't want to see this game tied on a wild pitch. Turnbow got Feliz to ground to Hardy, and this ballgame is over!

Prince Fielder made a comment after the game that I thought was funny. People have been speculating that he's not hitting dingers because he's no longer eating meat. He responded by saying, "You guys (reporters) eat meat all day, and you can't hit a ball".

I can't tell you much about the Mets game, other than they won tonight in Washington, 7-2. I was peeking at the score throughout the night, but gave the Brewers most of my attention on this night. From what I read, Johan looked good, going seven innings and holding the Nationals to two earned. Each team will look to sweep their respective two game series tomorrow.

April 24

Not much to write about today. The Brewers could never get the bats going vs Jamie Moyer, and David Riske gave up two runs in the 8th, after Jeff Suppan pitched beautifully. Suppan went seven innings, gave up only five hits, and allowed only one run. The Brewers were not able to score against Brad Lidge in the 9th, and the Phillies leave town with a split.

The Mets carried a 3-0 lead in the bottom of the 5th, but the Nationals would put 10 runs up in the next three innings. The score was 10-5 when it was all said and done. So, no sweep for the Mets either. I taped the Office, so I'm gonna watch that, and Brett Favre is on Letterman tonight. Not to mention the very beautiful and talented Tina Fey. Call me!

April 25

I have the Mets game on in the background as I write tonight, but I'm not doing a ton of baseball writing. I'm writing a letter to my daughter. You won't see it in this book, but it's important that I mention it, if I seem distracted lately. Thank goodness for baseball....

Tonight's Mets/Braves game is intriguing because of the pitching matchup. The Braves send Jair Jurrjens to the mound vs Mike Pelfrey of the Mets. These are two young men the NL East better get used to seeing for a long time. I saw something in the 3rd inning that I don't think I've ever seen personally. Jurrjens walked Luis Castillo to load the bases, then went on to walk the next three batters to bring in 3 straight runs. But if you take away the four consecutive walks in the 3rd, Jurrjens pitched very well. He went 6 innings, gave up only two hits and struck out 4. Pelfrey struggled a bit tonight, and the Mets bats fell silent again, as the Braves took game one tonight, 6-3.

Speaking of silent bats, the Brewers and Marlins went scoreless through nine, meaning the Brewers would play extra innings for what seems the millionth time this season. Yovani Gallardo looked great again today, going seven scoreless and striking out 5, lowering his ERA to 0.64. In the tenth the Marlins touched Guillermo Mota for three runs, and the Brewers could not get to the Marlins bullpen, and the Marlins took game one, 3-0. The Brewers were wearing their 1982 throwbacks tonight, but I don't remember that being advertised, nor do I see it mentioned in their 2008 media guide. Maybe they're just springing it on the fans randomly, based on the team's record when they advertise the old uniforms. I don't have the numbers, but it's not good. And it certainly wasn't good tonight.

I have to spend the rest of tonight preparing for tomorrow's Money Conference. It'll be a long day, highlighted by Reggie White's son, Jeremy, speaking to the attendees, and plugging his book. Maybe next year, the Money Conference invites Jimmy the B's son to plug his book. Yeah, right!

April 26

I was able to leave the Money Conference a little earlier than I thought I would, so I ran home for about an hour to change clothes and check on the Mets. It looks like we won today, on the strength of a seven strikeout performance by John Maine, over five innings. A Carlos Beltran two run double in the 4th put the Mets ahead for good. The Braves would add a run later, but the Mets held on to win 4-3, using six pitchers.

Tonight, I will be joined at the game by Jill, Gina and Jordan, who is my sister's God son. Jordan is about 16, and I spent about a year watching Jordan during the day when he was around two years old, maybe a little younger. It's been a long time since I've seen him. Jill had to wait for Jordan outside as he was getting dropped off, so Gina and I walked in to sit down for a bit. I realized as we were taking the escalator upstairs that I left my wallet in the car. It looks like I will not be enjoying any dogs tonight.

It looks like a huge crowd tonight, easily a sell out. I've been looking forward to the game all day, and as I take in the sights and smells, I notice that Gina is already lost in her book. Jill called from outside to let us know she'll be in by the 2nd inning or so. Before the game even gets underway, four people have been asked to leave the game after being asked four times by the usher to surrender the beer they snuck in. Later in the game, another guy would be thrown out for throwing a bottle. There's a reason the NCAA doesn't sell beer at their events.

Hanley Ramirez, who is one of the best young players in all the game, comes in to tonight's game with a batting average of .333 and 7 homers. Make that 8 homers, as Ramirez hits a moon shot off of Carlos Villanueva to open the game. But, that's all they would get in the first. The Brewers were unable to score off big Mark Hendrickson in their half. Hendrickson is one of eleven athletes to have competed in both the NBA and major league baseball. For those of you unfamiliar with it, the NBA stands for National Basketball Association, and it used to be a major sports league based out of North America. I went to wikipedia recently to look up what year they folded, and apparently, they still play games! How neat!

Jill and Jordan arrived in the top of the 2nd. I asked Jordan if he remembered me, and he said he did, but certainly not from 1994. He plays baseball himself, and will be trying out for the varsity team this summer. He would like to be the closer and play some left field. Whenever you want to see a game, Jordan, let me know. In the bottom of the 2nd, the Brewers had loaded the bases with one out, and the batter was Villanueva. There was something I noticed as Villanueva stepped in the box. Dale Sveum, the Brewers current 3rd base coach, and hero of Easter Sunday 1987, was talking to Prince Fielder, who was on 3rd. I notice that as Sveum was talking, Prince's head snapped up really quick, and I knew at that moment that the squeeze was on. And sure enough, it was, as Villanueva got the bunt down, and Fielder scored to tie the game. The crowd went nuts, as Gina read on.

One of things I love most about baseball is the way children connect to the game. The pace of a baseball game is often mocked as being "way too slow", but I think it's perfect, in the sense that fans of all ages have time to dissect and wax poetic about the story that is being told on the field, without missing any of it. You don't get that a lot in football, and certainly not basketball. To my left, I see a group of five kids, and they seem to be entertained by everything presented to them. They have a different comment for each Brewer that steps in the batter's box, and they do a different dance for each player's entrance music that blares through the Miller Park speakers. I notice two of them enjoying dogs (must be nice to not forget your wallet), and one of them is sharing nachos with his dad. Later in the game, Jordan starts proposing trades that the Brewers should make. "What if we traded Fielder, Braun and Hart to the Yankees for A-Rod?" After I explained why that couldn't work, he said, "What about trading Bill Hall for David Ortiz?" I asked, "Where would we play Ortiz? There's no DH in the NL." "Oh", he said. "Nevermind." Gina picked her head up from her book to throw out the occasional, "Uncle Joe, isn't J.J. Hardy cute?" She's my 12 year old niece, and I don't have the heart to simply say, "No", so I just add, "He plays a good shortstop."

In the bottom of the 3rd, the Brewers added two more runs, first on a Prince Fielder single, then on a J.J. Hardy sacrifice fly. So the Brewers head into the 4th inning up 3-1. My sister came through for me in the 4th by offering to feed her idiot brother. I went with the jumbo dog instead of the two regular hot dogs, based on the one bite from Saturday night.

There was an interesting play in the 5th inning. Mark Hendrickson hit a leadoff triple to center, that got by a diving Gabe Kapler. If it were anyone on the Marlins but Hendrickson, it would have been an inside the park home run. With one out, Dan Uggla hit a long fly ball to left field. Ryan Braun retired Uggla, and Braun rifled back in towards Kendall. But Hendrickson was jogging in, and was nearly out at the plate when the ball arrived to Kendall. That would have been embarrassing for Hendrickson. It was a great throw by Braun. That sacrifice fly made the score 3-2 Brewers.

The Marlins would tie the game in the 8th off of Salomon Torres. The damage could have been much worse, but Torres induced a double play ball, with the run scoring on the DP. In the bottom of the 8th, the Marlins would go to left hander Renyel Pinto to face Fielder. And just like he did vs Cole Hamels in the 8th inning on Wednesday night, Fielder hits a solo HR, this time to left center, to take the lead. I'm high-fiving nieces, sisters, sons of sister's friends, "cougars", ushers, old men, EVERYONE.

Eric Gagne came on in the 9th, and struck out the side, allowing only one hit to notch his seventh save of the season. Another great night at the ball park! Good company, good pitching, clutch hitting, great crowd (minus a few a-holes), and a Brewers win. As great as the game was, all I can think about walking back to the car, and driving back home, was the jumbo dog.....

April 27

By the time Jill arrived for the Brewers game today, the Mets were already up 4-0 vs John Smoltz in their game vs the

Braves. A common courtesy that I abide by is that if someone is coming over for the Brewers game, that I don't spend the whole game going back and forth between the two games. The same goes during the NFL season. If I have company coming over for the Packers game, I don't keep switching back and forth between the Packers and Browns games. As my mom and Mike read this, there eyebrows twinge in disagreement. I'm getting better, and it certainly will help this season that the two teams combine for nine prime time games. I'll be able to see more full Browns games this fall than I ever have been able to. So as the Brewers game starts, I follow the Mets game on cbssports.com.

Not much scoring again today, but the Brewers did carry a 1-0 lead into the sixth inning. Manny Parra looks like he's pitching well enough to keep his spot in the rotation. With Ben Sheets scheduled to go on Tuesday at Wrigley, many are speculating that either Parra or Bush will go back to Nashville to make room for Mike Cameron, who will make his Brewers debut that evening. Parra would end up giving up a couple of runs in the sixth, and the Marlins now lead the game 2-1.

Ned Yost wanted to get Craig Counsell a start today, with the idea that he get around two starts a week in the infield. Counsell spelled Hardy earlier in the week, and Yost had to decide to sit either Hall or Weeks, both of whom have played every game thus far in 2008. Yost decided to literally pick names out of a hat, and had Bill Hall draw the name that would sit today. Hall drew his own name, and Yost would be quoted as saying, "Bill Hall benched himself today." Hall would enter the game in a double switch in the sixth, and made the most out of the very first pitch he saw at the plate, hitting a towering home run to left to tie the game. As if I need to tell you, the Brewers would end up going extras again. I might as well have called this book, "The Tenth Inning" because of all the tenth innings I've written about. Today's tenth inning didn't go the Brewers way, but it went well for a former Brewer. Wes Helms hit a lead off homer off Seth McClung that would prove to be the game winner today. The fish take today's rubber game, 3-2 in ten, and the Brewer's end up losing three of their last four games on this homestand.

The Mets took today's game with the Braves, 6-3, on the strength of two Carlos Delgado home runs. After four weeks of action, the Mets are 13-11, and a game and a half back of the Marlins in the NL East. The Brewers are 14-11, a game and a half behind the Cards, and two games back of the Cubs. In a scheduling quirk, the Brewers return to Wrigley on Tuesday, where they opened the season, and the Cubs will not visit Miller Park until late July.

April 28

It's a light schedule in the majors, and the Brewers have a scheduled off day, before they start their series with the Cubs tomorrow night. The Mets and Pirates got rained out. I took some time to read about who the Browns and Packers drafted this weekend. The Packers drafted two quarterbacks, Brian Brohm of Louisville and Matt Flynn of LSU. The Browns didn't have a day one pick, but ended up getting Wisconsin WR Paul Hubbard on day two. It looks like my fantasy football league is ready to be renewed on cbssports.com, and I'll get on that in the next couple of weeks. We enter our 16th year this fall, and we are planning a reunion of some sort in January of 2009. I'm thinking of roasting my good friend, Mike Schwingle, like they do on Comedy Central. We'll try to get the likes of Jason Tietz, John Koloske and maybe a Gary Schwingle to playfully take jabs at Mike, and I've written some stuff already. Maybe we can talk Bea Arthur to flying to Milwaukee for the occasion, and I'm almost certain we could get Jon Lovitz and Andy Dick.

April 29

Tonight's pitching matchup at Shea is a dandy. Johan Santana is going for the Metropolitans, and Ian Snell is throwing for the Pirates. It looks like the weather will cooperate tonight, after last night's rain out. I am hungry for baseball, with very little going on last night. This is also a big night for the Brewers, as Ben Sheets returns to the hill after missing his last start, and Mike Cameron will make his Milwaukee Brewers debut tonight, playing centerfield and batting second. Gracie has been asleep since I got home, and I can tell from looking at her room that she had a great time. To borrow a phrase from my dear Grandma, her room "looks like a cyclone hit it."

Nate McLouth, the Pirates lead off batter tonight, quickly deposited the second pitch he saw from Santana into the right field stands for a home run. Jason Bay would hit one out as well in the 4th. As good as Santana is, this is his weakness, always amongst the league leaders in home runs allowed. So the Mets will be playing from behind tonight.

The game time temperature at Wrigley tonight is 41 degrees, which would be downright balmy for most Packers/Bears games, but damn cold for baseball. Most everyone is wearing the long sleeves tonight. Mike Cameron's first at-bat in a Brewers uniform was a memorable one, as he nearly went deep, doubling high off the wall in left field. Ryan Braun reached first after he struck out swinging, as strike three was in the dirt, and got by Cubs catcher, Geovany Soto. Prince Fielder hit a towering sacrifice fly to give the Brewers an early lead. The Cubs got two runs right back in the bottom half...2-1 Cubs.

Checking back with the Mets, Ryan Church continued to stay hot, hitting a long HR off Ian Snell to tie the game in the bottom of the 4th. Church is now hitting .316 with 3 dingers. In the 5th, the Mets added two more, highlighted by an RBI triple by Jose Reyes. It would remain 4-2 Mets through seven innings.

The Brewers were able to put three up on the Cubs in the 3rd. Prince Fielder added his second sacrifice fly of the game to tie it, Corey Hart tripled home Ryan Braun to take the lead, and Bill Hall singled home Hart to make it 4-2 Brewers. The Cubs came right back to score two in their half of the 3rd, and after three innings, the Brewers and Cubs were deadlocked at 4 a piece.

Duaner Sanchez would walk Adam LaRoche with the bases loaded in the 8th inning to bring the Pirates within one. Billy Wagner would come on in the ninth to attempt to notch the save, but a costly Jose Reyes throwing error would lead to Freddy Sanchez singling home Brian Bixler to tie the game. It would be

Wagner's first blown save of the year. But David Wright would bail out the Mets as this game would go extra frames tonight. With the bases loaded in the bottom of the 11th, Wright hit a towering single down the right field line to give the Mets the win tonight. The win puts the Mets at 14-11, and they pull within a half game of the Marlins in the NL East.

The Brewers scored in the top of the 5th to give Ben Sheets a 5-4 lead to work with heading to the bottom of the inning. Sheets would leave after 5 with the lead in tact, only allowing three hits, but walking a career high seven batters. The Crew would add a run in the sixth, and three more in the seventh to increase the lead to 9-4. Salomon Torres would inherit the sizeable lead in the bottom of the seventh, but struggled tonight, giving up three runs on four hits, and the Brewers now found themselves only up two, 9-7. J.J. Hardy drove in the Brewers tenth run of the evening in the 8th, and Eric Gagne pitched a scoreless ninth to give the Brewers a win in the series opener, their third win in four games thus far at Wrigley in 2008.

April 30

It was an ugly night of baseball. Let's just say they both lost, and move on.

2. Not Looking Good

May 1st

Today we'll be driving up to Wrigley Field for the rubber game in the Brewers/Cubs series. The Brewers will try to rebound from their 19-5 loss last night. The pitching matchup will be a great one, as Yovani Gallardo will hook up with Carlos Zambrano. Game time is 1:20pm. It's about 10:30am as I start to head to Chicago, and I can tell the traffic is going to be awful. I hit a bunch of construction that I wasn't planning on, and I don't hit Addison until about 12:55. Of course, it takes forever to find a parking space, and I settle for a tight spot about twelve blocks away from Wrigley. I hook up with Schewe on the corner of Addison and Clark as the national anthem is being sung. By the time we reach our seats, the Brewers have already been retired in the top of the first. Matt and I bought a couple of SRO tickets to a Cardinals/Cubs game last August, and we'll probably make this an annual deal. He's a huge Cubs and Bears fan. We are joined today by his wife, Erika, Michael Weber and his girlfriend, and TJ Lindwall. I asked Schewe what TJ stood for, and he told me that it stood for Tommy John. I wish I had a lefty's name, like Sandy, or Whitey, or Fernando.

There's a good mix of Brewers and Cubs fans in the stands today. Right in front of us is a married couple wearing matching Brewers regalia. Behind us, a family of six, here to see a Brewers win. The wind is really blowing out to left field today. With eight right handed batters in the Brewers lineup, we may see some serious long balls today. Time for a beer...

The Cubs would strike first today, in the bottom of the third inning. Carlos Zambrano, who is a great hitting pitcher that comes into today with 12 career home runs, looked down right silly trying to check his swing on a 1-1 curve ball from Gallardo. Before I can get the phrase, "What was that, Schewe?" out of my mouth,

Zambrano hits an opposite field home run to left. I've said it once, and I'll say it again. I hate facing Zambrano, but I'd love him on my team(s). The guy is a competitor, and I love his passion for the game.

Both teams had a hard time coming up with big two out clutch hits this afternoon, and the Brewers didn't tally until the top of the sixth, when Ryan Braun hit his 4th home run of the season. Off the top of my head, it seems like it's been about three weeks since his last bomb. After the Brewers half of the sixth, it was time to head downstairs for a jumbo dog and some nachos. The food at Wrigley is not the best, but today, it tasted great.

Every Brewers fan in the stands took a collective deep breath in the bottom of the sixth. Cubs outfielder Reed Johnson tried to bunt for a hit, and Gallardo and Fielder both converged for the bag at the same time. As Fielder tagged Johnson out, Gallardo tripped past a diving Johnson, and appeared to badly twist his knee. He stayed down for several minutes, and eventually finished the inning, but not before the Cubs rallied for two runs to take a 3-1 lead.

As I'm sitting in the stands today, I can't help but notice just how many Kosuke Fukudome jerseys and t-shirts I see worn by adoring Cubs fans. He's been a Cub for barely a month, and he's already the most popular player on the team. He's 4-4 today, and he's hitting .348 for the season, so the numbers add up. Amongst the various Cubs fans is a fan behind me who gets really excited whenever the Cubs hit any sort of fly ball. On at least four occasions in the first six innings, I've heard him exclaim, "OH MY GOD" as a Cub is hitting a lazy fly ball. A guy in front of us jokes that he must have attended the Chip Carey school of broadcasting…"SWUNG ON AND BELTED…to shallow left, the shortstop squeezes to retire the side."

One of the great traditions of seeing a game at Wrigley is singing "Take Me Out to the Ballgame" in the middle of the seventh. Most, if not all ballparks partake in this tradition, but there's nothing like the way it's done at Wrigley. Since Harry Carey's passing in 1998, the Cubs have traditionally had a celebrity or well known personality lead in the rendition, and today, Bob Uecker has been asked to take the lead. Uecker uses an interesting angle in his version. He is one of the few people that the Cubs ask to lead in "Take Me Out to the Ballgame" that is employed by the opponent, and instead of saying, "It's root, root, root for the home team, if they don't win it's a shame", he sings, "I'll root, root, root for the Brewers, and you do the same for the Cubs". It's always fun to hear the division amongst fans in the stands. While Uecker is saying, "Brewers" with all the Brewers fans in attendance, Cubs fans try to drown in out with a monstrous "CUBBIES". Nothing like an afternoon at Wrigley....

In the top of the 8th, the Cubs replaced CF Reed Johnson with Felix Pie for defensive purposes, a move that would go on to haunt Lou Pinella. Not because Pie shouldn't be in there, but he should be replacing Soriano in left, and not Johnson in center. The Cubs would call upon Kerry Wood to shut the door today. This is his first appearance vs the Brewers since giving up three runs in the ninth on Opening Day. At this point, most of the fans are rising to their feet to see how this one unfolds, and the first pitch Kerry Wood delivers is a slider that grazes Craig Counsell. Yost would go to his bench and ask Gabe Kapler to pinch hit for Brian Shouse, who only threw one pitch to Daryle Ward before picking off Kosuke Fukudome to end the 8th inning. Kapler would hit a fly ball to deep left, but it looked playable all the way. However, Alfonso Soriano would badly misjudge it. Score it a double, and the Brewers have ducks on the pond with nobody out, and Jason Kendall coming to the plate. Now everyone is up! Kendall grounded an 0-1 slider past Wood. Ryan Theriot would cut it off before it ended up in centerfield, but Counsell would score and Kapler advanced to third, bringing the Brewers to within one. Rickie Weeks would walk to load the bases, which prompts a visit from Cubs pitching coach, Larry Rothschild. Whatever advice that was given was taken to heart, as Wood got Mike Cameron to strike out on four fastballs. Ryan Braun, who homered in the sixth, would send an 0-1 fastball to deep right field, scoring two, but Weeks was gunned down at home for the inning's second out. The Brewers fans are going crazy, as we've gotten to Wood again. Fielder would tap a grounder to second to end the inning. Here comes Gagne for the save.

Despite walking the leadoff batter, Gagne would settle down, striking out Geovany Soto, and inducing a game ending double play to Felix Pie. The Brewers have now won 4 of 6 games with the Cubs, all in Chicago, and seven of their remaining ten games with the Cubs are at home. They pull within a game of the Cubs, and trail the Cardinals by only a game and a half.

And now for the worst part of seeing a game at Wrigley: the drive back. There is no Mets game tonight, so I won't be in a rush to get back home. I assume the traffic is going to be bad, and I've got a lot of music in the car to keep me company.

May 2nd

The Brewers suffered a major setback today, before a pitch was even thrown in Houston. It was learned that Yovani Gallardo torn his ACL during the sixth inning yesterday, and will require season ending surgery to repair it. This is a huge blow, as Gallardo was proving to be an ace in the making, and the team will miss his 1.80 ERA and ability to eat up innings. The team recalled Dave Bush to take his spot on the roster, and will most likely pitch next Wednesday in Florida. In other news, the Brewers designated Derrick Turnbow for assignment today, meaning his days with the Brewers are most likely over. If he clears waivers, the Brewers can send him to AAA, but Turnbow would most likely decline that, becoming a free agent. I think a change of scenery may do him well.

On the field tonight, the news wasn't much better. Ryan Braun got things under way, hitting a two run homer in the first, and Mike Cameron would hit his first home run in a Brewers uniform in the fifth inning, giving Carlos Villanueva a 4-0 lead to work with, entering the home half of the fifth. But it was all down hill from there, as Hunter Pence would hit a two run homer in the fifth, and then Villanueva would give up back-to-back-to-back homers in the sixth to Tejada, Berkman and Lee to give the Astros a 6-4 lead. Hunter Pence would add his 2nd home run of the night in the 8th, and the final would be 7-4 Houston. In an incredibly surprising game note, the last time that a Brewers starting pitcher other than Ben Sheets has won a game was Saturday, April 5th, when Manny Parra beat San Francisco at home. That's amazing!

        The Mets came into their game with Arizona owning the D-Backs in Arizona. They've beaten them in 11 of their last 12 games played at Chase Field. But the Diamondbacks have the best record in baseball at 20-8, and have a record of 11-3 at home. So something had to give tonight as John Maine faced Micah Owings. The Mets jumped off to an early lead, scoring 3 in the first, led by a leadoff Jose Reyes triple. They added another run in the 2nd, to give the Mets a 4-0 lead. Maine would give two right back in the bottom half, but pretty much settled down after that. Maine would go 6 tonight, and only give up those two second inning runs, while striking out six. Ryan Church added two hits tonight, including his 4th homer, to raise his team leading batting average to .324. David Wright dropped a two run bomb in the sixth to give the Mets a 7-2 lead, and that's how it would end tonight. The Mets beat Micah Owings to give him his first loss of the season. We now trail the Phillies by a half a game in the division. My rotisserie league team has climbed from sixth to second place in the past few days. If I can just find a way to convince my boys that a .248 batting average is not sexy, I may just make a run at this.

May 3rd

        I had to work until 1:30 today, then I enjoyed some Cheesecake Factory for lunch. Schwingle and I loosely committed to seeing "Harold and Kumar Escape From Guantanamo Bay" later tonight. The Cubs/Cardinals will dominate the national games this weekend, as they are the Fox game today, and will be the ESPN Sunday Night game tomorrow. The Mets have a 3:40 CST start today, but have a tough assignment in the 6-0 Brandon Webb. Mike Pelfrey toes the rubber for the Mets.
        The Diamondbacks lead the Mets 5-2 through five innings. Mike Pelfrey did not have it today, giving up nine hits and walking four in his five innings of work. Frankly, he was lucky to only give up the five runs that he did. The D-Backs would end up leaving

eleven men on base today. In the sixth, Carlos Delgado got the Mets back into the game, hitting a 3-run HR off Webb to bring the Mets to within one, 5-4. The game would remain close for a few more innings, until the D-Backs put a 5 spot up in the 8th, and would win by a final of 10-4.

I was in the kitchen making a roast beef and cheddar sammie when I heard Brian Anderson exclaim that Rickie Weeks led off tonight's Brewers game with a long home run. If you're familiar with Minute Maid Park at all, he hit that goofy train in left field. What a clout! Schwingle arrived a few innings later, at this point, the Astros have tied the game at one a piece. We have now fully cemented our plans to see the movie at 9:35 this evening. In the fifth inning, the Astros explode for five runs, on the strength of back to back home runs by Astros pitcher Brandon Backe and leadoff hitter Michael Borne. The Brewers got one back in the sixth, but that would be the end of the scoring tonight, as the Brewers would go on to lose this one, 6-2. The only Brewers regular currently hitting above .300 is Corey Hart, at .309. Listen to some of these averages, and keep in mind, we are now in the first week of May (Weeks, .197, Fielder, .250, Hall, .225, Hardy, .228, even Braun's .279 is far below expectations). The Crew will try to avoid a sweep tomorrow, sending Ben Sheets to the hill.

The movie was just what Mike and I needed tonight. Neil Patrick Harris returned to play himself, and David Krumholtz reminded me that words are funny. Never forget the power of laughter. Thank *you,* Harold and Kumar. Thank *you.*

May 4th

If you haven't figured it out yet, I tend to write more if the teams I'm writing about play well. If the teams struggle, I have less motivation. I would have loved to spend a lot of time telling you that Mike Cameron hit two home runs today, and that Sheets left the game in the seventh with the two run lead, but instead, I'm just going to fast forward to the part about Gagne blowing a two run lead in the ninth by walking three, and allowing two hits. This is Gagne's fifth blown save out of fourteen chances thus far, a percentage of 64%. Seeing as we are only 3 ½ games out of first, this really stresses the importance of having a reliable closer, which we do not. This is the first time the Brewers have been swept all year, and to a much inferior team in the Houston Astros. The Crew will take tomorrow off, and will then head to Florida for a three game set with the surprise Marlins.

The Mets got a solid start out of Johan Santana today, going six, striking out 8 and allowing the Diamondbacks only one run. He left the game with a 2-1 lead, but Joe Smith gave up a two out RBI single to Mark Reynolds to tie the game. The Mets were able to touch Arizona reliever Chad Qualls for three in the top of the ninth, and Billy Wagner came out for his seventh save of the season. We remain a half a game back of Philadelphia in the East, and head to Los Angeles tomorrow for a three game set.

May 5th

The Brewers had a scheduled day off today, and the Mets thought they had the night off. The bats never showed up, scoring only one run on five hits vs Chad Billingsley and the Dodgers. The Mets lit up Oliver Perez for three dingers, including the first major league home run for a kid named Blake DeWitt. The loss puts the Mets at 16-14 on the season.

Here's a bombshell for you: my wife and I are separating. It hurts to say that. It hurts a lot. But it's for the best. I'm sorry, Heather. I will always love you.

May 6th

Two phuckin' hits for the Brewers tonight. Scott Olsen hasn't allowed a run against the Brewers in 16 innings this year. The final was 3-0 Marlins. Sound familiar? We are now 16-16 and five games back of the Cardinals. Now I know it's May, but the Brewers just don't look like contenders at this point. Three of our four infielders are hitting .226 or lower, and we're still not getting consistent pitching out of the starters. Suppan gave up eleven base runners in five innings tonight, and was lucky to only have given up three runs. Yost was tossed in the 4th after arguing balls and strikes, but that did not light a fire under the team.

The Mets and Dodgers spent the first half of their game trading leads back and forth, and the Dodgers took the lead for good after Blake DeWitt hit an inside the park home run that Ryan Church almost caught, but thought was gone. His hesitation allowed DeWitt to circle the bases and give the Dodgers a 5-4 lead in the fifth, a lead that would hold until the end.

Hey, it's only May 6th, so I'm not panicking. I see that all of the National League playoff teams from last year were at .500 or worse on May 6th last year. Tomorrow is a new day...

May 7th

The Mets played an afternoon game in Los Angeles today, and looked to avoid the sweep vs. the red hot Dodgers. My boy, John Maine took the hill for the Mets, and Brad Penny would go for the Dodgers. It was a busy day at work, but I did make an effort to check in on the score from time to time. It was all good news for the ol' Metropolitans. The Mets scored 4 runs in the 2nd inning, added another in the 3rd, and chased Penny with six in the 5th inning. Ryan Church hit his sixth home run of the year in the sixth inning, to give the Mets a 12-0 lead. John Maine was brilliant today, going 8 1/3 before being scored upon in the ninth. The

Mets would go on to win today, 12-1, and leave L.A. on a positive note, heading back to Shea this weekend. The team will take a day off tomorrow before opening a series with the Cincinnati Reds.

Last year, the Brewers looked like a team that knew they could beat you each night. In the first three weeks of this season, they played like a team that *thought* they could beat you, and lately, they are playing like a team that is trying not to lose. Dave Bush made his first start since being recalled from Nashville, and in typical Dave Bush fashion, looked unhittable for four of his six innings pitched, but would give up 3 spots in the 3rd and 6th innings. The only offense the Brewers could muster was a two run homer by Rickie Weeks in the top of the sixth, the team only managed to collect five base hits, and would lose this one, 6-2, in front of a capacity crowd of 10,405 in South Miami. I'll never understand why a franchise would ever be awarded to a city that lacked a strong fan base or a stadium deal. I understand a stadium is being discussed right now, but I'm not sure how much difference that'll make. It's a strange situation. The franchise has a history of building a champion, selling off the parts next season, alienating their fan base, stinking for a few years, rebuilding with youth, winning another championship and repeating the steps over and over. Whatever the case may be, the Marlins are in the thick of the NL East, currently a half a game behind Philadelphia for the division lead. The Brewers are now 4 games back, and have fallen below .500 for the first time this season.

May 8th

Happy birthday, Gina! I love you! Do me a favor, though, and stop growing up so fast!

I'm writing tonight from Madison, as I am spending a couple of days here for some quarterly sales training. It's about 11:00pm, and I'm watching the latest "Costas Now" on HBO, which originally aired about ten days ago. Tonight's episode is a live town hall edition which features hot-button topics broken into five segments: Sports Talk Radio, The Internet and the Impact of Bloggers, Sports Television, Athletes and the Media and A Discussion on Race. Some good stuff was bantered about, and it makes me want to get HBO again.

After day one of the training, my colleague Greg Stimart and I went out searching for a place to watch the Brewers/Marlins game. We decided on Old Chicago, and arrived at the restaurant about 10 minutes before first pitch. Dinner is on the company, but not drinks, so we ask the waiter while we are ordering if we could have three separate checks (one for me, one for Greg and one for drinks). He says they can't do that. We can put a man on the moon, clone sheep, and successfully pull off peanut butter and jelly in the same jar, but they can't accommodate three separate checks. Fair enough.......We decide on the Signature Trio as an appetizer, which includes Italian nachos, Sicilian pepperoni rolls and cheese garlic bread, and we each order a custom calzone. I haven't been to Old Chicago since I lived in St. Paul in 2002, and it was as good as I remember. The TV that was in the corner did not have FSN (I searched three times over), and the bar area seemed pretty full (where the game was prominently displayed), so we decided to skip out after dinner and find a place to watch it. We decided to head back to the hotel that we were staying at, and they also did not have FSN on the TV in the lobby. We got back in the car and headed to Applebee's. Madison is completely non-smoking now, which I love, so I can now comfortably sit at a bar at watch a game without getting sick from smoke. We found a place right away, asked the bartender if we could switch one of the TV's that had the Celtics/Cavaliers game on to the Brewers. She obliged, but stressed there would be no sound. The score was 3-0 Marlins in the 3rd as we settled in. We ordered a few beers and a couple of tasty appetizers, and waited patiently for the Brewers to turn things around.

We barely touched our nachos and boneless honey bbq wings as the game went on. In the top of the 4th, Carlos Villanueva helped himself out with an RBI single, his second hit of the night. But after Villanueva gave up a three run homer to Matt Treanor in the bottom of the 5th, we agreed that it was time to head back to the hotel. The score was 7-1, and neither of us was going to touch any more of the food we ordered anyway. While we were walking towards the car, I joked about us stopping somewhere for some more food before we turn in for the evening, and Greg suggested we get some waffle cones from Dairy Queen. Once I got back to the hotel, I looked for a final before spending the rest of the night with Bob Costas. 7-2, Marlins. Six straight losses for the Brewers, and we have dropped to 4th place, five games back of the Cardinals. I'm taking Amber to the game tomorrow night, and they better turn this around soon.

May 9th

I got a nice workout in this morning before the second day of training. I have now lost 20 pounds since March 10th, and I'm feeling better than I have in a long time. Who knows, I may have to get into playing shape again and provide the Brewers with some much needed starting pitching depth. The training session let out a little early today, so I picked up Amber earlier than planned, and started to head to Miller. We parked at Jamie's tonight (thank you, sir), due to the fact that tonight would be a sellout, and the parking already looked thin driving in. Jamie paid me for the Billy Joel tickets, and that reminded me......it's Billy Joel's birthday today! It's 5/9, and he turns 59. What do you call that, a golden birthday or something? What is that called? It's also Prince Fielder's birthday today, and I am predicting that he goes yard tonight.

As we are walking towards our seats, I notice that the Mets have been rained out vs Cincinnati tonight. Since the Reds do not return to Shea for another series this season, it looks like the Mets and Reds will play a day/night doubleheader tomorrow. The Cards were already up 1-0 when we arrived, and the people sitting in our section are still talking about the 450 foot home run that Albert Pujols just hit to left center. There are always a lot of Cardinals fans at Miller Park for Brewers/Cardinals games, and tonight is no exception. I would say it's 50/50 in our section.

Manny Parra struggled mightily in the 2nd, allowing an RBI single to his counterpart, St Louis pitcher Todd Wellemeyer and walking Cesar Izturis with the bases loaded to give the Cardinals an early 3-0 lead. I didn't think it would happen this early, but the conversation with Amber turns to Kenneth Craig and Frau Moore mid way through the second.

In the middle of the fourth inning, we agree that it's time to get some food. This weekend is "Spring Madness" at Miller Park, which means half price tickets and dollar dogs. Because of the dollar dogs, the jumbo dogs are not on tonight's menu, so I go with two dogs and a Mike's Hard Lemonade. Amber went with a brat, cheese pizza and a Mike's Hard Lemonade. For those of you scoring at home, that is two mentions of Mike's Hard Lemonade (now three), in case the fine folks at Mike's Hard Lemonade (four and counting) want to contact me about free product due to the generous free advertising I am providing tonight. By the time we get back to our seats, the Brewers had put two on the board in the fourth. We ask the friendly couple next to us for some play by play, and it sounds like Corey Hart doubled home Ryan Braun with one out, and would later score on a Todd Wellemeyer wild pitch.

So the score is 3-2 Cardinals in the fifth, and the ushers have started handing out the all star ballots. My apologies to Dale Wegner and my ex-wife Suzy, but this story has to be told. This is one of Mike Moser's favorite stories, I told it to Amber tonight, and I'm telling you now. Back in 2000, the last year at County Stadium, Suzy, Dale, Mike and I took in a Brewers game one summer night. To give you a little bit of a background, Suzy and I were separated later that year, and there had been a strain on the marriage for some time. That night, as the all star ballots were being handed out, I looked at Mike as if to say, "enjoy". We all had our ballots in hand, and I asked Dale who he would be voting for from the Brewers. After spending a couple of minutes on his ballot, it was on to mine. I pulled out my ballot, and went right down the line, from catcher to outfielders, taking several minutes to dissect each choice that I was making. But instead of pulling out my keys or politely asking for a pencil so I could cleanly remove the "chads" from the ballot, I proceeded to poke my entire finger through the ballot, and this would lead to my entire fist by the third or so entry. After the stunt, I enthusiastically handed by ballot to the usher, begging that he make sure this ballot gets to where it needs to, because I want to be heard. This was clearly an attempt to make Moser laugh, and to piss off Suzy, and although I regret doing this in the presence of Dale, this story has become one of my calling cards.

In the sixth, I offered Amber $1000 to tackle a sausage of her choice during the incredible edible sausage race. She did not take me up on that offer, although there were a couple of people in our section that drank enough to do it for peanuts, had they been offered the same thing. There really is no reason to want to see someone tackle a fake sausage in front of 40,000 people, especially after seeing Randall Simon knock over the Italian sausage at a game in July of 2003. I was with my niece that night, and had to explain to her that she "fell". Still remember that like it was yesterday….

The bullpen did a great job getting the Brewers to the bottom of the ninth, going four innings, allowing only three hits and not allowing the Cardinals to add to their 3-2 lead. In the Brewers half of the ninth, Jason Isringhausen would come on to save this one for the Cards. He entered tonight's game with a 1-3 record, including 4 blown saves and an ERA in the low 7.00's. But he retired Corey Hart and Bill Hall on successive pitches to begin the ninth, and fans started to file out as it looked like the Brewers would drop their seventh straight game. Amber and I would get to our feet, but we ain't going anywhere just yet. After taking Izzy's first offering for a called strike, Hardy would single cleanly to center to keep the Brewers alive. Gabe Kapler was announced as the pinch hitter for Brian Shouse, who worked a scoreless top half of the ninth. Kapler took ball one before depositing a 1-0 fastball to right field for a base hit, and now the Crew has two on with 2 out for Jason Kendall. The crowd is buzzing at this point, knowing that a single could tie this game. Izzy wasn't even close on the first three deliveries to Kendall. Kendall would take strike one on 3-0, but a 3-1 cutter would miss badly to load the bases for Rickie Weeks. We have some major drama tonight at Miller Park, and everybody is on their feet to see how this one will end. I'm basically pleading with Weeks to leave the bat on his shoulder until he sees a strike. He takes the first offering from

Isringhausen, and it's low for ball one. Weeks swings on 1-0, and I nervously grab my head as he follows through. I'm in disbelief as he ignores my advice, but just as quickly as I panic, I realize that he's just doubled down the left field line to score Hardy and Kapler to beat the Cardinals. Another amazing finish! The last two games I've seen in person were come from behind wins in the ninth in huge division games. Great game. Now let's keep this going!

May 10th

The first game of the Mets doubleheader will not be televised today on mlb extra innings, however, the Brewers and Cardinals are the national Fox Game of the Week, and have a start time of 2:50 today. I will be following the Mets on cbssports.com, as I keep an eye on my rising rotisserie league team. I am within 4 points of Matt Weiss for the top spot, and I need to find some stolen bases and improve the batting average.

I still remember the first fantasy baseball league I ran in 1990. It was a four team league consisting of Mike Moser, Scott Moser, Phil Hohlweck and myself. We drafted in the Moser basement at the end of May, with the understanding that we would start the season on June 1st. And for some reason unknown to this day, we ran that league for three years, and always started our season June 1st. Looking back, it wasn't really a fantasy league or a rotisserie league. There was no head to head schedule. We just had a cumulative point total for the season. And here was the strangest thing about what we did. We gave our lineups *after the games were played!* I would get the paper the following morning, and ask the boys who they played the night before. What trust! I think Mike won that season. I still remember some of my team. Howard Johnson, Darryl Strawberry, Bob Welch (yes, the year he won 27 games), Bobby Thigpen (indeed, the year he saved 57 games)....The scoring system was weird as well. We awarded four points for a home run, and one each for an RBI and SB, and pitchers were awarded one point for each win and save, and a -1 for a loss. If your pitcher threw a no hitter......5 points, which was equal to a solo HR! But we were kids, what do you want from us?

This year's rotisserie league is my first stab at running a baseball league in fifteen years. I've been busy with the football league, but I thought the time was right to extend the brand that is Fugazzi. It's a 12 team, 6x6 rotisserie league, and I think it's going pretty well so far.

Gracie and I went outside to play some wiffle ball for a bit, and when we got back inside, I checked on the Mets, and am happy to tell you they are up 10-3 in the sixth. It's looking like Johan is going to get his first home win as a Met. The Brewers game will be starting in a couple of minutes on Fox, and the network is doing something pretty neat. Fox is pairing Dan McLaughlin, the television play by play man of the Cardinals, with Bill Schroeder, the long time color analyst of the Brewers, to call the game today. Ben Sheets is getting the start today for the Brewers, and he has yet to lose a game this year. The Cards will counter with Joel Pineiro.

The Mets were able to finish off the Reds to take game one of their doubleheader with the Reds. The final was 12-6, and they will start game two around 6:10pm tonight.

Skip Schumaker initiated the scoring today, with an RBI groundout to Weeks. The Cards added a couple of runs in the 4th to make it 3-0 in front of another sell out crowd at Miller Park. Sheets would settle down after that, going seven while only allowing the three runs, and striking out six. He didn't get any run support today, leaving with a 3-0 deficit as the Brewers entered the bottom of the seventh. There have been two constants in Sheets' career with the Brewers, injuries and lack of run support. Today, the Brewers have some work to do to assure that Sheets doesn't join the loss column.

The Cardinals had all kinds of trouble finding the plate in the seventh, as Cardinal reliever Kyle McClellan would walk in two runs with free passes to Jason Kendall and Mike Cameron. The Brewers now found themselves back in the game, and in the 8th, former Brewer Ron Villone was called upon to face one batter, Prince Fielder. All Villone threw to Prince were fastballs, and

Fielder belted a 2-2 meatball into the right field stands to tie the game. I instinctively gave my daughter a playful "Rock-Bottom" on the couch, followed by a good minute of tickling. The Brewers have tied the Cards!

Eric Gagne would be asked to come and preserve the 3-3 tie in the ninth. Same old shit......single, single, ground out, walk, pop out, two run single by Ryan Ludwick, before retiring Adam Kennedy to end the inning. All the Brewers could muster in the ninth was a Ryan Braun double. The final is 5-3 Cards.

Not much to say about the Mets second half of their doubleheader. They only mustered 4 hits vs Bronson Arroya, and lost 7-1. I thought the Brewers had been underachieving at the plate. Check out some of these uncharacteristic batting averages some of the Mets are carrying.....Reyes (.246), Wright (.271), Beltran (.233), and Delgado (.234). This has got to improve for the Mets to have a shot this year.

SNL is new tonight. Shia LaBeouf is hosting. No idea who that is, if I'm being honest. I said the same thing when he hosted last year. I still don't know why I know his name. Since there are only two first run episodes left this year, we will give the kid a chance.

May 11th

Happy Mother's Day to the moms of the world as Major League Baseball busts out the pink bats once again. Bill Hall has made a living out of hitting home runs vs the Mets on Mother's Day, using the trademark pink bats. He's gone deep the last two years, and who could ever forget the walk off bomb on Mother's Day in 2006.

Today, the Mets look to take game three vs the Reds as Oliver Perez battles Johnny Cueto, who has struggled of late. Well over 49.000 fans packed into Shea Stadium to see the Mets jump off to an early lead. Luis Castillo's RBI triple gave the Mets a 1-0 lead, Carlos Beltran doubled home Castillo and Moises Alou doubled home Beltran to give the Mets a 3-0 lead right off the bat. In the fifth inning, Carlos Beltran would go deep to give the Mets a 5-0 lead, and Ryan Church would make it back-to-back jacks, extending the lead to 6-0. Perez would not be scored upon until the sixth, giving up his only three runs on the day in that sixth inning. Perez only gave up three hits all day, and struck out 8, but walked four on the day. All in all, it was a pretty solid performance for Perez. The Mets would add two in the sixth, and the bullpen would not allow a run in helping the Mets secure a series win over the Reds, winning today, 8-3. This gives the Mets a record of 19-16, still three behind the Marlins.

After the game last night, Eric Gagne told the media that he didn't deserve the ball in the 9th inning, and Ned Yost took those comments to heart today, announcing that Gagne would be removed from the closer's role for the time being. The team would go with a closer by committee until Gagne can work out whatever he needs to work out.

Jeff Suppan would do everything in his power today to make sure it didn't come down to the bullpen. Suppan has always pitched well at Miller Park, whether it's been as a member of the Pirates, the Cardinals or the Brewers. Braden Looper would start for St Louis, and the Crew would get to him early with 2 first inning runs. The Cards would get one back in the third to pull to within a run, but Ryan Braun would hit an absolute skyscraper in the bottom half to give the Brewers a 3-1 lead. Braun looks like he's starting to see the ball really well as of late, as the batting average has now climbed to .281. So well in fact, that he would homer again in his very next at bat. Braun has now tied Bill Hall for the all time franchise lead in pink bat dingers with two. After going seven strong today, Jeff Suppan gave way to David Riske, who gave up a solo shot to Ryan Ludwick in the 8th to bring the Cards to within two, at 4-2. The Brewers added a run in the bottom of the 8th on a J.J. Hardy double to left field. So the Brewers head to the ninth up 5-2, and Salomon Torres is called upon to save this one for Suppan. Torres would allow a double and a walk, and Yost would go to his lefty, Brian Shouse to try to shut the door.

He's not kidding when he says committee. Shouse would allow an RBI single to make the score 5-3, but he was able to get Adam Kennedy to ground out to J.J. Hardy to end the game. After losing six straight, the Brewers have taken two of the first three from the Cardinals, with game four tomorrow night.

We watched the last couple of innings at the Milwaukee Ale House that recently opened in Grafton. Would you like a quick review of the calzone I had? Tasty.

May 12th

The Nationals start a three game series at Shea tonight, marking the return of Lastings Milledge to Queens. This would have also marked the return of Paul LoDuca, but he's been on the DL for some time. The Nationals manager, Manny Acta, was a 3rd base coach for the Mets for two years as well. All kinds of storylines to follow.....The Nationals and Mets would trade runs for the first four innings, then the wheels came off quickly for the Mets, allowing 3 three runs in the 5th, and five in the 6th. Throughout the game, the Nationals could be seen chanting like a bunch of little leaguers in their dugout, and one wonders if this got to Nelson Figueroa, as he gave up six runs, four of them earned, through five tonight. Jorge Sosa was just as bad, if not worse, giving up four earned in his one inning of work. David Wright's home run in the seventh was too little, too late, and the Mets would lose tonight, 10-4. Figueroa and Sosa were optioned to New Orleans after the game, and the Mets called up Claudio Vargas to be the team's fifth starter, and Fernando Tatis to give a spark off the bench. Tatis has tallied 12 home runs in the Pacific Coast League thus far for New Orleans, tops in the league. In another move, the Mets activated Matt Wise from the DL, and sent Angel Pagan to the DL with a left shoulder contusion.

The Brewers take the field tonight looking to take three of four from the first place St Louis Cardinals. The pitching matchup favors the Cards as they send their ace to the hill, Adam

Wainwright, the guy who stymied Carlos Beltran and the rest of the Mets in the 2006 NLCS. The Brewers go with Dave Bush tonight, who is looking to improve on his 0-4, 6.70 ERA.

Rick Ankiel and Ryan Braun would each put their teams on the board with two out solo home runs in the first inning. For Braun, that's three home runs in his last four at bats, and this one *still* hasn't landed yet. The Brewers continued to hit Wainwright hard all night, exploding for five runs in the 3rd inning, and connecting on two more solo shots later in the game. The first of those two was yet another Ryan Braun moon shot, his 4th homer in two games, becoming the first Brewer since Geoff Jenkins in 1999 to hit multiple home runs in consecutive games. Bill Hall would hit the other one, his eighth of the year. Dave Bush had his good curve ball working tonight, and would go six innings en route to his first win of the season. A couple of late Cardinals runs brought the final to 8-3 Brewers. Guillermo Mota was credited with a save because the tying run was on deck when he entered the game. It seems like every Brewers reliever has at least one save this year. I think I may even have a save for the 2008 Brewers. Let me double check that...ah, nope, I'm still a banker. Shit.

May 13th

Pancakes.....yum!

My boy John Maine is pitching for the Mets tonight. Let's see how I am doing on my pre-season prediction of him going 27-3 with a 1.31 ERA. He comes into tonight with a 4-2 record and an ERA of 3.00. So all he has to do is go 23-1 the rest of the way, and who cares what his ERA is if he can go 23-1 the rest of the way. I tell you what.....if he can do that, I will grow a perm and a giant porno moustache and wear it for a year.

Maine looked like an ace tonight going six, allowing only one earned run on two hits, and striking out five. The Mets out hit the Nationals 14-4, but tonight was the Ryan Church Show, as

Church would go 2-4 with a double and HR, and 4 RBI. Church is easily the MVP of this team thus far in 2008, anchoring the team with 8 homers and a .324 batting average. And yes, he is on my rotisserie team, and he's not coming out of my lineup anytime soon. The Mets are now 20-17, two behind the Marlins. I spent most of the night following this game, mainly because I was curious on how the Mets would respond to the Nationals cheerleading during last night's game.

By the time the Mets had wrapped it up, I checked in on the Brewers, and was pleasantly surprised to see them leading the Dodgers 5-3 in the seventh. As I scour the world wide interweb for details, the boys on TV mention that Gagne is ready to close again. Apparently, Yost and the coaching staff addressed a mechanical flaw they noticed, and now they are ready to give him the ball again in the ninth. The box score tells me that Ryan Braun continues to be all-world, as he has doubled, tripled and driven in two already. Bill Hall went deep again, giving him nine on the season, and Carlos Villanueva went six tonight, giving up two earned runs and did not walk a single batter. Suddenly, after over a month of no wins from starters not named Ben Sheets, the Brewers are in line for the third straight win from their rotation. Salomon Torres pitched a scoreless 7th and 8th, and continues to be my choice to be this team's closer going forward. His ERA is under 3.00, he can go multiple innings, and he's done it before, albeit for the Pittsburgh Pirates.

I actually do feel uneasy as I see Gagne jogging out to the mound to try to notch this one for the Crew. It was only three nights ago that I heard this guy say, "I don't deserve the ball", and now he's gonna get a chance tonight, vs the team he excelled with for eight years. The first Dodgers batter, Russell Martin, singles to left, and I'm really longing for the days of Dan Plesac at this point. What is Doug Henry up to these days? Mike Fetters? I'm losing my mind. Blake DeWitt would reach as Russell Martin was retired on a force play at second. The Dodgers are now going to their bench, as Joe Torre (classy) sends Mark Sweeney to the plate to pinch hit for Chin-Lung Hu. Sweeney would fly out to right field for the second out. My stomach is still not right. Andrew Jones, who has been struggling mightily, had the night off, but is being asked to pinch hit for Cory Wade. Jones would walk after battling Gagne for ten pitches, and now the go ahead run is at the plate in the person of Juan Pierre. Pierre has had a resurgence as of late, reclaiming the starting left field job that he lost in Spring Training. You would figure that Pierre would be more patient with Gagne, but offers at the first pitch he sees, and pops up to Hardy to give the Brewers their third straight win. As Jason Kendall meets Gagne on the mound, you really can sense a huge weight being lifted off the shoulders of Gagne, as he more or less falls into the arms of Kendall. The team is starting to show signs of life, having won four of five from two pretty good teams. The bats are waking up a bit, and the starting pitching as been really consistent on the home stand. The Brewers have climbed above .500 again.

Yost mentioned in his post game address that Gagne is his closer, and the bullpen tends to struggle if each pitcher doesn't know from game to game what their role is. So I guess time will tell if Gagne is fixed.

The new Weezer album has been bumped up to a June 3rd release date, due to a bunch of the album's songs being leaked to the internet. I listened to a couple of them tonight. They are definitely returning to form in their quirkiness. I look forward to the release. Speaking of new music, I bought the new Death Cab For Cutie tonight. This is a really good band, and they've put out another really good album. It's called Narrow Stairs, and you should run out and buy it right now. Go! This book will be here when you get back....

May 14th

Driving to work this morning, I realized that I forgot to make my famous Fugazzi Fiesta Dip for Teller Appreciation Day. Joe's making brats and burgers, Stephanie is making a taco casserole, Hope is making a special trip to the grocery store for all the fixings, and I'll be walking into the branch with a bag of Doritos. I'm no damn good, and I never will be.

I took the household to Chili's tonight, and they had the Brewers game on a couple of the screens in the bar area. Between delightful tastes of my chicken club tacos and nachos, I was sneaking peeks at the game from a far. Parra vs Penny. My daughter is beyond high chairs and booster seats. She's sitting next to me coloring, taking little bites of her full size chicken tenders and hot fries. She's even cognizant of the game being on, pointing to the TV several times, and physically turning my head to the left, saying, "look, dada, look.....baseball players!!" I haven't replaced Chi-Chi's in my heart, but Chili's comes pretty close. Who am I kidding? No restaurant will ever come close. Chi-Chi's was a friend, not just an American-Tex-Mexican restaurant. I'll never forget October 2, 2004. My 29th birthday. I call Chi-Chi's in Brookfield to make a reservation for 8 to celebrate. I get an automated message thanking me for years of patronage. I go to their website and find that they've gone out of business. I haven't fully recovered from that heartache.

By the end of dinner, it's 4-1 Brewers in the sixth. On the way home, we stop somewhere to get better fitting shoes for Gracie. It was Walmart, so sue me. Heather's idea, I'd much rather be on my way home listening to Bob Uecker take me the rest of the way. As we get back to the car, I find that the Dodgers scored 2 in the 7th inning to cut the lead to 4-3. As we are walking in the door, Guillermo Mota is approaching the mound for his second save opportunity in three nights. While Yost did stress that Gagne is his closer, he's thrown 60 pitches in the last few days, and he's getting the night off. After retiring the first batter, Mota would go on to walk the next batter, then give up a single and a two run double to Juan Pierre to give the Dodgers the lead, and me a migraine. Another run would score as I'm looking for the Advil. After a 1-2-3 bottom half, I quickly switched over to Raging Bull on AMC. Maybe psychologically, seeing Jake LaMotta's rage would somehow curb mine. That, and I'm a huge fan of black and white, early 80's Cathy Moriarty. Huge fan...

The Mets are still not putting big enough dents in the scoreboard, losing tonight to the Nationals, 5-3. They managed only six hits. Claudio Vargas carried a shutout into the sixth inning, but the Nats tied it in the sixth, and lit up the Mets for 4 in the seventh. Two late inning tallies would not be enough to unseat Washington tonight.

I know it's still mid-May, but color me frustrated through a quarter of the season. The Brewers are at 20-20, only four games out, but have blown six saves, and still aren't getting consistency from their starting eight. The Mets are 20-18, 2 ½ games back, but seem to lack that bravado the team has had the last few seasons. It doesn't change my commitment. It's a long season, and there is a ton of baseball to be played. What I need is some Game Six and some Easter Sunday to get the juices flowing again. But then I'd have to walk all the way down the hall and into the bedroom.......oh, sweet itunes, you've seduced me again, you fantastic whore...

May 15th

I love pitching. Look, I've never try to hide that from you. I love twirling a ball with one hand and having my glove on the other, whether I'm at a game, sitting on the couch, in the passenger seat of a car, at a picnic, wherever. I feel calm when I've got a hardball in my grasp. I would have given anything to be at either Shea or Miller for one of the games this afternoon. Each game was scoreless through six innings, and Mike Pelfrey carried a no-hitter into the seventh. I couldn't help but pace around as I noticed that online. Aaron Boone put an end to my pacing quite quickly, singling off Pelfrey in the 7th inning. The Nationals were unable to score in the inning, but would score in the 8th to make it 1-0. Again, the Mets could barely muster a thing on offense, collecting only five hits today, and making Jason Bergmann look like Walter Johnson. The final from Shea today, 1-0, and the Nationals have just taken three of four from the Mets.

Ben Sheets was dominant for the Brewers today through six innings, and even collected the Brewers first hit in the third inning, but in the seventh, the Dodgers touched Sheets for six runs, including three long balls by Andruw Jones, Jeff Kent and

Gary Bennett, yes, thee Gary Bennett. Ryan Braun would later hit his first home run as a multi-millionaire (more on that in a bit), but it would not be enough, as the Dodgers would take this one, 7-2.

Back to Braun….Earlier today, it was announced that Ryan Braun had signed the richest contract in baseball history for a player not yet eligible for arbitration. Braun has yet to play a full season in the bigs, and today signed an 8 year, $45 million contract. He is the reigning NL Rookie of the Year, and clearly one of the rising stars in this league, despite the move to left field this off-season. When I forwarded the official press release to my sister, she almost lost it. Now one would say that Braun could have made a lot more on the open market, but like he said in his press conference, "There's not much you can't buy with $45 million." It will be interesting to see what the Brewers do with Prince Fielder, who last year, became the youngest player ever to hit 50 home runs, and finished in the top five in the NL MVP race. Ben Sheets is also a free agent at the end of this season, and I really wonder if he'll be here next season. Plenty of teams will make a push for him in July if the Brewers are no longer players in the NL Central. It will be a very interesting next couple of months for the Brewers on and off the field.

As for this weekend, major league baseball kicks off the interleague portion of their schedule. The Mets will face the Yankees at Yankee Stadium, and the Brewers will make their first trip to Fenway Park since 1997. Despite each teams' struggles as of late, if I can't get excited for this weekend, then I'm writing the wrong book…..

May 16th

Wouldn't you know it…..the only two games rained out today are the Mets at Yankees and the Brewers at Red Sox. The Mets and Yankees will play a home and home twin bill in June at each other's park, which doesn't bid well for the Mets, who have been swept in each of the other two home and home doubleheaders with the Yankees over the years. The Brewers and Red Sox will play their doubleheader tomorrow, with game one being featured on Fox as their national game. With no games tonight, I think we're going to give the Pizza Shuttle a try, and see if we can realistically tackle that 28 incher. $500 is $500, and way you slice it.

May 17th

We leave for Chattanooga tomorrow morning at 4:00am, so today, we'll be spending a lot of time packing for the trip, loading the van and generally taking it easy. I always look forward to seeing the in-laws, but I never look forward to 13 hours in a van. We've decided not to split the driving over two days like we normally do, so there will be no frequenting of the Cracker Barrel in Mt Vernon, IL this time around. Damn! I'm being sarcastic.

After dropping three of four to the Nationals at home, it is really important for Johan Santana to come out today and make a statement against the Yankees. It didn't look good early, as Derek Jeter would go yard in the first to give the Yankees an early 2-0 lead. The game cannot be found on the mlb ticket, so I am following it online between the parenting, the packing and the what not. The Mets were able to string together three runs in the top of the 5th off of Andy Pettitte to give Johan a 3-2 lead. Pettitte would give way to Kyle Farnsworth in the seventh, and the Mets took advantage of the pitching change. Jose Reyes hit his 3rd HR of the year, and David Wright would hit a two run shot, giving the Mets a 6-2 lead. Santana would surrender solo HR's to the Bronx Bombers in the 7th and 8th to cut the Mets lead to 6-4, and the Mets would add an insurance run in the ninth, making it 7-4. Billy Wagner was called on to shut the door in the ninth, and did just that to earn his ninth save of the year. Wagner has yet to allow an earned run all year, and continues to be a vocal leader for the Mets in the clubhouse as well. This is a huge win, regardless of what either team's record is. It's always good to win at Yankee Stadium.

The Brewers were down 4-0 to the Red Sox in the 2nd inning, so I decided to take a nap, because I was going to leave at 6:00 to take Gina out for her belated birthday night of Taco Bell and a movie. When I woke up, the Brewers were down 4-2, on the strength of a Mike Cameron home run in the seventh. Schwingle sent me a text message while we were at Taco Bell to let me know that the final was 5-3 Red Sox. The second game of the doubleheader would be played while we watched the Chronicles of Narnia sequel. I was disappointed to see that Andy Samberg and Chris Parnell were not in our theater enjoying it with us. It really is all about the Hamiltons, baby....

We got home from the movie around 9:45. Here's a quick summary of game two. The Red Sox blew a 5-0 lead, as the Brewers put up 3's in the 6th and 7th, but Salomon Torres gave two right back in the bottom of the seventh, and the Sox would go on to win game two, 7-6, and sweep the Brewers in today's double-dip. The Brewers have now lost 4 in a row, and our now officially in last place in the NL Central. They are not the only surprise last place team in major league baseball at this point. The Yankees, Tigers, Mariners and Padres are all in the cellar as well. Four of the six teams I predicted to win their divisions are in last place, and the other two, I had going to the World Series, the Mets and Red Sox. The Mets are in 4th, only two and a half back, and the Sox are a game and a half up on the Rays. That is correct. The Tampa Bay Rays are the surprise team in the major leagues thus far, five games ahead of the Yankees in the AL East.

Steve Carrell is hosting the season finale of SNL tonight. I know I should be heading to bed, but I'm not driving until about 9:00 tomorrow, so I'm going to take it in, and sleep in the van until it's my turn to drive. I will have limited access to the internet for the next eight days, and little to no access of major league action on the television, but I should have plenty to write about. We will be seeing a Southern League game on Monday night as the Mississippi Braves visit Chattanooga, and we will be attending the Mets game at Turner on Thursday night.

May 18th

We woke up at 3:30 in the morning, and hit the road a little after 4:00am. The ipod was charged, chalk full of new weezer songs and zesty playlists. Heather was driving while Gracie and I napped in the back, and then I took over the wheel around 9:00 or so, after a stop at the McDonald's in Effingham, IL. I enjoyed a couple of breakfast burritos, Heather ordered a bacon and egg bullshit something or other, and Gracie enjoyed a hash brown. After a couple of hours of driving, Heather and Gracie each fell asleep for a little bit. When Heather awoke, she asked where we were. I must have rocked a little too hard to the weezers, because it turns out I missed an exit, and set us back about an hour. I just kept going down 57 South, and never thought to ask what exit to look for. We ended up in Missouri. Here's a little trivia for you. I lost something in Sikeston, MO, and it wasn't my wallet. I'm pretty sure it was Sikeston. I remember it was October 6, 1996, and that Late Night with Conan O'Brien was on in the background. Yeah, do the math. I was 21. But it was always a dream to save myself for my bosses' administrative assistant. I'm old fashioned that way.

Once we got turned around, we drove back on 57 North until we found the exit for 24 East that I missed. Heather lost faith in my abilities to get us to Chattanooga in a timely fashion, and took over the driving after about an hour or so. Because of the nearly two hours I cost us, and the hour we lost to the time zone change, we ended up in Chattanooga around 6:30. After greeting Tracy and Kathy (Heather's parents), and unloading the van, I checked in on the Brewers to see if they could avoid the sweep. It turns out, they could not, however, the bats awoke from their long nap. The Brewers were able to put up seven runs on the strength of 4 home runs, two of which were hit by Ryan Braun, who has hit four since he signed his new contract. But Carlos Villanueva pitched terribly, giving up six runs, five earned, over four innings. Mark DiFelice made his major league debut relieving Villanueva, and gave up three runs on five hits in his only inning of work, and the Sox would win by a score of 11-7. I can just hear the Milwaukee media and sports talk shows in Milwaukee, calling for

Ned Yost's head. The Brewers are now 20-24, at the bottom of the NL Central, and still have seven games left on this road trip.

Speaking of managers on the hot seat, there were rumors heading into the weekend that Willie Randolph's status as the Mets' skipper was dependant on how the Mets faired in the series vs the Yankees this weekend. Friday was washed out, the Mets took yesterday's game, and the tonight's game will be featured on ESPN. I planted a seed with Tracy, casually mentioning that "I think the Mets *may* be on tonight on ESPN", while shrugging my shoulders, as if to say, "But I don't care". The game would eventually find it's way on to the Norrell television set in the third inning with the game scoreless. The Mets would put an end to that nonsense in the fourth, tagging Chien-Ming Wang for four runs in the top of the fourth. This set off a series of friendly pointing to Tracy on my part, pointing that insinuated that my team was going to put a similar beat down on his team, the Braves, in their four game series kicking off on Tuesday. He was more humble. The Yankees scored two in the bottom of the fourth, on a two run bomb by Hideki Matsui. Ryan Church hit a dinger off Wang in the sixth. I just said dinger and Wang, Beavis. The Mets would blow this one wide open in the eighth, scoring six runs, to give the Mets an 11-2 win and a series sweep of the Yankees. Jose Reyes went yard for the second straight game, and it looks like Randolph gets to keep his job.

May 19th

First full day in Chattanooga, and there is no Mets or Brewers games to speak of today. The Mets begin a four game series with Atlanta tomorrow with a day/night doubleheader, and the Brewers will kick off a three game series with Pittsburgh. I am officially retiring the jeans that I wore to Tennessee on the drive down here. I bought them a size too big to begin with, and with the weight I've been losing, I look like a complete asshole pulling them with up every ten feet that I walk. So I stopped by the local

K-Mart this afternoon to pick up a couple of pairs of shorts and shirts to compliment said shorts. Say that fast five times....SAY IT, I ask of you....

Tonight, I took in the Mississippi Braves/Chattanooga Lookouts game at AT&T Field, not to be confused with AT&T Park in San Francisco. This is a beautiful diamond, which was built in 2000. It's signature feature is it's hilltop location, and the stadium is uniquely designed so that most of the seats are located on the first base side. I scored the game tonight, but I will spare you of full play by play, due to the fact that neither you or I will know of many of these players in the future, and half way through the game, I met two big baseball fans sitting in front of us, and ended up talking to them from the fourth inning on. There names were Christa and Nicole, and Christa happens to be a huge Mets fan. She loves her some David Wright, and also still has love for Paul LoDuca and Mike Piazza. Nicole is a Red Sox fan. I told her that a current member of the Red Sox pitching staff shares a last name with me, and gave her three chances to guess which one. Her guesses were Schilling, Wakefield and Burkett. I told her it was Matsuzaka, and that I was 2/15th's Japanese. Nicole, now you know the truth.

It is an amazing night for a game, and I'm really getting lost in the sounds (the pop of the glove, the crack of the bat, the chatter in the stands and on the field), the sights (the beautiful sunset, fathers and sons shelling peanuts, the players in the dugout, anticipating a night of ball), and the smells (the dirt, the grass, the dogs, and my glove under my nose). This is heaven. What is more enjoyable than a night of baseball? Right before the starting lineups are announced, Henley's "Boys of Summer" blares over the sound system, and I know someone is thinking of me. I am counting 71 unique advertisers on the outfield wall, there are six ceremonial first pitches tonight, all kids, and the field looks breathtaking. As I look through the scorecard, I notice that Chris Bosio is the Lookouts pitching coach, and Franklin Stubbs is Mississippi's hitting coach. Bosio and Stubbs were teammates on the Brewers in 1991 and 1992.

In the bottom of the 3rd inning, the Lookouts held the Hardee's Thickburger Race down the third base line. Basically, two children rolling giant plastic cheeseburgers down the line, with a chance to win........Hardee's food, I'm guessing. I guess that's how these promotions work. This reminded me of the time a few years back when Tracy and I were asked to do a "dizzy bat" competition at a Lookouts game, and Tracy wouldn't do it, but I agreed to it immediately. I lost, but couldn't help to think that I was on a minor league baseball field. What I should have done was said, "Enough with this dizzy bat stuff, let me see what this mound feels like". In the fourth inning, Louie the Lookout asked me to do the chicken dance on the Lookouts dugout with a bunch of children. That......didn't happen.

The Lookouts scored four times in the third inning off of Braves starter Jerome Gamble. Gamble looked great in the first two innings, but was really hit hard in the 3rd. He's got a great fastball/curve combo, but I don't think he uses his curveball enough. Gamble was originally drafted by the Red Sox, and also spent a season in the Brewers' organization in 2005. He's now getting a chance with Mississippi to extend his career.

The Lookouts starting pitcher tonight was Ben Jukich, a 6'5" lefty, coming into tonight with a 3-2 record, and an ERA of 2.34. Jukich threw six innings, allowing one run, and striking out 8. He also helped himself at the plate, singling in the fourth and going on to score to spark the Chattanooga rally. The Lookouts would score one more time in the 8th, and would win this game tonight, 5-1. Ironically, the Lookouts turned a 4-2-3 double play in this game, which is the area code for Chattanooga.

As for Christa and Nicole, they will be at the game on Thursday at Turner Field. I did get their e-mail addresses, to tell them more about this book, and hopefully, they are both enjoying it at this moment. It's always good to meet baseball fans from different parts of the country. Thanks for chatting with me tonight. And as a side note, I mentioned that Nicole was a Boston Red Sox fan earlier. Well, Jon Lester no-hit the Royals tonight in Boston. What a story! Lester beat cancer a few years back, and now he has become the 18th Boston pitcher to throw a no-hitter. That is 18 more than my Mets have thrown. We followed the last few innings on her cell phone. It was a great night to be a baseball fan, indeed.

May 20th

    The internet has definitely changed the way that I follow baseball, and sports in general. As a kid, I remember grabbing the sports section during breakfast, and spending a lot of time going over each box score, seeing who homered, scoring our rotisserie league long hand, checking out the west coast summaries. If a player was traded, you read it in the paper. If an all star was placed on the disabled list, you read it about it in the "transactions" section. Now, all of this information is at our fingertips instantly. Don't get me wrong, I love the instant gratification, following at-bats as they happen, getting real time fantasy updates, reading up on trades and moves as they happen. But I also miss the anticipation of opening the paper, and slowly scouring the pages, reading each headline, getting familiar with the league leaders, finding your guys in **bold** or *italic*.

    I will be leaning heavily on the Chattanooga Free Press and the ESPNews bottom-line this week, with limited access to the internet. I think I may get back into a routine of picking up a paper on the way to work, because I've enjoyed the time I've spent this morning, reading up on the upcoming day/night doubleheader that the Mets and Braves are playing in Atlanta today.

    I guessed wrong in thinking the second game of the doubleheader would be on the television, and as I was trying to find cartoons for Gracie, I stumbled upon game one, with the score 3-1 Braves in the 5th inning. John Maine is already out of the game, having given up eight hits and walking three in four plus innings. Scott Schoeneweis would give up a sacrifice fly to Kelly Johnson that would give the Braves a 4-1 lead. Since I didn't plan on watching this game, I leave the game on outside, and find Gracie some SpongeBob on the big screen. I checked in from time to time, but Tom Glavine was his old self today, going six, only allowing a run on three hits before conceding to his bullpen. They were able to hold the Mets at bay, and the final for this one would end up being 6-1, giving Glavine his 305th career win. It's really nice out today, so we're going to blow some bubbles outside and take in this gorgeous weather.......tonight, we'll spending an hour or so at a birthday party for Tracy's buddy, Kenny. When we get back, we'll check in on the night games.

In game two, it was more of the same for the Mets. An early deficit of 4-0 in the 3rd would remain that way until the 8th, as Braves starter Jorge Campillo held the Mets scoreless over six, only allowing three hits in the process. Claudio Vargas was the starting pitcher for the Mets today, and he would only go five. The Mets made it a game in the 8th, scoring twice off of reliever Blaine Boyer, but Matt Wise gave the runs right back in the bottom of the 8th. I'm basically checking this game online every 20 minutes or so while we enjoy a screening of Evan Almighty on cable. The final would be 6-2 tonight. Swept by the Braves today...I need some comfort food. Sonic anyone?

The Brewers got back on track tonight, beating the Pirates 7-2. Manny Parra went 5 2/3 of shutout ball, striking out six, before handing it over to the bullpen. Jason Bay touched Eric Gagne for a homer in the ninth to spoil the combined shutout, but a win is a win, and it's good to start the series off on a positive note. I'm reading the attendance tonight was only 11,761 in Pittsburgh. I just don't get it. Yes, the Pirates haven't had a winning season since The Civil War, but come on!

I'm watching season one of "Human Giant" on DVD tonight, now that everyone is in bed. Very funny stuff. I'm taping a season two marathon on TiVo back home, and will enjoy it when I get back. And I'm dead serious when I say that when MTV officially releases "The State" on DVD, I will take two weeks off, grow a giant beard, and go through each episode without sleeping. It shouldn't take two weeks to do that, so I'll probably watch each episode multiple times. It's going to happen. I've been waiting for years.

May 21st

    Good news / bad news. Which would you like first? OK, we'll start with the good news. The Brewers won in Pittsburgh again. Ben Sheets improved his record to 5-1, lowered his ERA to 2.92, and went the distance. Now here's the bad news. The Mets got their asses handed to them, 11-4. The Willie Randolph rumors are spreading rampantly, and word is that Gary Carter is openly campaigning for the Mets' manager job through the sports talk radio circuit. Several Mets players have acknowledged that all of this talk of Randolph possibly getting fired is affecting the play on the field. They don't want to see him fired, and Wright and Beltran have specifically said that the players need to step up and start performing like they know they can. Hopefully, Johan can stop the bleeding tomorrow, and the Mets can avoid a sweep. We'll be there tomorrow night, and I plan to give the full story again.

May 22nd

    Despite the Mets poor play in the first three games of their series with Atlanta, I am very excited to get to Turner Field tonight. Tracy and I are here with Tracy's friend, Bubba, and his son, Jeremy. We got to the stadium at about 5:30, and talked it up with fans in the parking lot over some beers. There are plenty of Mets fans here, so I don't feel alone in my road Mets jersey and cap. When we make it in the stadium, we sit for a bit to check out our view. Very sweet tickets down the first base line. I forgot how huge the scoreboard is here. Easily the biggest I've seen, and they utilize it well. As we watch the tail end of batting practice, I grab a dog and a beer, and take in the beauty. I could not ask for a better pitching match-up, as the Mets send Johan Santana to the hill vs Tim Hudson of the Braves. Hudson pitched for the Braves the only other time I saw a game at Turner, in 2006 vs the Nationals. The Nationals won that game, but I remember Hudson pitched really well. I will once again do my best in giving you the entire story tonight.

(Top of 1st) Tim Hudson sets up Reyes beautifully with three straight fastballs, getting the count to 1-2 before going to his sinker, and getting Reyes to strike out swinging. I like that Reyes looked aggressive against the equally aggressive Hudson. Luis Castillo showed bunt on the first pitch from Hudson, then laid one down on 2-0, but it wasn't a great bunt, and Castillo has lost a step in recent years, and was out by a couple of feet. Hudson threw nothing but fastballs to David Wright, and Wright would ground to short to end the inning. We just couldn't get anything going in the first, and 9 of Hudson's 10 pitches were fastballs.

(Bottom of 1st) Omar Infante, the Braves' shortstop tonight, sends a 1-2 changeup to deep left, clearly fooling Tracy and other Braves fans in thinking that he got all of it. Marlon Anderson made the play at the warning track to retire Infante. Mark Kotsay slapped the first pitch he saw into centerfield for a single. This brings up Chipper Jones, who leads the planet with a .412 batting average. Kotsay hasn't been much of a threat to steal in years, and he doesn't have much of a lead at first. Jones works the count to 3-1, and hits a bullet to Reyes, as the Mets turn a 6-4-3 to end the inning. That's what I like to see. Nice. Very nice.

(Top of 2nd) Carlos Beltran must have taken advice from Hank Aaron tonight. Aaron always looked breaking ball, because he knew that nobody could throw a fastball by him. After three consecutive fastballs from Hudson, Beltran belted an 80 MPH changeup to right center for a solo HR. As I am boyishly taunting Tracy with some good natured trash talking, Carlos Delgado took the first pitch he saw to left field for another home run. I didn't even see it! But I'm smiling none the less, as the Mets suddenly lead the Braves 2-0. Have I mentioned how much I love this game? Marlon Anderson tries to catch the Braves off guard, and attempts to bunt for a hit, but McCann would throw to first and get him by a few steps for the innings' first out. Brian Schneider has a great at-bat vs Hudson, seeing 7 pitches, but would be called looking for the second out. Endy Chavez, whose bobble head sits atop my big screen TV at home, hits a soft fly ball to left, and shows great hustle to stretch it to a double. Santana comes up, and hits it hard to short, but is retired at first to end the inning. Hopefully, Santana won't need much more than the two dingers he was given earlier in the inning.

(Bottom of 2nd) Mark Teixeira led off the inning by hitting a dribbler in front of the plate, but Brian Schneider couldn't pick it up cleanly, and Teixeira reached on the error. Jeff Francoeur fooled the crowd again into thinking they'd just seen a home run, as Marlon Anderson retires him on the warning track for out number one. I'll even admit, I thought that one had a chance. Brian McCann would hit a lazy fly ball to right for the second out. The next batter is Matt Diaz, who is playing left field tonight. He looks at a couple of fastballs that are low and away, and rips a 2-0 fastball to left to extend the inning. Kelly Johnson now steps to the plate with two on and two out, with a chance to put the Braves on the board. Johnson would work the count to 3-2, than promptly deposited a single to right that would score Teixeira. Diaz advanced to 3rd. Tim Hudson, who is not a great hitting pitcher, struck out to end the inning. So the Braves got one back, big deal...2-1 Mets.

(Top of 3rd) The Mets would go down pretty quietly in the 3rd. Jose Reyes popped up to short, and if you know me at all, you know I can't stand the popups. Castillo and Wright each grounded out to second basemen Kelly Johnson. The Mets 1-2-3 hitters are now 0-6 in this game. Tracy is enjoying what looks like a very tasty bratwurst, but I'm still full from earlier.

(Bottom of 3rd) There's a couple sitting next to me, they are clearly Braves fans. I have to ask...it's a great night, the Braves are going for a sweep, we're in a beautiful ballpark. Why don't the Braves draw well here? From the looks of it, I would guess there are about 25,000 people here, tops. The gentleman I asked said that since the Braves were so dominant for 15 or so years, that the fans take it for granted. It also probably hasn't helped attendance in the past that most of their home games were on television, even before FSN started airing nearly every game a while back. I just don't understand how this place isn't packed tonight. We'll get an official word on the paid attendance later. The first two Braves hitters in the 3rd, Omar Infante and Mark

Kotsay, each flied out to Endy Chavez in right. Chipper Jones singled on the first pitch he saw, raising his average to something like .850. Mark Teixeira singled to left, and Chipper is clearly one base at a time tonight, after taking one on the shin last night. Tracy still holds animosity towards Scott Schoeneweis for plunking him. Jeff Francoeur flied out to left to end the inning, marking the sixth fly ball out that Johan Santana has recorded in three innings.

(Top of 4th) Tim Hudson took a different approach this time around when pitching to Carlos Beltran. Instead of feeding him fastballs, then getting burned on a changeup, Hudson started off with a changeup for strike one, and came right back with another one, with Beltran bouncing to Kelly Johnson for the first out of the 4th. Hudson made no such adjustment with Delgado, serving him five straight fastballs to run the count to 3-2, than eventually getting Delgado to strike out swinging on a rare Hudson curveball. Marlon Anderson would ground out to short to end the inning. Hudson has now retired that last seven Mets he has faced since the Chavez double in the 2nd, and eight of the outs he has recorded have been groundball outs.

(Bottom of 4th) This is my kind of game so far. Two pitchers that work quickly, throw a lot of first pitch strikes, and attack hitters. Johan Santana has retired the first two Braves hitters on three pitches, getting McCann to ground out to Delgado, and Matt Diaz to fly out to Endy Chavez. Santana would also go right after Kelly Johnson, but Johnson would single to center for his second hit of the evening. Johnson would be left stranded, as Tim Hudson would softly tap back to Santana to end the inning. Between innings, the Home Depot Tool Race is being shown on the big screen. We have the sausage race in Milwaukee, Pittsburgh has the pierogie race, Washington has the racing presidents, and Atlanta has racing tools. What ever happened to just showing baseball related items between innings? By the way, the hammer won.

(Top of 5th) Here's a little observation…the female Braves fans that I see tonight, for the most part, are hotter that the female Mets fans. Last year, at the Brewers/Mets game in Milwaukee, the female Mets fans were hotter that the female Brewers fans I saw. But what does that even mean? Hotter. Moving on to baseball, Brian Schneider saw three pitches from Tim Hudson, and was called looking once again. Endy Chavez would take a fastball for a ball, before fouling the next one back. Hudson pulled the string on 1-1, and Chavez lifted a fly ball to right, easily playable for Jeff Francoeur. Johan Santana ripped the first pitch he saw to deep right, and Francouer snagged it on the edge of the warning track to give Hudson another 1-2-3 inning. As the Braves jog back in to take their swings, Billy Joel's "Tell Her About It" begins to blare from the sound system. I'm starting to feel spoiled now, as I sit in this beautiful ballpark, my belly, full from delicious hot dog goodness, the weather perfect, my team is up 2-1, and the familiar sounds of Billy Joel providing the soundtrack. Life is good.

(Bottom of 5th) Santana was able to rid of the Braves in very quick fashion in the sixth, retiring Omar Infante, Mark Kotsay and Chipper Jones on 8 pitches. Infante bounced quietly to Reyes. Kotsay hit a screamer back up the box. The ball was deflected off of Santana's glove, and fielded by Reyes, who threw to Delgado for the second out. Chipper Jones hit a long fly ball to center, but Beltran made the play look easy, as he always does, as the Mets carry their 2-1 lead into the sixth inning.

(Top of 6th) Heading to the sixth, I'm feeling a big inning for the Metropolitans. Hudson has retired 10 straight, but the Mets will send Reyes, Castillo and Wright to the plate. These guys are due to do something big, and my gut says now is the time. Well, it turns out that my gut is a liar. Jose Reyes fell to 0-2 in the count, and fouled a couple of pitches off to stay alive, but would ground out to Kelly Johnson to start the inning. Luis Castillo also battled Hudson, and would get the best of him, singling to left field to give the Mets their first base runner since the 2nd inning. As David Wright approached the batter's box, Tracy predicted that he would ground into a double play to end the inning. Damned if he wasn't right, as Wright would bounce a 2-2 sinker to Kelly Johnson for a 4-6-3 double play to end the inning. I'm starting to think about grabbing another dog, or taking a shot at one of those brats, but I'm witnessing a really good game, and I don't want to leave it now. If I'm hungry later, there's always Sonic. I've already enjoyed a couple of their bacon cheeseburgers this week, and their cheddar jalapeno poppers are tasty, tasty, deep fried and breaded joy-filled slices of heaven. What I mean, is that they taste good.

(Bottom of 6th) Santana continues to work quickly, getting Mark Teixeira to line to Luis Castillo on the first pitch to start the inning. Jeff Francoeur saw a good mix of fastballs and changeups, and he would pop up in foul territory to Brian Schneider on a 1-2 changeup. Brian McCann singled up the middle to keep the inning alive, but Matt Diaz hit into a 5-4 force out to end the inning. Santana is rolling, and has yet to allow an extra base hit thus far.

(Top of 7th) As we head to the top of the seventh, it suddenly looks like it could pour here any minute now. Hopefully, the weather will be kind to this great pitching matchup. Carlos Beltran leads off the top of the 7th by singling to center. Hudson makes a couple of attempts to pick Beltran off of first, but Beltran is able to steal second easily on a 2-1 slider to Carlos Delgado. Delgado would fly out to Kotsay on the next pitch. With Beltran on 2nd and one out, Marlon Anderson has a chance here to extend the Mets lead, and give Johan Santana more of a cushion to work with. But the Mets run their self out of a chance to score, as Anderson bounced to short, Beltran was caught in no man's land as Infante tossed to Johnson, and Johnson threw to Jones to retire Beltran on the very rare 6-4-5 fielder's choice. Brian Schneider bounced out to Kelly Johnson to end the inning, and it's time to sing, "Take Me Out to the Ballgame". I traditionally don't sing along, I more or less mouth the words, but I do take the time to stretch out these rickety old legs.

(Bottom of 7th) The Braves fans begin to start a heavy dosage of that annoying chopping and chanting nonsense that I hate. And, I gotta tell you, it's much more annoying in person than it is on the TV. I hope like hell that fans in Milwaukee did not take part in this when the Braves played their in the 50's and 60's. Kelly Johnson digs in against Santana, already 2-2 with a couple of singles. Johnson would make it 3-3, doubling to center to give the Braves' fans something to get excited about in the seventh. Tim Hudson is going to hit for himself, since he's pitching marvelously tonight. He squares to bunt, and Santana's first offering nearly takes his head off. The park floods with boos as Hudson hits the deck, and Tracy starts making threats to Santana. After fouling off the next two pitches on bunt attempts, Hudson is able to lay one down, successfully moving Johnson to third with one out. Omar Infante steps in, as the fans begin to slowly rise to their feet, trying to rally their hometown Braves to tie this game. Infante fouls off the first pitch, an 81 MPH changeup. The next pitch is a fastball, and Infante crushes it to center to score Johnson, and the game is tied. Infante would advance to second on a wild pitch while Santana was dealing to Mark Kotsay, and now the Braves are in good position to take the lead. There's a young girl whistling behind me, and my ears are beginning to ring. Kotsay singles to right, but Infante is held at 3rd, and we are now looking at 1st and 3rd with one out for the scalding hot Chipper Jones. Every Braves fan in the stadium is on their feet, and the whistling won't end. We're all here to have a good time, so I'm not about to make a scene, but damn, my Lord, please stop with the whistling. The whistling is making me long for the chops, and speak of the devil, now I have both as Jones steps in. And they would go nuts as Jones singled to right on an 0-1 fastball to give the Braves a 3-2 lead, as Kotsay advances to 3rd. Randolph looks like he's going to stick with Santana to try to get out of this mess. Mark Teixeira than singled to left to score Kotsay, and it's now 4-2. Randolph still hasn't made a move to his bullpen, despite Santana giving up five hits in the 7th, and allowing three runs. Jeff Francoeur would bounce into a 1-6-3 double play to end the inning, but the damage has been done. The score is now 4-2 Braves, entering the 8th.

(Top of 8th) The Mets are now playing from behind for the first time all night, as Endy Chavez steps in to face Hudson to start the 8th. Ryan Church has grabbed a stick, and is in the on-deck circle to hit for Santana. Chavez looks at ball one, a sinker low and away. Hudson comes in with a fastball, right down the middle for a called strike. Chavez would ground back to Hudson on a 1-1 fastball, and he would be retired easily by Teixiera. Ryan Church is booed mightily as he approaches the batter's box. I suppose he's starting to get treated like an all-star, as he carries a .315

batting average into tonight's game. Church was not in the starting lineup tonight, nor was he last night, after suffering a mild concussion on Tuesday night. I guess I'm a little surprised to see Church hitting tonight. A concussion, after all, is a traumatic brain injury, and if I suffered a concussion, I'm not sure if I'd be up for facing 90 MPH fastballs two days later. But Church stepped in against Hudson, and singled to right to bring the tying run to the plate. How's this for drama......Jose Reyes up with one on and one out, with the heart of the order coming up. After a pickoff attempt, Hudson delivers a changeup to Reyes for strike one. Hudson missed on an 0-1 fastball to even the count. Reyes would foul off a 1-1 fastball to make it 1-2. The crowd is anticipating a strikeout, but Reyes hits a slow dribbler down the third base line, that Brian McCann can not handle, and now the Mets have two on with one out, for Luis Castillo. Castillo is 1-3 with a single, and while there is activity in the Braves bullpen, Hudson remains in the game to face Castillo. The first delivery to Castillo is a fastball called for a strike. The 0-1 is grounded back to Hudson....Phuck! It's 1-6-3 double play to end this rally. More whistling! Damnit !! They announce the attendance as 30,348, and I'm not so sure.

(Bottom of 8th) Pedro Feliciano is on to pitch the 8th for the Mets. He gets Brian McCann to go down on strikes to start the frame, and gets Matt Diaz to strikeout as well. Kelly Johnson, who is 3-3 with an RBI and a run scored, battles Feliciano, but would ground to Delgado, who flipped to Feliciano to retire the side. Now, c'mon bats, let's do this!

(Top of 9th) Manny Acosta is coming on to pitch the ninth for the Braves, and he will face Wright, Beltran and Delgado. Acosta finds himself in the closer's role for now, with Rafael Soriano on the DL for the Braves. Wright looks at a called strike, a 95 MPH from Acosta. The next delivery looks like a slider, and Wright sends it to left for a base knock. OK, I'm on my feet now as Beltran steps in. Acosta misses on a changeup for ball one, then comes back with another one that Beltran fouls off. A 1-1 fastball misses low for ball two. The 2-1 delivery is ripped to right, but Kelly Johnson snags it, and doubles off Wright at first for a double play. I thought I'd be looking at 1st and 3rd with nobody out, and now the bases are empty with two out. It's up to Carlos Delgado to keep this alive to avoid a four game sweep. He looks at a fastball for ball one, but Acosta gets Delgado to hit a high fly ball to center, and Mark Kotsay squeezes it to end the game.

Just like last July at Miller Park after the Tom Glavine game, I have a long walk back to the car, as Braves fans heckle me and tell me that I suck. I'm sure the Willie Randolph rumors are going to dominant the media for a while, as the Mets fall to a game under .500. The team now travels to Colorado for a weekend series.

After we get back to Chattanooga, we did stop at Sonic for some comfort food. I said to the guys that despite my team losing, I thought it was a great game, and the only thing that got to me was that annoying whistling. Well, it turns out, the whistling was not coming from a young girl. It was Tracy, the whole time, as he proceeded to demonstrate.

The Brewers were not able to pull off the sweep of Pittsburgh, losing tonight 8-4. They start a four game series with Washington tomorrow night.

May 23rd

I spent some coin at the local "Steve and Barry's" this afternoon. Everything in the store is $9.98 or less. Jeans, shoes, t-shirts, polos.....it's like a Ponderosa. The only place where you can get a steak, pepperoni pizza, macaroni and cheese, chicken wings, a salad, a bowl of jello and bottomless root beer, all for $11.

You're probably thinking that the baseball wasn't that great if I'm spending time giving free advertisement to Steve and Barry's and Ponderosa. That would be a correct assumption. We spent the evening watching "National Treasure: Book of Secrets", starring Nicolas Cage, and I would excuse myself every now and then to get updates. The Brewers called up Russell Branyan and reliever Tim Dillard today, placed Eric Gagne on the disabled list, and optioned Tony Gwynn back to Nashville. During tonight's game, the Brewers out hit the Nationals 8-3, but were outscored 5-1. You don't see that every day. In Colorado, Billy Wagner gave up his first earned run of the year in blowing the save vs the Rockies. I tried to follow the extra frames as long as I could, but decided to go bed with the score tied at 5 in the 12th inning. I awoke the next morning to see that they lost in 13, extending the losing streak to five games. Sports Illustrated is now referring to them as the New York Mess.

May 24th

Today is our last full day in Chattanooga before we drive back to Port Washington tomorrow morning. Tracy and I spent this morning picking up and delivering vegetables for the big Ruritan Club event tomorrow afternoon. Afterwards, we spent an hour or so cutting firewood, but I wasn't confident in my abilities to handle the chainsaw, so for the most part, I just loaded the truck with said firewood. My forearms are on fire as I'm writing. We also talked for a bit about life, and he gave me some valuable advice. I didn't get a chance to tell you in person, Tracy, but I appreciate your thoughtfulness, and I consider you a friend and a brother.

The Mets/Rockies game was one of the featured games on Fox today, and the Mets wasted no time in taking control of this one early, scoring five runs in the 1st inning. I wish I could have seen this, because this is what I've been looking for all season. A Reyes single, a Castillo walk, a double steal, another walk to Wright, and a three run double by Beltran to start the game. David Wright and Carlos Delgado would add home runs in the 2nd and 9th innings respectively, and Claudio Vargas turned in his best start in a Mets uniform, going seven strong innings, only allowing 2 runs on 4 hits. Today's final was 9-2.

Tonight we enjoyed some Papa John's and huddled around the TV to watch Blades of Glory. I have to say, not Ferrell's best work, but I'm not really into ice skating, and that may have leant a hand in the reasoning. For me, Anchorman is still the essential Will Ferrell film. From what I've seen, Step Brothers, which comes out this July, looks hilarious, and makes me want to buy a sweater vest. I checked in on the Brewers from time to time, and it looks like Seth McClung made the most of his first start in the Brewers' rotation. He was not scored upon until the 5th inning, when he gave up a 2-run HR to Lastings Milledge, and left the game with a 3-2 lead. The Brewers added some insurance runs late, on a Jason Kendall double and a Mike Cameron homer. Salomon Torres, who I'm guessing will take over the closer duties for the time being, came on in the ninth to notch his second save of the season. The final tonight was 5-2. Because of the long ride back tomorrow, it's time for this baseball fan to hit the sack.

May 25th

Just like a week ago, we hit the road at around 3:30am for another full day in the minivan. I made a promise not to get us lost today, and I kept that promise for my share of the driving. After about 9 hours on the road, and a couple of stops at McDonald's, we are able to find the Brewers game on the radio, albeit a grainy transmission. Not a lot of good news early on, as Manny Parra would allow the first run of the day to score on a wild pitch. The Nationals would add three more in the fourth, on the strength of an RBI double by Lastings Milledge, and a two run double by Wily Mo Pena. Parra would allow a 2-run HR to Aaron Boone to make the score 6-0 Nationals in the 5th.

Tim Redding entered the 6th inning with a shutout and a large lead to work with, but the Brewers would get to him early and often in the 6th. Prince Fielder led the inning off with single up the middle, and Corey Hart followed with a 2-run HR to dead center. Russell Branyan, who is making his first start with the team since returning to the club, doubled to right field. Branyan will probably see a lot of right handed pitching at third base, while Bill Hall will most likely continue to face the lefties. Mike Rivera popped up to the catcher for the first out, and Craig Counsell lined out to left for out number two. Joe Dillon pinch hit for Mark DiFelice, who took over for Parra in the 5th, and singled home Branyan to make it 6-3. Rickie Weeks was hit by a fastball from Redding, and with the tying run coming to the plate, Manny Acta went to his bullpen, calling upon Saul Rivera to stop the bleeding. But the Brewers would hit him hard as well, with Mike Cameron doubling home Dillon and Weeks, and Gabe Kapler singling to score Cameron. Suddenly, we are tied at 6 a piece! Prince Fielder, who led off the inning with a single, ends the inning by lining out to right field, but the damage has been done.

The game was pretty uneventful for the rest of the drive home, but as we were bringing the luggage in, I was hit with a one-two punch that left me down for the count. The first thing I did was turn the end of the game on, and it's still 6-6 in the bottom of ninth, but the Nationals have men on 1st and 3rd with only one out. The first score I see on the bottom of the screen reads Mets 1 Rockies 4, Final. I check cbsports.com for the summary, and Aaron Cook went the distance, holding the Mets to just four hits. While I am reading about this, Guillermo Mota throws a wild pitch to score the winning run for the Nationals. Both the first and last runs scored by Washington today were on wild pitches. That is tough a pill to swallow.

Taking a look around the majors going into Memorial Day, the Devil Rays have a half game lead on the Red Sox in the AL East, the White Sox lead the AL Central by 2.5 games over the Twins. The Angels lead the AL West by 1.5 over the A's. Boston leads the Wild Card by two games over Oakland, and Seattle holds the worst record in all of baseball, a huge surprise to me. In the National League, the Marlins still lead the NL East by 2.5 over Philadelphia and Atlanta, with the Mets 5.5 out at 23-25. In the Central, the Cubs and Cardinals share the top spot, with Houston a game out, and the Pirates, Brewers and Reds all within a game of each other towards the bottom of the division. The Brewers are six games back, but have played the least amount of home games in the majors thus far, so things should turn around for the Crew, as they play really well at home. In the NL West, the Arizona

Diamondbacks lead the Dodgers by 3.5 games, with Colorado, San Francisco and San Diego far behind. St Louis holds the wild card lead, with a one game lead over Houston, and the Padres are the worst team in the National League, record wise.

Based on what happened last year in the National League, nothing has been determined by a long shot. I still feel the Mets will pull it together and take the East. Getting Pedro back will be a huge lift, and Jose Reyes is really starting to get hot. There is a lot of magic left to be seen at ol' Shea. As for the Brewers, there are still a lot of concerns. They hold the worst AVG and OBP combined in the big leagues for their 1 and 2 hitters, the starting pitching has been inconsistent, and the bullpen has taken a hit lately, losing Riske and Gagne to the DL. You wonder if the league has figured out how to pitch these young guys, as Braun's average is down from last year, Fielder's power numbers are way down from last year's pace, and Bill Hall continues to struggle vs right handed pitching. J.J. Hardy isn't seeing nearly as many good pitches to hit in the 7 hole as he did hitting 2nd, and Rickie Weeks' .202 batting average simply isn't cutting it as a leadoff hitter. I wouldn't mind seeing Hart and Hardy at 1-2, and Cameron and Weeks at 6 and 7. It seemed to work last year.

'Sup, Carson? I live for your prank phone calls to "Meredith".

May 26th

Ah, Memorial Day…the unofficial start of summer. It's a beautiful day, but where is the ESPN triple header I'm used to seeing? And eight teams have today off? That doesn't seem right…..The Brewers will try to gain a split in D.C., as Ben Sheets takes the hill. The last time out for Sheets, he went the full nine in Pittsburgh, only allowing a single run. Sheets had another solid outing today, going six innings, and allowing two runs, striking out six without walking a batter. But he left the game down 2-0, as the Brewers could not figure out Jason Bergmann, who struck out eight over 5 2/3 without allowing a run. The Brewers were able to get to the Washington bullpen in the 7th, thanks to a Jason Kendall single that scored J.J. Hardy. Joe Dillon, pinch hitting for Sheets, reached on an error by Dmitri Young, which scored Hardy to tie the game. In the 8th, Prince Fielder hit a long sacrifice fly to center to give the Brewers the lead, but Dmitri Young redeemed himself by going yard against Brian Shouse in the bottom of the 8th. This game would end up going extras, and today it was the Brewers coming out on top, with Gabe Kapler singling home Prince Fielder in the 11th, and Salomon Torres slamming the door for the save. So after getting swept by Boston to start the ten game road trip, the Brewers take four of the last seven, and will now return to Milwaukee to try to build on the momentum built today. 18 of their next 24 games are at home, and a lot of ground can be made up if we play well.

The Mets continued their recent slide, dropping their seventh game of the last eight played since sweeping the Yankees. Jose Reyes stayed hot at the plate, hitting solo homers in the first and second inning against Florida starter Rickie Nolasco. But a costly Reyes error in the 3rd led to four Marlins scoring, giving the fish a 6-3 lead. The final score would be 7-3, as the Mets fell to 23-26, 6.5 games behind Florida in the East.

Well it wouldn't be Memorial Day without a cookout and a game of catch. My mom grilled dogs and burgers, and a good time was had by all. Schwingle and I played catch for about ten minutes, and then we headed back to my place for some RBI Baseball 3 on the Nintendo Entertainment System. Mike was the Brewers. I was the Mets. How appropriate! We have been talking about doing this for a while, and I'm sure we'll be doing this more in the future. Tonight, we will be competing in a seven game series, with the replica WWF championship belt on the line. I refuse to say WWE. Here's a brief summary of the series....

(Game One) Mookie Wilson goes yard in the 5th, Robin Yount returns the favor in the 6th, and Darryl Strawberry singled home Keith Hernandez in the bottom of the 12th as the Mets take

Game One. Roger McDowell is the winning pitcher, the loser is Chuck Crim.

(Game Two) Mets win 4-1. Darryl Strawberry would hit the first of three triples that he would end up hitting in this series. Ron Darling defeats Teddy Higuera.

(Game Three) Bobby Ojeda and Jesse Orosco combine on a seven hitter as the Mets take game three, 1-0. Ron Robinson pitched well for the Brewers, but not good enough. One more win, and the gold will be draped around my sexy waist.

(Game Four) Doc Gooden, Roger McDowell and Jesse Orosco combine on another shutout as the Mets complete the sweep of the Brewers, winning 2-0. The Mets outscore the Brewers 9-2 in the series, and I remind Mike that I am his RBI daddy. A challenge has been made by Mike for a rematch on Thursday. I'll be ready.

May 27th

Never underestimate the importance of an ace. Having lost 7 of 8 coming into tonight, the Mets turned to Johan Santana vs Florida in game two of an important series at Shea. The Marlins would counter with young lefty Andrew Miller, who was acquired from the Tigers this off-season in the Dontrelle Willis/Miguel Cabrera trade. Your ace gives your team its best chance to win every five days, and the Mets really need a win tonight. The bats came out early and put a 3 spot on the board in the 1st. Santana now has a three run lead to work with, and we all know how good he is with a lead. The Marlins got one back in the 2nd to make it 3-1. In the 5th inning, Fernando Tatis singled home David Wright to extend the Mets' lead to 4-1. Tatis finds himself hitting .429, filling in nicely for Ryan Church, who is still nursing the concussion. Cody Ross went deep in the sixth to make the score 4-2. The Marlins added one more run in the seventh to pull within one. In the bottom half of the seventh, Ramon Castro delivered his second RBI knock of the night, giving the Mets a 5-3 lead they would not relinquish. Santana was vintage Santana, going seven strong, scattering 8 hits, and striking out seven in the process. Billy Wagner came on to secure his 10th save, lowering his ERA to 0.43 on the year. 5 ½ back in the East, as they go for the series win tomorrow night.

The Brewers start a nine game homestand tonight, and all nine games will be against teams with winning records. They start with three vs Atlanta, and then it's three vs Houston, before they finish with three vs Arizona. Tonight, the Brewers will face Tim Hudson, who pitched great and got the win last Thursday vs the Mets. The Brewers send Dave Bush to the hill, and I wonder which Dave Bush we'll see. Bush has the stuff to be a very good starter in this league, but tends to give up the big inning too often. Last year, he was among the league leaders in total scoreless innings, but it's those big innings that have cost him some wins and some ERA love. Bush would give up solo homers to Kelly Johnson in the first, and Gregor Blanco in the second, so early on, it didn't look good for the Crew. But Bush would really settle down, and pitched great the rest of the way, going 7 innings, and not allowing a single run to score from the 3rd through 7th. The Brewers entered the bottom of the seventh down 2-0, with Hudson still hurling for the Braves. Russell Branyan led off the inning by doubling to right center. J.J. Hardy would single to center to score Branyan, and awaken a crowd of 29,000 plus that had been waiting all night to see the Brewers score. The Brewers were not able to plate Hardy in the 7th, and it didn't look like they would muster anything in the 8th, with Hudson still in the game. Mike Cameron flied softly to left field to start the inning, and Ryan Braun grounded weakly to second base for the second out. With the shift on, Prince Fielder singled easily up the middle to keep the inning alive. Corey Hart doubled to left, but Fielder was not able to score. The Braves decided to walk Branyan intentionally to get to J.J. Hardy. It looks like the fans are on their feet, and I'm pacing around here in my apartment. Hardy looks at a fastball for strike one. Hudson comes right back with the cheese, and Hardy smokes it up the box, and it bounces straight up off the mound, as

Fielder scores to tie the game. I just pedigreed one of Gracie's stuffed animals on her "Little Tikes" coloring table. She's asleep, you know I'd never do that in front of her. Jason Kendall would pop up to end the inning, and that would be the end of Tim Hudson's night. The Brewers got to him for eleven hits over eight innings. This game has a very similar feel to the game I saw in Atlanta five days ago. Only two walks all night, and no errors, all in all, a very well played game thus far. Salomon Torres was able to dispose of the Braves on seven pitches in the top of the ninth, after replacing newly acquired Julian Tavaraz, who pitched a scoreless 8th. In the bottom half of the ninth, former Brewers reliever Jeff Bennett was called on to hold the Brewers scoreless, and get the Braves to a tenth inning. If you remember, Bennett was the Brewer who wore his bill flat, and really low above his eyes. He is no longer sporting this look in Atlanta. The first Brewers hitter would be Bill Hall, who came in defensively in the top of the ninth as part of a double switch. Hall needs to take advantage of these late inning appearances to warrant more playing time. Tonight, Hall would have to battle from an 0-2 count, but he did come through, hitting a broken bat blooper to right to reach on a base hit. Rickie Weeks was asked to move Hall over with a bunt, and laid down a beauty to do just that, setting the table for Mike Cameron. Hall, noticing that Bennett was showing him any attention, was able to steal third on a 1-0 pitch to Cameron. Cameron only saw fastballs from Bennett, and after two more balls that were low and inside, Bennett finally hit the inside corner to make it 3-1. Cameron swung and missed at ball four, which was also low and away. On 3-2, Cameron hit a fly ball to left center, definitely deep enough to send Hall home. The throw was a good one, but Hall evaded it to score the winning run. Another pedigree to the giant pink bear, this time on the floor.....

Trenni Kusnierek was able to get in a word with Hall after the game. It was great to see Hall contribute tonight, and boy was it great to get back home. A quick word on Kusnierek : I am a fan. Trenni, if you ever want in on my fantasy football league, you're in. I don't even care who I have to kick out. Sorry, Schwingle. I know we're friends, but it's Trenni Kusnierek. You'd do the same for me if it was your league, and you were trying to court Paul Stanley.

May 28th

It's extremely hard to win games when you only get three hits, but it's not impossible when you can hold your opponent to four. Tonight, Jeff Suppan pitched eight shutout innings, and left the game with the score 0-0 in the bottom of the eighth. This was definitely the Jeff Suppan that carried the Cardinals to the 2006 World Series as the NLCS MVP. Suppan has always pitched well at Miller Park, with a career record of 15-3 in Milwaukee. If the Brewers could score in the eighth, it would put Soup in line to add another win to that record. J.J. Hardy would walk to lead off the inning, and Jason Kendall successfully bunted him over. The Braves would go to their pen, calling on Blaine Boyer to try to keep the game scoreless. Braves starter JoJo Reyes pitched as well as Soup did for us. I always like to see a young rookie go toe to toe with a proven veteran. Boyer struck out Joe Dillon, which set the stage for Rickie Weeks to do something special. Weeks would triple to score Hardy, as the crowd at Miller erupted. Weeks has been hovering around .200 for most of the year, but his walk to strikeout ratio continues to improve. The more Weeks can put the bat on the ball, the more chances he'll have to help the Brewers win games. Salomon Torres, who has been lights out since assuming the closer duties, pitched a scoreless ninth to give the Brewers a 1-0 win. The team has now won three straight, and they are playing with the confidence that seemed to be lacking earlier in the season, even as recently as ten days ago.

The Mets provided some late inning heroics of their own tonight. After giving up a three run homer to Cody Ross to give the Marlins a 5-4 lead in the sixth, the Mets would stare at the bottom of the ninth down by the same score, with Florida closer Kevin Gregg coming on to save it. Coming into tonight, the Marlins were 25-0 when leading after 8, and the Mets were 0-25 when trailing after eight innings. But Endy Chavez led off the inning with a solo shot to right, giving the Mets a much needed shot in the arm. But the Marlins would strike back, in the top of the 12th, as Alfredo Amezega would homer to put the Marlins up 6-5. So now, the Mets would have to come from behind twice from the ninth inning on to assure a win tonight. Twice in four innings, when it hasn't happened all year, is a lot to ask for. But the Chavez homer in the ninth has the team loose, and the fans are going crazy, in anticipation of the bottom of the 12th. David Wright walked to start the inning, and Carlos Beltran singled to left, advancing Wright to 3rd. With men on 1st and 3rd with nobody out, I do believe it's time for Gracie and I to put our rally caps on. Damion Easley struck out, and the next batter would be Fernando Tatis. This feels like a late season game. It even has a playoff atmosphere to it. Imagine my reaction as Tatis lined a double to left, easily scoring Wright. The relay throw was botched, and Beltran was also able to score to win the game. The Mets, much like the Brewers, look like they are enjoying baseball again, and this is a big win, taking two of three from the NL East leading Marlins. Oliver Perez and the bullpen combined on 16 strikeouts, easily a season high. Hopefully, this momentum will carry into the four game set with Los Angeles, which marks Joe Torre's return to New York.

May 29th

When the season starts, I always choose a handful of day games to see, and today was one of those games. We grabbed some breakfast before hand, and I'm gonna be here again on Saturday, so I didn't go crazy on food. One jumbo dog, and one Italian, both very good. The Brewers didn't really give us much to cheer for today, losing 8-1. Most of the damage was done in the fifth, as the Braves put up a 5 spot, on the strength of a Mark Teixeira three run homer off of Seth McClung. The only offense that the Brewers were able to muster was a solo HR from Russell Branyan in the bottom of the fifth. But, I'll take an afternoon of good company, good food, great weather and major league baseball any day. The Astros come into town tomorrow night to start a three game series.

After the game, the Brothers Schwingle and I headed back to my place for another night of RBI baseball. We picked up Lenny's on the way. I haven't had Lenny's since the night of the Academy Awards, and I've been craving it for months. Great New York style pizza, the tastiest jalapeno poppers on this planet, and a great staff that always makes me feel welcome. Between Lenny's and Tomaso's, my pizza hungers will never go unsatisfied, and in my mind, these two establishments make Mequon, WI the pizza capital of the world.

Mike and Jeff would play each other in a best of five to determine who gets to play me. Tonight, Mike was the Giants and Jeff was the White Sox. Jeff would take game one, but Mike would win the next three to advance. So, it would be Giants/Mets for the championship. I am following the actual Mets game on cbssports.com, and it's all good news. I turn to Mike and say, "Ever heard of David Wright? Two bombs." Mike owns Wright in my league, and is slightly ahead of me in the standings. That will change soon. But I hope Wright continues to knock the cover off the ball like he's doing tonight. The Mets collected 13 hits tonight in beating the Dodgers 8-4. With the Mets game in the books, it's time for me to school young Mike on how to play RBI. Just like in our last series, I take game one, 2-1, and I feel a sweep coming on. I don't have the same roster though, as I accidentally chose the 1990 Mets instead of the 1986 Mets, which means no Lenny Dykstra, no Ray Knight and no Gary Carter. So this isn't a true rematch, since Mike is not the Brewers, and I am not the '86 Mets. Mike came back and took game two. Jeff is entertaining my daughter, so I can show a little bit of emotion, and I'm probably coming off as crabby with the loss. I'm still competitive, even when playing a video game. So, I drop a game, not a big deal. What I wasn't expecting was to drop the next three. I can't blame the pizza, because we all enjoyed the same delicious goodness, but Lenny's does have a calming effect on me, and I must have lost my focus. I was soft tonight, and did not put Mike away like I know I can. The next series will be held inside of a 15 foot high steel cage, we will save the pies until after the series, and I will regain my championship!

May 30th

Since I won't be able to see my daughter much tomorrow, she gets all of me tonight. We spent the night coloring, playing basketball, listening to Union Pulse and enjoying some popcorn. She fell asleep on my chest shortly after asking for milk (not one sip taken), at around 10:00pm. I didn't even check on the games until after they were done.

The Mets had a 5-4 lead heading to the 8th, but Aaron Heilman gave up four hits without retiring a single Dodger, and they all scored. The Dodgers would score 5 runs in the 8th, and would win the game 9-5.

The Brewers game provided better news, as Mike Cameron and Ryan Braun would hit back to back jacks in the first, and Prince Fielder added a long bomb in the fifth, en route to a 5-1 Brewers win tonight. Manny Parra struck out six Houston batters over six innings, improving to 3-2 and lowering his ERA to 4.72. The Brewers have now won 4 of 5, and are sitting at 27-28. I'll be at Miller Park tomorrow for the much anticipated bachelor party of one Frank Crivello. Will he sing Maroon 5's "This Love" at the top of his lungs like he did the last time we attended a game together? God, I hope so. The kid has pipes.....

May 31st

Before I head to Miller Park for Frank's bachelor party, I had to take care of some long overdue business, and get my haircut. Whenever Elif cuts my hair, it looks really good, and she "musses" it up, and makes this white bread, Wrangler wearin' momma's boy look sexy. But whenever anyone else cuts my hair, they always want to give me a part on the side, and I end up looking like Dan Goddamn Rather. What *is* the frequency, Kenneth? I mean, I really want to know.

I got to Miller Park around 3:15, and met the gang near the Sausage Haus. Frank's brother, Rob (don't give me this Robert bullshit......you're Rob Crivello, and in my mind, you still have that super-sexy jet-black mullet) had Joey Bueno's catered in, and we all ate very well. Burgers, Italians, chicken, those chips with the seasoning, and plenty of beer. I nearly choked to death again (gotta learn to chew that food......it just tastes......so good). I also developed a new strategy for drinking beer. I can't stand beer when it is anything less than ice cold, so instead of pouring full cups, I only get a couple of ounces at a time. It does mean more trips to the keg, but I can use the exercise. There were about 50 of Frank's closest friends there, and ya damn right I talked up this book to a bunch of them, but I spent most of my time with Phil and Greg. Phil is one of my oldest friends, and Greg enjoys House of Pain. Greg used to be a close friend of mine, and he and I used to wage classic games of strikeout vs. each other in the early 90's. In our most memorable game, he was the Cubs and I was the Brewers, he beat me in the bottom of the 16th inning on a Mark Grace walk off. When that game ended, it was almost completely dark out, and we spent the rest of the night at his house, most likely playing nerf basketball and making prank phone calls. Greg was also my partner when Moser challenged me to a game one weekend. Mike chose Phil as his teammate, and asked me to find anyone I'd like. I chose Greg, and Greg and I won that game 20 to 5. I don't hold many victories over Moser in my life, but I remember that one. In 20 years of basketball, I've probably beaten him seven times, and I don't think I've ever beaten him at Madden's. Ever. EVER!

As we approached our seats, I notice on the out of town scoreboard that the Mets have taken care of the Dodgers today, 3-2. The seats we have are right down the right field line, about 15 rows back. Great seats! Phil, Greg and I try to find three seats that are together, and it felt like old times. Matt Gitzlaff was with us tonight as well, and he reminded me of the time I told him that I would buy him a candy bar if he took a.........you'll have to call me directly to get the end of that story.

123

Tonight is a sell out, and we will start to see a bunch of those in the coming months, especially on weekends. They gave away a J.J. Hardy poster, and I'm sure my niece, Gina will hang it up tonight. You can also tell by all the matching shirts that there are a lot of groups out tonight. In about the 4th inning, the words, "The Brewers welcome the Frank Crivello Bachelor Party" showed up on the scoreboard, and I felt like a minor celebrity for a moment. So *that's* how that feels, David Faustino.

With the Brewers trailing 1-0 in the 5th, Ryan Braun hit an RBI single scoring Rickie Weeks to tie the game, and Prince Fielder quickly untied it by hitting a towering homerun to right field. There is nothing more pure than seeing my good friend Rob giving stereo high fives as Fielder rounds the bases. It's even better to see the same quantity of high fives after a two out walk. It's baseball enthusiasm at it's finest. At the end of five, the Brewers now lead 3-1. Ben Sheets, who is most likely going to represent the Brewers at Yankee Stadium in this year's All Star Game, is pitching great again. He has great command of his fastball and curveball tonight. In the 6th inning, Russell Branyan hits one of the longest home runs I've ever seen, into the 3rd row of the Dew Deck in right field. They said it was 462, and I say it was longer. Branyan owns the longest home run I've ever seen at Miller Park, when he hit a picture of himself on the scoreboard on Opening Day in 2005. That was the 2nd of two dingers he hit on that day. The longest home run I've ever seen was in 1990 at County Stadium. Cecil Fielder hit a ball about 507 feet over the left field bleachers off of Dan Plesac. It was just an incredible show of strength. Branyan's home run gave the Brewers a 4-1 lead.

There was talk of the guys leaving early for a surprise party that Todd Asmondy was throwing for his fiancée, but with the game going so well in the Brewers favor, and Sheets working quickly, most of the group stuck around to the end. Sheets entered the ninth with a 4-1 lead, and got both Kaz Matsui and Miguel Tejada to fly out to Corey Hart on a total of five pitches. Salomon Torres is warming up in the Brewers bullpen, but I gotta think that this will be Sheets' game to finish tonight. The capacity crowd of 42,913 is now on their feet, to watch Sheets go the distance and secure game two of this important series within the division. His pitch count entering the inning was 102, and although he was able to quickly dissolve of the first two batters, Lance Berkman battled for a total of 11 pitchers before walking. Ned Yost rushed to the mound, and called for Torres, and a very animated Ben Sheets let Yost and the crowd know how he felt about being pulled, just one out short of his 2nd complete game in his last three starts. Sheets flipped the ball to Branyan and walked back to the dugout without saying a word to Yost. This was not a popular move, but at 118 pitches, it is understood by this banker / author. Torres was able to retire Carlos Lee on two pitches, and the first guy on the field to greet his teammates was Sheets. I love seeing that kind of passion from this team. Hopefully that kind of emotion can spill onto the rest of the team, and I think it is really starting to. 5-1 and 4-1 wins vs the Astros to guaranty a series win, with game three scheduled for tomorrow afternoon at 1:05 pm.

Fellas, it was good to see all of you again. Frank, best of luck in your marriage, and I look forward to hearing your soccer talk show in the near future on my radio dial. Phil, I'll see you very soon, say hi to Lincoln and Erika for me. Greg, do what you do, just do what you do, and that's all the Baby Jesus ever wanted of you. Rob, thanks for having me, we will talk very soon, and thank you for lending your ear to me at the tailgate.

3. There Is Still Work to Be Done

June 1st

Berries and cream, berries and cream, I'm a little lad who loves berries and cream!! Forgive me, but I didn't get much sleep last night, and when I don't get enough sleep, I slip in and out of singing commercial jingles to myself. I also get cravings for foods I don't normally crave, and this morning, I wanted nothing more than to have a plate of tomato alfredo, and chase it with some s'mores. Don't ask.

Gracie woke me up this morning, and wanted a rematch for the basketball game we played on Friday night, as she grabbed my hand and walked me right to her basket. She's developing a habit of just throwing the ball square at my face and laughing her heart out. She must get a kick out of the way I react, because it gets her every time.

The Brewers took care of business today, scoring four in the 1st, chasing Shawn Chacon after one inning, and then putting up five in the 4th. Dave Bush had his second consecutive great start, giving up one run in the 1st, then scattering 3 hits the rest of the way, going 7 innings in this 10-1 Brewers win. So the Brewers return the favor and sweep the Astros, and are now a game over .500. They are starting to hit and pitch at the same time, and are winning games convincingly. It's good to see. May has always been a bad month for Milwaukee, so hopefully we can see more of this for a while.

The Mets were featured on ESPN tonight, facing the Dodgers in the fourth game of their series from Shea Stadium. Johan Santana gave up a run in the first, but the Mets got one right back, and in the third, busted out five runs to give Santana more than enough. Carlos Beltran and Ryan Church went deep to pace the scoring for the Mets. In winning tonight, Santana ran his record to 7-3, and lowered his ERA to 3.20. The Mets are also a game over .500, and get Pedro Martinez back on Tuesday night. It's always good to get a win on the "world wide leader".

June 2nd

With the Brewers coming off of a sweep of Houston, the NL West leading Arizona Diamondbacks come in for a three game set to finish off the homestand. Doug Davis makes his return to Milwaukee, and the Brewers will counter with Jeff Suppan, who had his best start of the year last week vs Atlanta. Both pitchers had good stuff tonight, but Davis was a little bit better, leaving the game with a 3-1 lead in the 7th inning. After Davis was pulled, the D-Backs started to give the game away. With two on and nobody out, Jason Kendall was asked to sacrifice. He laid down a pretty good bunt, but Arizona reliever Chad Qualls tried to get Bill Hall at 3rd, and the throw was late, loading the bases. The big break would come during the very next at bat, with Gabe Kapler pinch hitting for Soup. Kapler hit a bouncer to Arizona third basemen Mark Reynolds, whose throw home was way off the mark, scoring both Hall and Hardy to tie the game. Sometimes it's better to be lucky than good, and the Brewers are definitely lucky to be tied at this point. In the 8th, Guillermo Mota set the Diamondbacks down in order, setting the stage for Prince Fielder in the bottom of the inning. Fielder would lead off the inning, hitting a long home run to dead center off of Doug Slaten, who only faced one batter tonight. Salomon Torres slammed the door in the ninth to record his sixth save of the season. The Brewers have now won 7 of their last 8 games, but the Cubs keep winning as well, and we remain 7 back in the Central.

Not much to say about the Mets tonight, as they continue their Jeckyl and Hyde routine. After taking 3 of 4 from the Dodgers at Shea, they lose tonight in San Francisco, 10-2. Oliver

Perez only retired one more batter than I did tonight, facing eight batters, allowing five hits and walking two more.

But my focus tonight has been less about baseball, and more about "rawk", as the new Weezer album comes out tomorrow. It is a couple of minutes after midnight, and I keep checking itunes to see if it's available for immediate download, but it looks like I'll have to wait until tomorrow. As I get ready for bed, I put on some Dick Prall, and daydream about one extra bowl of cornflakes.

June 3rd

I have an e-mail from itunes this morning, and it's time stamped 1:37am. It says that my Weezer pre-order is available for download. I feel like Ralphie when he found his BB gun behind the tree as the pop nuggets transfer to my ipod, and I just hope to God I don't shoot my eye out today. After giving it a couple of listens in the car and at work, here is a short review...

Weezer (The Red Album) is probably their strongest record since Pinkerton, with the album's first track, Troublemaker, rekindling the sound of The Good Life. The Greatest Man That Ever Lived (Variations on a Shaker Hymn) is one of the most ambitious Weezer songs ever recorded, coming in just under the six minute mark, and providing many different flavors to please your ear drums. You can hear some Beatles influence, some Queen, even some Fred Durst, among others. The song features police sirens, piano and a falsetto vocal from Rivers Cuomo not heard from him since Hash Pipe. The first single, Pork and Beans, is Weezer at its finest, with a great hook and a very catchy chorus. What makes this album stand out from previous Weezer efforts is that every member of the band has songwriting credits, and they all sing lead vocals on at least one song. Pat Wilson, who is the bands drummer, sings and plays lead guitar on Automatic, and Rivers has been quoted as saying that the best guitar playing on this record was by their supposed drummer. This track has a Maladroit feel to it. Scott Shriner, the bands bass player, wrote the music and sang lead on Cold Dark World, which is one of the standout tracks on the album. He also sings one of the bonus tracks on the deluxe version, the name of the song being King. I think this song is good enough to have made the album. Miss Sweeney, another bonus track, sounds like it was taken directly from the Green Album sessions, and features a very unique vocal style from Rivers. All in all, I recommend this album to all Weezer fans. If you're a non Weezer fan, you can go to hell, my friend. Wait, come back, I'm kidding, you stay right here, nobody's going to hell. But give it a listen, or I will kick your dog. And if you don't have a dog, I will push the smallest member of your family down.

The Brewers and Diamondbacks continued their series tonight at Miller Park, with Randy Johnson facing Seth McClung. Mark Reynolds, last night's goat, doubled home Orlando Hudson to give the snakes a 1-0 lead in the 4th. That is all Seth McClung would allow through six innings, and he even singled twice off of the 6'10" future Hall of Famer. One would wonder if McClung will be used as a pinch hitter, or even as a designated hitter in a future interleague game. Ryan Braun gave McClung a lead in the bottom of the sixth, by hitting a two run bomb off Johnson. The Brewers added two in the 7th, and hit a couple of homers in the 8th (Fielder and Hardy) to give the Brewers a 7-1 lead. Tim Dillard and Brian Shouse held the Diamondbacks hitless in three innings of relief as the Brewers held on to a 7-1 win tonight. The team is now only a game behind the Diamondbacks for overall record, the same Diamondbacks that had the best record in baseball three weeks ago. That honor now belongs to the Cubs, who have now won nine straight. The last time the Cubs had the best record in baseball this late in the season…1908.

Tonight is a huge night for the Mets, as Pedro Martinez returns from the disabled list. This will be a huge lift for a staff that has been very inconsistent as of late. The Mets and Giants swapped runs in the first, and then the Mets exploded for a season high 8 runs in the fifth. There must be something in the air, as Pedro also had two singles tonight, giving my teams' starting pitchers four hits total tonight. Pedro gave the Mets a quality start, going six and giving up three. Scott Schoeneweis gave three back in the ninth, but the Mets hung on to win 9-6. My boy John Maine is going to throw a no-hitter tomorrow. He is. HE IS!!

June 4th

I was not able to follow the games today. It looks like I missed a lot. The Brewers swept the D-Backs by winning today 10-1. Corey Hart hit a three run inside the park HR, and Manny Parra struck out eight over seven innings, only allowing four hits. The Brewers are now 4 games above .500, and have won six straight. They'll take tomorrow off, and start a three game set in Colorado on Friday night. John Maine did not throw the no-hitter that I predicted yesterday, but the Mets did put up a three spot in the 1st inning today in San Francisco. Maine held the Giants in check over six innings, as the Mets would go on to win, 5-3. After getting killed in game one, we take the final two to take the series, and will now head to San Diego for a four game series with San Diego. Without having to face Peavy, Maddux or Young, the Mets should be able to get some wins this weekend.

June 5th

I promised Heather that I wouldn't use this book as a diary about our marriage, and I certainly won't to that. It's not fun to write about, and I know it wouldn't be fun to read. But the fact is, we are getting a divorce, and it's hard on everyone. The writing may run thin for a couple of days. Gracie, Heather, Mom, Dad, Jill, Gina, Tracy, Kathy…each one of us will come out of this a stronger person. Each of you will always be family to me, no matter what happens. I love you all. And to Amber, Schwingle, Moser, Gilly, Phil, Jamie and Sean…Thank you for supporting me and for being the best friends a man could ask for.

The Mets lost tonight 2-1 at San Diego on a walk off HBP. Scott Schoeneweis walked three to get to that point. This is a hard loss to swallow.

June 6th

Tonight was my first night visiting Gracie in the apartment that I used to call home. It is a little awkward, and I don't know all the ground rules. Can I go in the fridge? Should I answer the phone if it rings? I don't have any clothes to change into, so I'll look like Bobby Banker all night, chasing Gracie around in khakis and a long sleeve collared shirt. When I left Port Washington, the Brewers were up 4-1 in the 7th. I was shocked to see a 6-4 Rockies win on my cell phone when I got home. I checked online for an explanation. Mota took over in the 8th…faced four batters…single, single, double and triple. Shouse came in, and gave up a homer to complete the cycle for Colorado. The bullpen blows another Ben Sheets win, and we waste back to back jacks by Russell Branyan and J.J. Hardy.

The Mets lost 2-1 again. A Johan Santana throwing error led to two runs scoring in the sixth. They scored the second run as unearned, even though it was his error. I can see if another guy botches one, you don't want to pin that on your pitcher, but I always assumed that they would score that as an earned run if the pitcher commits the error. The Mets are now sitting at .500, all alone in fourth place, six games behind Philadelphia. At what point to you stop saying, "It's early and they'll come around".

June 7th

It's Groundhog Day, and I'm Bill Murray. At least that's what it's felt like the last three days. The Padres beat the Mets 2 to 1 once again tonight. It's their fourth straight 2-1 victory, and the first time in Major League history that this has happened. Tonight, Scott Hairston took Pedro Feliciano deep in the bottom of the tenth to end it. Old Lady Karma wants me to work harder for my marriage, and is taking it out on my book. Who's going to buy a book about a high priced 4th place team, and a 3rd place team in a small market? You. The answer is you. But, hey! Now you can tell people you know an author. It may even get you laid.

The Brewers lost tonight 7-2 in Colorado, continuing the trend of playing great at home, and not so great on the road. Colorado has one of the worst records in baseball, and are currently without Matt Holliday, but that doesn't matter if you can't score runs. Giving up 5 runs in the 1st doesn't help either, Dave Bush! Taylor Buchholz pitched a scoreless ninth, lowering his ERA to 1.67 over 32 1/3 innings. His K/BB ratio is 25/8. Before there was a Clay Buchholz, I was rooting for Taylor during his stint with the Astros. When he got his first Major League win, I emailed everyone I knew. I know these guys aren't related to me, but I feel a connection to them, especially being pitchers. After Clay no-hit the O's last year, I cried, and then hugged my mom as if he was in the family. And it's neat to think that they were both in the World Series last year, even though neither of them pitched. It makes me feel old to know that there are Major League Pitchers named Buchholz, and they are ten years younger than I am. I like to think that I broke my arm to help make room for these guys. And while you make think that sounds silly, it gives me peace. That's what I'm going with.

June 8th

The Brewers hang on today to take game three, 3-2. Everyone pitched great. Jeff Suppan is now 4-4 with an ERA of 3.78. Carlos Villanueva got out of a big jam in the 7th, and Salomon Torres recorded five outs to get the save. He is the fuckin' closer, people! They better give that job to him on a permanent basis. Now the Brewers head to Houston after a day off tomorrow, and will try to avoid getting swept there again. Getting a couple of wins there will put some serious distance between us and the 'Stros. The Brewers will be without Rickie Weeks, as he was placed on the disabled list after suffering a sprained left knee on Saturday night. The Brewers have recalled infielder Hernan Iribarren to take his spot on the roster.

San Diego swept the Mets. It wasn't 2-1, but I'm stunned either way. The Mets carried a 6-4 lead into the 8th inning. Pedro was not his best today, giving up 10 hits over 5 innings, but the bats put up five runs in the first four innings, and the bullpen was given a two run lead to protect. Billy Wagner was asked to record a four out save, and gave up a 3 run pinch-hit home run to Tony Clark, who I believe celebrated his 91st birthday earlier this week. I am in shock, I really am. I always seem to have really high hopes for the Mets in the off-season, especially this season. After getting so close in 2006, and having a commanding lead last year, only to blow it in September, I really thought this collection of talent would put it together this year. We have a great mix of young studs and proven veterans, and I thought we would bully through this division by adding Johan Santana, and getting back a healthy Pedro Martinez. We are now 30-32, and 7.5 back. Now I really need to cuddle up with some Game Six.

June 9th

I did watch Game Six last night, but only from the 7th inning on. 1986 really was a special year for the baseball fan in me. Prior to the start of the season, the Brewers acquired Rob Deer from the San Francisco Giants, and as a ten year old, I knew little to nothing about players traded here. But it didn't take long to label him as my new favorite Brewer, as he would hit home runs in his first two at bats in a Brewers uniform, both off of Tom Seaver, and one of them completely leaving Comiskey Park. My mom instantly loved Deer as well, and not just because of his pop. She had a huge crush on him. Some days, I don't know who she loved more, Jake Roberts, Elvis or Deer. It was neat for us to have a common interest in a player, and often times, we would get seats in the right field bleachers, where Deer played in four of his five years in Milwaukee. Ironically, later that year, Gorman Thomas was brought back to Milwaukee for the rest of the season, so for half a year, my two favorite Brewers of all time were teammates. The '86 Brewers only won 77 games, and finished in sixth place, but pieces were starting to be put in place to turn the team around.

Of course, the 1986 baseball season was especially memorable for me because of the Mets championship campaign. They coasted through the regular season, going 20-4 in the month of April, winning 18 of 19 games during one amazing stretch, and never really looked back. They started to build a reputation as a team that played "dirty", but really, they just played hard with a lot of determination. I can see why other teams would hate excessive curtain calls, but this team knew they were good, and weren't afraid to tell the world. They even made a music video, midseason. Some of the worst acting I've ever seen, I still youtube it from time to time. On July 22nd, Ray Knight brawled with Eric Davis in the tenth inning of a game in Cincinnati, and the team rallied to beat the Reds in the 14th on a Howard Johnson home run, making the Mets even more of a target for other contending National League teams. But in the end, the Mets took the East by an overwhelming 21.5 games, clinching the division on September 17th vs the Cubs. The team would win 108 games in the regular season, to finish with a winning percentage of .667.

This would setup a National League Championship Series vs. the Houston Astros. I remember the league championship series that year were televised on ABC, with Al Michaels doing play by play in the American League, and Keith Jackson called the National League games. Michaels' call of the Dave Henderson home run off of Donnie Moore is still one of the most memorable calls I can remember. The Sox were down 3-1, and three outs away from elimination. Henderson beat Moore, and the Sox would go back to Boston and take games 6 and 7 to advance to the World Series.

In game one of the NLCS, Mike Scott, who dominated the National League with an 18-10 record, and an ERA of 2.22, beat the Mets 1-0, only allowing 5 hits. Bobby Ojeda and the Mets would beat Nolan Ryan in game two, 5-1, to even the series at a game a piece. Game three would go down as an all time Mets classic, as the Mets would trail 4-0 in the 2nd inning, but would tie the game with 4 runs in the sixth. After giving the lead back the next inning, the Mets would enter the ninth down by one. But Lenny Dykstra hit a walk off homer off of Houston's closer, Dave Smith, to give the Mets a 2-1 series lead. Mike Scuff, I'm sorry, the family name is Scott. Mike Scott beat the Mets in game four, 3-1, this time surrendering only three hits. Game five went 12 innings, with the Mets winning 2-1, to take a 3-2 series lead back to Houston.

Game Six of the NLCS is another all time classic, as the Astros would tag Bobby Ojeda for three runs in the bottom of the first, and Bob Knepper would hold the Mets scoreless for the first eight innings. The Mets would enter the ninth, down 3-0, with Mike Scott staring at them for a potential game seven in Houston. The last thing the Mets wanted to think about was facing Mike Scott in a deciding game, in Houston. He was nearly unhittable in games 1 and 4. In the top of the ninth, Lenny Dykstra led off the inning with a triple, and Mookie Wilson quickly singled him home to put the Mets on the board. Kevin Mitchell grounded out, advancing Wilson to 2nd. Keith Hernandez would double home Mitchell to pull the Mets within one. Knepper's night was done, and he got a huge ovation on the way to the dugout. Dave Smith was called upon to save it for Knepper, in an effort to get the Astros to a game seven. But he would walk Carter and

Strawberry, to set up a Ray Knight sacrifice fly. The game would remain 3-3 until the 14th inning, when Wally Backman would drive in a run to give the Mets the lead. The Mets called upon their closer, Jesse Orosco, to get the final three outs. But this game would be far from over, as Billy Hatcher would homer off the left field foul pole to tie the game. It seemed like this game would go on forever, but I loved every minute of it. In the top of the 16th inning, the Mets scored three times to take a 7-4 lead, and nearly gave that lead up, giving up two runs to Houston, before Orosco finally got Kevin Bass to strike out to end the game, and put the Mets in the World Series. At the time, I had yet to experience anything like what happened that night. The Mets were in the World Series!!

As exciting as the two league championship series were in 1986, the 1986 World Series was something else. So many story lines, so much drama. The Red Sox would win the first two games, at Shea, to take a 2-0 lead back to Boston. Game one was similar to game one of the NLCS, another 1-0 loss. Bruce Hurst pitched a complete game four hitter, and Ron Darling pitched equally well for the Mets, giving up only an unearned run in the 7th, caused by a Tim Teufel error. In game two, the Sox out hit the Mets 18-8, and beat them 9-3. Now the Mets would have to win four of the next five games to win the Series, and the first three of the remaining games would be played at Fenway Park. The Mets got the jumpstart they needed in game three, when Lenny Dykstra led the game off with a home run off Dennis "Oil Can" Boyd. The image of Dykstra barking at himself and pumping his fist as he circled the bases will forever be branded in my memory. The Mets would put four up in the top of the first, and sailed to a 7 to 1 victory behind a strong performance from Bobby Ojeda. The Mets dominated game four as well, on the strength of two Gary Carter home runs over the Green Monster, and seven shutout innings from Ron Darling. The visitors take the first four games of a World Series for the first time ever, setting up an all-important game five. Bruce Hurst would go the distance again, beating the Mets 4-2, while Doc Gooden continued to struggle in the post season. Gooden would only go four innings, yielding four runs on nine hits. The Mets would now have to go back to Shea and win the next two games to win their first world championship since 1969.

    Game Six. What can I say? My first-born son is going to be named Game Six. If I could legally change my last name to Nineteeneightysix, we'd be all set. I'd give anything to go back in time, and be able to sit in Shea Stadium on Saturday night, October 25th, 1986. To this day, I cannot watch this game without my mascara running down my face. There are so many memories. In the top of the 1st, with Bill Buckner hitting, a man by the name of Michael Sergio parachuted on to the field with a "Go Mets" banner. The crowd went crazy, and I still remember thinking that tonight was going to be a special night. He was greeted by two of New York City's finest, and escorted out of the stadium, through the Mets dugout and clubhouse. When he walked past the players, Ron Darling actually made an effort to shake his hand. They showed Dwight Evans in the on-deck circle, and the look on his face told everyone watching that this was an event. The world tonight revolved around Flushing, NY. This really set the tone for an unforgettable night. The pitching matchup was Roger Clemens vs Bobby Ojeda. The Sox would score single runs in the 1st and 2nd innings, and the way Clemens was hurling, they probably wouldn't need much more. Clemens carried a no-hitter into the 5th inning, but the Mets battled and battled, scoring first on a Ray Knight single, then on a run scoring double play ground out by Danny Heep to tie the game. A throwing error by Ray Knight led to the Red Sox taking the lead in the 7th. Roger Clemens would be pulled for a pinch hitter in the 8th; prompting John McNamara to hand the ball to Calvin Schiraldi to get the last six outs of the World Series. Lee Mazzilli, who entered the game in a double switch last inning, singled to lead off the inning. He motioned to the dugout with his arms as if to say, "Is someone pinch running for me", but he would stay in the game. Lenny Dykstra would lay down a bunt to advance Mazzilli, but the throw to 2nd was in the dirt, and everyone was safe. The crowd is so electric at this point of the game. Wally Backman also laid down a great bunt, and Schiraldi had to go to first to retire Backman, setting up a 2nd and 3rd with one out situation with Hernandez and Carter coming up. They gave Hernandez a free pass, to set up the force, as the Mets fans chant "Gary, Gary".

The first three pitches to Carter were way off the mark, as the crowd is going crazy. Vin Scully would chime, "Oh, this'll kill you" right before the 3-0 delivery, which Carter lined to left, caught by Jim Rice, but scoring Mazzilli to tie the game. Ray Knight is now off the hook for the 7th inning error, and it's a brand new ball game.

The game remained tied at 3-3 through nine innings. In the top of the tenth, Rick Aguilera, who came in to pitch in the ninth, gave up a lead off homer to Dave Henderson that got outta here in a hurry. Aguilera gave up the most home runs on the Mets in 1986, and this was the worst possible time to give one up. Vin Scully would comment that after the home run, "It is so quiet in New York, that you can hear Boston." Aguilera would strike out Spike Owen, and Calvin Schiraldi, who hit for himself (with Don Baylor and Tony Armas still on the bench). Wade Boggs would double, and Marty Barrett would single him home to give the Sox a 5-3 lead. Bill Buckner would hit for himself, and was hit by a pitch before the Sox were retired to end the inning. It should be noted that the Red Sox would often pull Buckner late in games in favor of Dave Stapleton as a defensive replacement. Buckner's nagging injuries were well known at the time, but the Sox probably figured that it would have meant a lot to Buckner to be on the field when they clinched the series.

In the bottom of the 10th, the Mets first two hitters were retired quietly, with Wally Backman flying out to Jim Rice and Keith Hernandez flying out to Dave Henderson. Shortly after Hernandez flied out, NBC would name Marty Barrett as the game's MVP, and the scoreboard at Shea would read, "Congratulations to the 1986 World Champion Boston Red Sox" for a moment. Vin Scully commented that it looked like Dennis Boyd would now have tomorrow night off, as he was scheduled to pitch game seven. Gary Carter would fall to 0-2, before singling to left field. I've read different variations of what happened in the bottom of the tenth that night, but one thing I've seen on multiple occasions that humored me was that Carter said to first base coach Bill Robinson, "No way I'm making the last out of the (expletive) World Series". I've also read that while Gary Carter was up, Kevin Mitchell was making plane reservations while he and Keith Hernandez were sharing a beer in the clubhouse, drowning in their sorrow as the season was ending. After Carter reached base, Mitchell was summoned to pinch hit, and again, I don't know that it's true, but it sure makes for a great story, had already taken off his jock strap, and hit without one that night. Mitchell would also single to put the tying run on base. Ray Knight would single to right to pull the Mets within one run, putting Mets base runners on 1st and 3rd with two outs for Mookie Wilson. John McNamara would call on Bob Stanley to shut the door. Kevin Mitchell would score on the infamous wild pitch to tie the game, setting up one of the most incredible endings in baseball history. With Knight now on 2nd base, Mookie Wilson worked the count to 3-2, before hitting a slow grounder towards Bill Buckner. The ball would go through Buckner's legs, and roll into right field, allowing Ray Knight to score. It's hard to capture all of this on paper, you really have to sit down with me one night and watch this game from start to finish to really understand what an amazing night this was, and how important it was and still is to me. When I watch game six, I still watch it like it's the first time. I can never walk away from it. I even pause it when I use the restroom so that I don't miss anything. Game seven was washed out on Sunday night, and was rescheduled for Monday night, October 27th. For the 41st time in the 1986 season, they had to come from behind again, overcoming a 3-0 deficit to eventually win 8-5, giving the Mets their 2nd championship in their 25-year history. The game winning RBI belonged to Ray Knight, who homered to lead off the 7th, giving the Mets their first lead of the night. The home run was hit off of Calvin Schiraldi.

Three months after experiencing the ultimate high in seeing the Mets win the World Series, in the fashion that they did, I experienced the ultimate low, as the Cleveland Browns were beat by the Denver Broncos in the AFC Championship Game in Cleveland. This game is simply known as "The Drive", as John Elway drove the Broncos 98 yards to tie the game, and went on to win in overtime. Looking back, I think that needed to happen for me to really appreciate what happened back in October. I think had the Browns won, I would have started to take winning for granted, and maybe not have enjoyed it as much. But that loss to Denver puts everything into perspective. Sometimes you win, and sometimes you lose. Losing always hurts, but the losses make you hungry to win again. And when you win it all, nothing is sweeter.

June 10th

OK, spending time last night rehashing game six is giving me a new sense of hope for 2008. Yes, the Mets are struggling, and it's going to be hard to make up 7.5 games while chasing three teams, but it's the last year at Shea, and the Mets have certainly come back from larger deficits in the past. See 1969. We open a three game set with Arizona tonight, and some home cooking may do us some good. John Maine did not have his best stuff tonight, but he was given an early 5-1 lead, so things looked great for awhile. The Diamondbacks scored twice in the 5th, ending Maine's night, and would tag Claudio Vargas for two in the 6th, before a lengthy rainfall delayed the game for well over an hour and a half. With the score 5-5 in the 7th, I checked to see how the Brewers were doing in Houston. Roy Oswalt was pitching for the Astros, and he's always been something of a Brewers killer in his career. Nothing new tonight. He went seven, striking out ten, and a four run Astros 7th would cap a 6-1 win tonight for Houston. The Brewers did bat Corey Hart leadoff, and J.J. Hardy in the 2 hole, moving Mike Cameron and his .215 batting average down to 6 in the order. With Weeks on the DL, the Brewers opted to play Bill Hall at 2nd for the first time in well over two years. Russell Branyan is still hitting over .300, and this may be Hall's only chance to crack the lineup these days. Tonight's only run for the Brewers was courtesy of a Ryan Braun solo home run, his team leading 17th of the year. He's slowly starting to garner some All Star rumblings, with his 17 bombs, 48 RBI's and a .293 batting average. Seth McClung did not pitch that bad, but two throwing errors tonight were costly.

The Mets game resumed after my daughter was asleep, the news wasn't good the rest of the way. Mets relievers were hit hard, and the Diamondbacks would score four runs in the last two innings, as the Mets would lose tonight, 9-5. That's five straight losses for the Metropolitans. Three under .500, but I will not give up hope. Not after what the Phillies were able to do last season. I have to treat every game like a precious snowflake. I just wish these snowflakes could pitch better after the 7th inning.

June 11th

Wednesday nights are going to be hard on me for a while. This will be the one day during the week that I will not be able to see Gracie. For now, Heather wants to take one night a week and spend that with Gracie exclusively, which I'm ok with, because she needs her more than anything right now. I'd be lying if I said that I didn't miss tucking in Gracie, and having her wake me in the morning by poking me in the head, asking to play basketball. God, do I miss that. While I do miss her a ton, I know that Heather needs to be close to her, and I can't in good conscious have Heather feel lonely right now. My extended time with Gracie will come soon enough. I can really use this time to reconnect with my niece, Gina, who has felt the effects of me not being around as much. She knows about what's going on, but it hurts too much to bring it up with me. Yesterday, she gave me her new cell phone number, and simply said, "You can call me anytime you want". I cried all the way back home. Life is complicated. I can honestly say I have no regrets about my decision, because of the long term good it will do for everyone involved, but the short term pain is real, and shouldn't be ignored. Everyone is hurting, but time heals all wounds.

Thank God for baseball! People want to say that professional athletes are overpaid. Not me. The entertainment value of a baseball game, football game, rock show, etc, is priceless. Think of all the people who work all day, tough jobs, I mean really tough jobs, people with big families, who look forward to these games as a way to release stress. It's great to lose yourself in the moment of these games, even just for three hours, to make those stresses easier to deal with tomorrow.

With all of my stresses as it relates to not seeing Gracie as much, the Mets and Brewers picked a great night to give me something to smile about. The Mets had a 3-0 lead heading to the ninth, but when Mike Pelfrey walked the leadoff batter, the lead was handed over to Billy Wagner. Wagner gave up a single and a three run homer to Mark Reynolds to tie the game. I don't have access to my beloved mlb extra innings package, so I cannot give the finger to the television the way I'd like to. But cbssports.com gives a pitch by pitch description of what's happening, and when I saw that Carlos Beltran hit a walk off two run shot in the bottom of the 13th, I did a series of post WrestleMania Hulk Hogan poses to a room of no one. I wish I could have seen it. I'm going to become very good friends with mlb.com in the coming months, and their video highlights of nightly games.

The Brewers and Astros played a little beer league softball tonight, combining for eight home runs, five of which were hit by the Brewers (Mike Cameron, Russell Branyan, Jason Kendall, and two by Corey Hart). Hart's average is now above .300, and he and Hardy combine for a 5-8 night, with 4 RBI and three runs scored. The Brewers have to keep Hart and Hardy at the top of the order. Hart is a natural lead off hitter, who is also the best base runner on the team, and Hardy is going to see better pitches hitting in front of Braun and Fielder. This should have been a no-brainer all year. Manny Parra got knocked around a bit, but pitched well enough to improve his record to 5-2. The final was 10-6, and the Brewers will go for a rare series win on the road in tomorrow afternoon's game.

June 12th

Stunned. I'm stunned. Heading into the 8th inning, the Mets led the Diamondbacks 4-0, after Johan Santana gave the team 7 innings of scoreless ball, allowing only three hits and striking out ten. Maybe his best start wearing the orange and blue. Joe Smith gave up two in the 8th, and Billy Wagner gave up

142

two in the 9th, blowing his third straight save opportunity. The guy didn't give up an earned run for something like seven weeks, and now is ERA is up to 2.33. I remember Wagner having a stretch like this with Houston a while back, but I didn't care then, because he wasn't wearing the clothes that I root for. Aaron Heilman gave up a sacrifice fly to Miguel Montero in the 10th, which would be the game winner this afternoon. Hey, I understand the Willie Randolph rumors aren't going away anytime soon, but it's not his responsibility to get outs late in games. The bullpen has to take ownership.

The Brewers picked up where they left off last night, and hit another four home runs today (Fielder, Cameron, Hart and Kapler). Three of those home runs were hit in the 2nd inning off of Houston starter Brian Moehler, who really got hit hard today. Ben Sheets struck out 9 Astros over seven innings, only allowing three runs before the bullpen gave up a few to make the game close near the end. The Brewers did win this one, by the score of 9-6, and it was an important win for a few reasons. Taking two of three in Houston is huge, after being swept here less than a month ago. This also gives us momentum heading into a 9 game homestand against American League opponents (Minnesota, Toronto and Baltimore). We are back to four games above .500, but still not gaining any ground. The Cubs still hold on to baseball's best record.

I reconnected with an old friend today. Bob Douglas was my supervisor when I worked in Firstar's call center in the late 90's. He quickly became a good friend of mine, and for reasons that escape me at this time, we fell out of touch about four years ago. A few days ago, I asked his ex-wife how I can reach him these days, and called him on the way to Gracie's tonight. We talked for about ten minutes, caught up on the last four years, and loosely committed to seeing a game in early July. I look forward to it. Hey, Bob...what was your "cheese" name. I remember I was Parmesan, and Bill was Mozzarella. Wait a minute...Bobby Romano. That's it. Good times...

June 13th

Today is Friday the 13th. What would Joe say? WC!
Speaking of WC, Will Clark was born on Friday the 13th. I never
got into the superstition of Friday the 13th. Nor did I enjoy the
movies...

I gave Heather the Brewers tickets tonight, and I'll be
taking Gracie out for pizza, and meeting Amber to plan Mikey's
birthday get together. It sounds like we'll be taking our boy to
Chili's, then doing some mini golfing, and then chasing the putt-
putt with some midnight bowling. What do you get a 32 year old
man that has everything? Gift certificates to Leonardo's and
Tomaso's, that's what. After dinner, I took Amber to see Brown
Deer. Where I grew up, where I played baseball, and there just
happened to be a Brown Deer High School varsity baseball game
going on, so we dropped in and stayed a while. Gracie was an
angel, sitting on my knee for most of the game, commenting on
what she saw. I was pleasantly surprised to see that the
concession prices were comparable to what they were when I was
a kid. Where can you get 50 cent bags of popcorn anywhere else
these days? The Falcons did not win, but we had a lot of fun.
Gracie found a puddle that she just had to introduce herself to
before we left. By the time I got her back home, she was asleep,
and the Brewers and Mets games were already in the books.
The Brewers got smoked 10-2 in front of about 38,000 fans
tonight. Kevin Slowey pitched brilliantly tonight for the Twins,
giving up two runs on five hits over eight innings. Dave Bush did
not pitch poorly, registering a quality start of six innings, three
earned, but two Bill Hall errors in the 7th led to five unearned runs
to score off of Tim Dillard. Sadly, I've changed my mind about
Hall. It's time to go. I was a huge critic five years ago, but
believed he could turn it around, and he did, even leading the
team in home runs in 2006. But the .217 average and 15 errors
cannot be overlooked anymore. Yes, Hall has been the
consummate team player, and he's done everything the team has
asked of him as far as flexibility. But this game is about results,
and he's not providing major league results.

The Mets got back on track with a 7-1 win tonight over the Texas Rangers. One can't help to get nostalgic about Rangers/Mets games at old Shea. Takes me back, yes it does. OK, I'll stop being a smarty pants. It's never happened. This is the Rangers first ever, and last ever series at Shea. Oliver Perez had his best start in weeks, going 7, striking out 8, and not allowing a single runner to score after he gave up a first inning solo home run to Josh Hamilton. Hamilton has 72 RBI thus far, which easily leads the planet. Ryan Church and Moises Alou were each placed on the disabled list today, which will mean more playing time for the likes of Fernando Tatis, Endy Chavez and Marlon Anderson. There is also talk of acquiring Trot Nixon from Arizona in the next few days.

As I write tonight, I would be remiss if I didn't mention that Diane DeLeon will be leaving the Fugazzi Fantasy Football League after 11 years in the league. Diane has been a model owner, winning 2 championships in her first five years, and will be sorely missed. We will never be able to replace someone like Diane, and collectively, the Fugazzi wishes her and her family all the best. When Diane joined the league in 1997, before the league had its own website, and I was scoring this long hand on Monday mornings, Diane would give me her lineup each week in a new and fun way. One week, it would be on a Wheaties box, the next it would be in an Archie's comic book. The NBA and the WWF had the 80's, and the Fugazzi Fantasy Football League flourished in the mid to late 90's. Don't get me wrong, I still enjoy it a ton, but we just got together more often than, and that's what makes a league great, is getting together for games, talking trash, commenting about Pat's hair and betting moustaches on what team will score more points. We will be having our 15th anniversary this fall, and extending the brand by offering a supplemental scoring only league as well. August 17th is draft day. It won't be the same without Diane and the Moratz's.

June 14th

I was thrown a real life curveball tonight, as tonight was supposed to be the night that we went out to celebrate Mike's 32nd birthday. However, it was not meant to happen as planned. I took my daughter and niece out to Sussex to see my dad at his new apartment. We spent a nice afternoon there, enjoyed some Tony Marroni's pizza, which dad says has been named the 7th best pizza in the world. It was good, but it was no Leonardo's. On the way back to Port Washington, I got a little lost in the rain, and could not make out any of the street signs. Between reading the mapquest directions and trying to find Main Street, I hit a pothole, and blew the front tire on the passenger's side of my car. I tried to get back to dads on the flat, but it only did more damage, completely shredding the tire. I parked across from a car wash, called dad, and tried to stay calm for Gracie and Gina. I immediately knew that I had to cancel tonight, and started to call Chase, Jeff, Amber and Mike. I could tell Mike was disappointed. He deserved a fun night, and I feel like I've blown it for him. My dad came through, and let me take his car back, so that I could get the girls home safe and sound. The plan would be to come back on Sunday, replace the old tire with the temporary, and get to a Tires Plus to replace both front tires. On the way home, I called Mike to apologize again, and he suggested that Amber and I stop over later in the evening for some nachos, the end of the Brewers game and a hour of Rock Band on the Xbox 360. Done deal. I will never pass up nachos.

When we got to Mike's place, Jeff Suppan was in the midst of holding on to a 3-1 Brewers lead, and it seems like as soon as we were offered beverages, the Brewers would give up a run at a time, eventually giving up the lead in the ninth. The Brewers would enter the bottom of the ninth down 4-3. It looked like the Brewers would go down quietly to end the game, but Russell "the Muscle" Branyan hit one out off of Joe Nathan, to the opposite field, as our small group of interested fans in the living room watched on (myself, Mike and Amber). In the bottom of the 10th, it looked as if Prince Fielder hit one out to end the game, but the ball was ruled in play, and Fielder ended up with a triple. They showed the replay several times, and it was hard to tell if the ball hit the yellow line on top of the fence, or just below it. Apparently, it doesn't matter, because the ball didn't go over the fence. See, I always thought the yellow line was a home run, but according to Ned Yost, "It's just a yellow line, and it has to go over the fence." Fielder was stranded at third to end the inning. In the 12th inning, the game got away from the Brewers, as Julian Tavarez gave up four hits and walked three while giving up four runs. The Twins would add one more off Mark DiFelice, and the final tonight would be 9-4 Minnesota. It was a frustrating loss in front of a sell out crowd at Miller Park.

The night would end with me providing lead vocals for Weezer's "Say It Ain't So" on Rock Band, and I scored a 98% as the top performer in the band. I tried my hand at each instrument, and ironically, couldn't figure out the drums, even though it runs in the family. In the car, I can drum the hell out my steering wheel and dashboard, but couldn't figure it out in Jeff's bedroom. I faired pretty well playing the bass. This game is addictive, and our paths will cross again.

No Mets game today. They were rained out, and will play two vs the Rangers tomorrow. Goodnight from the corner of 46th and Good Hope. I love Jesus.

June 15th

How does that Dave Attell joke go again? The one about the guy who's in a plane crash, and survives, but then is almost immediately killed by another plane that crashes in the same location. This is almost how I feel today. Happy Father's Day. Mike and I took Gracie back to Sussex to meet my dad by the car, to put the temporary tire on, and find a place to replace it. My dad and I changed it while Mike played with Gracie, and it was neat to share that moment with my dad. It made me want to break out the gloves and have a catch. Once we were all set to go, I drove the car up and down the driveway, just to check everything out and make sure the alignment wasn't out of whack, and everything seemed fine. We only drove about 10 miles before the temporary blew as well, leaving the three of us stranded on the corner of Silver Spring and Lovers Lane. Oh, and I can't find my wallet. I called my sister to see if I left it at Heather's place when I arrived this morning. I had. She came out to bring it to me. Many, many thanks, Jill! Called a tow truck ($85), and drove the car two blocks away to the nearest Goodyear. $85 for that! Did I just buy that guy cocaine for that price? I could've pushed the car that far, and not been tired afterwards. The Goodyear was closed, so now I'm thinking of selling this story to Warner Bros, and I'm gonna check to see what Chevy Chase is up to these days. National Lampoon's Father's Day: coming to theaters next summer. Just the way I want to spend Father's Day, and now I have to take tomorrow off to come back out here for a third straight day to address these repairs. Since I don't have a ride back to Greenfield, Mike took me back to Port Washington and hung out with me for the afternoon, so that I had a ride back home after Heather got home. I played with Gracie, Mike took a cat nap, and there was some baseball on the TV, naturally. I notice there are no light blue bats for prostate cancer awareness, like the pink bats that are used on Mother's Day. Just wristbands. I'd like to see the light blue bats next year.

Since it is Father's Day, I'm going to be brief today, as time spent with Gracie is at a premium these days. The Mets split a doubleheader with the Rangers. In game one, they came back from 8-3 down, only to lose 8-7. John Maine was not his best, and the bullpen continues to really struggle. In the nightcap, Willie Randolph elected to pinch hit for Pedro Martinez in the sixth with the bases loaded in a 2-2 game, and the move paid off, as Robinson Cancel hit a two run single to give the Mets the lead. Martinez had his best start of the year, and the bullpen did not give up a single base runner over the last three innings, giving the Mets a 4-2 win, and a series win over Texas.

The Brewers game today was very similar to the Mets second game with Texas. We got six solid innings from Seth McClung, took the lead for good in the sixth on a two run HR by Mike Cameron, and the bullpen only allowed one base runner over the last three innings. The final score was also 4-2, as the Brewers salvaged game three from the Twins. Next year, I have to make sure that I get out to one of these Brewers/Twins games. Next week, I'll be seeing the Blue Jays on Tuesday night and the Orioles on Saturday night.

If you'll excuse me for a moment, I need a hug and a kiss from my daughter. This weekend was challenging, but I will not let a couple of flat tires break me. I am a very lucky man. Gracie signed her Father's Day card to me and Gina gave me a homemade card that I will put on my refrigerator when I get home. Mike and I are going to grab some Tomaso's before he drives me home. Nothing cleanses the soul like a 16 inch sausage and pepperoni thin crust from Tomaso's. Life is good.

June 16th

Happy birthday shout outs to Tupac, Joan Van Ark, Calvin Schiraldi and Mike Schwingle. There's an eclectic bunch of folks for you. I think my parents were married on June 16th. These are some of the random things one can think about while they are sitting in the waiting area at Goodyear while their car is being worked on. $400 down the drain. There goes a portion of the baseball trip. I haven't made up my mind just yet, but it looks like I'll have to sacrifice Cleveland and Detroit. I will do everything in my power to make all the dates, but it doesn't look good.

There is no Brewers game tonight, as the Crew has the night off, before starting a three game set with Toronto tomorrow night. I will be attending the game with Jill, Gina and Gracie. It'll be Gracie's first game of the year, and I am very much looking forward to it. The Mets play tonight in Anaheim, and due to my new living arrangements, I will not see much of the game. Tonight seems like a great night for potty training, watching some SpongeBob and snuggling with Gracie on her bedroom floor.

Then it'll be off to bed early tonight. I'll get a Mets final first thing in the morning, before I head to work.

June 17th

Bob Picozzi gave me the news I was looking for this morning during the ESPN radio SportsCenter update. The Mets kicked off their series against the Angels with a 9-6 win, with Carlos Beltran homering twice, and Mike Pelfrey pitching well to secure the victory. I wasn't expecting to hear that Willie Randolph had been fired at 3:15 am, just hours after the end of the game. Pitching coach Rick Peterson and 1st base coach Tom Nieto were also let go. I understand that the rumors have been floating around for weeks, but the timing just seems unusual. The Mets just finished a homestand on Sunday. So, they make Randolph travel 3000 miles to L.A., he manages the team to a win on the road against one of the elite AL teams, and then he's fired, just like that. Look, I'm not stunned that he's been fired; I just don't get the timing. Minaya says he knew on Monday that Randolph was going be fired, but didn't want to make an announcement before the game, or risk having anything leak during the game, out of respect to Randolph. He did not want Randolph in uniform, knowing he was managing his last game with the Mets. But why wait until after one game of a west coast series? Shouldn't this have been done on Sunday night? Certainly, if Minaya knew Monday morning, he knew Sunday evening. While I am not surprised, it still seems pretty early, considering they just got Pedro back, the starting pitching as a whole looks like it's coming around, and we are only 6.5 games back. You hate to see managerial changes midseason, but there have been a handful of teams that have made changes during the season, and have gone to the postseason the same season. You only have to go back to 2004, the year the Astros fired Jimy Williams the day after the All Star Game (played in Houston), and Phil Garner was hired, and got the Astros to a game seven of the NLCS before bowing out to St Louis. The year before that, the Marlins fired Jeff Torborg, and hired Jack McKeon to finish out the season, and all they did was beat the Yankees to win the World Series. And don't forget 1982. The Brewers fired unpopular manager Buck Rodgers, and replaced him with long time hitting coach Harvey Kuenn, and that '82 team pushed the Cardinals to a game seven in the World Series. The 1982 Brewers are still one of the most celebrated World Series losing teams of all time. So, the season is not lost. Jerry Manuel takes over as interim manager, and now we have to get back to work. Manuel will have 93 games to make up 7 games in the standings. The talent is there. The team has underperformed, but the talent is there. And for Pete's sake, it's the last year at Shea; this is not how this was supposed to go down. Now, let's get pissed off, and win some fuckin' baseball games! Amber's asking me to watch my language...let me try that again...Let's get *angry*, and win some fuckin' baseball games! There, that's better. Pissed is a dirty, dirty word...now the children can enjoy this.

Tonight, Manny Parra takes the hill for the Brewers against the AL East's last place Toronto Blue Jays. Lyle Overbay makes his first return to Milwaukee since 2005. Overbay was a fan favorite during his stay in Milwaukee, hitting .301 in 2004, while hitting a team record 53 doubles that year. Overbay had to leave to make room for Prince Fielder, and I think everyone knows how that has worked out thus far. Gracie is behaving like an angel tonight, taking in all the sights and sounds that the game has to offer. She loved the pregame fireworks, and would see many more fireworks tonight. For the 2nd time in less than a week, the Brewers would hit five home runs in a game. Prince Fielder got the fireworks underway in the 2nd, hitting a towering home run to right field. In the 3rd, I left to get some popcorn for Gracie, and a jumbo and Italian for myself, and missed something you don't see too often at the ballgame. And that is a Craig Counsell home run. I got to see him circle the bases on one of the monitors after I heard the crowd go wild. If Counsell is going deep, it feels like it's going to be our night. In the 4th, Russell Branyan continued his hot hitting, taking Dustin McGowan deep to give the Brewers a 4-0 lead. This was Branyan's 8th homer in less than a month, and he's hitting .304. Ryan Braun would go deep in the 6th to extend the lead to 5-0 nothing. We left the game in the top of the 8th because Gracie was starting to nod off. Braun would go yard again, just after we left. I apologized to Jill on the way home, but it was a mutual decision to leave, so I didn't feel that bad. Manny Parra pitched 7 scoreless innings, and Mark DiFelice retired the last six Toronto batters, striking out a pair, to give the Brewers their third shutout win of the year, 7-0. The Cubs and Cardinals each lost tonight, pulling the Brewers to within 7.5 of the Cubs, and 4 of the Cardinals for the Wild Card.

As for the Mets, they played a sloppy game in Jerry Manuel's first night as interim skipper, committing three errors in the process. Santana was not himself tonight, and the bats couldn't get anything going. Jose Reyes left tonight's game in the 1st inning for precautionary reasons after feeling stiffness in his left hamstring. He shouldn't miss any more time.

It's an early bedtime for me tonight, because of tomorrow's early wake up time. We're gonna listen to an album on the ipod by a band named Islands, and the album is called Arm's Way. This is my midyear choice for 2008 album of the year. Way better than their last one...

June 18th

The news tonight was good across the board. Russell Branyan homered again, quietly becoming one of the feel good stories in the bigs in 2008. After being placed on waivers by the Brewers in January of 2006, Branyan was signed by Tampa Bay, and spent a few months there before being traded to San Diego. Less than a year later, San Diego released him, and he signed with Cleveland and reported to their AAA team in Buffalo. He played one game in Buffalo before being traded to Philadelphia. Branyan would hit a game winning home run in his first at bat with the Phillies, in a 3-2 win over Washington, before being designated for assignment two weeks later. This led to him being traded for the third time in 13 months, this time to St Louis. He spent a month there before filing for free agency, and signed a minor league contract with Milwaukee in February. Branyan's .300 plus batting average and 12 homers at AAA Nashville warranted the Brewers calling him up in May, especially with Bill Hall struggling at the plate. In his two brief stints with Milwaukee since 2004, Branyan has hit three of the five longest home runs in the history of Miller Park, and I've seen two of them in person. One of them was Opening Day in 2005, when he hit his own picture on the scoreboard, and the other one was the one that reached the Dew Deck the night of Frank Crivello's bachelor party. Hopefully he can keep this up.

Ben Sheets and the Brewers would never trail tonight, with the Brewers winning a 5-4 contest that stayed close all night. The win puts Sheets' record at 8-1, with a 2.74 ERA. Surely, Sheets will be representing the Brewers at Yankee Stadium in this year's All Star Game. I think Sheets and Braun are the two obvious choices this year. The Cubs and Cards lost again, and now the Brewers finds themselves only 3 out of the wild card chase, and 6.5 out of the division lead.

When I left Port Washington tonight, the Mets were down 4-3 to the Angels in the sixth inning. Heather was out with friends watching the Brewers game, so it gave me a chance to catch a good portion of this game, and I got to tuck Gracie in tonight. When I got home, I followed the rest of the game online, with Arm's Way playing in the background. When David Wright singled home Jose Reyes, who scored three runs tonight, in the top of ninth to tie the game, I looked for something to pedigree, but all of Gracie's stuffed animals are still with Heather, so I gave one of Hogan's leg drops to a red suitcase. Damion Easley homered in the top of the tenth to give the Mets the lead, and Billy Wagner pitched a perfect inning to notch his 16th save of the season, giving Jerry Manuel his first managerial win in five years. Some takeaways from tonight...earlier in the game Jose Reyes popped up to the 2nd basemen, and was almost on 2nd base when the out was finally recorded. That's the kind of hustle this team needs. Even though it was a can of corn, we need to see this kind of passion and desire all the time. That kind of play rubs off on the rest of the team, and is extremely contagious. Taking 2 of 3 from the Angels, in L.A., is a huge step in the right direction for a team that has underperformed thus far in 2008. This is still a winnable division. Way to go, boys…

June 19th

April 15th, 1987: The only no-hitter in Milwaukee Brewers history. Juan Nieves threw it against the Baltimore Orioles, and in the process, the Brewers extended their record to 9-0 to open the 1987 season. This was one of many memorable moments of the Brewers 1987 season. They ended up winning 13 games in a row to start the season. The 12th win was especially memorable, as the Brewers were down 4-1 heading into the ninth. Rob Deer hit a 3 run homer to tie it, and Dale Sveum hit a two run homer later in the same inning to win it. To this day, this is probably my greatest Milwaukee Brewers memory. And it was on Easter Sunday. Teddy Higuera was starting to establish himself as a premier left handed starter in the major leagues, at one point pitching 32 consecutive scoreless innings during that season. Paul Molitor's 39 game hit streak had baseball fans of all ages on the edge of their seats throughout most of July and August. Had it not been for a 12 game losing streak in May, the Brewers may have made a legitimate push at the playoffs in 1987. There have only been a handful of seasons since then where the Brewers have been in contention into September, and this year may be one of them. There's a reason why I'm feeling nostalgic for 1987 today.

The Brewers hosted the Blue Jays this afternoon, looking to sweep the Jays, and win their fourth straight game. Dave Bush was today's starting pitcher, facing his old team for the first time in his career. The Brewers were able to score early and often for Bush, giving him a six run lead after three innings. Russell Branyan homered yet again, and he's pretty much won the 3rd base job if you ask me. It hasn't been much of a platoon at all lately. And this is justified, as Branyan now has ten homers in less than a month, and is hitting .306. Bill Hall has been getting the occasional pinch hitting opportunity, and now and then will spell Branyan late in games, but he's not getting much of a chance to start. In the fifth inning, one of the strangest things you'll ever see, or hear on the radio, happened with Prince Fielder hitting. Fielder hit what sounded to us like a routine double to right field. However, Alex Rios, the Blue Jays right fielder, jogged towards the wall, putting up his hands to let the umpires know that the ball was stuck in the wall. But the 2nd base umpire was motioning palms down, which means the ball was still in play, and Fielder made it all the way around for an inside the park home run. This is Fielder's second career inside the park homer, as he hit one last year off of a speaker in Minnesota on Father's Day. This is also the Brewers' second such home run this month, with Corey Hart hitting one on the previous home stand. So going into the sixth inning, the Brewers were now up 8-0, giving Dave Bush a huge cushion to work with. Traditionally, this is where a pitcher may start to lose his focus a bit, maybe hang a few up in the strike zone, but that would not be the case today. Bush worked a 1-2-3 sixth, and son of a gun, if he isn't throwing a "you know what". Don't make me say it. You know what happens when someone says it. After doing the same in the seventh, the boys and I started to get really excited. Phone calls and e-mails started to pour in, everyone knowing the unwritten rule. Are you listening? Check out the bottom line! Oh my God!! Six more outs! This is so exciting. It was. It felt like 1987. We felt like kids. We were acting like children. It was great, until Lyle Overbay tripled to lead off the eighth. Then we were babies. Big babies. I can't remember the last time a Brewer entered the 8th with a no-hitter. Four years ago, Ben Sheets carried a perfect game into the seventh against the Angels. It may have been Odell Jones in May of 1988. He lost his bid with two outs in the ninth. With the no-hitter gone, Bush would try to preserve the shutout, but Overbay would score on an Alex Rios single to make the score 8 to 1. There is nothing to worry about, though. We're up 8-1, heading to the ninth, and the bullpen has been pretty good as of late. If you're a diehard, you remember what happened next. Lyle Overbay hit a two run homer with two outs, and then Tim Dillard followed that up by walking the next batter, and giving up a single before being pulled for David Riske. Riske walked the first batter he faced, and then gave up a grand slam to Joe Inglett, who entered the game as part of a double switch in the 6th inning. Are you kidding me? We went from a no-hitter and an 8-0 lead to a nail biter within a half hour. It's 8-7. What in thee hell just happened. Who is Joe Inglett? Salomon Torres was then brought in to restore order to the universe. He gave up a hit, bringing the go ahead run to the plate in the person of Matt Stairs, another former Brewer. Would this be a day of former Brewers breaking our hearts? Overbay did break up the no-no, but Stairs would strike out, giving the Brewers the sweep in a game that had all the elements. The Brewers are now 39-33, and if this news isn't good enough on its own, the Rays just completed a sweep of the Cubs, and the Royals did the same vs the Cardinals. The Crew now trails the Cards by two games for the wild card, and the Cubs by 5.5 games in the division. It feels like 1987. Get excited, Brewers fans! It's shaping up to be a fun summer.

Today was a travel day for the Mets. They start a three game set with Colorado tomorrow night.

June 20th

The Baltimore Orioles are visiting Miller Park for the first time ever this weekend, and playing in Milwaukee for the first time since the 1997 season. They are surprisingly in the mix in the AL East, at 37-34 coming into tonight. Jeff Suppan, who normally is a great pitcher at home, had one of his worst starts ever at Miller Park, giving up 6 runs in 1 2/3 innings. But the Brewers were able to chip away, hitting two run homers in the 1st (Hardy) and 3rd (Fielder), and the Brewers were only down 6-5 heading into the 4th inning. The Brewers had every opportunity in the world to win tonight, but could not get the big hit late when it counted. The Brewers stranded eleven base runners tonight, and had the bases loaded with nobody out in the ninth. The score was 8-5 Orioles, when Yost pulled Branyan in favor of Bill Hall against the left handed closer for the Orioles, George Sherrill. Sherrill got Hall on strikes, and got Gabe Kapler to ground into a double play to end the game. The team did show a lot of fight tonight, and this can hardly be categorized as a heartbreaking loss, especially when you give up six runs in the first two innings. We lose a game in the standings, as the Cubs and Cards both win tonight.

The Mets would face the Rockies best pitcher tonight, Aaron Cook, who came into the game with a 10-3 record. John Maine was on the hill for the Mets, and he has pitched much better than his 6-5 record would indicate. The Mets hit Cook hard all night, putting up five runs in the 2nd, including a Carlos Delgado home run. Trot Nixon hit his first home run in a Mets uniform in the 3rd, and when Cook's night was all said and done, he had given up six runs on twelve hits over seven innings. Maine was touched for a two run homer in the first, but settled down, and would not allow another Rockie to cross home plate the rest of the way, as the Mets took game one tonight, 7-2. With Philadelphia struggling as of late, the Mets find themselves only 4.5 back, with a record of 36-36.

June 21st

My boy Mikey and I took in the Brewers game at Miller Park tonight. We both have had a long week, and it's nice just to sit, enjoy a game, indulge in the fine tastes the folks at Klements have to offer, maybe have a beer. Tonight is a sell out, and the Brewers look to start a new winning streak tonight vs the Orioles. Seth McClung, who has pitched really well since cracking the starting rotation, wasn't scored upon tonight until the 7th inning, when he gave up a two run homer to Oscar Salazar. I'm not even sure Oscar Salazar has a wikipedia page. The Brewers entered the 7th up 3-0, so McClung left the game after allowing the home run still up 3-2. Brian Shouse faced four hitters tonight, striking out two, and not allowing a single base runner. Salomon Torres worked a scoreless 9th, earning his 11th save of the season, giving the Brewers their 40th win of the 2008 campaign.

David beat Goliath tonight in Colorado, as Ubaldo Jimenez went 8 innings, giving up only 2 hits, while Pedro Martinez gave up 6 runs in 4 1/3 innings, as the Rockies beat the Mets 7-1. We got out hit 14-4. Not much fun writing about that. Seacrest. Out.

June 22nd

Baseball took a backseat today. My daughter and niece spent the day with me in Greenfield, and I love them more than baseball, weezer, nachos, SNL, the Browns, itunes and Al Pacino movies combined. I took them to the mini golf course right down the road from me, but we were behind a group of about 14 teenage girls, so we never made it on the course. We entertained ourselves on the practice green for about 20 minutes, before heading back to my apartment for an afternoon of swimming. I have never seen Gracie happier than I did today as we chased Gina around the pool. The smiles became giggles, and the giggles became big belly laughs. The belly laughs would shortly turn into big tears, as we had to get out of the pool quickly with the storm clouds upon us. Gracie nearly cried herself to sleep while I dried her off, and would only calm down for her favorite juice, while she sat on my lap. We took a drive back to Port Washington, and stopped at McDonald's on the way. My baby loves her hot fries and chicken. She fell asleep on the way home. It was a great day with my girls.

The Mets and Brewers each secured series wins today. The Mets beat the Rockies 3-1 on the strength of Mike Pelfrey's 5 2/3 scoreless innings pitched. Five walks would contribute to him leaving early, but the bullpen did its job, holding the Rox to 1 run over 3 1/3 innings. Now the Mets are back to .500 at 37-37. The Phillies lost again, so the Mets are only 3.5 back in the NL East. The Brewers won today 7-3, hitting four home runs in the process. The last two knocks were provided by Prince Fielder, who is quietly catching up to Ryan Braun for the team lead. Braun is at

20, and Fielder is at 16. Manny Parra improved to 7-2. The
Brewers are 41-34, and only 2 games behind the Cardinals for the
NL Wild Card. Only the Cubs have had a better record in the last
month than the Brewers, and Milwaukee now holds the sixth best
record in all of baseball. I have Brewers fever!

June 23rd

The Mets lost tonight to the world's worst baseball team,
the Seattle Mariners. The Mariners were my pick to win the AL
West, and they came into tonight with a record of 26-49. The
pitching matchup was Johan Santana vs Felix Hernandez. If you
told me that Hernandez out pitched Santana, that wouldn't
surprise me. However, I would be surprised if you told me that
Hernandez would hit a grand slam off of Santana in the 2nd inning.
That's exactly what happened, and it was the difference in a 5-2
Mets loss. Santana's ERA is still a very solid 2.93, but a lack of
run support has led to a 7-6 record thus far.

Ben Sheets worked tonight like a man who knows he's in a
contract year. I hate to say that, but it's true. He's in a contract
year, and he's clearly going to test the free agent market at the
end of the year. And he should. He's 9-1 with a 2.59 ERA, and
he may just start the All Star Game for the NL, at the pace he's at.
And sadly, unless the Brewers can match the Yankees, Red Sox,
Mets or Dodgers dollar for dollar, he's gone. I hope I'm wrong. He
went the distance tonight, struck out seven, did not walk a batter,
and only allowed four hits in a 4-1 Brewers win in Atlanta. The
Brewers now find themselves only a game and a half behind St
Louis for the Wild Card.

The thing I will remember most about tonight has nothing
to do with baseball. Shortly before I left for the night, my daughter
sang Itsy Bitsy Spider and the Alphabet for my mom and sister,
without missing a beat. Right after she was done, she hopped up
on my lap, and said, "Dada, sing music?" I put Pork and Beans on

for her, and she sang the chorus with me, all three times, and clapped at the end of the song. She then proceeded to punch me in the face. It was the hardest I've ever seen Jill laugh, and my mom couldn't help from laughing as well. It was one of those once in a lifetime moments, where we went from a sweet father / daughter moment, to an act of rage in seconds. But what made it funny was she wasn't mad. She just thought to punch me. Maybe I wasn't giving her as much attention as she wanted. I wish you could have seen Jill; it was a truly priceless moment. I won't see Gracie until Thursday, because I will be in Madison tomorrow night for a presentation, and Wednesday night is Heather's night with Gracie. This makes me sad, but I will have her for the full weekend coming up, and I very much look forward to that. Thank you, Heather. Gracie will be in good hands, and I hope you enjoy your much deserved free time.

On a sad note, I'd be remiss if I didn't mention the passing of George Carlin. His bit on the differences between baseball and football is brilliant, but I'm not going to attempt to rehash it for you. You can find it online, I recommend watching it. Thank you for the laughter. You were the best.

June 24th

Driving back from Madison tonight, I heard Bob Uecker talking about the Mets during a break in the action. He mentioned that Jerry Manuel has recently lifted the ban on facial hair that Willie Randolph had placed on his team during his tenure as manager. He then informed me that they lost again tonight, 11-0 to lowly Seattle. The last thing he said before returning to the game was that facial hair doesn't matter, if you're good, you'll win. Fortunately for the Mets, every team in the NL East lost tonight, and they remain only four games back of the Phillies, who have now lost six straight games.

The Brewers were up 4-1 by the time I left Madison. Dave Bush pitched well again, coming off of the near no-no against Toronto last week. The Braves committed four errors tonight, and it's certainly hard to win games when that happens. The Braves made a game of it in the ninth, as Mark Teixeira hit a two run homer off Salomon Torres to make it 4-3. But when Torres got pinch hitter Corky Miller to softly line out to J.J. Hardy to end it, it put the Brewers at 43-34 for the season. It also put the Brewers within 5 games of the Cubs, whose 14 game home winning streak was put to an end tonight against Baltimore. Jeff Suppan goes for the sweep tomorrow afternoon. Damn, this is fun!

June 25th

It was a busy day on campus, so we didn't get to hear much of the Brewers game today. We led the game early, but the Braves came right back to tie it, and took the lead for good in the 5th. The Braves would end up taking today's contest, 4-2. Some quick notes…Julian Tavarez did not accept his AAA assignment to Nashville, and is now a free agent. Tavarez struggled in his short stint with Milwaukee, but you got to think that he will catch on somewhere else. Ryan Braun has been nursing a sore right hand as of late, which might explain his .256 batting average in June, but he will most likely not miss any time. The team takes tomorrow off, before heading to Minnesota to round out this year's interleague schedule. I'm sure Bill Schroeder and Bert Blyleven will wager on who has to milk a cow if their respective team wins the series. Those wacky ex-ballplayers!!

The Fugazzi Fantasy Football League named Demond Stewart as the new owner of its Steelers franchise tonight. Demond takes over a franchise that has two championships, but hasn't made the playoffs since 2001. To celebrate, Demond and I enjoyed some Bar Louie appetizers tonight, and I washed it down with some blueberry lemonade. Who's ever heard of such a thing? It was good! And it turns out, Demond is a Mets fan, so we were both delighted to see the Mets get off to an early 8-0 lead tonight, on the strength of a solid John Maine start, and two David Wright home runs. The final would be 8-2, but the Mets did not collect a single base hit after the third inning. No ground gained, as the Phillies finally won a baseball game, shutting out Oakland 4-0 tonight.

No Brewers or Mets tomorrow night. After I get back from my time spent with Gracie, I'm going to spend the night telling you about August 19th, 1987, which for me, signified much more than Ned Yost turning 32 years old. Wow, that makes me feel old. Morten Andersen turned 27 that night. Yikes!

June 26th

I just finished my final season of bird league, and next year, it would be time to graduate to the animal league. I had seen a few of their games. The hitters were bigger, the pitchers threw harder, everyone was faster, and the baseball was better. I couldn't wait. Summers were always spent playing a ton of baseball, whether it was our "street league", games of strikeout with Greg and Mike, or pickup games at the high school. The street league games were primarily played right in front of my house and usually included anywhere from three to eight of us. We played almost every day. The regulars were Mike and Scott Moser, Phil Hohlweck, Tim Miller, Johnny Bakula and I. We also had a handful of kids that would play on occasion. Names like Ben Ebert, Wesley Wilhite, William Hopkins, David Bakula, Jason Klinger, Ronnie Borth (or as Mike and I called him, Donnie Booth) and even Kenneth Craig graced our street league "diamond" from time to time. There was even a kid who threw a no-hitter in a four inning game that I was playing in as "all time outfielder". I can't remember his name. Adam something or other.

I couldn't get enough of baseball. Playing it. Watching it. Talking about it. It dominated my life. I had no interest in girls at the time. I didn't care how I dressed, or how my hair looked. My life was all about pitching against the Dean School wall, playing catch with my friends and going to the batting cages. It was the purest thing in my life. And next summer, I was going to be pitching in the animal league.

The night was Sunday, August 19th, 1987. The first day of school was on Monday, August 27th, so this would be the last weekend that we could do what we wanted without having to get ready for the 6th grade. Peter Duvernell and Joe Riche were over at my house, and we got a call from my best friend Sean Prude, asking us to come over to his house for a big pick up game. We were all stoked to play. I asked my mom if we could go, and she said no. It was going to get dark soon, and driving from 65th and Darnel to Northridge Lakes on our bikes would be a pretty long distance on our bikes. I asked a couple of more times, and she still said no. I was embarrassed that I couldn't go, knowing that Peter and Joe would go either way, and I was disappointed. I asked one more time, promising to be safe, and mom finally gave in, telling me several times not to be out to late, and to be super safe riding my bike there. I promised I would.

We would take 60th Street to Brown Deer road, and then take Brown Deer road all the way to 74th Street, before getting to Sean's place. After successfully crossing Brown Deer road, the only thing I remember next was flying off my bike and crashing down on the pavement. Eyewitnesses have said that as I crossed 60th street, I hit a car, and it didn't look like either of us saw each other, but all I remember is being in the air. I immediately got up, and ran towards the grass to lay down. I was in shock. Joe rode back to the house to tell my mom what had happened, and Peter stayed with me. I wasn't sure if I was injured, and the only thing I could think to say to Peter was, "Tell Sean I don't think I'll be able to play tonight". My mom would later tell me that Joe arrived at the house, and all he said was, "Joe was hit by a car". My mom was hysterical. She had a friend drive her to the scene of the accident. They hit a red light at the corner, and she ran out of the car towards where I was laying. When I saw her, I started sobbing. I knew at the time I disappointed her, but I was old enough to realize that she was in pain from seeing her son lying on the ground. We got to the hospital, and the tests indicated that I had shattered my right shoulder in two places, and further tests would indicate that I had a cyst in my right shoulder, further damaging my arm. A couple of weeks later, I asked the doctor how long it would take to recover. He said that because of the cyst, my right arm would never heal properly without a new procedure that was being done, but the procedure was not covered by insurance. I told him that I was a pitcher, and he said that it wasn't too late to learn how to pitch left handed. I knew I'd never make it in the bigs hitting. I wasn't a bad hitter, but I knew I could pitch well. I didn't have the blazing fastball, or much of a curve, but I knew how to pitch, and I could locate. Maybe it was having elders praise me at an early age, maybe it was the early success I had, but for the last few years, I had convinced myself that I'd be playing baseball for a living, and this news crushed me.

I noticed shortly after the accident, my grades started to fall from A's/B's to B's/C's, my language got worse, and I would become angrier quicker and more often that normal. I felt like my life was taken from me, and I started to carry an "I don't care" attitude towards life. I remember in the summer of 1988, when I met my new teammates for the first time, now playing for the Bucks, instead of the Falcons, I felt out of place. I knew I couldn't pitch anymore, at least for now, and I'd have to make another contribution to the team. Towards the end of the year, my coach could tell that not pitching was bothering me, and while my throwing style would now look awkward, I no longer had anymore pain, and he wanted to see what I had, possibly for next year. Right after our last game, I pitched to a catcher for the first time in about 11 months, and I knew that night that I could once again be a competent pitcher in little league, but I could never pitch in the bigs. It took a full year to realize, because I wanted to see for myself what I could do before giving up on the dream.

There was one game in particular that I remember, and think about a lot, where I came up with the bases loaded, and down one, after the last four of our batters walked to bring us to within one. After the four walks, the Beavers changed pitchers, and brought in Jason Schroeder to face me. I don't remember ever seeing or hearing about Jason pitching, and I knew in my heart that I would either draw a walk to tie the game, or I'd knock the shit out of the ball against a pitcher who looked scared, and I'd be the hero. I struck out swinging to end the game. I was already down, and now I was out. One last chance to be a hero, and I failed.

The last two years in the animal league were fun. I had already accepted the fact that my dream would not be fulfilled, and I just wanted to enjoy my last two years playing ball. I played a year of freshman baseball in high school, but I could never make it as a hitter, and that was it. A couple of years of slow pitch softball followed, but that could never fill the void.

I think about that August night in 1987 every day. Every day since then, I think about my mom telling me no, and me insisting that I would be ok. Every day I think what could have been. I'm 32 now. Even had I not been in that accident, would I have been good enough to pitch in the bigs? Thinking back, probably not, since I had the cyst, but I never got the chance. Pitching was the one thing I could get completely lost in, and it was taken from me before the age of 12. Every day, I wonder.

But, a lot of people that love me often remind me that things may have been different had the accident not happened, not just baseball related. Would I have met either one of my wives? I learned a lot about myself from Suzy and Heather, and while neither of my marriages worked out in the end, they each prepared me for the next chapter in my life, and I feel that I came out of each a better person. Would I have a beautiful daughter had I not been in the accident? Possibly, but how much would I see her if I were on the road constantly. Would I have been able to maintain such good friendships with the Mikes, Phil, Sean, and meet new such great people like Andy, Jamie, Joe, Heather and Amber? Probably not. I've learned over the past 21 years to learn to let go, and appreciate the place that I'm at in my life. I educate kids about finance for a living. Is it as exciting as calling Shea Stadium my place of employment? Of course not. But I know I'm making a difference in people's life, and I've never been booed in fifteen years of banking. I've found peace, but that doesn't mean I don't think, "What if?"

I was asked recently by a very special person in my life, "Would you trade everything you have now for what you could have had in baseball?" I would have answered that question differently fifteen years ago, certainly ten years ago, and maybe even five years ago. But today, I can honestly say no way. And here's why. Whether I played baseball for a living or not, baseball has always, and will always be a huge part of my life. Every night, I come home and slip a glove on, and grip a baseball, either in front of a game on TV, or while listening to Uecker on the radio. The average career lasts three years. What would I have done after I was done playing ball. How jaded would I have been had I had a taste of the big time, and it was taken from me? I have my health, I have a beautiful daughter, great friends, a wonderful future, and I still have baseball. Baseball never left me. It'll always be with me. Trade everything? No way. I have it all. I'm King.

June 27th

The Mets had their home and home doubleheader with the Yankees today. Game one was at Yankee Stadium at noon, and game two was scheduled for 6:00 at Shea Stadium. In game one, Carlos Delgado drove in nine runs in a 15-6 rout of the Evil Empire. Carlos Delgado, Carlos Beltran and David Wright drove in all 15 of the Mets runs. What a great start to the weekend!

Our plans to see the Guffs with the Milwaukee Symphony Orchestra were washed away by rain, so I took Gracie and Amber to Tomaso's for dinner. I have Gracie for the entire weekend, for the first time since to moving to Greenfield, which I am very excited about. This will also be Amber's first dining experience at Tomaso's. Dinner was fantastic as always, and dessert was a whole lot of yummy in our tummies. The Brewers game was on at the restaurant, and while we were enjoying our evening, we couldn't help but notice that the Brewers were up 6-3 in the 5th at one point. Someone at the bar mentioned that the Brewers had hit four home runs thus far, and Corey Hart hit two of them. Someone else asked why I was wearing a Mets hat. I told him about this book project, and he asked when it was coming out. I've been telling everyone March, and that's what I told him.

As Gracie was getting used to her new surroundings, I checked online to get an update on the Crew. They blew it. The final was 7-6, but the Cubs lost again as well, so no ground lost. The Mets were shutout 9-0 at Shea, as Pedro's ERA ballooned up to 7.12. Gracie ran herself to sleep a little after midnight.

My beautiful daughter, Grace Naomi Buchholz

My first trip to Shea Stadium, July of 2007

Jesus and I at Shea in July of 2007

Mike and I posing after a catch, July of 2008

Freeway and I, hanging out at a local bookstore

This book could have very well been about Tomaso's...

...and Leonardo's. Maybe I'm a pizza polygamist?

Could we see Gina in a Boston uniform in the near future?

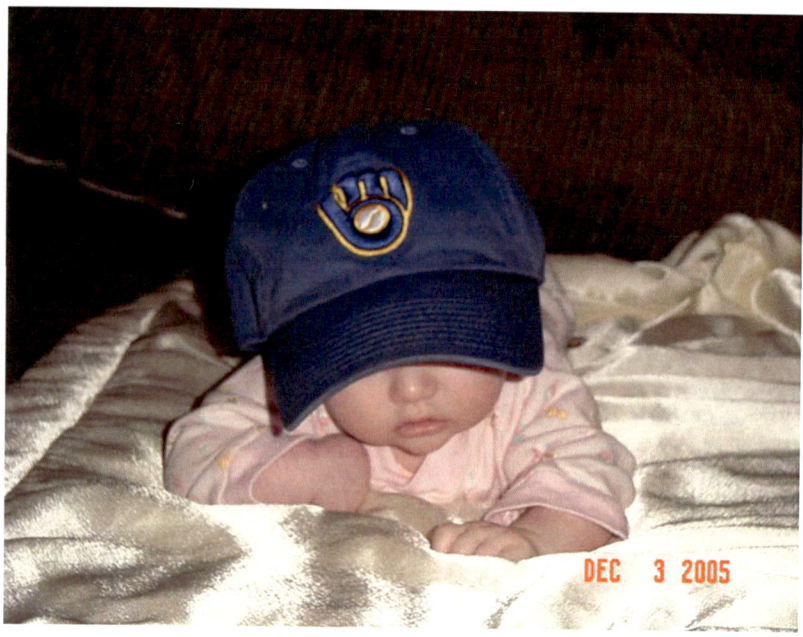

It's clear to me who Gracie's favorite team is

With my boys, Mike and Jamie, at Katz's Deli in New York

Mike, Amber and I attending the Billy Joel show at Shea

Tracy and I at Busch Stadium, July of 2008

A big reason why St Louis was my favorite destination of the baseball trip

Victory Park in Indianapolis, July of 2008

Tracy and I at Wrigley Field, July of 2008

Sean and I at Progressive Field in Cleveland, July of 2008

Great seats and a great night for a ballgame in Cleveland

Beautiful Miller Park, an hour before first pitch

Tracy and I at Miller Park, our final destination

My father and I

My three gloves, my two loves

June 28th

Gracie was up early this morning, and she kept walking me towards the patio door, a sure hint that she wanted to go swimming. It was a little too cool to swim today, so we played hard indoors through the early afternoon. After a big lunch, Gracie took a long nap, and I took my spot on the couch to watch the Cubs/White Sox game on Fox. The Yankees/Mets were also featured on Fox, but the Milwaukee markets would get the Cubs game today, which was fine, because the Cubs have been struggling as of late, and it might be fun to see them lose if the Brewers can take care of business tonight. The Mets were delayed by rain anyway. I fell asleep for a bit, but awoke in time to see the Cubs lose, but I saw the Mets lost as well, so all news is not good news thus far.

We were invited to Amber's father's house for a grill out tonight. This would be the second time meeting Lynn, and the first time meeting his wife, Linda, and Amber's brother, Dustin. The game was on in the house, and the Brewers were up 5-0 when we got there. They scored all five runs in the first three innings. The brat I had tonight may have been the best brat I've ever had. To me, nothing screams summer more than a brat and Brewers baseball on the radio. I also enjoyed some pickled okra, which Amber would not even look at. The Brewers hung on to win, 5-1. Manny Parra improved his record to 8-2, while lowering his ERA to 3.95. Does Parra have an outside chance at making the All Star team? I would say he has a chance.

Eric Gagne was activated from the DL today. When asked by the media what role Gagne would assume, Ned Yost only said, "reliever". Certainly, the Brewers are not going to relieve Salomon Torres of his closer duties now. He is 12 of 12 in save opportunities since taking over full time as the team's closer.

After Gracie fell asleep, we watched The Score with Robert DeNiro and Edward Norton. I forgot how much I liked this movie. DeNiro makes some pretty good DeNiro faces in this one, and Edward Norton does the Edward Norton thing pretty well. Before heading to bed, I read on mlb.com that the Dodgers beat the

Angels tonight without recording a single base hit. This has only happened five times since 1900, and the first time it's happened since the Indians beat the Red Sox in 1992. Jared Weaver gave up an unearned run in the fifth, caused by his own throwing error, and was lifted for a pinch hitter after six no-hit innings. Major League baseball does not recognize this as a no-hitter, not because the Angels lost, but because they were the road team, they did not pitch nine innings tonight. Very unusual, but from what I read, it was a great game.

June 29th

    I took my daughter to the park today. It was great to see her playing with kids her age, running and laughing, having a great time. It's the best feeling in the world, seeing your kids happy. But today, I had my first real run in with a mean kid trying to bully my little girl. She was about 5 years old, and was riding a Barbie scooter. She kept telling everyone to move, and when my sweet jewel of a daughter tried to touch her scooter, she screamed, "Get away from it!" I did the right thing by walking Gracie over to the nicer kids, but I wanted to do was kneel down by the bully, and say, "Hi, sweetheart. Stop being mean to the other kids. By the way, you are probably going to be pregnant when you're 15, and I'm pretty sure you won't know who the dad is until the three of you end up on Maury one day." I hate mean kids.

    Kevin Slowey continued his 2008 interleague dominance of the Milwaukee Brewers, tossing a three hit complete game shutout this afternoon, giving the Twins a 5-0 to take the series. The Twins take the season series against the Brewers with the win, going 4-2 vs us this season. Ben Sheets suffered his first road loss of the season.

    The Mets and Yankees were featured on TBS this afternoon. Oliver Perez gave the Mets exactly what they needed today, going seven strong innings and striking out eight in a 3-1 win. Today's game was the first Mets/Yankees game this year that the home team won. The Mets took 4 of 6 from the Yankees this season, which is something to build on going into the second half of the season. With the Phillies losing to Texas, the Mets find themselves only 3 games out in the NL East.

Both the Brewers and Mets are at the mathematical halfway points in their schedules. The Brewers are 44-37, and the Mets are 40-41. I would say the Brewers are pretty much where they thought they'd be. I just don't think they thought they'd have the third best record in the NL, and still be in third place in the NL Central. Only five teams in baseball have a better record overall (Cubs, Cardinals, Angels, Rays and Red Sox). The Mets are obviously not happy with the 40-41 record, and they've already fired their manager, but they have to be happy only being three games out. There is a lot of baseball to be played, and the Mets always play well at home in the second half of the season. My goal at the beginning of the season was to see the Brewers and Mets face each other in the National League Championship Series, and the way the NL is looking, it is still a possibility. The Brewers still have 10 games left with the Cubs, 7 of those games at home. They will have five more home games in the second half of the season than they did in the first half, and the Cubs will have five less home games in the second half than they played in the first half. The Brewers also figure to be a player in the C.C. Sabathia sweepstakes, as the Indians are now in last place in the AL Central, and the Brewers have the prospects to throw at Cleveland. The question is, can we sign him long term. He would be a phenomenal addition to this staff. The Mets have simply underachieved, and I still think they have enough talent to take the NL East running away. I'll go to battle any day with Johan, Pedro and Maine as my top three starters, and guys like Wright, Reyes and Beltran have what it takes to lead this team to late October baseball. The key is getting off to a quick start to the second half of the season. The Brewers open up with 4 at Arizona tomorrow night, before returning to Miller Park for ten games against Pittsburgh, Colorado and Cincinnati. The Mets next eight games are on the road against St Louis and Philadelphia, a very critical road trip.

Looking at how the divisions currently stack up, the Rays have a half game lead over Boston in the AL East, with New York 5.5 back, the Orioles 7.5 back, and the Blue Jays 10 back. I see this being a three team race, but I think the Rays are playing well enough to take this. In the AL Central, the White Sox lead the Twins by 1.5 games, and the Tigers are only 5 out. The Indians and Royals are each 9.5 out, and look to be out of it. The Angels lead the Athletics by 4.5 games in the NL West, and the Rangers by 7.5. The Mariners still have the worst record in baseball, at 31-50, and are 17.5 back. Sleepless in Seattle, indeed.

In the National League East the Mets trail the Phillies by three games, and the Marlins by two, clinging to third place, just ahead of the Braves, who are 4 out, and the lowly Nationals, who are 11 back. The Brewers are 4.5 back of the Cubs for the division, and two back of the Cardinals for the Wild Card lead. The Astros, Reds and Pirates are all playing rock/paper/scissors to see who will take last in this division, as I thought they would. The Diamondbacks still lead the NL West, but are only 41-41, and have really fallen on hard times lately. The division is awful this year, and the Dodgers, who are five games under .500, are only 2.5 games back. The Giants are five back, and the Rockies and Padres are both 9.5 back. Despite this being a terrible division, I'm going to make a prediction right now. If the Padres and Rockies play each other this season in a play in game like they did last season, I will shave my eyebrows. That's right, I will Tom Crean it, and I will purchase a billboard on I-43 to show the world.

June 30th

Eight years ago today, one of my all time favorite Mets moments occurred. Trailing the Braves 8-1 heading to the bottom of the eighth, and 8-2 with two outs in that inning, the Mets went on to score 10 runs in the inning, including a tie breaking three run home run by Mike Piazza. Moser was watching the game and when he called, I knew it was him (caller ID), and all I could think to say was, "I'm going to loot town, cuz daddy needs a new VCR!!" It was unbelievable. Piazza officially retired a little over a month ago, and he'll go down as one of my all time favorite Mets. Who can ever forget the game winning home run he hit the night major league baseball resumed its schedule shortly after 9/11, also against the Braves. He's easily a first ballot hall of famer, and one of, if not the greatest hitting catcher of all time. Not bad for a 62nd round draft pick, made as a favor to Tommy Lasorda.

Tonight, there were no Mets fireworks to speak of, as the Cardinals scored in each of the first five innings, seven runs in all, to beat the Mets 7-1. Maine wasn't sharp at all tonight, allowing ten base runners in only 4 innings pitched. Don't look now, but Kyle Lohse, who almost didn't make the Cardinals roster this spring, is 10-2 with a 3.67 ERA. Not the way the Mets needed to start this very important road trip.

The Brewers got off to a quick start tonight in Arizona, grabbing a 2-0 lead, but giving it right back in the bottom of the first. The game remained 2-2 until the 5th, when the D-Backs touched up Dave Bush for three runs. They would trade runs late, but the Diamondbacks would hold on to win 6-3. As I'm typing, the Cubs are up 9-0 on San Francisco in the 8th, and I'm not staying up any later to see how that one ends up. I'm gonna assume the Cubs will hold on, but maybe the Giants can conjure up some of the magic Mike Piazza and the Mets provided in 2000. I'm still not staying up.

4. That's What I'm Talking About

July 1st

Foxsports.com posted a list, with pictures, of the seven greatest moustaches in baseball history. The list included 4 relief pitchers, 2 of my favorite first basemen ever, and Sal Fasano, a journeyman catcher currently with the...who knows. If I have to look it up, is it worth mentioning? I'm not even sure he's in the league anymore, to be honest. The four relievers listed were Al Hrabosky, affectionately known as "The Mad Hungarian", Rollie Fingers, Rich "Goose" Gossage and the late Rod Beck. The two first basemen were Don Mattingly and Keith Hernandez. Damn, Keith Hernandez is a sexy beast, and he'll be the first to tell you. And I'm 100% straight. I love the ladies, but Keith Hernandez is a sexy beast. I would have left Fasano off the list, and included someone like Pete Vukovich, Cap Anson or Dennis Eckersley.

The Mets called up Tony Armas in time for tonight's game against St Louis, and he will be asked to take on Todd Wellemeyer in game two of a four game series with the Cardinals. Armas was in a hole early, down 3-1 entering the 4th inning, but the Mets would chip away at Wellemeyer, scoring two in the 4th, and three in the 5th. David Wright added a homer off St Louis reliever Brad Thompson in the 6th inning to give the Mets a 7-3 lead. The Cards got one back in the bottom half of the inning to make it 7-4. The bullpen was able to hold the three run lead, and give Armas the victory in his first big league start of the season. Still 3.5 back as the Phillies won tonight, and within 2 games of the Marlins.

The Brewers opened the month of July by bullying a future Hall of Famer. They put up six runs in the first two innings against Randy Johnson, including two home runs by J.J. Hardy, who's been knocking the cover off the ball since being moved back to the 2 hole. The D-Backs got to Suppan in the 4th and 5th, and the Brewers led 7-5 after 5 innings. They would swap runs late in the game, but the Brewers would hang on tonight, 8-6. There were only 21,736 fans in attendance at Chase Field to see this game. That blows me away. Yes, the Diamondbacks are struggling, but they are in 1st place, the Brewers are hot, and this could be a playoff preview. I don't get, but maybe it's not for me to understand.

July 2nd

Andy Fefer is one of my oldest friends, and earlier this year, he asked me to stand up in his wedding, which is scheduled for August 30th of this year. Of course I said yes. He was a groomsman in my first wedding, and I'd do anything for the boy. I took off from work today to get fitted for my tuxedo, and get some other things done that have been sitting on my plate for a while.

While I didn't pay too much attention to the games tonight, I could not get away from two huge rumors near and dear to Wisconsin sports fans. The first one was inevitable. Brett Favre has apparently expressed interest to Mike McCarthy about returning this season. Amber and her mom, Susan, did not believe me when I broke the news, and even sent the waitress to the bar to confirm. We'll have to watch this story as it unfolds, and for the record, I would support his decision to come back. Look, it's Brett Favre. I don't think he should have retired in the first place. I'm glad he didn't wait until the end of June to announce his intentions, but I think it was too early for him to say he's done. We were so close to getting to the Super Bowl, and we have the talent to get back. I do feel for Aaron Rodgers if Favre comes back, but the bottom line is, we love Brett Favre, and we know he can still play. If he decides to return, we should embrace the decision. He's Brett Favre! The other rumor swirling around town is that the Brewers are close to completing a deal for Cleveland

Indians pitcher and reigning A.L. Cy Young award winner, C.C. Sabathia. The Indians really want Matt LaPorta, and I've even heard J.J. Hardy's name being thrown around. I don't think we should give up either of those players. We have enough talent stockpiled in the minors where we wouldn't have to give up LaPorta, and there is a lot of uncertainty as to whether we can sign Sabathia long term. I'd hate to see the Brewers give up the farm for Sabathia if we can't sign him. But, the Brewers haven't made the playoffs since 1982, and ownership may want to take a shot with this roster to see if they can't win it all this year, especially with the long term futures of Sheets and Fielder up in the air.

The Brewers got single runs in the 6th, 7th, 8th and 9th to hold off the Diamondbacks, 4-3. With the score 2-2 heading to the 8th, Rickie Weeks homered to give the Brewers a lead, but David Riske gave it right back by allowing a home run to Justin Upton. Mike Cameron was the hero tonight, singling home a run in the ninth to give the Brewers the lead for good. He also drove in the tying run in the seventh. Salomon Torres notched his 15th save of the season.

Pedro Martinez gave up four runs in the 1st against St Louis. The Mets got to Cardinals starter Joel Pineiro by the 3rd inning, and tied the game in the 4th. The Cards got one back in the 5th off Pedro, who's ERA is now 7.39. I think it may be time to start worrying about Pedro. The numbers don't lie. The Mets scored three in the 7th to take a 7-5 lead, but the bullpen blew that quickly and Carlos Muniz gave up a walk off dinger to Troy Glaus to end it. I'm glad I didn't see the end of this game.

July 3rd

If the Brewers miss the playoffs by one game this year, let's all look back on July 3rd for answers. Today, the Brewers took a 5-0 lead into the bottom of the ninth inning, and lost 6-5.

The Diamondbacks scored all six runs in the ninth, and did it all with nobody out. Guillermo Mota, who has been tipping his pitches as of late, faced three batters (two hits allowed and one walk). They all scored when Brian Shouse relieved him, and gave up a three run double to the only man he faced, pinch hitter Chad Tracy. Salomon Torres came on, and also couldn't retire a batter giving up three consecutive hits to hand the game to Arizona. We were listening to this game at work, and it really looked like we were going to wrap this one up easily, and take 3 of 4 from the NL West leading Diamondbacks. But it wasn't meant to be. When I watched the highlights on Baseball Tonight later that night, it looked like the Diamondbacks had won another World Series, the way they celebrated at home plate. It would have been fun to see, had I not been a Brewers fan, but this is a very frustrating loss to say the least.

The Mets needed tonight's game against St Louis to earn a split in their four game series, and they came out swinging, scoring three in the 1st and 6 in the 3rd, eventually winning big, 11-1. Had the Mets blown an 11 run lead to the Cardinals on the same day the Brewers blew a five run lead in the 9th, I don't know what I would have done, but it would not have been pretty. This I know.

July 4th

Happy 4th of July! I'm surprised to only see three day games on the major league schedule today. I thought I'd see a ton of day games on the docket. The Brewers hosted the Pirates in one of those three games, and Amber, Mike and I took in the game, getting there early to take in some batting practice. The Brewers treated the sell out crowd of 41,463 to a big win, 9-1. Ben Sheets got the win, extending his record to 10-2. He only went 5 2/3 innings, and was unusually wild today, walking three, and going deep in the count several times. Carlos Villaneuva went the rest of the way to earn his first save of the year. It was an amazing day at the park. I went with a jumbo dog and nachos today, and it surely hit the spot. Bill Hall and J.J. Hardy provided the pop, each going yard off Pittsburgh starter Tom Gorzelanny. J.J. Hardy has quietly raised his average to .292, clearly benefiting from hitting second. The Sabathia rumors are still going strong, and it sounds like the Brewers and Dodgers are the frontrunners.

I didn't get to follow game one of the Mets series in Philadelphia tonight, and was upset to find out that they lost in the bottom of the 9th on a walk off Shane Victorino single off of Duaner Sanchez. A great start by Johan Santana was wasted, as he went 8 innings, allowing two runs on six hits, striking out six without walking a batter. The final was 3-2 Phillies. The Mets are now 5.5 games back of Philadelphia. But even a Mets loss can't ruin this day. We got to see a great game at Miller Park, played some catch before after the game, and saw a great fireworks display in Pewaukee. What more do you need?

July 5th

I took my daughter swimming this afternoon, and spent most of the evening singing and playing with her. After a full day of activities, she wound down around 8:00, and watched one of her Winnie the Pooh movies while clutching a pillow on the floor. While she was falling asleep to the Pooh, the Tigger, the Eyeore and the what not, I followed the end of the Brewers game online. The radio we have here at the apartment doesn't get AM stations to clearly, or else we'd definitely be listening to Uecker tell us the story. This will change soon, as the playoff push comes to fruition. Prince Fielder drove in the winning run in the bottom of the 9th to give the Brewers a 2-1 win. Winning pitcher: Eric Gagne! The Cubs blew a 4-2 lead in the 9th earlier today in St Louis, so the Brewers are now only 3.5 back in the Central, one game behind the Cardinals for the Wild Card. The Brewers and Pirates honored the Negro Leagues, and donned the old throwbacks tonight. I may have to get me a hat. They are white with black stripes and a solid capital M on the front.

The Mets were down 4-3 in the 7th tonight, scored three in the 8th and three in the 9th to take game two vs Philadelphia, 9-4. What's funny is that after the Brewers game, I got so excited about how they won, I forgot to follow the end of the Mets game. I didn't know how this game ended until it occurred to me to check mlb.com during a commercial break while watching SNL. I was pleasantly surprised to see the comeback win. It's like finding a $20 in your pants when doing laundry. Not exactly, but I'm sure you get my drift.

July 6th

Happy birthday to you. Happy birthday to you. Happy birthday, dear Amber. Happy birthday to you. Hope you enjoyed the cupcakes. And thank you to Schwingle for preparing a great dinner tonight. Beef tips and noodles, a loaf of Italian bread and salad. I can't wait to try the tortellini.

I took Gracie to the park this morning, the same one we frequented last week, sans the bitchy six year old bully. She had a blast, kicking around a soccer ball with a young boy I would guess is just a little older than her. After about a half hour of playing, she ran up to me and said, "I want some lunch" with a straight face. It was priceless. After we ate, I drove her to Mequon and dropped her off with my mom. I turned the game on, and heard Uecker tell me the Brewers were tied 4-4 in the 2nd. Hardy and Braun hit back to back homers in the 1st, as the Brewers scored four, and the Pirates got 4 right back in the 2nd off Jeff Suppan. The Pirates took the lead in the top of the 3rd, but the Brewers quickly tied it with two of their own in the 3rd. By the time I got back to Greenfield, J.J. Hardy had homered again, giving the Brewers a 10-6 lead through four innings. This is the 2nd time in less than a week that Hardy has gone deep twice in a game, and the 4th time in his young career. The Brewers added a run in the 6th, and the bullpen pitched six scoreless innings today, giving the Brewers a 11-6 win, and a sweep of the Pittsburgh Pirates. The Cubs beat the Cardinals, which means the Brewers have inched percentage points ahead of St Louis for the National League Wild Card lead. Also, there are reports online that state the Brewers are very close to striking a deal with Cleveland for Sabathia. A deal could be announced as early as tomorrow. For what it's worth, Matt LaPorta was held out of the lineup today in Huntsville, a sure sign that something is brewing. It's great to see the Brewers as potential buyers before the trading deadline. I'm so used to them losing the big names in July and August (Vaughn, Seitzer, Sexson, Lee, etc...)

The Mets had a 1-0 lead over the Phillies heading to the 8th inning, when rain delayed the game for just less than three hours. We were at Summerfest for a couple of hours when I decided to check my cell phone to see if the game ever did resume. It turns out, the Mets added a run in the 9th, but Billy Wagner blew the save, giving up a two run homer to Jayson Werth in the bottom of the ninth. Fernando Tatis hit a two run homer in the top of the 12th, which proved to be the difference as the Mets pulled to within 3.5 of the Phillies today. After the update, it was time to find some eats and some good music. We enjoyed some cheese curds and mozzarella sticks from Saz's while listening to Greg Koch & the Other Bad Men at the Harley stage. Then we walked around for a bit, and listened to a band called Band X for a couple of minutes. They were not bad, doing a cover of the Foo Fighters' "The Pretender", which is one of the best rock songs released in the past two years, if you want my opinion. I ended up getting an Italian roast beef sandwich to round out my eating for the night, as 311 played us out. I'm not that familiar with them, but naturally, everyone there was, and I felt like I was about 78 years old. We listened to them for about 40 minutes before heading back to our car.

This was a great weekend. The Brewers are now firmly a player in the National League playoff picture. The Mets bounced back from Friday's loss to take two straight from Philly, to pull within 3.5 games of the top of the NL East, I got to spend the weekend with my daughter, and was blessed with great company for most of today. Billy Joel is in ten days. Can't wait!

July 7th

Well, it's official! The Milwaukee Brewers are the talk of the baseball world. This morning, a press conference was held to announce that the Brewers have traded four minor leaguers to Cleveland for CC Sabathia. Matt LaPorta will be heading to Cleveland, along with Zach Jackson, who came to the Brewers in the Lyle Overbay trade a few years ago, and a couple of Class A pitchers. The Sabathia trade is easily the biggest in-season trade the Brewers have made since acquiring Don Sutton in late August of 1982. Sutton went 5-2 in his seven starts down the stretch, including the division clinching start against Baltimore on the last day of the season. Sabathia is the reigning AL Cy Young award winner, and currently leads the majors in strikeouts with 123. The 1-2 punch of Sheets and Sabathia should be one of the most formidable in the whole league. Now, there a lot of questions as to whether we should have mortgaged so much for a guy who is a free agent at the end of the year, and will command a ton of money in the off season. But the way Doug Melvin and the Brewers are looking at this is, we have a shot to win the whole thing, this season, let's do it! The city is tired of rebuilding for the future; we have the talent, let's take a chance, and make a serious run at not just making the playoffs, but winning the World Series. The bottom line is, if we can make the playoffs, we are going to be tough to beat with Sheets and Sabathia going back to back. The Brewers were very high on LaPorta, but had doubts about his glove, and figure that he is better suited as a DH on an American League team. Sure, it's going to be tough to keep Sabathia, or Sheets for that matter, but with the talent that we have now, why not take a stab at winning it all. The fans have already responded by coming out in droves to eat up tickets for the upcoming series with Colorado. Sabathia will be making his debut with the

Brewers tomorrow night, which will actually give him 2 starts before the All Star Game. To make room for Sabathia, the Brewers have placed Jeff Suppan on the DL. Most likely, either Dave Bush or Seth McClung will be replaced in the rotation once Suppan returns.

Ryan Braun also made a big splash in the last 24 hours, surpassing Alfonso Soriano, Kosuke Fukudome and Ken Griffey, Jr as the leading vote getter among NL outfielders, and will start for the National League in left field at this year's All Star Game at Yankee Stadium. Ben Sheets was also named to the team, and could very well start that game, as his last start before the break is Wednesday night. Corey Hart is among five players listed on the final ballot for the last spot on the NL roster. The other four players are David Wright, Carlos Lee, Aaron Rowand and Pat Burrell.

The Brewers were not able to turn all of this positive energy into a win tonight on the field. Ubaldo Jimenez dominated the Crew over seven innings, not allowing a single run, and only giving up 3 hits. The Rockies had a 4-0 lead going into the bottom of the 8th, when Taylor Buchholz took over for Jimenez. Buchholz is among the league leaders in holds this season, and has an ERA of 1.70. The Brewers were able to load the bases for Ryan Braun against Buchholz, and Braun hit a scorcher up the middle, but Clint Barmes had him played perfectly, and turned a 6-3 double play, allowing one run to score to make it 4-1 Colorado. Prince Fielder would homer immediately after the double play, to awaken the Milwaukee crowd and pull the Brewers to within one. Brian Fuentes, however, got the Brewers in order in the ninth to lock up a win for Colorado.

In the fifth inning, Robb Edwards introduced Sabathia to the Miller Park crowd, and he was greeted to a huge standing ovation. We didn't pull it out tonight, but the atmosphere at the park was amazing, and just imagine what it's going to be like tomorrow when CC Sabathia makes his Brewers debut. It was noted during the press conference announcing the trade that Sabathia wanted to be referred to in print as CC and not C.C. No explanation was given.

The Mets got me all sexed up tonight as well, taking an 8-0 lead in the 3rd inning, hitting the snot out of the ball against Adam Eaton, who usually pitches pretty well against New York. The Mets led the Phillies 10-1 going into the bottom of the sixth, and nearly blew it, giving up 8 runs over the last four innings, but they did hold on to win 10-9, taking the last three games in a critical series in Philadelphia. We are now 2.5 back. The Mets did get some bad news today, as it looks like Moises Alou and Ryan Church could both be out for the season. Let the Barry Bonds rumors begin...now.

July 8th

The Cubs answered the Brewers tonight by acquiring Rich Harden from Oakland for next to nothing. Sean Gallagher, Matt Murton and two scrubs I've never heard of will head to Oakland in exchange for Harden, who is 5-1 with a 2.34 ERA this season. He has missed a month of this season to injury, and has a history of missing starts, but when he's on, can be a very effective pitcher. I still like Sheets and Sabathia over Zambrano and Harden in a seven game series.

The Brewers damn near broke a franchise record for walk up ticket sales for tonight's game vs the Rockies, with Sabathia making his first start for the Crew. My boy Mikey brought some Lenny's, and nothing beats a night of baseball and pizza. In the first, Ryan Braun hit an absolute missile to left field for a three run homer, igniting a playoff like atmosphere in the stands. The Brewers added a run in the 3rd to give Sabathia a 4-0 lead. The Rockies would chisel away at the lead, scoring 1 in the 4th, and two in the 6th, but Sabathia put an end to the rally in the 6th by striking out the last batter he faced, Brad Hawpe, with runners on 1st and 3rd. The Brewers added three runs in the 7th, highlighted by a Bill Hall two run single that once again lit the sell out crowd up. The bullpen combined for three scoreless innings to give the Brewers a 7-3 win, Sabathia's first W in the National League. The

Cubs and Cardinals both won tonight, leaving the Brewers four out of the division lead, and a half game back of the Wild Card.

Tim Lincecum of the Giants is gracing the cover of this week's Sports Illustrated, and they referred to him as a 170 pound man child. The timing of this could not have been better for Mets fans, if you believe in the SI curse. Lincecum came into tonight with a 10-1 record, and an ERA of 2.66, and was simply out pitched by Mike Pelfrey of the Mets. Carlos Beltran hit a three run homer in the first (like Braun for the Brewers) that got the Mets fans off their feet quick. That would be all Pelfrey needed, but the Mets weren't done, adding home runs from Carlos Delgado and Fernando Tatis later in the game, to give the Mets a 7-0 win tonight. Pelfrey was lights out, going 7 innings, only allowing 3 hits, and not walking a single batter. He is now 7-6, and his ERA is at 3.93. With Philadelphia losing tonight to St Louis, the Mets are now a game and a half out.

It's a funny game, baseball is. At the end of May, it was looking like the Brewers were going backwards, falling to four games under .500, and being swept out of Fenway Park. The media and fans were calling for Ned Yost's head, and the season looked lost. The Mets fired their manager, and the team lacked the fire that they'd possessed the last couple of seasons. It certainly didn't look like I'd have much to write about for the last four months of the season. Now, the Brewers are 50-40, and a half game behind St Louis for the Wild Card, and the Mets have won four straight, and find themselves within footsteps of the NL East lead. Get your popcorn ready…

July 9th

Nobody, but nobody makes banana bread like a Sue Benson. Only three ingredients: bananas, flour and love. Yummy in my tummy. And while I'm throwing out compliments, because I have food on the brain, Kathy Norrell makes the world's finest bacon. Her secret? Just the right combination of pork and kindness. Get a tournament together with some big name sponsors, and I guarantee that my baby's momma's momma walks out with the blue ribbon for bacon preparation.

Joe, Jamie, Pat and I attended the Brewers game tonight, and I had every intention of scoring the game, and giving you the play by play tonight. But Guillermo Mota gave up 4 runs late, in a tight game, and I destroyed the scorecard in a fit of rage. Early on, it looked like we were going to see a little bit of history, as Ben Sheets first seven outs tonight were recorded via the strikeout. The fastball was popping tonight, hitting 97 a couple of times in the first two innings. Bill Hall hit a monster home run off of Glendon Rusch, yes, thee Glendon Rusch, whose fastball looked like Andy Filo's tonight. I know they referred to him as "Fast Finger Filo", but that was in the fifth grade. I make fun, but Rusch out pitched Sheets tonight, only allowing one run over six innings. By the time Mota entered the game, it was 4-3 Colorado, and Mota gave up four hits, two of which cleared the outfield wall for what the kids these days are calling "moon shots", giving the Rockies an 8-3 lead. Jamie and I went back and forth on what the definition of awful pitching was. I claim Mota's been awful, and he likes to think he's been "memorable", because when a reliever struggles, you seldom remember the good. Look, he's stunk lately, and it's getting to the point where I can't trust him late in games. On a positive note, the food at Miller Park was in mid-season form, as the Italian and Jumbo Dog I had were quite tasty. Pat has informed us that he is leaning towards making Tom Brady the first ever pick of the yet-to-be-named scoring only fantasy football league I'll be launching this fall.

The Mets got another shutout tonight over the Giants, extending their winning streak to 5 games. Johan Santana only went five innings, giving up only hits, but looked very good. The bullpen did not surrender a single base runner through the last four innings. Jose Reyes raised his batting average to .301 with his 1-3 performance tonight. Despite going 0-4, David Wright remains neck and neck with Corey Hart for the final NL roster spot in this year's All Star Game. The voting ends tomorrow afternoon and the winner will be announced at 3:00pm CST. I'll be happy with either one winning the final vote.

July 10th

It's Thursday. What does that mean? Day baseball, and this afternoon, the Mets and Brewers wrap up their series with San Francisco and Colorado respectively, while I enable financial dreams, tell the story and spread the word.

The Mets were looking for a sweep of the Giants in an effort to run their winning streak to six. It was John Maine vs Barry Zito. To this point in the series, the Giants have yet to score a run. Fernando Tatis provided a two run double in a three run 3rd inning, giving Maine a 3-0 lead to work with. Maine gave up a run in the 4th, and two in the 5th before being pulled. Neither starter entered the 6th inning today, while combining to walk 11 batters. Entering the 7th, the game was tied at 3-3, and Fernando Tatis came up huge again, hitting a two run homer to break the tie, and give the Mets the lead for good. Tatis went 3-5 on the day, with four RBI. With Alou most likely out for the year, and Church on the shelf for a while (possibly the year), Tatis picked a great day to stand out. Don't look now, but the Mets have won six straight, and our putting themselves in position to take over the NL East lead before the All Star break. Who would have thought that would have happened six weeks ago?

The Brewers provided many thrills for Andy and me today. After Colorado scored off Dave Bush in the 1st, it was all Brewers the rest of the way. We knocked around former Brewer Jorge De La Rosa to the tune of seven runs over 3 and 2/3 innings, six of those runs coming in the 4th inning. Corey Hart and J.J. Hardy added home runs later, and Gabe Kapler tied a Brewers record by hitting three doubles today. But the day belonged to Dave Bush, who only allowed one run (unearned), and struck out a career high

13 batters in his eight innings worked. It looks like he may have saved his job today, as he has pitched really well as of late, especially at home. The final was 11-1, as the Brewers earned a split against Colorado. Their record is now 51-41, and the Cubs and Cards both lost this afternoon, so the Brewers are the current Wild Card leaders, and are only 4 behind the Cubs for the NL Central lead and the best record in baseball. The coolest thing that happened today was off the field. During the post game press conference, Corey Hart was talking about his day at the plate, with his child on his knee, when out of nowhere, ten to twelve of his teammates doused him with champagne, congratulating him on winning the final vote for the National League All Star team. It was so cool to see such team unity, and Hart didn't look like he was expecting it. It is certainly a special time to be a Brewers fan.

Today is my dad's birthday. Although he can probably name as many current Brewers as my daughter can, he'll get a kick out of being mentioned throughout this book. We haven't been to a game yet at Miller Park, and I would certainly like that to change soon. Just one game would be neat. What do you say, dad? We don't have to play catch, but could we? I've got the first round of dogs.

July 11th

The Billy Joel show at Shea Stadium is five days from today. I don't want to ruin any surprises, so I'm not checking online to see what guests may be in store for the show, or what songs Billy may play that he normally wouldn't. This will not be like any other show. The Beatles played Shea…twice! And after all, these are the last concerts ever at Shea. I'm sure there are going to be some big names there on Wednesday, whether they join Billy on stage, or just want to be a part of it like all of us.

The Mets must be feeling all the electricity in the air, because they are the hottest team in baseball. After taking the last three games in the big series in Philadelphia, they just swept San Francisco, and tonight, hung on to beat Colorado in a great pitching duel. Aaron Cook and Oliver Perez matched each other for six innings, each giving up one run. Perez had control problems, walking six, but got out of jams all night. The game remained knotted at 1-1 until the 8th, when Damion Easley hit a solo shot off of Taylor Buchholz. Billy Wagner struck out two in setting the Rockies down in order to give the Mets their seventh straight win. Philadelphia won in 12 tonight, so the Mets remain 1.5 back.

The Brewers blew a golden opportunity tonight, blowing a 5-2 lead in the seventh. A Mike Cameron error and a Manny Parra wild pitch led to two unearned runs crossing the plate, and the Reds went on to take the lead in the 8th. It was a sloppy game for the Brewers, committing three errors and throwing three wild pitches. Francisco Cordero pitched a scoreless 9th to lock up a 6-5 win for the Reds. This loss stings a bit, because the Cubs and Cardinals won. But the loss doesn't hurt too much, because we made s'mores tonight. S'mores can heal any kind of pain. So tasty, and fun to make!

July 12th

It's kind of rainy today, so I have no plans of taking Gracie out to play. We're probably gonna make it a day of coloring and watching Monsters, Inc. My daughter loves Jack Goodman and Willy Crystal in animated form. She does not act the same when I put in King Ralph or City Slickers 2. I can't explain why. Amber and I put up the bunk beds for when Gracie and Gina spend weekends here. I think I may want to put my Spawns on the top bunk for now. I'm sure Amber would love to walk into the room and see 50 "action figures" staring back at her.

All the Mets did today while we put up the bunk beds and played with Gracie was one-hit the Rockies for their 8th straight win. This is their 3rd shutout in the last five games. Pedro gave up the lone Colorado hit in the 4th inning, before leaving the game in the 5th with shoulder stiffness. I'm being told there is nothing to worry about. Jose Reyes hit his 10th homer of the season in the win. Philadelphia got pasted during the national Fox telecast, as Arizona beat them 10-4, pulling the Mets to within a half a game. David Wright, who was beaten out in the Final Vote for the NL all star game, was added to the roster today, replacing Alfonso Soriano on the roster. Soriano has been on the DL for nearly a month. This gives the Mets two all stars, Wagner and Wright.

The Brewers suffered another frustrating loss to Cincinnati tonight in front of their third straight sell out crowd at Miller Park. The Crew entered the 9th down 4-2, but Eric Gagne gave up back to back homers to Adam Dunn and Edwin Encarnacion to lead off the inning, and the Reds would add two more off of Gagne and Mota to blow the game wide open. Gagne's ERA is 7.33, and Mota's is 5.77, and yet the Brewers still feel comfortable shelling them out late in close games. The Cubs blew a 7-0 lead in the 8th and 9th against the Giants, but won the game in ten innings, so the Brewers now trail the Cubs by 6 games. St Louis lost in extras to Pittsburgh, so we remain a half of game back in the Wild Card race.

July 13th

Three days until the Billy Joel show. I was going to wait a while to do this, but today, I picked up the 30th Anniversary edition of "The Stranger", which includes a remastered copy of the original album, a CD of the first time he played Carnegie Hall, a DVD of his performance on "The Old Grey Whistle Test", and a bonus CD of five songs performed at Nassau County Coliseum. The collection also includes a 48 page booklet, and a small replica of hand written lyrics from 1977. Best Buy had this on sale for $29, and I simply couldn't resist. I am officially in Billy Joel mode heading into Wednesday night.

The Brewers game today was indeed one of the highlights of the 2008 baseball season, especially for Milwaukee Brewers fans. CC Sabathia was making his second start as a Brewer, facing Homer Bailey of the Reds. The Brewers needed to win today to avoid a sweep of the Reds, who've been playing pretty well as of late, improving their record to 46-49. The Reds would score in the 2nd and 3rd, each time on a sacrifice fly, to take an early 2-0 lead. In the bottom of the 3rd, Sabathia stepped up with one out, and helped out his own cause by hitting his third career home run, and second of this season, to deep right field. Jill and I went nuts, and the crowd was also going crazy at Miller Park. It was great to see the guys in the dugout react as well. The guy has been here less than a week, and he's already made huge contributions to this team.

In the 6th inning, Gabe Kapler tied the score at 2-2 with an RBI single. Sabathia worked a 1-2-3 7th inning, and the crowd was pleased to see him hit for himself in the bottom half of the inning. Why take him out of the game at 2-2? Good job, Ned. Sabathia got out of the 8th unharmed, but the Brewers were unable to score in the 8th. Surely Yost would have brought in Torres to face the Reds in the 9th had the Brewers scored, but with the game still tied at 2, Sabathia would enter the 9th with a chance to hold Cincinnati at bay, and put himself in a position to win again if the Brewers could score in the bottom half. Sabathia was brilliant in the 9th, striking out the side, and finishing the day with 9 punch outs, while only walking one. He threw 122 pitches, and 82 were for strikes.

Bill Hall led off for the Brewers in the bottom of the ninth, and as he stepped in, I schooled Jill on how much Bill Hall likes to hit in the ninth inning at home vs the Reds in his career (see 2004). Hall led off the inning with a single, off of a right hander (David Weathers). Mike Cameron would be asked to lay down a sac bunt, and he laid down a beauty, but Weathers and Paul Bako couldn't communicate on who should pick up the ball, and Weathers quickly picked and threw to first, but in the dirt, and past Joey Votto, advancing Bill Hall to 3rd base, and Cameron to 2nd. Jason Kendall was walked to load the bases with nobody out, and I was begging for the Reds to call upon Francisco Cordero to try to save this one. Nothing would be sweeter than to win this one with Cordero on the hill for Cincinnati. For a moment, I was hoping that Yost would send Sabathia up to hit for himself against Cordero. It would have been great theater. But Yost would call upon Craig Counsell, who is a career .420 hitter with the bases loaded, and can beat you in several different ways. He makes great contact and has good speed, so there are a few different ways to approach the at bat. He took the first pitch he saw deep to right, deep enough to score Bill Hall on a sacrifice fly, and both Hall and Counsell were mobbed on the field. The happiest Brewer out there was easily Sabathia, who was given the opportunity to go the distance, and was rewarded with his 2nd win in two starts. It was an incredible scene at the end of the game. The Cards won, so we remain a half game back of St Louis for the Wild Card, but the Cubs lost, so we are only five back at the break. After the All Star break, the Brewers get an additional day off on Thursday, before heading to San Francisco for three. Milwaukee's record at the break is 52-43, on pace to win just under 90 games.

I made myself a promise this morning. If Philadelphia lost to Arizona today, I would watch the Mets game against Colorado tonight at a local establishment, to see if I could witness them take sole possession of 1st place in the NL East. They were featured on ESPN tonight, as the last game of the 1st half of the season. However, if the Phillies won, I would return to Greenfield, get some George Webb's to go, and follow the game online while enjoying my new Billy Joel box set. The Phillies did in fact beat the Diamondbacks, so I returned home, picked up a couple of double cheeseburgers and some chicken tenders from the Webb's just down the road, and enjoyed the Billy Joel DVD. I had the box score refreshing on the computer, and checked on it from time to time. How's this for finishing the first half of the season? Mets 7, Rockies 0, there 4th shutout in 6 games. Pelfrey went 8 scoreless. The Brothers Carlos each went yard. 9 wins in a row, heading into the All Star Game!!! And I'll be at Shea in three days!

July 14th

      The home run derby was tonight. I am no longer enchanted by this event. Rick Reilly pointed that that tonight's derby featured 8 white guys, and no Yankees. Either way, by the end of the first round, I'm usually all homered out. Ryan Braun was one of the participants, and advanced to the 2nd round before bowing out. Josh Hamilton, who may be one of the best stories to come out of baseball in the last ten years, hit a record 28 home runs in the first round, including 12 in a row at one point without recording an out. Hamilton ended up facing Justin Morneau in the finals, and Morneau won it, despite hitting about 20 less homers combined through all three rounds. The totals carry over from the first to the second round, but those totals do not carry over to the finals. I watched the whole thing, but could have very easily turned over to Monday Night Raw, if their writing was half of what it used to be.

      The big news of the day was that Ben Sheets was named as the National League starting pitcher for tomorrow night's game. Cliff Lee of the Cleveland Indians will oppose him. This will be the first time that a Milwaukee Brewer pitcher has started an All Star Game. He has definitely earned the right. Lee is a nice story as well. He finished 4th in the AL Cy Young voting in 2005, and within two years, was pitching so poorly, that he was optioned to AAA Buffalo last July. He was recalled on September 1st last year, but only appeared in 4 games from Sept 1st on, and was a non-factor in the Indians run to the ALCS. This year, he pitched his way back into the Cleveland rotation, and so far, has amassed a 12-2 record with a 2.31 ERA. We'll see how much of the game I end up watching, as I have to be up around 4:00am on Wednesday to get ready for our trip to Shea.

July 15th

Here's a brief summary of tonight's All Star Game from a guy who has to get up in about three hours to drive to the airport, then try to stay awake for the next 30 hours...
Ben Sheets pitched 2 scoreless innings, striking out 3. Carlos Zambrano also pitched 2 scoreless innings. Through 4 innings, there was no score. In the top of the 5th, Matt Holliday homered off of Ervin Santana to make it 1-0 NL. Lance Berkman hit a sacrifice fly in the 6th inning to give the NL a 2-0 lead, and Dan Haren completed his 2 innings pitched in the bottom of 6th to hold the 2-0 lead for the National League. For a moment, it looked like the NL would finally win one of these things. 1996 was the last year they won. Edison Volquez, who was traded for Josh Hamilton in the off-season, gave up a two run homer to J.D. Drew to tie the game in the 7th. Jonathan Papelbon gave up an unearned run in the 8th, caused by a throwing error by Dioner Navarro, to give the NL a 3-2 lead. Papelbon was booed all inning by the Yankees fans. He had made some comments yesterday about how he deserved the ball in the 9th if the AL needed to shut the door, and then quickly retracted those comments, saying that Rivera should close, out of respect to the "elder statesmen". Tongue, I'm sure was planted firmly in cheek. Billy Wagner gave up an RBI double to Tampa Bay rookie Evan Longoria to tie the game in the bottom of the 8th inning. Both teams had plenty of chances to put the game away late. The game would end up going extra innings, and Aaron Cook loaded the bases in the 10th, with nobody out, but was able to get out of the inning unscored upon. Cook would pitch another two more innings, as the game remained scoreless through 12 innings. Mike and I promised each other we would go to bed after 12 innings, but broke that promise in unison. There's no way I was going to turn this game off now. It doesn't matter how much sleep I'll be losing, or what's going on tomorrow. This is the best All Star Game I've ever seen, and I have to see out it ends. The game would go into the 15th inning, still tied at 3-3, when Joe Buck started to wonder aloud if this game would end up in a tie like the infamous game in Milwaukee in 2002. Entering the 15th inning, each team was down to their final pitcher. The AL had Scott Kazmir on the hill, who

threw 108 pitches on Sunday, and was not even scheduled to pitch tonight, and the NL was down to Brad Lidge. Buck mentioned that Kazmir would only be able to go a maximum of two innings, and if the game went into the 17th inning, J.D. Drew would end up pitching for the American League. I later learned that David Wright would have pitched for the National League had it gone to the 17th. But in the bottom of the 15th, Michael Young hit a sacrifice fly to right field, giving the AL yet another win in the mid-summer classic. The AL has secured home field advantage in the 2008 World Series, I have to wake up in about three hours, and I ate way too much pizza tonight. Ryan Braun, Corey Hart and David Wright combined for a 1-9 clip tonight, with five strikeouts, with the only hit coming from David Wright in the 13th. The two teams combined for 34 strikeouts. I don't care how many innings were played, that is a lot for an All Star Game. All in all, it was a great game, but a disappointing finish for a fan of the National League.

July 17th

No games on the major league schedule yesterday, as it was the day after the All Star Game. But that doesn't mean that it wasn't a huge day. Yesterday, we flew to New York for the first of two Billy Joel shows at Shea Stadium. They originally referred to the show as the Last Play at Shea, but now they are calling it the Last Double Play at Shea, due to the 2nd show that was scheduled for tomorrow night. We landed at LaGuardia around 10:00am, and walked around Chinatown for a bit. As I'm typing this, I don't know if that's a racist term, or if that's indeed what it is referred to as. Maybe I should have done some fact checking before I included it in the book. My apologies in advance.

We met Jamie and Alisa at Katz Deli for lunch. This is indeed where the famous scene from When Harry Met Sally was shot. We'll just call it the enthusiastic Meg Ryan scene. There were pictures of celebrities all over the wall, and I am assuming they were all pictured with "Katz". We all ordered Philly Cheese steaks, except for Jamie. He enjoyed a reuben. I tried something called "beer" to wash down the tasty sandwich. The sandwich, as well as the beverage, was yummy. We then headed to Times Square, and walked around for a bit. We ended up in a giant Toys r Us, which brought smiles to everyone's face. My good friend Jesus suggested we head over to Junior's for some primo cheesecake, and that is exactly what we did. Many sweet treats were enjoyed, and I indulged in a pineapple ice cream soda. Shortly afterward, I committed to buying some Fanta pineapple soda as soon as I got home.

It was then time to take the 7 to Shea for the show. We got there around 6:30. I had an extra ticket, and sold it for well under face value to a guy who insisted I was a cop. I hope you had fun, buddy. The show started an hour later than scheduled, but that didn't surprise me. When I saw the Boss at Miller Park in 2003, he started almost 90 minutes later than scheduled. By 9:00, the mood was set for an amazing show. The only thing that was wrong was that fatigue was already starting to set in, due to the lack of sleep on Tuesday night. Billy came out to a roaring applause, and kicked off the show with the Star Spangled Banner, a fitting introduction to a show at a baseball stadium. The set was huge, and I noticed a full string section, a full horn section, and four scoreboards that would show the concert and random Mets highlights throughout the show. After the national anthem, Billy went right into "Miami 2017 (Seen the Lights Go Out on Broadway)". Already two songs in, I knew tonight would be special. It felt like no other show I'd ever been to. After Miami 2017, Billy started going through his normal set as of late..."Angry Young Man", "My Life", "Everybody Loves You Now", etc.....he didn't ask us to vote on a song tonight, but he did take a poll as to how many Mets fans were in attendance. Thousands of people roared. Then he asked how many Yankees fans were here, and the applause was noticeably louder for the Yankees fans. That disappointed me. We are in Shea Stadium, after all. Then he asked, "Who doesn't give a shit either way", and there were a number of people who responded jovially to that. One of the early highlights for me was when Tony Bennett came out after the first verse of "New York State of Mind" to join Billy for the rest of the song. I grew up with Tony Bennett being played on 8-tracks as a kid. My Grandma was a big fan, and that was a huge thrill to see one of her favorites singing with my favorite. I won't lie to you; it brought a tear to my eye. Don't judge me, a man can cry at a show. As the song commenced, Bennett got a huge ovation from the capacity crowd. Later in the set, John Mayer joined Billy and played guitar on "This is the Time", a song I've never heard at a live show. About 40 minutes later, Billy started talking about the Mets, and how well they've been playing lately. He then said the next song is appropriate, because they are our "Boys of Summer", and he introduced Don Henley. I'm sure Amber flipped over in her seat. It would have been neat to see her reaction. The final guest of the night would be John Mellencamp, who came out and sang "Pink Houses" while the crowd danced and sang along. During "River of Dreams", Billy broke into "A Hard Day's Night", prompting people to wonder if Sir Paul was in the house. He was not, but that didn't stop Billy from doing two more Beatles songs during his encore, "She Loves You" and "Please Please Me". After the two Beatles tunes, he put the harmonica on, and it looked like he was going to go straight into "Piano Man", but he serenaded us with "Take Me Out to the Ballgame" first, then "Piano Man". The last song of the evening was "Souvenir", which features the great line, "Every year's a souvenir that slowly fades away". It was a perfect ending to an unbelievable show. After the show, we headed to a pizza parlor called Famiglia's, right in the heart of Broadway. Great pie, but I was so tired, I couldn't enjoy it like I normally would. Shortly after 3:00am, we headed to the airport to hang out until it was time to board the plane. And by hang out, I mean sleep uncomfortably. But as I sit here right now, I can't help but daydream about what a great time I had, and how amazing Friday night's show will be.

The Mets played in one of only four games featured on the docket tonight, as they started a four game series in Cincinnati. I basically slept from 9:00 to 5:00 today, and have been writing ever since, while following this game online. It looked like the Mets 9 game winning streak was going to come to an end, however, they put a 4 spot in the top of the ninth against Francisco Cordero, which brings a huge smile to my face. Billy Wagner got the last three outs to notch his 23rd save of the season. The win puts the

Mets at 52-44, and they now share the NL East lead with Philadelphia. In a word, amazing! Shea is going to be rockin' next week when Philly comes in for a three game set.

The Cardinals won tonight, so the Brewers will enter their three game set with San Francisco a full game behind the Cards for the Wild Card. CC Sabathia takes the hill tomorrow night. It is shaping up to be an incredible second half of the season.

July 18th

I haven't seen Gracie since Monday night, so the Mets/Reds game took a backseat to father/daughter time. We shared a peanut butter sandwich and a banana. Most of it was consumed, but some of it was rubbed into the couch. It was great to see everyone after being away. The Mets lost tonight 5-2, ending the ten game winning streak. But I'm the big winner tonight. I got something like five kisses from Gracie, all random.

CC Sabathia threw his 2nd consecutive complete game in a Brewer uniform, as the Brewers took a lopsided game from the Giants, 9-1. Prince Fielder and Mike Cameron each homered. The Cubs lost, which means the Brewers are within 4 games of the NL Central lead. Still a game behind the Cards...I'm reading online a rumor about the Brewers trading for Ray Durham. I wonder how low the Rickie Weeks batting average would have to dip before a move like this would be made. Durham is currently hitting .293, which is higher than any current Brewers starter. He's 36, but would be a valuable addition to a team already deep in the leadership department. We'll see what happens. I can't imagine we'd have to give up a major leaguer for him.

July 19th

Today was not a good day. Driving to work this morning, my car stalled on 43 N, about a half a mile away from work. No flat tires this time. I have no idea what's wrong. Maybe the battery, I know it's been a while since my last oil change…my neglect has probably caught up to my five year old Chevy Cavalier. I had to have the car towed again. I may as well be a sponsor for Lou's softball team next year with the money I've been forking over to them lately. Goodyear closes at noon, so I won't have my car back until Monday at the earliest. I'm completely stressed out. Who knows how much this is going to set me back. And I leave for the baseball trip on Wednesday morning. This sucks. Unfortunately, I'm in no mood to enjoy baseball today. Since I have no car, I stayed in Port tonight with Gracie. While I didn't follow too much of the games, Gracie's company cheered me up, as always, and my mom treated me to Tomaso's. It's always good to have people that love you close by when you're in a funk. And nothing turns that frown upside down like Tomaso's pizza, located in Mequon, WI, USA. Tomaso's: Isn't it time you had some?

The Mets lost today 7-2, but Philly lost as well, so we only remain a game out. The Brewers came from 4-1 down to score 4 in the 6th to take a 5-4 lead. The Giants quickly tied it, but the Crew put up 2 in the 7th and 1 in the 9th to beat the Giants, 8-5. Ben Sheets was not great, giving up 9 hits over 5 innings, and did not figure into the decision. He did help himself with an RBI double. That is not a misprint. Prince Fielder's moon shot into the drink was the difference tonight. Fielder is the 2nd Brewer to hit one into McCovey's Cove, as Russell Branyan did it in 2005. The Cubs lost again, pulling the Brewers to within three games.

July 20th

I had dinner tonight with the staff from the 5 O'clock Club in Pewaukee, the restaurant that Amber works at on Fridays and Saturdays. We all met at Crawdaddy's for some Cajun cuisine. I had a chicken sandwich. I'm loyal to things I recognize. Not much of an oyster guy. When I left Port tonight, the Mets were locked in a 5-5 deadlock with the Reds, and I pumped my fist in joy as I checked the score on my phone, to see the Mets pulling it out in 10 today, 7-5. The Phillies lost, which means that when these two teams meet at Shea on Tuesday night, they will each come in with a record of 53-46. Should be a great series, and Johan is going on Tuesday.

When we arrived at the restaurant, Manny Parra was weaving a 5-0 shutout in 7th inning. Corey Hart and Ryan Braun each homered. Parra would finally be scored upon in the 8th, but he totally out pitched Tim Lincecum today, going 7 2/3 innings, striking out nine, and only allowing two runs. Ryan Braun would add a two run double in the 9th, and the Giants also put up two in the 9th, but it wasn't enough, as the Brewers completed the sweep of San Francisco, 7-4. Parra has now won 8 straight games. The Cubs won today, and the Cardinals completed a 4 game sweep of the Padres. No ground gained today; however, the Ray Durham deal was officially announced after the game. He will join the club tomorrow night in St Louis, and will wear # 5, which is of course Geoff Jenkins' old number. It didn't take long for that to be recycled. # 17 still hasn't been re-issued (Gantner), although it is not officially retired. I find that interesting. Durham will not automatically become the starting 2nd basemen, but will certainly spell Weeks, and be used off the bench to add a spark. I certainly think that Weeks has to step up his game though. We'll see how he reacts to this deal. Maybe this wakes him up.

July 21st

I got the call from Goodyear this afternoon. I don't know enough about cars to explain everything that needed to be fixed, but I can tell you that I dropped about $1300. But I now have "peace of mind". What can you do? I can't let this bring me down. I leave for the baseball trip in two days, I have my health, Mike treated me to Leonardo's tonight (and a pineapple Fanta), and Amber also surprised me with a pineapple Fanta. A good friend knows how to cheer you up, and they both remembered how much I enjoyed my treat in Times Square. Thank you!

The Brewers were featured on ESPN tonight, but we watched it on FSN, because it got blacked out in the Milwaukee market. I'm not sure why that is. It was a road game. It must have something to do with FSN wanting us to see their ads. Seth McClung was handed the ball tonight, and gave up two in the 1st, before settling down for good. The game was 2-0 until the 5th, when Rickie Weeks hit a three run homer to give the Brewers a 3-2 lead. I can just imagine what was going through his head as he circled the bases. About 24 hours ago, the Brewers acquired a solid 2B, possibly to replace Weeks, and he responds by going yard in a huge game. The Brewers would hold onto a 3-2 lead until the 9th, however, Salomon Torres was not able to save this one, allowing a sacrifice fly to Skip Schumaker to tie the game. But Bill Hall came up huge in the 10th, leading off the inning with a solo HR to give the Brewers the lead. They would add two more, and Torres was able to protect the 6-3 lead, and the Brewers are now percentage points ahead of the Cardinals for the NL Wild Card lead. The win is the fifth in a row for the Brewers, the last four on the road.

The Mets were off tonight, as they prepare for a huge series with Philadelphia at Shea this week. I'm sure last September's collapse will be on the minds of most Mets fans as this series kicks off. It's important to take this series, and not just because of the impact it will have on the standings. Taking two of three here will give them momentum heading into another important series against a team the Mets seem to struggle with, the St Louis Cardinals.

July 22nd

In October of 1986, I experienced the highest of highs when the Mets beat the Red Sox in Game Six, and eventually, went on to win the World Series two nights later. Less than three months later, I experienced the lowest of lows as John Elway drove the Broncos 98 yards to tie the Browns in the AFC Championship Game, and eventually beat them in overtime to advance to the Super Bowl. Tonight, I experienced a small taste of both feelings, within an hour of each other. Naturally, these games tonight were on a much smaller stage than what the World Series and Super Bowl can offer, but my heart strings were tugged back and forth regardless.

Johan Santana got the start tonight against newly acquired Joe Blanton for the Phillies. Blanton recently came over from Oakland in a trade that will strengthen Philadelphia's rotation heading down the stretch. Santana was brilliant tonight, going 8, and only allowing 2 runs while not walking a single batter. The Mets had a 5-2 lead heading into the ninth, but were without the services of Billy Wagner tonight, who is still battling left shoulder spasms. Jerry Manuel called upon Duaner Sanchez to get the last three outs. Sanchez could do no right, as he gave up three straight singles to load the bases. Manuel would then give the ball to Joe Smith. Smith did his job, inducing a ground ball to Jose Reyes, but Reyes could not beat Shane Victorino to 2nd as a run scored to make it 5-3. Pedro Feliciano would come in, and allow back to back doubles to So Taguchi and Jimmy Rollins to give the Phillies a 7-5 lead, and they would add another later in the inning. The final was 8-5 Phillies. Joe Smith was "credited" with the loss, and he was the only Mets reliever who did what he was supposed to do. The Mets are now a game behind the Phillies in the NL East. It's too bad we wasted the great start by Johan, but it really hurts to blow a three run lead in the 9th to your arch rival, especially at home.

Jeff Suppan made his return from the disabled list tonight, and got the start in game two of a big series with the Cardinals. Last night, the Brewers pulled even with the Cards for the NL Wild Card lead, and a win tonight would give us the outright lead. Suppan was rocky at first, but would settle down as the night progressed. The Brewers were opposed by Kyle Lohse, who came into tonight with a 12-2 record, with an ERA of 3.35. Lohse was dominant; having only given up one hit over the first six innings, and carried a 3-0 lead heading to the 7th. Prince Fielder would drive in the first Brewers run of the night in the 7th, and Rickie Weeks and J.J. Hardy would each plate a run in the 8th to bring the Brewers even with the Cards. I left Port Washington in the middle of the 8th, because of the early start to tomorrow's day. As I was putting gas in the car, Bill Hall went deep again, this time in the top of the ninth, to put the Brewers ahead for the first time tonight. Hall homered to put the Brewers up 4-3 last night as well. I wonder if he still wants out of Milwaukee. Salomon Torres struck out the side in the bottom of the ninth to give the Brewers their sixth straight win.

Tomorrow morning, we will drive down to Mt Vernon, IL to meet up for the start of our baseball trip. Tracy and I will be heading to St Louis tomorrow night to see CC Sabathia pitch. Then it will be off to Indianapolis Thursday, Wrigley Field on Friday afternoon, Cleveland on Saturday night, Detroit on Sunday afternoon, and then finishing with the Cubs and Brewers at Miller Park on Tuesday night. Monday will be a day of relaxation. I don't plan on spending a ton of money on this trip (thanks, car!), so I'll be bringing an appropriate hat for each game, and yes, I'm bringing the glove. Zest body wash? Check. Toothbrush? Check. ipod? Check. I think we're all set. And you can bet I'll get Tracy to sing the Bee Gees' "Nights on Broadway" with me while we're on the road.

July 23rd

We left for Busch Stadium as soon as we got to Mt Vernon, so that we could take in the stadium, get some good pictures and see batting practice. The stadium is beautiful, the atmosphere is great for baseball, and the fans here are really nice. I'm wearing a Brewers shirt, and instead of people looking like they want to beat me, I've had several people ask me if my drive in was safe. I've always sided with the Cubs as it relates to the Cubs/Cards rivalry, but that may change. I have a new found respect for St Louis. This is a family friendly environment that I will be returning to soon. And it smelled like baseball heaven from the second we walked in. Our seats are in Left Field Landing, a new section to Busch Stadium down the left field line. There are 28 seats in the section, and food and drink are included with the price of the ticket. After a quick trek to the Cardinals Team Store, we settled in for the game. Here's the play by play....

(Top of 1st) Rickie Weeks led off the game with a blooper down the right field line, with Albert Pujols, Brenden Ryan and Ryan Ludwick all converging, but none of them able to get to it. Weeks pulled in with a double, and the Brewers are immediately in good position to take an early lead. Braden Looper was able to get J.J. Hardy on strikes, and Ryan Braun grounded out to Cesar Izturis, with Weeks advancing to 3rd. Looper walked Prince Fielder on four straight pitches, and he wasn't even close to giving Fielder anything to hit. Corey Hart would fly out to center to end the inning. Opportunity wasted, but it's early.

(Bottom of 1st) Sabathia takes the hill tonight coming off of consecutive complete game victories, and is 3-0 in a Brewers uniform thus far. He walked Brendan Ryan to start off the inning, and Ryan Ludwick bunted him over to second on the sacrifice. Albert Pujols would take some mighty cuts, but would ground weakly to Sabathia, and would be retired, with Ryan advancing to 3rd. Troy Glaus flew out to deep left field to end the inning.

(Top of 2nd) This seems like an appropriate time to indulge in some of the fine foods available to us tonight. It looks like we have access to bottomless brats, dogs, nachos, soda, water and beer. It's set up "buffet" style, and everything looks great. Tracy and I each grab a plate and our beverages of choice, all while keeping an eye of the game. The Brewers went down pretty quietly in the 2nd, with Bill Hall (getting another start against a righty) grounding out to 2nd, Mike Cameron grounding out to short and Jason Kendall flying out to center.

(Bottom of 2nd) Here is a quick take on the food: The dog was good, the bratwurst was very good, and the nachos were solid. I will definitely be heading back for some more in the 5th or 6th. And I've noticed that food tastes really good when you pay for it six months in advance, which I've never really done before. Sabathia was able to get Yadier Molina on strikes to start the inning. Joe Mather, a utility man getting the start in left field tonight, hit a line drive to Weeks for the 2nd out of the inning. Cesar Izturis grounded hard back to Sabathia to end the inning. A couple sitting next to Tracy noticed he was wearing Tennessee orange, and told us that he and his family were from Knoxville, and now lived in St Louis. There names were Dipal and Britney. Good people and they are also brand new parents of a beautiful baby boy. It was good to meet you!

(Top of 3rd) CC Sabathia led off the inning by striking out, and he certainly wasn't cheated on his swings. I like watching CC hit, because he looks like he's trying to go deep every time, which I don't mind from a guy like him, because he has the capability to do it anytime he grabs a stick. Rickie Weeks singled to left, but was quickly picked off by Looper while J.J. Hardy was up. Hardy would single, and now the Brewers have one on with two out, instead of 2 on with 1 out for Braun. Braun singled to center, which would have scored Weeks, and Fielder was hit by a pitch to load the bases for Corey Hart. Hart looked anxious at the plate, but hit a lazy fly ball to right to end the inning. The Brewers have now stranded five base runners over the first three innings.

(Bottom of 3rd) LaRussa is still hitting his pitcher in the 8 hole, and Braden Looper starts off the 3rd inning by looking at a called 3rd strike. Skip Schumaker hit a grounder down to Fielder, which Prince would take himself for the 2nd out. Brendan Ryan hit a fly ball to Ryan Braun to end the inning. No score heading to the 4th.

(Top of 4) I really like the scoreboard here in St Louis. Not only do they have every game on the board at once, they rotate four games at a time, where they show a detailed account of who is up, who's on base and how many outs there are. There is also a running line on the bottom of the scoreboard with constant updates of who has homered, winning and losing pitchers, injuries, etc. Bill Hall led off the 4th with a fly ball to Joe Mather, who squeezed it for out # 1. Mike Cameron doubled to left field, but the Brewers were unable to capitalize, with Jason Kendall flying to center and Sabathia striking out to end the inning.

(Bottom of 4th) Jeff has been taking good care of us tonight, asking if we need anything to drink, and letting us know food will be served for another half hour or so. He has made us feel welcome all night, and yes, I will be heading back for some more grub in a moment. Ryan Ludwick struck out swinging to start the inning, and Albert Pujols would ground out to Billy Hall for the 2nd out. Troy Glaus would hit a weak roller up along 1st, and Jason Kendall was all over it, throwing to Fielder to retire the side. There is still no score here in St Louis. Time to eat again...

(Top of 5th) Rickie Weeks led off the inning by grounding out to 2nd as I filled my plate with nachos and one last brat. Have I mentioned how much I enjoy the brats here in St Louis? We'll most definitely be enjoying the Left Field Landing seats again in the future. As we settled back in, J.J. Hardy hit one out, just over the fence in left field, to give the Brewers a 1-0 lead. Hardy's batting average is at .293, as he has really turned his season around. Ryan Braun would triple down the right field line, and it looked like the Brewers were in business to add to their lead. Looper chose to pitch to Fielder, and got him on strikes. He looked like he checked his swing on strike three, and Ned Yost agreed, as he would be tossed while telling the home plate umpire what he thought. He was rung pretty quickly coming out of the dugout. Tracy and I wonder if he had to make a deuce, or if he had a hot date that he wanted to tend to. Corey Hart walked after Yost exited, but Bill Hall grounded to short to end the inning. But the Hardy dinger gives Sabathia a 1-0 lead heading to the bottom of the 5th.

(Bottom of 5th) Sabathia was able to get Yadier Molina to ground out to Fielder to start the inning. Joe Mather flew out to Braun, and Cesar Izturis grounded out to J.J. Hardy. I asked Tracy to take a look at the St Louis hits column, than begged him to not say a word. He knows the rules. I'm starting to get texts from people, but I refuse to read them, for obvious reasons.

(Top of 6th) Mike Cameron led off the inning with a solid base hit up the middle. The new pitcher for St. Louis is Kelvin Jimenez, as a double switch has been made, with Brendan Ryan moving over from 2B to SS, and Aaron Miles taking over at 2B. Jason Kendall was hit by a pitch to give the Brewers two on with nobody out. CC Sabathia laid down a good bunt, but the Cardinals were able to get Kendall at 2nd, with Cameron advancing to 3rd. Rickie Weeks came up big, hitting a towering sacrifice fly to left to score Cameron and give the Brewers a 2 run lead. Hardy hit into a fielder's choice to end the inning.

(Bottom of 6th) The final from Shea tonight is Mets 6 Phillies 3. Jose Reyes hit a three run homer to give the Mets the lead for good, and they now move back into a first place tie with Philadelphia. CC Sabathia has retired fifteen straight Cardinals since he walked Brendan Ryan to lead off the game. The first batter for St Louis in the 6th is Aaron Miles, who came into the game in the top of this inning. Miles flew out to Braun on the first pitch. Skip Schumaker would ground out to Hardy, and with two outs, Brendan Ryan would come to the plate. Ryan has walked and flied out to left. Ryan would work Sabathia deep in the count, and hit a scorcher, just past a diving Prince Fielder, to break up the no-no. The Cardinals fans erupted as Ryan rounded 1st. Sabathia retired seventeen straight batters before the first St. Louis hit of the night. So, we won't see history, but what we are witnessing is a hell of a major league baseball game, with the NL Wild Card hanging in the balance. Ryan Ludwick hit a hot shot down the 3rd base line, which Bill Hall was able to stop from going into left field, but Ludwick would reach base with the Cardinals' second hit. With two on and two out, Sabathia was able to get Albert Pujols to fly out to shallow center. Pujols is now 0-3 tonight. He came into the night hitting .450 vs lefties (45-100). At the end of 6th, it is 2-0 Brewers.

(Top of 7th) Ryan Braun led off the 7th with a clean single to left field. Even though Sabathia has been completely dominant tonight, it would be nice to put up some insurance runs for him. Prince Fielder would strike out to temporarily quiet the Brewers fans in attendance. Corey Hart would pop up to Troy Glaus in foul territory for the 2nd out. Bill Hall drew a walk, before Mike Cameron flied to left to end the inning.

(Bottom of 7th) Josh Gracin, I want to say he's an American Idol contestant from yesteryear, led in the singing of "Take Me Out to the Ballgame". Nothing to write home about, but he was competent in his rendition. Sabathia walked Troy Glaus to lead off the inning, but was able to get Yadier Molina to ground into a 6-4-3 double play. Joe Mather grounded out to Billy Hall to end the inning. We are having a great time tonight, and the Brewers are six outs away from taking a two game lead in the NL Wild Card. The Cubs currently lead the Diamondbacks 4-3 in the 5th.

(Top of 8th) Jason Isringhausen is on to pitch for the Cards. A smattering of boos could be heard from the stands, as "Izzy" lost his closer's role a while back. Jason Kendall led off the 8th by popping up to second. Sabathia, hitting for himself, grounded back to the pitcher for the second out of the inning. Rickie Weeks singled to left for his third hit of the night, but J.J. Hardy would strike out to end the inning.

(Bottom of 8th) As a result of another St. Louis double switch, Adam Kennedy led off the 8th for the Cards. He would come in to play 2B, and Aaron Miles moved to LF, and Isringhausen would hit in Joe Mather's spot in the order. Kennedy struck out on three pitches. Aaron Miles came up with one out, and singled to right center. With the tying run at 1st, Skip Schumaker dug in to face Sabathia. Schumaker is 0-2 thus far. With Miles running, Schumaker would hit a long fly to left field, but Ryan Braun would make the play, with Miles returning to 1st. Brendan Ryan would step in against Sabathia. He's had success tonight against CC, walking in the 1st, and breaking up the no-hit bid in the 6th. But here in the 8th, with a chance to extend the inning, Ryan would pop up to J.J. Hardy in shallow left field to end the inning. Heading to the 9th, it is 2-0 Brewers.

(Top of 9th) I mentioned before that the Cardinals fans are great fans, and it doesn't look like any of them have left yet. As Ryan Braun steps in, I tell Tracy that I believe Brauny and Fielder were going to hit back to back jacks that would send these Cardinals fans back to their homes with their heads down. Braun came through, hitting a line shot to right field to give the Brewers a 3-0 lead. Fiedler never got the chance to hit one out, as he was hit by a pitch again. Who knows if Isringhausen was throwing at him? Fielder ended up not putting a single ball in play tonight, getting hit by two pitches, walking once, and striking out twice. Corey Hart reached base on a 6-4 fielder's choice, and would steal second base with Billy Hall up. Hall struck out, and Mike Cameron flew out to right field to end the inning. It looks like Sabathia is coming out to finish what he started.

(Bottom of 9th) The Cardinals will send the heart of the order up in the 9th, with Ludwick, Pujols and Glaus all chomping at the bit to make something happen. Ludwick would go down looking, and Pujols would go down swinging, as Tracy and I got to our feet. We were not the only Brewers fans in Left Field Landing, and the other two are also standing. I did not get their names. It's up to Troy Glaus. After looking at a couple of fastballs for strikes, Glaus would ground weakly to Fielder, who made the play unassisted to give the Brewers a 3-0 win, their 7th in a row, and a two game lead in the NL Wild Card race. What an incredible way to start our baseball trip.

Driving back to Mt Vernon, we listened to the end of the Cubs game, and they hung on to win tonight in Arizona. They put up six in the 8th to take a commanding 10-3 lead, and the final would be 10-6. The Cubs start a 4 game series at home with Florida tomorrow afternoon.

July 24th

This morning, we drove to Indianapolis, and I was pleasantly surprised to see that the hotel we were staying in had a

Damon's Grill in it. My eyes lit up. I haven't had Damon's in years, and used my boyish puppy dog eyes to plant the seed with Tracy that we should eat there later. It didn't go down exactly like that, but however it went down, it worked. After we checked in, we relaxed for a bit, and found a 3-par golf course in the phone book, and called for directions. Now, I suck at golf, but I think the more I do it, the more I'll enjoy it, and maybe some day, I'll develop a little bit of a game. The name of the place was Shortee's, and when we pulled up, we decided to hit a bucket at the driving range before we started on our nine holes. It was really nice out, and regardless of how well we were hitting, it felt great to be out in the sun. We walked past a good looking family who were also out enjoying some golf, and before you start giving me the eyebrow, by good looking, I mean fit, healthy, etc. Tracy and I each hit our bucket, and started to head back to the clubhouse to get our scorecards for the course. As we were walking back, I noticed that the gentleman that was with his family kind of looked familiar, but I couldn't immediately place him. It wasn't until I saw his son's shirt, with a GEORGE 3 on the back, that I realized that it was Jeff George. I can't tell you how many times I drafted Jeff George in the Fugazzi Fantasy Football League, and I consider myself a big fan of his. I walked up to him and asked if he was indeed Jeff George, and he said yes, so I shook his hand. It was great to meet someone I've "owned". I immediately called my friends to share my brush with celebrity.

On the course, I surprised myself with a par on the 1st hole, after sinking an 18 foot putt. How do I know it was 18 feet? Feel. I led by three strokes after one, and I think I can get addicted to this game really quick. Tracy took the 2nd hole, and I led by 1 going into the 3rd. I would take holes 3 and 4, and got my lead back up to three, heading into the 5th hole. Tracy would take the 74 yard 5th hole by one stroke, and pulled to within two strokes of my lead. We each bogeyed # 6, and I had a terrible 7th hole, losing three strokes to Tracy, and I now trail by one. We each bogeyed 8, and it was a one stroke contest heading to 9. Then I pulled a Kevin Costner in *Tin Cup*, and scored a 9 on the 9th. Tracy would have got a par on the 9th, had he not messed with me, and jokingly 7 putted the final hole for the one stroke win. I will get my revenge next Tuesday in Wauwatosa, my friend. But hey, I got a nice tan, enjoyed the weather, and there's still a ball game to enjoy tonight. Walking back from the 9th hole, I checked the Mets score, and was happy to see that they hung on to beat the Phillies this afternoon, 3-1. We are now all alone in first in the NL East. It's fun to say. First place in the East. I wonder if Willie Randolph is rooting for them, or hopes they have another historic collapse.

We headed back to the hotel, and did indeed get a table for two at Damon's. The Cubs beat Florida today, so for the moment, the Brewers are a game and a half back in the Central. They finish out there four game series with St Louis tonight, and will try to complete their first 7-0 road trip in franchise history. The Damon's was just like I remembered. I ordered some southwest spring rolls and an order of fries, with a side of blue cheese, like the old days. Tracy enjoyed some hot wings, and we mingled with the other patrons on the deck. Now it's off to Victory Field for the game....

We chose to come to Indianapolis because of all the great things I've read about Victory Filed online. The stadium was great, and not just for a minor league field. It had great sight lines, an extensive menu and a pretty good fan base. 11,110 people showed up tonight to see the last place Indianapolis Indians, the AAA affiliate of the Pittsburgh Pirates, beat the Charlotte Knights, who are the AAA affiliate of the Chicago White Sox, 8-3. Jimmy Barthmaier, the Indians starting pitcher tonight, only lasted 2/3 of an inning, after he took a line drive off of the wrist on his pitching hand. I figured the next hurler for the Indians would need all kinds of time to get loose, so I took this opportunity to get a dog and a beer. The dog wasn't bad, but it wasn't great. Maybe I was full from the Damon's. The starting pitcher for the Knights was named Charlie Haeger, and he was a knuckleballer, as we noticed while he was warming up prior to the start of the game. Haeger had a 3-2 lead heading into the 7th tonight, but Indianapolis would put up six in the 7th, their biggest inning of the year, to give the Indians a comfy 8-3 lead. We left in the middle of the 8th, but that lead would indeed hold up. We got some great pictures of the field under the lights on the way out. As we were leaving the game, the Brewers were down 3-2 in the 7th. As we were getting ready

for bed (early morning ahead for trip to Wrigley), we had Baseball
Tonight on in the background to see if the Brewers could mount a
comeback. Guess how many text messages I received when
Ryan Braun took Ryan Franklin deep for a two run homer to give
the Brewers the lead? Five. Franklin also gave up the go ahead
dinger to Hall on Monday night. He's had a rough week. Torres
came on to earn his 18th save, and the Brewers have done the
unthinkable. They have swept the Cards on the road in a four
game series. Eight straight wins for the Brewers and a three
game lead in the NL Wild Card race. Tomorrow morning, we'll be
driving to Chicago for the Marlins/Cubs game. It will be the only
game going on in the bigs, so there will be no scoreboard
watching, just people watching, and of course the game at hand.

July 25th

After stopping for "breakfast" at White Castle in
Indianapolis, we got to Chicago around 11:00, and promptly found
a guy waiting to give up his personal driveway space for a
handsome fee of $40. Could we have found a space down the
road without shelling out $40? Probably, but hey, we're on
vacation, let's spend our time enjoying ourselves, and not
worrying about how much parking was, or walking a mile to the
game. We enjoyed lunch at the Cubby Bear. My boy Tracy
enjoyed some wings again, and I went with a Chicken Tender
Melt. It was pretty good, and the restaurant was buzzing, hours
before first pitch. After lunch, we walked around for a bit, taking in
all the Wrigley has to offer, and then had a drink at Goose
Gardens. The waitress laughed me at when I tried to order a
Mike's Hard Lemonade, and Tracy laughed even harder at me
when I ordered a Cubby Blue Berry Ale. He was probably
embarrassed to be seen with me, ordering a fruity beer. But it
was really good, certainly quenching my thirst in the hot, hot sun.
I bought some sunglasses on impulse before we walked into the
friendly confines.

Our seats were all the way down the left field line, about twelve rows up. We had a great view of the filed. Today's starters were Ryan Dempster for the Cubs and Josh Johnson for the Marlins. Alfonso Soriano would also be making his return to the Cubs lineup today. He has been on the DL since early June. Florida scored first today when Josh Willingham hit an RBI double off Dempster in the 2nd. The Cubs got one right back on a Geovanny Soto homer in the bottom of the 2nd. Reed Johnson homered to make it 2-1 Cubs in the 5th. Tracy went out to get a dog right around that time, and I decided to pass on the Wrigley cuisine. I've never been impressed with the food at Wrigley. And, honestly, the fans are starting to get to me after six or seven visits here. I have great memories of the Cubs as a kid, but coming to a game at Wrigley is much different than seeing a game at Miller Park or Busch Stadium. I could never take my daughter here, at least not for a while. Tracy wasn't too impressed with his dog; however, we were both entertained by the vendors in our section. One in particular resembled Froggy from the Little Rascals, and screamed great lines like, "I got hot dogs here for Christ's sake" and "Have a hot dog, I'm not doing this for my health".

Jeff Samardzija made his major league debut relieving Ryan Dempster in the 7th, and struck out the very first batter he faced. But the Marlins did get to him, and Jorge Cantu doubled in a run to tie the game. In the top of the 9th, Jeremy Hermida was asked to come off the bench to pinch hit for Paul Hoover, the Marlins catcher. Hermida is the everyday right fielder for the Marlins, but was given the day off today. He promptly hit the first pitch he saw off of Bob Howry to Sheffield Ave to give the Marlins a 3-2 lead. That'll sober up these Cubs fans in a heartbeat. Kevin Gregg came on to get the last three outs to give the Marlins the win. If the Brewers win tonight, they will share the NL Central lead with the Cubs.

Immediately after the game, Tracy and I drove to South Bend, IN to grab some dinner at Roc's Sports Café. I had some OK nachos, and Tracy enjoyed wings (third time on trip thus far, 2nd time today), and a burger of some sort. We followed the Mets and Brewers games on ESPN as we ate. Mike Pelfrey beat the Cardinals tonight, 7-2, and the Phillies were beat by the Braves, so the Mets have a 2 game lead now in the NL East. The Brewers were up 1-0 in the 6th when we left the restaurant. We were on our way to the movie theater to see *Step Brothers* with Will Ferrell and John C Reilly. I turned my cell phone off during the movie (they ask you too, so others can enjoy the picture). The movie was everything I thought it would be. There were some great lines that I'm sure I'll use in my everyday life. I'll sure I'll buy this for Tracy as a Christmas gift this year, as something to remember our adventure by. When I got back to the hotel, I was disappointed to see the Brewers lost 3-1. The 8 game winning streak is over, but no ground lost in the standings with the Cubs and Cards losing today as well. We are sleeping in tomorrow morning before heading to Cleveland. Damn do I love the king size hotel beds, with the sheets tucked in tight, and the dozen or so pillows.

July 26th

We had a little bit of an adventure in Cleveland this afternoon. We could not find out hotel, so we pulled over on St Clair Ave to call them, to see exactly where they were located. We were looking for the Sheraton, but when Tracy called them, they answered "Crown Plaza". He looked confused, but they explained that they changed the name a while back, and it turns out, we were right across the street from them. But when we went in to check in, they told Tracy that they did not have a reservation for him. He provided a confirmation number and the name of the person he spoke with, and they told him they don't have anyone by that name working there (Tyra, I believe). They told Tracy they did not have any rooms available, and after a few cold stares, they were some how able to accommodate us. I'm not sure exactly how that works, but we went from not having a single room available to checking in to room 925 within minutes. Once we were situated, we met up with my oldest friend in the world, Sean. Sean and I go back to 1982. He and his father are the reason that I am a Cleveland Browns fan. Sean and his family live in Cleveland now, and the three of us met at Local Heroes for dinner. Local Heroes used to be Cooperstown, the restaurant owned by Alice Cooper, and it doesn't look that different, and the food is still pretty good. Tracy had, you guessed it, hot wings. I enjoyed a roast beef sandwich and some chipotle orange wings. For the life of me, I can't remember what Sean ordered, and I hope that doesn't make me any less of a friend. We talked for a while, and Sean shared some great news with us. He and his wife Jackie are expecting their second child this December. During dinner, the Cubs had lost their game with Florida in the 12th inning, giving the Brewers another opportunity later tonight to jump into first place.

We entered Progressive Field about 45 minutes prior to first pitch. The Indians hosted the Twins tonight, with Fausto Carmona returning from the DL to face Scott Baker. This is my 2nd time seeing a game here, and the first time for Tracy. Before we settled in, we made a quick stop to the Indians Team Store. The game was a blowout from "Play Ball!", as the Twins put up 6 runs in the 1st and 3 in the 3rd to take a quick 9-0 lead. We were already planning what to do after the game, possibly leaving early. I ordered a dog and a brat, but didn't finish either. They were both good, but I was still full from the sandwich at Local Heroes. After the Indians mounted a small comeback, scoring one in the 5th and two in the 6th, we decided to leave with the Twins up 9-3. We headed to Zocalo Mexican Grill for some drinks. Tonight was the first time I ever had "shots", as the kids call them. I believe it was Patron. I don't drink outside of a beer here and there at the ball game, and I didn't know what to expect. It had no real effect on me initially, but later that night, Tracy and I were engaging in an argument in the hotel lobby, about whether eating well after midnight will make you feel sluggish and make you want to sleep later. That's the stance I took as we were contemplating ordering a pizza at 1:30am. We had to get up at 7:00 the next morning, and I didn't think I could wake up that early if I'm downing a pizza at 2:00 a.m.

When we got back to our room, I saw that the Brewers came back from a 4-2 deficit to tie the Astros on a two run homer by Ryan Braun, and took the lead for good on a Bill Hall single in the 8th. The final score was 6-4 Brewers, and they now share the best record in the NL with the Cubs. Fernando Tatis provided some dramatics for the Mets tonight, hitting a home run in the 9th to tie the Cardinals, but Albert Pujols would hit a two run homer in the 14th inning to beat the Mets, 10-8. Philadelphia won a wild one with Atlanta to pull within a game of the Mets. With Philadelphia up 3 to 0, Atlanta scored nine runs in the 4th, only to give up seven in the 5th. The final was 10-9 Phillies. Now it's off to bed for us, as we head to Detroit tomorrow. I heard the food isn't great at Comerica. Maybe I should have ordered that pizza.

July 27th

Tracy and I enjoyed some McDonald's this morning before hitting the road. The plan for today is to hit Detroit around 11:00, pick up some merchandise in the gift shop, walk around and see what Comerica Park has to offer, and then see a no-hitter. If the no-hitter was gone before the 7th inning, we would leave to beat the traffic, and try to get back to Wisconsin before it got too late. We are looking at about a seven hour drive tonight, and we're both a little tired from last night. Both teams collected hits in the first inning, so we would not be witnessing history today. Comerica Park is nice, but I'm not connecting with it like I did Busch Stadium. There are some really neat statues, and a real sense of history displayed all over the place, but I'm not feeling it, for some reason. It may be the McDonald's settling in. Anyway, with the score 6-2 Tigers after 6 innings, we started to walk out. I would find out later on my cell phone that the Tigers hung on to beat the White Sox, 6-4. The dog I had was pretty good. It was a Ball Park Frank, and it may have been the best hot dog I've had thus far on the trip. That will change on Tuesday night, when we hit Miller Park. Not a bad stadium, but again, I don't see myself rushing back here.

The Mets had an easy time with the Cardinals today, as Johan Santana went the distance in a 9-1 win. David Wright homered, and raised his RBI total to 82, which is good for 3rd in the NL league. Jose Reyes collected two hits to raise his batting average to .302. The Phillies won another wild one from the Braves, 12-10, so the Mets hang on to their one game lead for the time being.

The Brewers were not able to build on their momentum from last night, and got smothered by the Astros, 11-6. Houston collected 16 hits, and scored 7 runs in the 5th, all off of Milwaukee starter, Jeff Suppan. Don't look now, but Suppan is 5-7 with an ERA over 5.00. He could be the odd man out if we make the postseason. He's proven in the past to be money in October, so hopefully he can turn it around. The Cubs won today, so the Brewers fall a game back in the Central. They still have a three game lead over the Cards for the NL Wild Card.

The biggest series of the season kicks off tomorrow night as the Cubs come into Miller Park for a four game series. It will be CC Sabathia vs Ted Lilly in the opener. All four games have been sold out for some time. I am going to get some things done at home, than head to Port Washington to see my daughter and then watch the game with Tracy. This is what we've been waiting for all season. We've taken 4 of 6 from the Cubs at Wrigley, now it's our turn to host the I-94 Series and show the world what we are made of. I think we have the talent to take 3 of 4, and we have our two studs pitching Monday and Tuesday. It should be an incredible atmosphere at Miller Park.

July 28th

Tonight's game between the Brewers and Cubs at Miller Park had everything you would want in a game between two teams that are running neck and neck in a hotly contended divisional race. The attendance tonight was 45,311, the third largest crowd in Miller Park history. CC Sabathia took the hill for the Brewers, who despite only having four starts under his belt in the National League, is already tied with teammate Ben Sheets for the NL lead in complete games with 3. The Cubs countered with Ted Lilly, who was on his game tonight. The Cubs plated one run in the top of the 1st, and Alfonso Soriano hit a solo homer to left field in the 3rd to give the Cubs a 2-0 lead. That's where it stood until the bottom of 6th, when J.J. Hardy and Ryan Braun hit back to back homers to tie the game. Braun's home run damn near cleared Bernie Brewer's slide. From the start of the game, it sounded like it was about 50/50 Cubs/Brewers fans, but Braun's bomb quickly quieted the Cubs fans and a thunderous applause shook the ball yard. After Lilly walked Prince Fielder, the Cubs went to Bob Howry to keep the game knotted at 2, but the first hitter he faced, Corey Hart, doubled home Fielder to give the Brewers their first lead of the night.

But in the top of the seventh, all momentum was lost as Derrick Lee stepped up with the bases loaded. It was widely known around major league baseball that Lee is a great hitter with the bases loaded, but he also hits into a lot of double plays. Sabathia was able to get Lee to ground to Hardy, for what all Brewers fans thought was an inning ending twin killing, however, Rickie Weeks' throw to first was well off the mark, and into the stands, scoring two Cubs. That would be the last batter that Sabathia faced, giving way to David Riske. The euphoria in the bottom of the sixth was now replaced by a cascade of boos directed at the young second basemen. The Cubs now lead 4-3. But a baseball game has a funny way of teasing with your emotions, and in the bottom of the seventh, Russell Branyan was asked by Ned Yost to pinch hit for David Riske, and promptly took Howry deep to tie the game at 4.

Heading into the ninth, the Cubs and Brewers were still tied at 4, and Yost brought in his closer to keep things that way. Salomon Torres, who has been lights out since assuming the closers role, was anything but that tonight, although this was not a save situation (like that matters). Torres walked three and gave up two hits, as the Cubs scored two in the top of the ninth. Carlos Marmol struck out two Brewers in the bottom of the ninth in route to his fifth save of the year.

Whether you were a Brewers fan, a Cubs fan, or just a fan of baseball in general, tonight's game at Miller Park was a great game. It had good pitching, timely hitting, and all the drama you could ask for. It will be interesting to see if the Weeks error in the 7th will cause Yost to replace him late in games with Durham or

Counsell. Durham is not a great defensive player himself, but most certainly an upgrade from Weeks. Counsell would be the more obvious choice in these situations.

Tonight in Miami, the Mets blew a golden opportunity to increase their lead over Philadelphia to a game and a half, as the bullpen combined to allow six runs after John Maine left the game in the fifth with shoulder stiffness. They took a one run lead (3-2) into the bottom of the eighth before surrendering five runs to the Marlins. Fernando Tatis hit an RBI triple in the 2nd inning, and raised his batting average to .322. New York remains a half game ahead of the Phillies, and a game ahead of the Marlins.

I see my boy Tracy falling asleep there on the couch, and that is my signal to put this baby to bed for the night. Tomorrow morning, we may hit the links again before heading to Miller Park for a little Ben Sheets/Carlos Zambrano, which I have been informed will be contested inside of a 15 foot high steel cage.

July 29th

The trade deadline is Thursday afternoon, and the Manny Ramirez rumors are circling the wagons. I hear Mets. I hear Dodgers. I hear Marlins. The Red Sox will certainly not trade him to an American League team. I've heard Pedro Martinez has been campaigning for the Mets to bring Manny in. I can honestly see any of these three teams making a strong bid, as he may be the best right handed hitter in the bigs in the past 30 years. Other smaller deals may get done in the next few days as playoff contenders continue to add those final pieces to their championship puzzle.

The Mets got a solid performance tonight from Oliver Perez, as well as the bullpen, scattering six hits and striking out eleven Marlins. New York took a 2-1 lead into the 8th, when Carlos Delgado hit his 23rd home run of the season to extend the lead to 4-1. Boy, Delgado is quietly turning his season around. I didn't think he had that many dingers, and the average is up to .263. We're gonna need that stick in these last two months or so. Billy Wagner did the honors in the 9th, notching his 27th save. The Phillies kept pace with the Mets by beating the Nationals, 2-1.

Tracy and I hit Miller Park around 5:00. I am sore as hell, for two reasons. First, we got in 18 holes today at Doyne Park. It was another 3-par, but remember, I am a lazy piece of trash, and my body isn't quite used to all the walking and swinging and such. Second, I did the splits falling on the way to the stadium just before entering. I slipped on some standing water, and went straight down, but initially was more concerned that I would get my glove wet. I did. Shit! I did appreciate the four Cubs fans laughing at me as I helped myself up. If I had a pair, I would have approached them, but I just kept walking, all the time fantasizing about kicking each of them in their cursed testicles. Steve Bartman, bitches! Leon Durham, assholes!

Tracy has been talking about hitting for the sausage cycle since I brought it up earlier in the baseball trip. Tonight, we each grabbed a chorizo during batting practice. It was my first chorizo at Miller Park, and my last. They served it in a tortilla with salsa, just not what I was expecting. In the 3rd, Tracy went with the brat and the dog, and was already proclaiming victory. We agreed last week that he only had to go with four of the five sausages to constitute the sausage cycle. Neither one of us were into getting a polish tonight. I didn't have much of an appetite. My head hurt, and I was in pain from the fall. The game itself was pretty good, until we left in the 6th to make sausage history. Tracy and I left for the concession stand together to get a couple of Italians, and as we waited in line, the Brewers went from being down 1-0 to down 6-0 in about ten minutes. The Cubs were hitting Sheets hard, and everything was finding a hole or a gap. Just so that there was no controversy, Tracy also got a piping hot pretzel to chase his four sausages, and as he finished his Italian, I proclaimed him the new King of Klements. He will pay for that tomorrow, on the road back to Chattanooga. Two nights ago, it was White Castle, and tonight, the sausage cycle…any toilet he christens in the next few days will not have a chance. Kathy, I apologize in advance for the smell.

With the score 6-0 in the 7th, we decided to leave. Tracy and Kathy have a long drive back tomorrow, and I have to get up early for work the next day. The baseball trip of 2008 is now in the books. We agreed to definitely do it again soon. Tracy told me on the way back that I will always be family. That meant a lot. You are my brother, Tracy. I had a wonderful time these past seven days.

The final tonight was 7-1 Cubs. After the first ever 7-0 road trip in franchise history, the Brewers are now 1-4 on the current homestand, and have squandered their two best chances at beating the Cubs in the series. We are now three back of the Cubs, but still a game ahead of the Cards.

July 30th

The Brewers and Cubs were featured on ESPN tonight, and this would have been a great opportunity for the Brewers to turn this thing around and take it to the Cubs in front of a national audience. But it wasn't meant to be. Manny Parra's night at the plate was much better that his night on the mound, as he was 2-2 with a double and a triple. In 5 1/3 innings pitched, Parra walked four and gave up eight hits, letting five runs cross the plate. The Brewers as a team was 0-8 with runners in scoring position, they are 1-15 so far in this series, and are an atrocious 3-60 with RISP in their last eight games. Corey Hart was quoted as saying that the Cubs are "the better team in July, but that doesn't make them world champs yet". The final was 7-2, as Prince Fielder hit his 21st homer of the season in the 9th, after the dust had settled. With the Cardinals winning tonight, the Brewers find themselves mere percentage points ahead of St. Louis for the NL Wild Card.

The Mets fell out of first place tonight, losing to the Marlins 7-5. Mike Pelfrey was not sharp, and the Mets also could not come up big when it counted. The Mets also do not look like they will be a factor in the Manny sweepstakes, as the Marlins look to be the favorites to land the slugger. Even if the Mets don't deal for

Man-Ram, they could still go after a corner outfielder after July 31st, assuming the player clears waivers. I've heard the name Raul Ibanez bantered about recently. We'll have to see what happens.

July 31st

     Swept...Cubs 11, Brewers 4. All the momentum gained in St. Louis last week is gone. The Brewers could have been as many as three games up on the Cubs by the end of today, but by getting swept, we are now right back where we were at the all star break, five games back. The Cardinals lost today, so we are still tied with them for the Wild Card lead, but getting swept by the Cubs at home really sucks. This was *thee* series that Brewers fans circled on the schedule when it came out last fall. There's not much more I can say. So I won't.

     The Brewers will head back on the road for three in Atlanta, before heading to Cincinnati next week. The Mets had today off, and will travel to Houston for a three game set. It was a year ago today that I got the idea to write this book, at the Mets/Brewers game at Miller Park, in Tom Glavine's attempt to win # 300. That night, I dreamt of a Mets/Brewers NLCS at the end of the 2007 season. Neither team made the playoffs, as they both blew huge division leads in the second half. As I look at the last two months of the season, the Brewers still have a chance to win the Central, but their confidence took a knee to the groin this week. They are still in good position to win the Wild Card, and I would like their chances in a short series with Sabathia and Sheets going back to back. The Mets find themselves a game behind the Phillies with 2 months left, and they seem to have turned it up a notch since making a managerial change in early June. They also have the pitching to do damage in the playoffs. It looks like my wish could still come true.

     A quick update as it relates to the trading deadline: Manny Ramirez was shipped to the Dodgers in a three team deal that sent Jason Bay to the Red Sox and four prospects to the Pirates. Another future hall of famer was moved, as Ken Griffey, Jr. was dealt to the Chicago White Sox. With Ivan Rodriquez being traded to the Yankees earlier in the week, that is three first ballot hall of famers moving to contenders in the last three days before the trading deadline passes.

5. Is This Really Happening? Yes!

August 1st

The Atlanta Braves found themselves in the rare position of sellers turning the trading fury that occurred over the past few weeks. They traded Mark Teixeira to the Angels last week, knowing they probably will not be able to sign after the season. With Chipper Jones on the DL, the Brewers were facing a very vulnerable Braves lineup tonight, as Jeff Suppan took the hill, trying to stop the bleeding from the sweep of the Cubs. The Brewers do have a seven game road winning streak they can try to extend as well. From the start of the game, the Brewers looked determined to turn things around, scoring two in the 1st, and another run in the 2nd. They knocked out Braves starter Chuck James in the 3rd, with home runs from Prince Fielder and Mike Cameron. Fielder has now homered in three straight games. The Brewers led 6-0 after three innings, and the score did not change until the 8th, when the Brewers added three more to make it 9-0. Jeff Suppan pitched seven shutout innings, before letting the bullpen finish off Atlanta, 9-0 the final. The Cubs lost this afternoon, so the Crew find themselves 4 back. The Cardinals won, and we remain tied for the NL Wild Card lead. CC goes tomorrow night, as the Brewers look for their ninth straight road win.

The Mets bullpen cost us the game in Houston tonight. Heading into the 8th, they were deadlocked with the Astros, 3-3, but Aaron Heilman gave up a grand slam to Mark Loretta to give the Astros a 7-3 lead. Jose Valverde retired the Mets in order in the ninth to seal the deal for Houston. Heilman is now 1-5, and the ERA is a shade over 5.00. I would have liked the Mets to go after a reliever or two yesterday, as it seems that the bullpen is the glaring weakness lately. With the Phillies losing, the Mets are still just a game back, but the Marlins are right there, a half a game behind New York. Johan is going tomorrow night, coming off his first complete game victory in a Mets uniform. We could use more of the same, and give the bullpen the night off.

August 2nd

Happy birthday wishes to Joe Dahms. Joe is going to be a father for the first time later this month, but don't expect him in my fantasy football league anytime soon. I think it's because we swear too much on the website, and we certainly do throw good taste out the window when it comes to posting stories and polls. Joe, just so you know, I will continue to aggressively pursue you for the league. I know you'd enjoy it, and we need good men like you. If you did indeed join the league one day, I'm sure the other 12 owners will get us confused like our co-workers in Madison and our members do, because of the shockingly similar ways our first names are spelled. Joe and Joey; mistaking that consistently is like mistaking the numbers 123 and 1234. If you were an accountant and did that...fired. OK, moving on...

The Brewers got more of the national spotlight today, as their game with Atlanta was the FOX game of the week. Before they took the field, the Cubs had already beaten the Pirates, so a win today would keep them within games games of the NL Central lead. The pitching matchup favors Milwaukee, as CC Sabathia opposes Charlie Morton. I can't tell you anything about Charlie Morton. I'm relying on mlb.com to tell me that he is making his 9th major league start this afternoon, and that thus far, he is 2-5 with an ERA of 6.56. But I've seen enough baseball games to tell you that none of this matters, and that we still have to perform inside the white lines. Talking about it ain't gonna accomplish anything.

Casey Kotchman got the Braves on the board with an RBI single in the 1st. Kotchman came over in the Teixiera deal last week. Sabathia allowed a leadoff single to Kelly Johnson in the 2nd, but after that, he would retire 16 of the next 17 Braves he faced. Unfortunately, Charlie Morton had only allowed one hit through six innings, a Craig Counsell single in the 2nd inning. Morton had a 1-0 lead heading to the 7th, but Prince Fielder got the Brewers on the board, finally, with a solo HR, to tie the game, and later in the inning, Jason Kendall came up huge with an RBI double, scoring Craig Counsell to give the Brewers the 2-1 lead. After the Brewers chased Morton from the game, Prince Fielder came up in the 8th and jacked a two run homer off of Rafael Soriano to give the Brewers a 4-1 lead. Sabathia came out to pitch in the 9th, but his pitch count was high, and after walking a batter with one out, Yost went to Torres to get the last two outs. Torres did allow an RBI single to Kelly Johnson to cut the lead to 4-2, but that is as close as the Braves got. Put another check mark in the win column for the Brewers. That is nine straight road wins, tying a franchise record. Sabathia is now 5-0 with a 1.88 ERA in six starts with the Brewers.

The news was not so good for my Mets tonight, as the gall damn bullpen blew another great start from Johan Santana. Santana handed a 4-1 lead to his pen, and Billy Wagner blew the save in the 9th, and Aaron Heilman gave the game away in the 10th. We are now two games out, and have actually fallen to third place, a half game behind the Fish. For those of you wondering, "gall damn" was what my Grandma used to say to keep it clean around us kids, also assuring her a cozy spot in heaven. I'll notice myself using it a lot myself these days, but I always chase it with an f-bomb or twelve, which pretty much cancels out the effort of saying "gall damn" in the first place.

August 3rd

Baseball is a game filled with superstition. There are rally caps. There's the idea of the pitcher not stepping on the white lines coming in and out of innings. Batters have all kinds of rituals at the plate, etc. Well, what ever I did today as a fan before the Mets and Brewers played, I will try not to do again, in the order I did them. You see, neither team scored a single run today as the Mets got swept by Houston, losing 4-0, and Ben Sheets and the Brewers were blanked by Atlanta, 5-0, ending Milwaukee's nine game road winning streak. So, never again, between the hours of 8:00 and 11:30 am on a Sunday morning, will I ever, in this exact order, wake my daughter, share a bowl of Reese's Puffs cereal with her, take a shower while she watches Winnie the Pooh Springtime with Roo on digital video disc, play soccer with her and Amber outside, draw various members of my family with Gracie on her Barbie etch-a-sketch, then give her some milk while I read to her as she falls asleep on my lap. Never again...it's bad luck!

August 4th

I have been resisting the temptation to comment about the whole Brett Favre situation, but I gotta get this off my chest. Initially, I was pretty intrigued about the idea of Favre coming back to the Pack. All along, I've empathized with Aaron Rodgers, and really wanted to see him succeed as the new Packers starting QB, but in my heart of hearts, I wanted to see Favre return for one more season. But this has turned into a joke. Both Favre and the Packers look ridiculous the way this has transpired. Whether he admits to care about it or not, Favre has tarnished his legacy. And the Packers have embarrassed themselves by alienating the greatest QB of our generation. Both sides need to take equal blame. Favre should not have retired so soon after the season ended, and the Packers should not have named Rodgers as the starter before camp opened up. Even if Favre was long gone, how does Rodgers assume the role as starter without having ever started a game in his NFL career? There has to be a reason that the Packers drafted Brian Brohm in the 2nd round, and Matt Flynn in the 7th round this past April. You want there to be competition in the pre-season to see who the very best players are at each position. I'm totally embarrassed by the whole situation. If Favre ends up in Minnesota or Chicago, the Packers are going to be the laughing stock of the league for years to come, and if Favre returns and isn't 110% committed to giving it his all, the team that takes a chance on him will look foolish too. I'm sure there is more to this story that we may never hear about, but there has got to be a reason why Favre walked away, so emotionally in early March. What a circus!

And speaking of unwanted drama, the Brewers got some attention tonight that they didn't want or need, in the form of an in-house scuffle between Prince Fielder and Manny Parra in the Brewers' dugout, during the 7th inning of the Brewers game at Cincinnati tonight. Parra was cruising early, carrying a no-hitter into the 5th, but gave up four runs in the 5th, and two more in the 6th before being pinch hit for in the bottom half of the inning. Parra and Fielder could be seen in the dugout exchanging words, when out of nowhere, Fielder shoved Parra, and then took a swipe at his head, before being detained by four or five teammates. The Brewers encountered something similar to this last season, on August 2nd against the Mets. Johnny Estrada and Tony Graffanino were seen shouting at Ned Yost in the Brewers' dugout, and both players had to be restrained by various players. When something like this happens, one of two things usually happens. Either it creates a spark in the clubhouse, and lights a fire under the team. Or, it divides the team, and can ruin team chemistry, and ultimately end a team's season. This team has too many leaders, and too much talent to let something like this affect them. Because these games are televised, every little detail is picked up on camera, and re-played on dozens of cable channels and hundreds of websites within hours. The reality of it is, this kind of stuff happens more than you'd think, but gets magnified in this TMZ society we live in. These are competitors, and you almost like to see this from time to time, to show us fans that they give a shit. Nobody got hurt, and now we move on. The Brewers wound up losing 6-3, but I'll be interested to see how they respond tomorrow night.

The Mets were off tonight, and start a three game series with the San Diego Padres tomorrow night. They will be without Billy Wagner, who was placed on the 15 day disabled list this afternoon to rehabilitate his ailing pitching arm. Aaron Heilman will get the first crack at closing for the Mets, per Jerry Manuel. The Mets have not recorded a single save this year by anyone other than Billy Wagner, so we'll have to see how this plays out. The bullpen has been a glaring weakness as of late.

August 5th

It's been 24 hours since the Parra/Fielder scuffle, and how have the Brewers responded? Well. Very well. The Brewers knocked around Edison Volquez all night, totaling 6 extra base hits, 13 hits total, and beating up on the Reds, 8-1. The highlight of the night came in the 7th inning. After Prince Fielder was knocked down in successive pitches by Cincinnati reliever Nick Masset, he drilled the next pitch about 410 to center field for a long home run, and then flicked his bat towards the dugout like it was a # 2 pencil. Dave Bush, who was recently named the 5th starter (home and away), looked great tonight, going seven strong innings, and striking out 7 in the process. Fielder has apologized about his actions, but will not apologize about the intensity. Again, if this wakes the team up, it's not the worst thing in the world. If you think Matt Gitzlaff and Jason Pawlowksi didn't have their differences in those Wrens dugouts in 4th grade, then you are kidding yourself. Ya Goddamn right they did, because they were competitors.

The Mets began a three game series with the San Diego Padres tonight, and so help me, if they drop so much as one 2-1 game in this series, someone's house is getting toilet papered. With the Mets down 1-0 in the 4th, Fernando Tatis hit a big fly over the left field wall to tie the game at 1-1. Tatis has been quite a story for the Mets, with a batting average of .316. He has been some kind of clutch since his early season call up. Adrian Gonzalez hit a solo knock in the sixth to give the Padres a 2-1 lead, and Mr. Tatis came up huge again in the bottom of the sixth, hitting a 3 run homer down the left field line off of former Brewers closer, Mike Adams. Tatis recalled Carlton Fisk, waving this one fair as he hopped out of the batter's box. The Mets added a couple of late runs, to take a 6-2 lead heading into the 9th. Temporary closer Aaron Heilman would come on in the 9th, but with a four run lead, this would not be considered a save situation. He was awful, giving up a walk, a single and a three run homer to Jody Gerut to make it 6-5. He only retired one batter. Joe Smith would come on and get the second out, and Jerry Manuel would call upon Scott Schoeneweis to get the final out and secure the win for the Metropolitans. The Marlins beat the Phillies, so the Mets remain in 3rd place, but only 2 back of Philadelphia for the NL East lead. Despite the 9th inning scare, this was a good win for the Mets. To lose another nail biter to the Padres would have been devastating for the Mets, and for one of you, with the toilet paper and all. What a jerk I am!

August 6th

As I'm getting ready to write about the Brewers game in Cincinnati this afternoon, and tonight's Mets game against the Padres, all I can do is stare at my monitor, in shock. The writing has been on the wall for awhile, but now that it's happened, and it doesn't seem real. Brett Favre is a New York Jet. It even feels strange to type it. Brett Favre is the starting QB of the New York Jets. The trade just went down a half hour ago, and I'm already getting a bunch of text messages from friends and family "breaking the story" to me. This kind of feels like when you break up with your girlfriend, and then you see her kissing someone else, and she's lost some weight, and now has a really cute haircut. The Packers are like family to its fans, and Favre has been a big brother to all of us for a long time. When he cried, we cried. When he laughed, we laughed. When he won a Super Bowl, we won a Super Bowl! And now, to picture him celebrating a TD as a member of another team just seems wrong. How could this happen? I guess if Joe Montana can leave the Niners for the Chiefs, Pete Rose can get his 4000th hit with the Montreal Expos and Paul Molitor can win a World Series with the Toronto Blue Jays, anything is possible.

Although I've wanted this drama to end for a long time, now that it has, I can't get it out of mind. It's hard to focus on baseball writing. The news tonight was mixed. The Brewers hung on this afternoon and beat the Reds, 6-3. Jeff Suppan pitched well, going seven strong innings. The Cubs and Cards also won today. The Mets were beat by the long ball tonight, as the Padres hit three of them in route to a 4-2 win at Shea Stadium. The Phillies shut out the Marlins, so we are now three back in the standings.

I will check espn.com tomorrow to confirm the Favre trade, and I still won't believe it. Most of my friends probably don't even know that it has happened yet, and will find out about it on the way to work. This story will dominate the world of sports for a while, but this will be my last mention of it in this book. That is, unless I get the "itch" to mention it later.

August 7th

I can already tell the role of closer for the Mets is going to be a revolving door until we can get Billy Wagner back. After Aaron Heilman gave up the three run homer to Jody Gerut on Tuesday night, Scott Schoeneweis was given the opportunity to close the door, and did get the job done that night. This afternoon at Shea, Schoeneweis gave up a home run to the very same Jody Gerut (who homered in all three games of this series) to blow the save and get several million Mets fans to wonder when the bullpen is going to get their collective heads out of their asses. Only the Braves have a worse bullpen ERA since the all star break (6.75). Heilman recorded the last two outs of the ninth, as the game went to the bottom of the ninth tied at 3-3. Thank goodness for the mighty David Wright, who hit a walk off two run dinger off of Heath Bell to win the game, and take the series against San Diego. I wasn't even aware of how the Mets won until I was driving to Port Washington earlier this evening. I also learned that Philadelphia lost, so the Mets are back to within two games of the NL East lead. This weekend, the Mets will host the Florida Marlins, with a chance to leap frog the fish and hop back into 2nd place, and hopefully the Pirates can go into Philadelphia and help us out a bit.

The Brewers have their first day off today since the all star break. They've played 20 games since then, which is the most games that can be scheduled consecutively for any team without their permission. In those 20 games, the Brewers were 11-2 on the road, and 1-6 at home. They start a short four game homestand, a wrap around series with the Washington Nationals, tomorrow night. The Cubs host the Cardinals this weekend, and I'm sure they will be on Fox and ESPN. As a Brewers fan, it's hard to choose who to root for, because you want to gain ground on both teams. Is it more important to cut into the Cubs' five game lead, or to build on the 1 game wild card lead you have on the Cards? Either way, the Brewers have to take care of business against the Nationals at Miller Park. Just like the Cubs series last week, Sabathia and Sheets go in the first two games of the series, and it is important that we make a statement. It would also be great to have some momentum heading into the west coast trip to San Diego and Los Angeles next week.

August 8th

Remember last Sunday when both the Mets and Brewers were shut out, and I vowed never to repeat that days events in that exact order ever again, in fear that they might get shutout again? Well, tonight was the exact opposite. The Mets opened their series with Florida by shutting out the Marlins, 3-0, behind seven solid inning pitched by Oliver Perez. Aaron Heilman got the last six outs, and the Carlos Delgado and David Wright added home runs, as the Mets pulled ahead of the Marlins in the standings, and within one game of the Philadelphia Phillies for the

NL East lead. The Brewers shut out the Nationals 5-0 behind another dominant performance by CC Sabathia. Sabathia is now 6-0 with a 1.58 ERA in seven starts with Milwaukee and his 4 complete games now lead the National League. The guy is going to get NL Cy Young votes at this pace. Can you say Rick Sutcliffe? Ironically, Sutcliffe, who went 16-1 with the Cubs in 1984, was also traded mid-season from Cleveland. Sutcliffe led the Cubs to the NL East pennant in 1984, before losing to the San Diego Padres in the NLCS.

So, with that being said, I will try to duplicate today to the best of my ability, hoping this leads to more shutouts. Here is a snapshot of what I did today...

Woke up at 7:20am, took a shower, ate one strawberry pop tart at the table, ate the other one in the car, washed them down with orange juice, got to work about 8:25am, had a chicken club from Burger King for lunch, made a ton of calls to students this afternoon, clocked out at 5:27pm, headed to Port Washington, split a ham and cheese sandwich with Gracie, sang "Talkin' Baseball" and "D-O-D-G-E-R-S" with her, and put her to bed around 10:10pm. If I can just do this everyday, the Mets and Brewers will be coasting into the NLCS. Gracie would then know two classic baseball songs by heart, I would bring in a ton of business to the credit union, and I'd probably get really sick of ham, not to mention Burger King. But it would all be worth it.

August 9th

I was sad to hear that Bernie Mac died this morning. Bernard Jeffrey McCullough, as he was known by close friends and family, will forever be linked to Milwaukee and the Brewers, as he played fictional ballplayer Stan Ross in the 2004 film *Mr. 3000*, which was filmed at Miller Park. In the film, Ross collects his 3000th hit, but then promptly retires, only to find out years later that he is actually three hits short of 3000. Ross decides to come back to the Brewers at the age of 47 to get the three hits he needs to get to 3000, and most of the movie takes you on the journey. The character ends up getting a sacrifice in his last at bat, leaving him one hit short of 3000, but the sacrifice propels the Brewers to 3rd place in their division. It was a selfless act by Ross, and he was rewarded by being voted into the Hall of Fame towards the end of the movie, and Ross would go on to rename his many businesses "Mr. 2999". I was at the filming the night they shot the footage of his 2999th hit, and his last at-bat. It was a neat experience. I wasn't able to see the filming for "Major League", for it was 103 degrees the day my mom and I were going to go. She took me to the park instead and threw batting practice to me. What an incredible mom I have. Bernie Mac will also be remembered for his role in the Ocean's trilogy as Frank Sutton. He was a very funny guy, and he'll be missed.

I've got my daughter and my niece for the rest of the weekend, and we're going to kick off the festivities by taking in the Brewers game against Washington at Miller Park tonight. They kicked off the short home stand on the right foot last night, getting a complete game shutout from CC Sabathia. Tonight, Ben Sheets goes up against Tim Redding, who has always pitched well against Milwaukee, whether it has been as a member of the Houston Astros or the Washington Nationals. We got to the game about 5:30, which was not in time to get our commemorative $1 coins, which were given out to the first 10,000 fans through the turnstiles. Gina did bring a book tonight, but I've challenged her not to read it *all* night. She has accepted the challenge. The first thing on Gracie's mind is getting a snack, as she sits like an angel in her chair, awaiting her popcorn. I can't believe she's still hungry, as the four of us split a box of macaroni and cheese and a Jack's pepperoni pizza less than two hours ago. I guess she's going to be like her dad in that aspect. While Gracie was enjoying her popcorn, and Gina read, Amber and I took in the game. The Brewers were able to put a 2 spot on the board in the 3rd, then came back immediately in the 4th and hit back to back homers (Durham and Hardy), to give the Brewers a 4-0 lead. All the while, Ben Sheets was mowing down batter after Washington batter. In the 5th, Corey Hart hit a long home run to center field to make it 5 to 0 Brewers. It's time for an Italian. I had a jumbo dog earlier, and damn was it good. Gracie is still working on her popcorn.

While Sheets and the Crew are rolling past the Nationals, the Mets took an early lead against Florida, scoring four in the 1st on a Carlos Beltran 2 run double and a Carlos Delgado two run homer. The Marlins scored two in the 3rd, and two in the 6th to tie the game, but the Mets put up three in the bottom of the sixth to take a 7-4 lead. Daniel Murphy hit a pinch hit home run tonight for the Mets, his first in the big leagues. Carlos Beltran hit a homer in the 7th to make it 8-4, and although the Marlins would battle back, scoring 2 runs in the 8th, it was not enough, and the Mets would beat the Marlins tonight, to extend their lead over Florida for 2nd place to a game and a half.

In the 8th inning of the Brewers game, Ben Sheets hit for himself with a man on 2nd, and was greeted by a thunderous applause for his efforts tonight. That applause became deafening as Sheets hit an RBI single to center field to make it 6-0 Brewers. Sheets would retire the Nationals in order for the complete game shutout, and ended the night with six strikeouts and no walks allowed. The Brewers have not allowed a run since the 3rd inning of Wednesday afternoon's game with Cincinnati. Some other notes from tonight...Ryan Braun left the game in the 2nd inning, after apparently aggravating his back while swinging and missing in the 1st. Gabe Kapler took over for him in left field. Also, tonight was the 12th straight sell out and 29th sell out of the season for the Brewers. It's great to see this building packed against teams other than the Cubs and Cardinals. This city is hungry for a winner, and right now, the Brewers look like they can play with anyone. The memories of the sweep against the Cubs are long gone, and the Brewers are on some kind of roll. The Cardinals beat the Cubs 12-3, so the Brewers are now just four games out in the NL Central.

After the game tonight, Gracie fell asleep around 11:00, and Amber, Gina and I made it a movie night. We watched *The Best of Will Ferrell, Volume 1*, *Shallow Hal* and *Men at Work*. Throw in some beer cheese, some Ritz crackers and a case of Coca-Cola, and what more could you want on a Saturday night. It was 3:45am before we went to bed. Amber had never seen the famous "cowbell" sketch before tonight, and although it seemed like she liked it, I don't see her making SNL a priority in the future. It's a staple in my life, so maybe I'll make more of an effort to listen to Kid Rock so that she'll watch that with me. The new season kicks off on September 13th, and I've read on multiple web sites that Robert Downey Jr. is hosting the season premiere, but nothing has been confirmed. I wonder if Brett Favre will host this year, now that he is New York's newest darling.

August 10th

I only got about three hours of sleep last night, as my niece's cell phone alarm went off at 6:45, which woke up my daughter. Gracie then found me sleeping on the couch in the living room, and proceeded to poke me firmly on the forehead in an effort to wake me up and watch some Pooh. After Amber and Gina awoke, we kicked the soccer ball around for a bit, had a catch and the kids got some swimming in while Amber and I listened to the ipod. Shortly after Amber left for Chicago, Gracie grabbed her sheet and pillow from the bunk beds, and pulled up in front of the TV, where Gina was watching "The Lion King", and fell asleep almost instantly. While Gina was watching the movie, I took some time this afternoon to look over some fantasy football rankings, as I have both of my drafts next Sunday. I also followed the Mets and Brewers games online. By the time Gracie awoke from her Sunday afternoon nap, the Mets were already down big, and wound up losing 8-2 today. Mike Pelfrey was hit pretty hard. The Brewers extended their streak of scoreless innings pitched to 29 innings, as their game with Washington was scoreless into the top of the sixth inning today. The Nationals did score in the 6th, which thrilled Nationals starter John Lannan, as he was carrying a no-hitter into the 6th. Lannan has been a hard luck pitcher for the Nationals this season. Despite a very good ERA of 3.40, Lannan has posted a record thus far of 6-11. In the bottom of the 6th, Corey Hart broke up the no-no with a single, and the Brewers were able to plate an unearned run due to a Ronnie Belliard error earlier in the inning. Today's starter was Manny Parra, who was making his first start since the one sided shoving match he had with Prince Fielder on Monday night. Parra was brilliant today, going 7 strong innings, and striking out nine batters. Eric Gagne took over in the 8th, and was not very good, giving up a double to Ryan Zimmerman, and home runs to Austin Kearns and Lastings Milledge to give the Nationals a 4-1 lead. I was listening to the game in the car as I drove the girls back to Port Washington, and after Gagne gave up the 2nd homer, Bob Uecker urged Brewers fans to stick around. "There's a lot of baseball left", said Uke. God knows Brewers fans are familiar with the team coming back from 4-1 late in games (Easter Sunday, 1987).

When we got to the apartment, I made sure Gracie hugged her mom tight before I asked Heather if we could watch the end of the game. The Brewers were able to load the bases in the bottom of the 8th, with just one man out for Mike Rivera, who despite only starting about once every two weeks, has posted a batting average of .333 thus far this season. Rivera came up huge today, hitting a rope down the left field line, easily scoring the two lead runners, and Mike Cameron would be called safe on the play at the plate, to tie the game at 4 a piece! A bigger hit Mike Rivera has not had in the major leagues, I'm sure he'd tell you. Heather and I watched for two more innings before I hugged Gracie goodbye, and I was now off to Star's place for more movie watching. You'd think after last night, I'd be all "movied out", but Star and I ordered some Domino's and watched *Fun With Dick and Jane* and *The Ten*, but not before finishing the Brewers game. When I left Heather's place, Salomon Torres just finished up his 2nd scoreless inning, and the Brewers were not able to capitalize in the bottom of the 10th. Carlos Villanueva pitched the next two innings (the 11th and 12th), and again, the Brewers were not able to score in their respective half innings. Guillermo Mota came on to pitch in the top of the 13th, and despite giving up one base hit, was not scored upon. The game was starting to look like it may go 22 or 23 innings, which would put our movie night in jeopardy. Gabe Kapler, who was playing today for Ryan Braun, stepped in to lead off the 13th against brand new Washington Nationals pitcher Luis Ayala, who was coming into the game with a 1-7 record and ERA over 6.00. Thus far, Kapler had had a rough game, going 0-6 with a run scored, as he reached base in the sixth on the Ronnie Belliard error. Star has been a good sport since I arrived almost an hour ago, as she is not a huge baseball fan, and we enjoyed some nachos and Mike's Hard Lemonades while we waited for the pies. What happened next was a defining moment for the Brewers 2008 season, as Kapler ripped a 2-2 pitch off the left field foul pole for a walk off home run. It was the first walk off homer for the Brewers all year, and the first walk off of Gabe Kapler's career. I threw my arms up like the Doorman usually does for a Brewers home run, and started to get text messages left and right from my Brewer fan friends. Heather emphatically stated, "Gabe Fucking Kapler", my sister said, "Yea, Brewers!" and Amber simply typed, "NICE". While the Brewers drew a season high thirteen walks in today's game, they also surrendered a season high sixteen base runners. This is a huge win and they've now won all five games since the night of the Fielder/Parra fight. Whether that has specifically fueled the team is anybody's guess, but it certainly hasn't hurt team chemistry. The Brewers and Nationals will play game four of this series tomorrow afternoon at 1:05pm.

The Cubs and Cardinals wrapped up their series tonight on ESPN with the Cubs winning 6-2. The Brewers will now go to bed tonight with a three game lead in the NL Wild Card chase. I know there is a lot of baseball left, but with the Brewers playing the way they're playing as of late, and the Mets only two games out in the NL East, I just want to grab my glove and find a pickup game tonight. This is what baseball is all about. The odds of finding a pickup game are very low, so I'll settle with watching *Magic, Miracles and True Believers*, *Harvey's Wallbangers* and I think a little bit of Game Three of the '86 series. This was the one where Nails hits the lead off homer at Fenway with the Mets already down two games to none in the series. Seeing him pump his fist as he rounds the bases still gives me goose bumps. Yep, that's what I'm doing tonight…

August 11th

The Brewers did something today that they haven't done in sixteen years, and had only done three other times before that in franchise history. The day after hitting a walk off home run (Kapler), the Brewers led off a game with a home run (Weeks). When it happened in 1992, Robin Yount hit a walk off against Baltimore, and Paul Molitor led off the next game with a homer. It's worth mentioning that Rob Deer hit a walk off against Minnesota in April of 1989, and Paul Molitor homered to lead off the next game as well. C'mon, you knew I'd get at least one more Rob Deer reference in, didn't you? The Weeks homer today tied the game at 1-1, and the Brewers would score six more times, while Dave Bush was once again dominant at home, in the Brewers 7-1 win today, which secured the sweep of the Nationals. Ryan Braun was out of the lineup again, nursing his sore back, but Gabe Kapler filled in nicely again, going 1-4 and scoring two runs today. The Brewers will now fly to San Diego and take on the Padres in a three game series before heading to Los Angeles to take on the Dodgers this weekend. They will be riding a six game winning streak into California.

The Mets originally were supposed to have today off, but instead played the Pittsburgh Pirates in a game that was postponed due to rain in April. In what has become the theme for the Mets season, the bullpen blew a great effort by the starter, Pedro Martinez, and dropped today's game, 7-5. The Mets led this game 5-1 heading into the 7th. Martinez went six innings, and only gave up three hits, but was pulled due to a high pitch count (four walks). Five different relievers gave up six hits and three walks over the next innings, as the Pirates scored three in the 7th and three in the 9th. Aaron Heilman gave up the three that counted, blowing his 3rd save, and dropping his record to 2-7. I'm not giving up on this year, but the Mets clearly have to improve the pen in 2009. They are too good a team to be losing this many close games. Fortunately, the Phillies and Marlins also lost today. The Mets travel to Washington tomorrow for a three game series. Who knows what might happen. The Nationals were a hot team before heading to Milwaukee, and after getting swept, they'll be looking to rebound against a divisional opponent. Manny Acta is a former Mets 3rd base coach, and I'm guessing he'll have his team ready to play.

August 12th

Johan Santana could very well have been 15-7 coming into tonight's game against the Washington Nationals, however, the New York Mets bullpen has blown six leads that Santana has surrendered to his relievers this season. Jerry Manuel may have had this statistic on his mind in the 7th inning tonight, as the Mets took a 3-2 lead into the bottom of the 7th. Instead of handing this one over to his pen, Manuel left his ace out there, which was really a no-brainer, as Santana's pitch count was in the mid 80's heading into the inning. But Santana's weakness is giving up the long ball, and Ryan Langerhans, the former Atlanta Braves outfielder, chose tonight to hit his first home run of the season, to tie the game at 3-3. Santana closed out the inning, and would leave the game with the score tied. In the top of the 8th, the Mets loaded the bases for Damion Easley. Washington reliever Saul Rivera threw a pitch that appeared to sail over Easley's head, and David Wright charged home to try to score. However, the home plate umpire ruled that the pitch hit Easley in the helmet, and there was no need for Wright to hustle in, as he was awarded home plate on the HBP. Manny Acta came out to argue that the pitch did not connect with Easley's helmet, but I'm not sure what his argument was, as Wright would have scored anyway had it been ruled a wild pitch. So the Mets now lead 4-3, but would the bullpen blow another Santana lead late? The question on everybody's mind is who will be closing games until Billy Wagner is right again. They certainly are not handing the ball to Aaron Heilman in the 9th anymore. Mets rookie Eddie Kunz could be an option. Hell, they may even move a starter to the bullpen, if they feel they have to. Tonight, it would be Pedro Feliciano getting that opportunity. After Joe Smith worked a perfect 8th, Feliciano did the same in the 9th to notch his first save of the year. The

Dodgers came from behind to beat the Phillies tonight, so the Mets find themselves only one game out.

I'll borrow some creative license from Limp Bizkit, and say the Brewers keep rollin', rollin', rollin, rollin'...After Jeff Suppan allowed a 2nd inning HR to Kevin Kouzmanoff, Mike Cameron hit one out in the top of the 3rd, and Prince Fielder hit a three run shot, his 27th, to make it 4-1 Brewers. Joey Gerut would homer in the sixth to make it 4-2, but the Brewers got that run right back in the 7th to make it 5-2. Suppan looked great tonight, going eight innings and only allowing the two solo homers and 4 hits all night. Salomon Torres worked a 1-2-3 ninth inning for his 23rd save of the year. The Cubs were rained out, so the Brewers do gain a half game tonight, and now trail Chicago by three games in the NL Central.

August 13th

All day at work today I struggled with where I should go tonight to watch the Brewers game. I went back and forth between Applebee's (the restaurant, as opposed to Appleby's Service Center on Port Washington Rd) and T.G.I. Friday's. Then someone suggested BW3's. Done! I happen to live about ten minutes from one, and it's located right next to a Chuck E Cheese, no less. When I arrived, I grabbed a table near the big screen, and took in the end of the Cubs/Braves game. It looks like the Cubs are going to sweep the Braves in a doubleheader today. They are up 6-0 in the top of 9th, with the bases loaded and nobody out. St Louis is currently up 5-4 on Florida. My Mets are up 12-0 in the 7th tonight at Washington, scoring eight runs in the 3rd. Gary Sheffield was placed on waivers by Detroit yesterday, and the Mets may be interested, although I doubt they'll bring in the diva. John Maine responded tonight to the rumors of him being moved to the bullpen by throwing 5 innings of 1 hit ball before being lifted. There is no reason to keep Maine out there with a twelve run lead, seeing this is his first start since coming off the DL.

As the Brewers game gets under way, I order twelve boneless wings to get this party started (six medium and six spicy garlic), and the tallest beer I've ever consumed. Tonight's pitching matchup is CC Sabathia vs Josh Banks. I don't know much about Banks, but he does remind me a little bit of Jake Peavy. He has good command and mixes his pitches well. NICE CATCH BALL GIRL! I notice that BW3's takes baseball seriously, as I've noticed signs posted that say NO JUKEBOX DURING BREWERS GAME. I can honestly see my mail being delivered here, and having a room of my own in the back. The Brewers go down quietly in the 1st.

These spicy garlic wings are great! I have yet to try a flavor here that I'm unhappy with. Maybe one day, I can use Amber's looks and charms to get the fine folks here to bring out an order of twelve wings, each with a different sauce. Jerry Hairston starts off the 1st singling hard up the box, past Sabathia. Here's a little trivia. Experts estimate the earth will blow up in 5 billion years. That damn sun! The Mets game is now a final (12-0). Brian Stokes pitched the final 4 innings to earn the save. Stokes was making only his 2nd appearance for the Mets this season. After the lead off single, Sabathia gets out of the 1st, with no damage done.

Prince Fielder...TO RIGHT AND DEEP! Fielder leads off the 2nd with his 28th of the season. He is now just two shy of Ryan Braun's team lead in big flies. Corey Hart follows by singling to left field. Coming into tonight, Hart was 22-28 in stolen base attempts, good for 85% for the season, but was gunned down by Nick Hundley on a great throw. Craig Counsell and Mike Cameron each draw a walk, which was followed by a Jason Kendall RBI single. Kendall and Cameron advance on the throw home, and the Brewers now lead 2-0. The Cubs game is now a final, and the Brewers have lost a game in the standings tonight before they can complete two innings of their own game. A CC Sabathia RBI groundout makes it 3-0 Brewers. Rickie Weeks pops out to short to end the inning. It is now time for some honey BBQ boneless wings and some chili con queso.

Sabathia takes the hill in the bottom of the 2nd with a 3-0 lead. I really hope we make a run at him in the off-season. I'm gonna say this...the Brewers can win the World Series this year. The talent is there. The starting pitching is there. We can put up a bunch of runs. We have the 4th best record in baseball, behind the Angels, Rays and Cubs, and surprisingly, the 2nd best road record in baseball behind the Angels. There are only 4 teams in baseball with winning records on the road (Angels, Brewers, Cardinals and Phillies). We can do this, and I think we can make a serious run at Sabathia. Nothing doing for the "Friars" in the 2nd...Klement's commercial. Beautiful.

The Cardinals have beaten the Marlins, and the Phillies are up 6-1 over the Dodgers in the 2nd. Gabe Kapler leads off the 3rd by nearly going yard, with a long fly ball to left field. Prince Fielder steps in the box, looking to do more damage. His home run totals by month thus far have been 4-4-6-6-8, which is always a good sign. And not to mention that it's only August 13th, and he's already hit 8 this month...the kid may push 50 again! He draws a walk, but Corey Hart hits into a fielder's choice to end the inning...Chili's commercial. Beautiful.

I have to get out soon and play baseball, whether it's an afternoon of the ground ball game, shagging flies with a local high school team, hitting the batting cages, a game of strikeout. Anything! Lying in bed with my glove and a ball isn't cutting it. Sabathia sets down the Padres 1-2-3 in the 3rd.

Craig Counsell draws a walk to lead off the top of the 4th. Why does Counsell look so bored? He's always looked bored playing baseball. I know that's certainly not the case, but it just looks that way. He steals 2nd base (all the while looking bored), but the Brewers are unable to score in the 4th. Chase Headley hits a one out double in the bottom of the 4th, and Edgar Gonzalez hits a sharp single to left, setting up a 1st and 3rd for Nick Hundley. Hundley hits a grounder to Hardy, we have a chance for two, but Weeks can't turn it, a run scores, and it's now 3-1 Brewers. Sabathia is able to get out of it with no further damage.

Chase Headley makes a great diving catch, off the bat of Rickie Weeks to open the 5th inning. J.J. Hardy walks (the 5th free pass for the Brewers thus far), and Gabe Kapler reaches on an infield single, and he and Hardy advance on a throwing error.

With men on 2nd and 3rd, the Padres will not pitch to Fielder in this situation, which loads the bases for Corey Hart. The Brewers have yet to hit a grand slam this season, and Hart is a career .130 hitter with the bases loaded (3-23). But tonight, Hart hits a screamer down the left field line, and as the ball bounces around, all three runs score, as Hart glides into 3rd with a three run triple. Banks' night is done. Why the haircut, Corey? What bet was placed and lost? The new pitcher for San Diego is Justin Hampson. Counsell pounces on the 1st pitch he sees, and hits a long sacrifice fly to center, scoring Hart and putting the Brewers up 7-1. Mike Cameron flies out to end the inning, but not before the Brewers put up a 4 spot to give Sabathia a hell of a cushion to work with.

And joining me the rest of the way is Hope Sterken, my manager at the credit union, and the biggest sports fan you'll ever meet (dripping sarcasm). The first two Padres reach on hard hit singles, and thus far, the Brewers have been out hit 7-5, but lead 7-1. Brian Giles hits a slow roller to Hardy, and also reaches, which loads the bases with nobody out. What the hell, Sterken? You're bad luck! Kouzmanoff pops up to short...one down. Adrian Gonzalez goes down swinging...two away. Headley hits a grounder to Counsell, and he steps on the bag to end the inning (still looks bored). Sabathia strands the bases loaded! You're not bad luck after all, Hope! Stay awhile and have some wings...

Not much happened the rest of the way, as the restaurant started to thin out near the end of the game. Sabathia ended up going seven innings, before handing it over to David Riske. Riske worked the 8th, and Guillermo Mota worked the 9th, as the Brewers wrapped up game two in San Diego, 7-1. We left in the top of the 9th, and I listened to the rest of the game in the car on the way home. Bob Uecker and Jim Powell were talking about the Brewers being undefeated since the Fielder / Parra fight, and Uecker said that the Brewers good play as of late has nothing to do with the fight. He talked to Robin Yount shortly after it happened, and Yount told him that people don't realize just how much stuff like that happens in the clubhouse, that we just don't see it on the field a lot. I suppose if you spend 8 months a year with the same guys, it's like having a bunch of wily brothers, and things happen. Uecker said if the fight truly caused the Brewers to start playing better, they would do it everyday. Good point.

August 14th

You can't ask for a better pitching matchup than the one the fans in San Diego were treated to this afternoon, as Ben Sheets faced Jake Peavy at Petco Park (gorgeous stadium, by the way...a must see...I'm also basing this opinion on pictures and video, as I have never been there. I'm drawn to the dimensions, as it is a classic pitchers park). The game is on in the background, but the focus is on origination, loan origination that is, and everyone is wondering if Baby Dahms will be on his way today. The game was exactly what you'd expect with Sheets and Peavy going at it, a fast paced scoreless game entering the 7th inning. Mike Cameron untied the game in the top of the 7th with an RBI single off Peavy. Unfortunately, Sheets unraveled in the bottom of the 7th, giving up three runs to the Padres. Mike Cameron got one back for the Brewers, hitting a solo HR off Trevor Hoffman in the 9th, but it wouldn't be enough, as the Padres won today 3-2, ending the Brewers 8 game winning streak. The Brewers will head to Los Angeles for a weekend series with the Dodgers.

The Mets were able to pull off the sweep of the Nationals, just like the Brewers did on Monday. They had a 5-0 lead heading into the 7th, and the Nationals scored 3 to make it a game, but the Mets put 4 up in the 9th to seal the deal. The final was 9-3. What makes this win especially sweet is that the Dodgers beat the Phillies tonight, pulling off a 4 game sweep, and the Mets are now a full game ahead of Philadelphia in the NL East divisional race. They will now travel to Pittsburgh for a three game set.

I've just been informed that young Ryan Edward Dahms has arrived. I can't help but notice that Joe and Nikki's son has the initials R.E.D., and Joe is one of the biggest Badgers fans I've ever met. It makes me want to have a son one day, and name him Maxwell Lawrence Buchholz (M.L.B). I can't wait to meet you, Ryan. Your dad is a great guy. You'll have to sit him down when you're older, and talk to him about closers. I'm sure you'll see it my way.

August 15th

My fantasy football drafts are in two days, and I haven't spent two seconds preparing for either one of them yet. Back in the old days, I'd get like three magazines in mid-June, spend about a half an hour a night taking notes, following up on team moves, injuries, highlighting lists, doing mock drafts, etc. This year, I have to remind myself where my pick is in the first round. The truth of it is, all the preparation has led to NO championships, so I may as well just wake up, clean the shit out of my eyes, have a bowl of cornflakes, take a shower, have one extra bowl of cornflakes, log in at 12:55 and draft a champion. I know the players, the site tells you the bye weeks, and if players are injured. It's all luck anyway, why spend all that time preparing when you have no real control over anything that happens. Last year, I had LT and Brady, and went 12-2 in the regular season, and I was outscoring my opponents by an average margin of 28 points, and when I made the playoffs, the Chargers pulled LT in the 2nd half, and Tom Brady chose that week to have his worst game of the season, and I lost. Preparing gives you a better chance, but it doesn't guarantee wins. Winning comes down to luck. Sorry Schwingle. You're not better at this than me. You're luckier. Had you *drafted* Ryan Grant last year, instead of picking him up mid-season, maybe I'd say you're better.

The Mets won their fourth straight game tonight, behind a solid start from Mike Pelfrey, who pitched 7 scoreless innings, before handing his bullpen a 2-0 lead. Jack Wilson hit a solo HR off of Duaner Sanchez in the 8th to pull the Pirates to within one, but Pedro Feliciano and Aaron Heilman got the last five outs to shut the door. Manuel is still giving the ball to Heilman late, huh? Billy Wagner should be back soon. The Phillies were winners tonight, so the lead in the East remains at 1 game.

With an early start to the day tomorrow (taking Gracie to the zoo), I didn't follow the Brewers game tonight, but I did check the final score after using the bathroom at 2:00am. Dodgers 5, Brewers 3; and still no Ryan Braun in the lineup.

August 16th

The Milwaukee County Zoo is having their annual Zoo Ala Carte extravaganza this weekend. This event combines everything you love about Summerfest and the Wisconsin State Fair, except I don't ever remember getting bit in the right eyelid by a goddamn horsefly at either of those events in the past. For about an hour, it felt like I was hit in the head with a baseball. But we had fun anyway. There is nothing in the world like seeing your children enjoy themselves, and Gracie had a great time seeing the monkeys, the fish, the elephants, etc. I got her some rainbow sherbet towards the end of the day, but she was more interested in playing with it than eating it. Today will be a multiple bath day for her.

After the day at the zoo, we enjoyed some appetizers at Champps, and I got to see a little bit of the Mets game, as well as some pre-season NFL coverage. When we left the restaurant, the Mets led the Pirates 6-0. The plan tonight was to do a whole bunch of grocery shopping, which would put a limit on the scoreboard watching. The same will apply tomorrow, with the drafts going on. The Mets wound up winning by a score of 7-4, and Philadelphia lost, so we now lead the NL East by two games. Sweet!!

The Brewers were down 2-1 for most of tonight's game, but J.J. Hardy hit a two run homer in the 8th to give the Brewers the lead. But in the bottom of the 9th, a Hardy fielding error led to the tying run crossing the plate for the Dodgers. However, in the 10th, Hardy redeemed himself by hitting an RBI single to give the Brewers the lead once again, and this time, the Brewers held on to win. Milwaukee's record is 71-53, and they are 4.5 back of the Cubs, and still 2 ahead of the Cardinals for the Wild Card. Still no Braun.

August 17th

The Fugazzi Fantasy Football League Draft: It's the Super Bowl, WrestleMania and the Grammy's all rolled into one, and today, we conducted our 16th such event. Matt Weiss took a Charger (LT), the Brothers Fefer took a Viking (AP), Schwingle took a few Packers (Grant and Driver), and I took Randy Moss and a couple of Browns (Anderson and Winslow). What I'm saying is that there weren't too many surprises. We held a 2nd draft in the early evening, for a newly created scoring only league, that I have aptly named "Son of Fugazzi". The first pick was Tom Brady, and I took Braylon Edwards in the 1st round, and Joseph Addai in the 2nd. I did select Aaron Rodgers as my backup to Eli Manning, because Manning has a bye the week I play Schwingle, and I want him to have to root for my QB. The two drafts combined took a little over three hours to complete. We draft online using cbssports.com, but in the past, we'd draft in Mike's basement, or at Jeff's house, and ONE draft would take nearly five hours. I've already set my lineups through week 9 for both leagues, because I don't care to think about it until baseball season is over.

Johan Santana has me daydreaming about one last tour of the playoff battlefield at Shea, as he threw his first CG shutout as a New York Met, a three hit masterpiece against Pittsburgh. The Mets hit two homers (Delgado and Schneider) in today's 4-0 win. The win gives the Mets six straight wins, as they still hold on to a two game lead in the NL East. With all the fun I've been having at the zoo and with the drafts, I haven't really followed any baseball this weekend, but this would have been a great game to see.

And from what I'm reading, the series this weekend between the Brewers and the Dodgers was a dandy. I just saw the Gabe Kapler catch from last night on mlb.com. That may be one of the best plays I've ever seen a Milwaukee Brewer outfielder make...ever! Kapler dove high above the left field wall to rob Russell Martin of a home run. His momentum almost carried him over the wall, which would have then been ruled a home run. Today's game was probably the best of the three this weekend, as far as sheer drama. The Brewers trailed the Dodgers 5-1 heading into the top of the 9th, and a James Loney fielding error sparked a 4 run rally, tying the game at 4 a piece. Ray Durham had a two run single to bring the Brewers within two, and Ryan Braun hit a two run homer to tie the game. This was Brauny's first start since last Saturday, and what a way to return to the lineup, hitting a game tying home run in his home state of California. The energy in that Milwaukee dugout must have been electric. But the beauty of baseball is how quickly a game can change. Just as fast as the Brewers came back from 4 to tie it, Carlos Villaneuva gave up a walk off homer to Andre Ethier to give the Dodgers a 7-5 win. It was Ethier's second bomb of the game, and the win today for Los Angeles pulled them into a 1st place tie with Arizona. If this is a playoff preview, it should be a great series. At week's end, the Brewers find themselves 5.5 back of the Cubs, but still maintain a two game lead over the Cards for the NL Wild Card lead.

Despite not giving baseball the attention she so deserves, it was a great weekend. I scored three weezer tickets (they are playing on my birthday in Chicago), the zoo was great, the drafts went well, and I now have a place to display my baseball books, memorabilia, gloves, etc. Thanks, Amber! I'm taking my niece to the weezer show. She will be so excited. Hell, I'm excited! Amber, are you excited? Scale of 1-10, and for the love of God, don't say 4 !

August 18th

The Mets finished their series in Pittsburgh this afternoon, looking for the four game sweep, and trying to extend their winning streak to seven games. John Maine, who didn't allow a run a run on Wednesday night, took the hill today against Paul Maholm. We were extremely busy at work, as our annual three weeks of registration started today, but never too busy to get a quick peek at the scores during down times. I'm kidding. I don't do that. That would be against policy. I wait until 5:15pm, and I call a friend, and ask who won the ball game. When I called my friend, we'll refer to him as...I don't know...Doug, he told me, via cell phone, that the Mets led 2-0 after five, but the bullpen gave up two in the 6th and three in 8th to blow it. Pirates 5, Mets 2. Maine again went five without allowing a run. Four walks brought the pitch count up, or else he would have gone longer. So the sweep wasn't meant to be, but guess what. Still in 1st, a game and a half ahead of Philadelphia. The Mets did trade for Washington reliever Luis Ayala late last night, in hopes of righting a mighty big wrong, and he will replace Eddie Kunz on the roster. He should be available for the series against Atlanta, starting tomorrow night. Thanks for the update "Doug".

The Brewers returned home tonight after a 3-3 road trip in California. Last year, around this time, people were speculating whether Ryan Braun would be the NL Rookie of the Year, and some people said, "Forget Rookie of the Year, he may be the NL MVP". It wasn't that crazy to think that, and in the end he did take the Rookie of the Year honors, despite only playing four months in the bigs. This summer, there is speculation that CC Sabathia may get some love for NL Cy Young, and my boy Steve Phillips of ESPN, and former Mets General Manager, said tonight that he could garner consideration for NL MVP! Entering tonight, Sabathia was 7-0 with an ERA of 1.55 in 8 starts as a Milwaukee Brewer, and was named the NL Pitcher of the Month in July. The NL Player of the Month in July, Ryan Braun, was once again in the lineup for the Brewers, the day after returning after missing seven games to injury. Sabathia, Braun and the rest of the Brewers kicked off a three game series with the Houston Astros, who recently won 8 straight games before dropping a few this weekend. Former Brewer Cecil Cooper is currently managing the Astros, and apparently, Coop is predicting that Houston will sweep us this week. "I'm predicting that, I'm going out on a limb. You heard it here first", said the former Milwaukee slugger. Cooper is also predicting the Astros will win 90 games. They'd have to go 28-11 the rest of the way. If either happens, I will legally change my first name to Cecil. You heard *that* here first.

After not seeing the any of the Dodgers series, I really looked forward to watching the Crew tonight, but the Browns are on Monday Night Football against the World Champion New York Giants. I know it's a pre-season game, but I gotta show some love to the Brownies. I did a lot of bouncing around. I didn't manage the remote well, as the Brewers scored 5 runs in the 4th inning as I was watching Eli Manning torch the Cleveland secondary twice for touchdowns. When I turned back, the Brewers were up 6-1, and as I got caught up in the baseball game, the Browns started to mount a comeback. Bad news coming out of halftime...Derek Anderson has suffered an apparent concussion. The day after I drafted him! Who do I drop for Brady Quinn? The Brewers went on to win 9-3, and wouldn't you know it, Sabathia went the distance again! He is now 8-0 with the Brewers, and going back to his last three decisions in Cleveland, he has now won his last 11 decisions. He also drove in two runs on a bases loaded single in the 4th inning. His ERA with the Brewers did balloon up to 1.60 tonight, so I'm sure Mike Maddux will talk to him about his mechanics. Why not talk MVP? Do the Brewers have the Wild Card lead without him? Some bad news coming out of tonight's game...Ryan Braun re-injured his rib cage, and may miss some more time. He left tonight's game after his at-bat in the 6th. Rickie Weeks also missed tonight's game with a sprained thumb, and could miss the entire Houston series.

The Browns ended up making a game of it tonight at the Meadowlands. They were down 23-3 after one quarter, but outscored the Giants 31-14 the rest of the way, with the final being 37-34 Giants. I'll have to keep an eye on the Anderson situation. Man that would suck if he couldn't start the season opener against Dallas. But, they are also very high on Brady Quinn, so we'll see what happens…Goddamn it, I just got rickrolled. You kids think you're so funny, don't you?

August 19th

My accident was 21 years ago today. I've long since dropped the whole "Why me" song and dance, but that doesn't mean I don't think about it every day. It's only natural. There are days when I smell a freshly cut grass or when I hear the pop of a hardball hitting a mitt, and I get lost in the game, and can't help but wonder what might have been. The game still enchants me. I'm 32, gonna be 33 in October, and I still love taking my glove to the game, still love tuning in to Uecker while I drive home at night. I still love playing catch, and it doesn't matter with whom. I will never turn down a game of catch. I still eat, breathe and sleep the game. A couple of nights ago, I pitched about four innings in my mind, while eating dinner. It keeps me young…keeps me on my toes. And despite work stoppages and escalating payrolls over the years, baseball has maintained its looks, and is still the prettiest girl on the block. She still makes my heart flutter.

You know what else makes my heart flutter? Come from behind wins at home against the Braves. That's what the Mets were up to tonight. After taking an early 2-0 lead against Atlanta, the Braves got three runs back in the top of the 3rd, and that's the way the score stood until the bottom of the 8th. Atlanta Braves starter Jo-Jo Reyes pitched well enough to win tonight, but his bullpen gave up five runs in the bottom of 8th, highlighted by a bases loaded, two-run double by Carlos Delgado, and a bases loaded, two-run single by Damion Easley. It was nothing doing for the Braves in the 9th, and the Mets wrapped it up, 7-3.

In Milwaukee, Ben Sheets made one bad pitch to Geoff Blum, but that proved to be the difference in the game tonight. The Brewers did grab an early 2-0 lead, with single tallies in the 1st and 2nd, and the Astros tied it in the 3rd with two of their own. But it was the change up served to Blum in the sixth that produced a three run homer to give the Astros a 5-2 lead, a lead they would not relinquish. Sheets doesn't throw the change up a ton, and tonight, it must have looked like a batting practice fastball to Blum, who knocked the hell out of it. Put a check mark in the column for reasons Sheets doesn't need a third pitch. He's the best two pitch pitcher I've ever seen, and when he's on, and he's mixing his fastball and curveball properly, he's almost unhittable at times. Sheets has a record of 1-5 since he made his start in the All Star Game. But he's also not getting the run support he was getting earlier in the year. With the Cubs winning tonight, we now fall 6 back of the Cubs, 7 back in the loss column.

August 20th

Just for the record, I want to make this very clear. I did not, did not receive any bootlegs of the two Billy Joel shows at Shea Stadium on 4 DVD's this afternoon, and I certainly am not enjoying them right now. No way. You must be thinking of someone else. Maybe someone that looks like me, but you're obviously mistaken. I am not currently enjoying the fairly decent video quality, not to mention the surprisingly high quality audio from these two historic shows on my DVD player. You got the wrong guy. How can that be me? I am writing this book right now! New York State of Mind, with guest vocalist Tony Bennett is not on in the background as I'm typing this. Nope. Sorry. I'm sorry!

This afternoon, the Brewers finished their series with Houston in a battle of crafty left handers. It was Manny Parra for the Brewers, who hasn't won in over a month and Wandy Rodriguez for the Astros. It was the Brewers 17th straight sell out at Miller Park, and Brewers fans should be proud of themselves. The Tampa Bay Rays, by far the biggest story in baseball this season, drew an average of just over 17,000 fans a game for their huge three game series with the Angels this week. The two best teams in the American League can't draw 20,000 fans for a game in Tampa, and Brewers fans continue to sell out Miller Park on a daily basis.

The Brewers treated the sell out crowd to a 5-2 win today; their fifth series win out of their last six, since being swept by the Cubs at the end of July. It was a great win, as several different players made key contributions. Parra went five, wasn't spectacular, but pitched well enough to leave the game after five innings with a 3-2 lead. J.J. Hardy hit a key two run homer in the 7th to give the Brewers a 5-2 lead, and Rickie Weeks returned to the lineup today, walking three times, and scoring each time he drew a walk. The bullpen was phenomenal today, and has pitched well as of late, which is rare, if you know your Brewers history. Historically, our bullpen usually starts to falter in mid-August. Over four innings, they only allowed one base runner. The Reds beat the Cubs, so the Brewers pull within five games. Over the next eight days, the Brewers have three days off, which is very rare, but they've only had one day off since the All Star Break, so it is well deserved. The Brewers have a weekend series at home against the Pittsburgh Pirates. No telling at this time if Ryan Braun will be available for that series.

Mike Pelfrey couldn't have chosen a better night to post his first major league complete game, as the Mets beat the Braves tonight, 6-3. Pelfrey was outstanding, only needing 108 pitches to dispose of the Braves, giving up only three hits all night. And it doesn't hurt when you put up five runs in the 1st, which the Mets did tonight against Atlanta starter Jair Jurrjens. If the Mets expect to have any success from here on out, they have to get quality starts from their rotation, as the bullpen is the most overused in the entire league. Pedro goes tomorrow night, in hopes of notching a three game sweep of the Braves. The Mets did sign former Tampa Bay reliever Al Reyes to bolster the pen, and Ryan Church is slowly making his way back to the big club, but it is unlikely that he will assume the starting right field position that he secured for the most part of the first half of the season. Church was having a breakout year for the Mets, before sustaining a concussion in Atlanta. You hate to see a player lose his job to injury, especially after the way he played for us, but Fernando

Tatis has filled in really well in right, and the platoon of Daniel Murphy and Nick Evans seems to be working in left field.

There are only 20 home games left for the Mets at Shea Stadium. Let's make the best of them, and hopefully there will be a few more in October.

August 21st

I gotta be honest. When I was at Turner Field at the end of May, and I witnessed the Braves sweep of the Mets, I wasn't too sure that my boys were going to be players in the NL East hunt. They even spent a few days in 4th place for a while. Fast forward to three months later, and the Mets are in the driver's seat in the NL East, looking to return the favor, and sweep the Braves tonight at Shea. Pedro Martinez struck out 6 in 7 plus innings of work, and would leave the game with the game tied 4-4 in the 8th. The bullpen did a great job keeping the Braves scoreless in the 8th and 9th, and in the bottom of the 9th, Carlos Delgado's fifth single of the night scored David Wright to give the Mets the sweep. Delgado and Wright were a combined 9-10 with 4 RBI and three runs scored tonight. Pedro pitched well, only really struggling in the 6th, when he allowed three runs to score. The Phillies lost tonight, so the win gives New York a 2.5 game lead in the NL East. Did anyone else see the Mets getting to 71-57 after Randolph was fired? They have completely turned it around under Jerry Manuel. The Mets will welcome the Houston Astros to town for a wrap around series this weekend.

No Brewers today, as they prepare for the Pittsburgh Pirates to come in to town for a three game series. The papers are saying that Ryan Braun should be in the lineup for Friday night's game. We will see.

August 22nd

There has been a free large pizza card from Tomaso's burning a hole in my wallet for months, so I took care of that problem tonight, and took Amber, Mom, Gina and Gracie out for dinner. As always, the food was great, and as always, they treat us like royalty. A great time was had by all. Naturally, the game was on at the bar, and there seemed to be a lot of Brewers fans in attendance tonight. By the time we left the restaurant, the Brewers had a slim lead in the 4th inning, 3-2. J.J. Hardy hit his 20th home run of the year to give the Brewers a 4-2 lead in the 5th. Hardy became the 4th Brewer to eclipse 20 homers this season, and when Corey Hart hits his next dinger, he will be # 5. The Pirates got one back in the 7th, on a solo home run by LF Brandon Moss, to make it 4-3, but the Brewers made a statement in the bottom of the 7th, scoring six times, tying a team high for an inning this season, to take a 10-3 lead. Ryan Braun, who did start tonight, showed a lot of hustle in the 7th, by scoring on a ground ball to 2B Freddy Sanchez. When Sanchez picked up the hard grounder off the bat of Prince Fielder, he lollygagged the throw to 1st, and Braun scurried home as the Pirates dugout looked on in disgust. The Pirates did get to Eric Gagne, and scored once in the 8th, but that was it, as the Brewers took the first game of the series, 10-4. Dave Bush had another solid start at home, improving his record to 8-9 on the season. If you compare that to 5th starters for the past six or seven World Championship teams, it's pretty similar. He's done pretty much what you expect from a 5th starter, and more, especially in the past three months. The Washington Nationals slaughtered the Cubs today at Wrigley. It was an interesting game. The Cubs led 4-0 after five innings, and the Nationals scored thirteen runs in the last four innings to beat the Cubs 13-5. With the Brewers win tonight, we are now only 4.5 games back. The Cardinals beat the Braves 18-3 (what's with all the softball scores tonight?), so we remain 2.5 ahead of the Cardinals in the Wild Card hunt.

The Mets made quick work of the Houston Astros tonight, only needing 2 hours and 18 minutes to complete the 3-0 shutout. Johan Santana's pitch count was the only thing between him and his 2nd consecutive complete game shutout, but he was dominant in his 7 innings pitched tonight. The Mets were able to get Santana an early lead tonight, with an RBI single by David Wright in the 1st, and a 2-run HR by Brian Schneider in the 2nd. After the Schneider HR, Roy Oswalt retired the next 20 batters he faced, but the bullpen was able to hold on to the 3-0 lead, to give the Mets their 4th straight win.

August 23rd

This afternoon, we spent the afternoon with my dad, and I was sad to find out that he is no longer in possession of "the magnet", which was the name he gave to his baseball glove. He doesn't remember packing it the last few times he's moved. I loved that glove. It took on a unique shape after all these years, but I still remember exactly what it looked, felt and smelled like. I have a very close relationship with baseball gloves. I still miss Phil Hohlweck's glove, and whoever is responsible for losing that will pay. Phil's glove seemed like it weighed about 30 pounds, but it had character. And Mike Moser's old glove, looked like it had been through several world wars, but I miss the hell out of it. I have three gloves in my "arsenal" right now. The one I played with for most of my little league days, which is huge, and has no padding. I call it "the gamer." It was a Regent. I'm not even sure they make gloves anymore. In 8th grade, I bought a Wilson, which I still have. It looks more like a traditional pitcher's glove, and is probably the glove most of my friends use the most if we are playing catch, because they don't feel safe using "the gamer", and I won't let them use my new one yet. I bought my first Rawlings last July, right before I saw my first game at Shea Stadium. It still isn't completely broken in, and I want that process to take a long time, for it was the first glove I ever bought myself. My comfort level has always been in the field, or on the mound. I was never much of a hitter, but I loved being in the field, glove in hand. It didn't really matter where I was playing. Naturally, pitching was what I loved most, but I also enjoyed playing shortstop, roaming the outfield, or manning first base. I always thought I'd be able to add "the magnet" to my collection. But today was a great day, spending a Saturday with my dad, watching Bull Durham in the afternoon and the Brewers/Pirates game at night. Amber and my dad seem to get along really well, as they loosely committed to taking a Harley ride together in the near future. Hey dad, when are we gonna have that catch?

The Brewers got on the board quickly tonight, scoring 2 in the 1st, and adding another run in the 4th, on Ryan Braun's 32nd home run of the year. The big damage was done in the 5th, with the Brewers putting up 3 runs, to take a 6-0 lead. The Pirates scored two in the 6th, and one in the 8th, before Brian Shouse stopped the bleeding in the 8th, and Salomon Torres slammed the door in the 9th for his 25th save of the season. This was the Brewers' 20th consecutive sell out, with another one expected for tomorrow. With the Cardinals losing tonight, the Brewers now hold a 3.5 game lead on St Louis for the NL Wild Card.

The news tonight for the Mets was not good. John Maine was tattooed for 8 earned over 5 and 2/3 innings, but that wasn't the worst of the news. It looks like the bone spur, which is causing him pain in his pitching shoulder may place him on the DL, and he could be lost for the season. The Mets were not able to generate much against Brandon Backe tonight, and the final from Shea Stadium was 8-3 Astros. The Phillies pulled within a game and a half of the Mets, with their win against the Dodgers.

August 24th

This afternoon, I scratched the itch I was talking about a few days back, and got out to the ballpark, played some catch, threw some batting practice to Amber (who is more than competent in the batter's box), and hit the cages for some slow pitch softball. It felt good to get out there. I seriously have to get back into a softball league next year, doesn't matter if it's a co-ed league, church league, whatever, I just want a fence, and I want to play under the lights. This is a goal for next year. Get back out there and play. I have a lot of work to do. Number one, I have to start heading back to the gym, and I have to start laying off the beer cheese. As soon as this book is done, printed and in your hands, I will start my workouts again.

The Mets wasted two Carlos Beltran homers this afternoon in an extra inning loss to the Astros. The Mets gave away this game on three different occasions, first blowing a 3-0 lead in the 4th inning, then after taking the lead in the 5th, they gave it right back in the 7th, and in the 10th, giving up a home run to Darin Erstad. The Mets were not able to score against Houston closer Jose Valverde in the bottom of the 10th, and the final was 6-4 Houston. Philadelphia won again tonight, so the lead is now a half a game. The Mets will try to earn a split with Houston tomorrow night, as Philadelphia will try to return the favor, and sweep the Dodgers, less than a month after Los Angeles swept them at Chavez Ravine.

J.J. Hardy made the most of J.J. Hardy bobble head day at Miller Park this afternoon. CC Sabathia was pulled after 6 innings and 96 pitches (a bit of a head scratcher), with a 2-1 lead. David Riske gave up a run in the 7th to cost Sabathia the win, but Mike Cameron hit his 23rd home run of the year in the bottom of the 8th to give the Brewers a 3-2 lead. What a 2nd half Cameron is having! He had five hits today, and is average is up to .257. Not great, but considering where he was just a month ago, it's amazing. Salomon Torres then became the 2nd Brewers reliever today to blow a save, giving up a run in the 9th to tie the game at 3-3. The game went into the 12th, still tied 3-3, when J.J. Hardy stepped up with Rickie Weeks on 2nd, and singled up the middle to plate the winning run. And despite Hardy collecting three hits, and Mike Cameron going 5-5, you cannot go without mentioning the job that Guillermo Mota did in the top of 12th to preserve the tie. After Carlos Villanueva pitched a scoreless 11th, he started the 12th by giving up a single and walking a pair of Pittsburgh Pirates (say that ten times fast). Mota inherited the bases loaded, with nobody out, and struck out Chris Gomez, and got Luis Rivas to ground into a 1-6-3 double play. Mota earned a standing ovation from a Miller Park crowd that, quite frankly, has given him a hard time all season. The win today gives the Brewers a record of 76-55, and their ninth series sweep of the season. They will take tomorrow off before heading to St Louis for a quick two game series.

August 25th

Look, the last few years, I've certainly learned my lesson about counting my chickens before they hatch. The Mets finished the 2006 season with the best record in baseball, winning the NL East by twelve games, and I remember as early as Memorial Day of that year, thinking they were shoe-ins to represent the National League in the World Series. But, it didn't happen, as Carlos Beltran watched an Adam Wainwright curve ball go right by him to end the NLCS. Then, last year, the Mets had a seven game lead on Philadelphia with seventeen to play, and again, I had them penciled in the NLCS at least, and not only did they relinquish the NL East crown to Philly, they came up one game short of the Wild Card as well. I was numb to it. I'm not even sure if I was sad, I was just numb that they could blow a seven game lead with seventeen to play. And this year, they played poorly enough in the first half of the season to get Willie Randolph fired. But since then, they've been one of the best teams in baseball, and yes, it's only August 25th, and they only have a half game lead on Philadelphia, but I have to admit, is this ever fun! The Mets have 16 games left at Shea, and they are in the pennant race. Nevermind what's happened, let's focus on 2008. The Mets have a chance to do something really special THIS year. But wait a minute!! So do the Brewers. The Brewers have the 2nd best record in the National League, and they also blew a substantial lead in their own division last year. And not to mention, they haven't been to the post season since 1982. This idea of the Mets and Brewers meeting in the NLCS seemed like a fun idea last year, and was definitely a possibility coming into the season, but I have to sit down and really process this. It is August 25th, and if the season were over, they would be meeting each other in the 1st round. The Cubs would draw the Diamondbacks, and the Mets would face the Brewers, because the Cubs and Brewers, by rule, cannot play each other in the 1st round. Now what? It kind of seems anti-climatic, after all I've written, they may have to play each other in the 1st round?? In a five game series?? So, one of the teams I love would have to knock out the other, with no guarantee of making the World Series. How would I feel about this? My vision was to have these teams meet in the NLCS, with the winner representing the National League in the World Series. If the Brewers eliminate the Mets, and then eventually lose to the Cubs, will I have wished the Mets won that series, thinking they would have a better shot at beating the Cubs? And vice versa, if the Mets beat the Brewers, and fall short of making the World Series, will I look back and wish the Brewers could have ended the Mets last season at Shea in the 1st round, so the Brewers could get the Cubs in a seven game series with Sabathia and Sheets each getting two starts? After almost five months of baseball, I still haven't answered these questions. Nothing has changed in the fact that I can and will not root against either team in the post season, under any circumstance. I still see myself having mixed emotions whatever happens. The true test will come next week, when the Mets make their only regular season trip to Miller Park to take on the Brewers. Will I look at the standings before the three game series, and make up my mind before first pitch on Labor Day as to who to root for, or will I follow my long standing rule of rooting for the home team in this series? I don't presume the Mets will have one of their starters going after his 300th win in this series, so I should be rooting for the Brewers to hold serve at home. One thing that I have noticed since sitting down to write this book, is that the people that I know that are Mets fans are far more open to me being a fan of both teams than my friends who are Brewers fans.

OK, I still have a while to think about this, and again, nothing has been clinched anyway, so I think I spent too much time talking about it in the first place. Tonight, Mike Pelfrey of the Mets did something that no Mets starter has done since 1995.

Before tonight, Bret Saberhagen was the last New York Mets starter to pitch consecutive complete games. I'm not even talking about complete game shutouts; I'm just talking about going nine innings. That blows my mind. And Pelfrey was one out shy of tossing back to back shutouts, in the Mets 9-1 win tonight against Houston. Carlos Delgado hit a pair of three run homers, raising his HR total to 28, and his RBI total to 90. Man alive, the media was writing this guy off three months ago! Tomorrow night, the Mets play their biggest game of the season thus far, as they travel to Philadelphia to take on the Phillies, still holding on to a half game lead. It will be Pedro Martinez vs Jamie Moyer. Treat this like a playoff game, boys. Go in to Citizens Bank Park and take care of business.

And the same goes for the Brewers. They have a 3.5 lead on St Louis, and getting another sweep of the Cardinals would put them up 5.5 games for the Wild Card lead. While a split is probably more realistic, they have to get at least one. Again, treat this like its October, and don't fall asleep at the wheel. Ben Sheets toes the rubber tomorrow night. Hopefully the bats will wake up. Sheets hasn't been getting great run support as of late. Tomorrow is heating up to be a great night of baseball. Where the hell is my glove? Go ahead, make your fun. I love this game.

August 26th

Five weeks ago tonight, the Mets blew a late lead to lose to the Phillies, and the Brewers won a huge game in St Louis. The exact same thing happened tonight. But this time, the Mets blew a seven run lead, and the Brewers win wasn't a nail biter, rather a blowout.

After taking a 7-0 lead in the 4th inning, the Phillies got one back in the bottom of the 4th to make it 7-1. Jimmy Rollins and Ryan Howard each hit 2 run homers in the 5th to cut the lead to 7-5. Pedro Martinez would leave the game with a lead after five, and the bullpen held the Phillies scoreless in the 6th and 7th innings. Duaner Sanchez gave up a run in the 8th, and Luis Ayala blew the save opportunity in the 9th, when Eric Bruntlett doubled home a run to tie it. The game would stay tied until the bottom of the 13th, when Shane Victorino led off the inning with a triple. The next two Phillies hitters were walked intentionally, to set up a force play at home. Charlie Manuel sent Brett Myers to the plate to pinch hit, and was clearly asked not to swing the bat, in hopes that he'd draw a walk to end the game. The count did go to 3-2 before Myers looked at a called strike three from Scott Schoeneweis. The next batter was Chris Coste, who entered the game in the 8th, and already collected three hits before entering the batter's box for the fourth time. Coste singled to center to end the game, and just like that, the Mets find themselves in 2nd place, when they were five innings away from coasting to an easy win, and taking a game and a half lead in the division. They have to bounce back with Johan Santana on the hill tomorrow.

The Brewers, who have won nine of thirteen against the Cardinals this season, and the last five games they've played at Busch Stadium, came into St Louis tonight hoping that they'd get a win, and take a 4.5 game lead in the Wild Card chase. Ben Sheets would take the ball tonight, and although he wasn't completely dominating, he did pitch six scoreless frames before handing it over to his bullpen. The Brewers would score single runs in the 1st, 3rd, and 5th before scoring two in the 7th on Ryan Braun's team leading 33rd home run of the season. The Brewers weren't satisfied with the 5-0 lead in the 9th, and put up a season high seven runs in the 9th, and would win this game 12-0. The Brewers collected 16 base hits, including seven for extra bases. Corey Hart's 38 doubles put him atop the NL leader board with Lance Berkman. The win puts the Brewers at 77-55, and with 30 games left, they look like they're in good position to capture the Wild Card. But as I've learned in the recent past, 30 games is a lot of baseball. And a 4.5 game lead ain't nothing at the end of August. You can't argue that the Brewers are one of the top three or four teams in baseball at this point of the season. A win tomorrow night would give them a 5.5 game lead in the Wild Card, with the lowly Pirates coming into Milwaukee on Friday. I am literally drooling right now.

August 27th

 I'm trying not to swear a lot in this book.........eff ewe see kay eye enn Cubs! They won again today, 2-0, to complete the sweep of the Pirates. Their record is now 83-50, which is the best record in all the land. The Brewers blew a golden opportunity tonight to stay within 5 games of the Cubs, as they blew a 3-0 lead, in what was an emotional game at Busch Stadium. Entering the 6th inning, the Cardinals were down three runs, when Ryan Ludwick got St Louis on the board with a solo HR off Manny Parra. It would be the only run that Parra would allow all night, as he left the game after six. In the 7th, Carlos Villanueva would load the bases, but got out of the inning with no damage done. As Villanueva walked off the field, he and Albert Pujols were barking at each other. Apparently, Villanueva said something in Spanish that Pujols did not appreciate. Whatever he said, it must have got the Cardinals pumped up, because they touched David Riske and Brian Shouse for four runs in the 8th, to take a 5-3 lead. The Brewers were not able to figure out Chris Perez, who struck out 3 Brewers in the 9th to earn his 6th save of the season. It looks like Perez could be the Cardinals closer of the future. While the loss is disappointing, getting a split here was the goal. After six straight wins at Busch, the Cards were due to get one back. The Brewers still have a 3.5 game lead, and won the season series, 10-5. It is the first season series win over St Louis in franchise history. They will take tomorrow off before traveling to Pittsburgh for a three game set. The Harley festival also kicks off tomorrow, so Milwaukee will be the center of the universe for four days, at least to folks who enjoy their Harleys. Speaking of which, I met a gentleman today named Paul who is from Milwaukee, but rides Yamaha's. His license plate says WHD, which stands for Why Harley Davidson? It sounds like he and I have a lot in common, as far as being from here, and being loyal to another "brand".

The Mets game in Philadelphia tonight got me dancing on the ceiling for a while (my apologies to Lionel Richie). After they took a 1-0 lead in the 1st, Johan Santana got bit by the long ball, as Ryan Howard hit a two run homer in the bottom of the 1st, and Jayson Werth hit a solo shot in the 2nd, go give the Phillies a 3-1 lead after 2 innings. I was violently going back and forth all night between the Brewers and Mets games, all the while entertaining my daughter, who I got to spend the night with. Thank you to the boys in Lynard Skynard for allowing this to happen. While tickling the laughs right out of Gracie, I missed Carlos Delgado hit his 29th homer of the year in the 6th inning to make it 3-2. Delgado would later tie it with his 30th homer of the year in the 8th, and Daniel Murphy untied it with an RBI double off of Brad Ridge. Brian Schneider added a two run single to give the Mets a 6-3 lead. Luis Ayala redeemed himself and notched the save, to put the Mets back in 1st. When the final out was recorded, Gracie and I chanted LETS GO METS several times before the tickle machine returned to get a few more giggles out of her.

My favorite memory from tonight had nothing to do with the pennant races I've been following all year, but it was witnessing my daughter come to attention anytime the Brewers game came back from commercial. She would hop up to the TV and copy whatever she heard from Brian Anderson. I heard her say "FSN Wisconsin several times, and even heard her say, "…and by Diggers Hotline" once. Once she starts learning all the players' names as quickly as she learns the ads, look out…

August 28th

I saw my friend Jim Hazard today, and was reminded that he is in a similar position that I am in. You see, Jim is a Chicago White Sox fan. The Sox are currently in 1st in the AL Central. Jim is also a Brewers fan, and naturally, he's hoping for a Sox/Brewers World Series, the same way I'm rooting for a

Mets/Brewers NLCS. I don't know anyone personally that has an emotional connection to the Rays or Angels, so I kind of hope the White Sox make it out of the American League, for good guys like Jim. I've had plenty a baseball conversation with him, and he is a true fan.

The Brewers and Mets each spent the day traveling, to Pittsburgh and Florida respectively. On Sunday night, both teams will travel to Milwaukee for a three game series, which will kick off on Labor Day afternoon. As I type tonight, the Mets have a one game lead on the Phillies, and the Brewers are 6.5 behind the Cubs, and 3.5 ahead of the Cardinals for the Wild Card. This very well could be a preview of the National League Divisional Series. Barring any rainout or injuries, Ben Sheets will lock up with Johan Santana on Monday. Just like earlier this season, I don't want either team getting swept. After the series in Milwaukee, the Mets have 15 of their last 22 games at home, so dropping two of three in Milwaukee wouldn't be the worst thing, because they can make that back with a ton of home games in September. I'm predicting the Brewers will win the Monday and Wednesday games, and the Mets will win Tuesday night. I don't know if I'm predicting that, or scripting that in my head. Either way, no sweeps guys!

August 29th

I *should* be at my good friend Andy Fefer's rehearsal dinner in Eau Claire tonight. The hats I choose to wear as financial mentor and # 1 dad prevented me from making the trip up tonight. He's getting married tomorrow, and as soon as I tell you about the amazing night of baseball I witnessed, I'm heading to bed so I get enough sleep for the ceremony. I have a four hour drive ahead of me in the morning.

Ryan Braun hit an opposite field three run homer in the 1st to give the Brewers a 3-0 lead, and then in a stunning move, the Brewers collectively told the Pirates that they were going to forfeit their at-bats for the next eight innings, and give Pittsburgh the next nine innings to score four runs for the win. Obviously, I'm kidding, but had they done that, they would have won either way. The Brewers did not score again, but Dave Bush and three relievers held the Pirates to one run scored all night, and did a great job getting out of jams, as the Pittsburgh would leave eleven men on base tonight. Eric Gagne returned to the team after his wife gave birth to their 4th child, and retired the only two men he faced tonight. They chose to name their son Harley Gagne. That can't be a coincidence. The Cubs stayed hot by winning their 7th straight, so we don't gain any ground on the division lead, however, the Cardinals lost, so the Brewers lead in the Wild Card race increases to 4.5 games.

Tonight, the Mets kicked off their series in Florida in "grand" fashion. Trailing 2-1 heading to the 9th, Florida closer Kevin Gregg was able to retire Robinson Cancel and Jose Reyes easily, and it looked as if the Marlins would take game one. But all Mets fans know that this team is Amazin' when they trail in the 9th, have no one on base, and are down to their final out. Luis Castillo kept the inning alive with a sharp single up the box after being down in the count 0-2. David Wright, who's been clutch all year, grounded a single into the hole in left field to put two on for the resurgent Carlos Delgado. Delgado never got a chance to do any damage, as he was hit by a pitch to load the bases for Carlos Beltran. Now, it's been documented and witnessed by a notary that I've been hard on Beltran since he looked at that Adam Wainwright curve ball in the 2006 NLCS. But it also needs to be said that there is no one I'd rather have roaming center field in Shea Stadium than Carlos Beltran. He's one of the best center fielders I've ever seen, and is clutch late in games, as well as October. Tonight, Beltran launched the first pitch he saw out of Dolphins Stadium for a grand slam as Gracie and I looked in amazement. The best thing was seeing all the Mets fans in Florida's stadium going nuts as Beltran circled the bases. What a thrill!

Then things got interesting. Luis Ayala, who is the closer de jour for the Mets, had already given one run back to the Marlins when he allowed a double down the left field line to Jorge Cantu, which should have scored two to tie the game, but Daniel Murphy played the double beautifully, and Alfredo Amezaga was held at 3rd. Wes Helms came up with men on 2nd and 3rd, and two outs, with a chance to single home a pair to win the game for Florida, but hit a weak grounder to Jose Reyes, who threw to Delgado to end the game. That was a 9th inning for the ages. The bullpen still scares the hell out of me, and I can't rely on grand slams to save us the rest of the year. But with all that said...one of the biggest wins of the year for sure.

August 30th

Andy and Deanne became man and wife today, in a beautiful ceremony in Eau Claire, a good time was had by all, and I just wrapped up my 8th hour of driving, and I am dead tired. You would think that the bar would have had the Brewers game on, as I did leave the reception area at around 7:30, right before the grand march, to try to get a score. No Brewers game. I forget sometimes that Eau Claire is really close to the Twin Cities, so for all I know, the bartender could give a shit about the Brewers/Pirates game. I left around 8:45, and got back home around 12:30. I'm tired as hell.

Here's a brief summary of what happened tonight...per the World Wide Web. I hope it's accurate, as I didn't catch a pitch of either game.

The Mets bullpen blew another one tonight, as Mike Pelfrey left with a 3-2 lead in the 7th. The Marlins scored one in 8th to tie it, and in the 9th inning, Aaron Heilman walked 4 batters in 1/3 of an inning, including the walk off free pass to Josh Willingham to win it. I'm glad I didn't see this one, I'm sure it would have pissed me off, and raised my blood pressure a couple of notches. I don't mind losing games, but I hate handing wins to teams. The loss was costly, as the Phillies beat the Cubs today, 5-2.

The Brewers continue to play like a world championship contender, as they hammered the Pirates tonight, 11-3. They scored 9 of their 11 runs in the 6th inning or later, and collected 16 hits. Jeff Suppan became the first Brewers starting pitcher in history to win five games in August, and CC Sabathia will have a chance tomorrow to do the same. With the Cubs losing, the Brewers find themselves only 5.5 back, and the Cardinals lost as well, so the lead in the Wild Card race increases to 5.5 games.

Rickrolled again! You know what they say...Rickroll me once, shame on you. Rickroll me twice, shame on me. Time for bed!

August 31st

Why in the world would a life long Brewers fan turn a game off in the 8th inning if the Brewers were up 7-0, and CC Sabathia was throwing a no-hitter? Can anyone answer that? The answer is...because one man, the official scorer in Pittsburgh, didn't see it that way. In the 5th inning today, Andy LaRoche hit a grounder back to Sabathia. Sabathia got to it quickly, and tried to bare hand it, but fumbled it, and LaRoche reached. It was clearly an error by Sabathia, but the scoreboard flashed "H" right away to the surprise of everyone (at least the Brewers fans). I was open-minded about seeing the replays, to see if LaRoche would have beaten it out, or if it would have taken an unbelievable play by Sabathia. But after looking at it several times, the ball was rolling slowly, and not spinning away from Sabathia, and when he got to the ball, LaRoche wasn't even half way down the line. He would have been out by about ten feet. After the ruling, I was hoping the Pirates would collect a clean hit later in the game, so that we wouldn't have to wonder "what if" for the rest of time. But that never happened. When Sabathia got Freddy Sanchez to fly out to Corey Hart to end the game, I was listening to the game in my car, and it felt like all Brewers fans had been collectively kicked in the stomach, knowing that history had been stripped from the record books. Even Uke said, "That should have been the 2nd no-hitter in Brewers history", shortly after the last out was recorded. I understand that the Brewers will appeal to Major League Baseball to have the call reversed, but even if they are successful in doing so, what makes a no-hitter great for the players are the butterflies that churn through your stomach as you count down the outs, and what makes it great for fans is to see the team celebrate that final out on the field. That has been taken from us, and the Brewers. Ned Yost was very animated, saying, "That's a stinkin' no-hitter that we all got cheated from". Ryan Braun said, "I think that 29 of 30 scorekeepers would have called that an error. I thought it was definitely a no-hitter". Sabathia was less animated than his manager and star teammate, saying, "We swept the series. I think that's the biggest thing and most important thing out of today. If they change it, they change it. If they don't, they don't. I'll be fine either way."

Whatever comes out of this, I believe that I witnessed a no-hitter today, and there is no question that I saw one of the best pitched games of my life. Sabathia struck out eleven, and walked three, and only allowed one base runner after the 3rd inning, the LaRoche "hit". Sabathia improves to 9-0 with an ERA of 1.43. This was his 3rd complete game shutout since joining the Brewers, and I'm starting to believe the hype about him being a NL MVP candidate. He has been more valuable to his team that any other player in the majors has been to theirs, no question.

Let's not forget that the Brewers have just swept the Pirates, their 10th sweep of the year, and have improved to 80-56. The Cubs and Cardinals each lost again today, and the Brewers now enter September with a 6.5 game lead in the Wild Card race, and only trail the Cubs by 4.5 games (with 6 more games head to head with Chicago).

The Mets gave up ten clean, uncontested hits today to the Marlins, but they knocked out twelve of their own, in beating the Marlins 6-2 in the rubber game of their series in Florida. The Mets brought out the heavy lumber early, with Carlos Beltran going yard in the 2nd, and Nick Evans and David Wright hitting back to back jacks in the 3rd. It was Evans' first major league homer. The Mets put up three in the 7th, chasing Scott Olsen from the game. Pedro Martinez went six solid innings, and five Mets relievers went three scoreless innings to seal the deal. New York heads into the last month of the season with a one game lead on Philadelphia. After the Mets series in Milwaukee, they head back home to host the Phillies in a huge weekend series.

I'm watching Baseball Tonight, and John Kruk thinks that Major League Baseball should reverse the call, and award a no-hitter to CC Sabathia. If John Kruk says no-hitter, than it's a no-hitter. Kruk is the industry standard when it comes to professional baseball analysis on this planet. While I am kidding about my opinion of Kruk, he's right. Even if the Brewers and their fans couldn't enjoy it as it happened, CC Sabathia threw a no-hitter today, and nobody will ever forget it, no matter how it goes down in history.

6. What a Ride

September 1st

Labor Day is one of my favorite days of the year. Labor Day to me means pennant fever, grilling out and looking forward to the upcoming football season. Today marks the first time that the Mets and Brewers have ever played a truly meaningful game against each other this late in the season. The Mets are coming off a series win against the Marlins, and the Brewers just swept the Pirates in Pittsburgh. The baseball world is still buzzing about CC Sabathia's performance yesterday, and it sounds like Major League Baseball will meet on Wednesday to discuss the possibility of changing the ruling and giving Sabathia credit for a no-no. I doubt anything will come out of it, but I hope I'm wrong.

This morning, I spent $12 on a new radio so that we can listen to Brewers games on the weekend. I'm sure I looked like Ralphie from "A Christmas Story" as I ran into our apartment, ripped the batteries out it's packaging, and placed them in the radio, hungrily looking for AM 620 on the dial. As soon as I found it, it was music to my ears, as I heard Bob Uecker welcome me to the broadcast of game one from Miller Park.

Now as you know, I've been asked all year who I'd cheer for if the Mets and Brewers faced each other in the playoffs, and over the last three days, I've gotten several e-mails as to who I'm pulling for this week. I'm going to take the advice of my good friend, Jesus Maldonado-Reyes, and not tell you…right now. He compares this dilemma I have to someone who is asked, "Who are you voting for in the upcoming election?" That's personal. A handful of my close friends know the answer, and have heard my explanation, but I will not be sharing that with the world…just yet. The fact is, I can say I love each time with all my heart, and I could never root against either franchise, but in all honesty, if you're putting a gun in my mouth, and making me tell the world who I'd rather see advance to the World Series in 2008, there is an answer. But I should let it be known, that the answer to that question would/could change from year to year, based on a number of different factors. If you're not satisfied with that answer, so be it. I think it is funny how the players that we love and idolize jump from team to team, sometimes on a yearly basis, showing absolutely no loyalty to a city, and I'm being chastised for being completely loyal to two teams.

The pitching matchup today was Johan Santana vs Ben Sheets. When these two men faced each other in April, Sheets got the best of Santana in a 5-3 Brewers win, as the Crew lit Santana up for three dingers. Miller Park was sold out for the 38th time this season, and for the 22nd straight game (a streak that will most likely end tomorrow night, with school starting). The Brewers got off to a great start, with an RBI double by Ryan Braun in the 1st inning. Braun would go on to collect three hits today. Ben Sheets looked as good today as he has since the All Star Break, going 5 shutout innings, before leaving the game in the 5th with a tight groin muscle. He didn't strike out a batter, but he only allowed three base runners. In the 6th inning, Prince Fielder would score on a Johan Santana balk to make it 2-0 Brewers. The Mets would score in the 7th to make it 2-1, and the bullpen (Gagne) gave up three in the 8th to blow the lead. Carlos Delgado, who is having a 2nd half for the ages, jacked a two run bomb to give the Mets the lead before they added another run later in the inning. The Mets bullpen was phenomenal today, going three innings, while striking out 5 and only allowing one base runner. The Brewers were not able to muster anything late, as the Mets took game one, 4-2. The good news is that the Cubs, Cardinals and Phillies all lost, meaning the Mets gain a game in the standings, and the Brewers don't lose any ground. Tomorrow night, I will be attending the game with Steven Forst, Demond Stewart and Jesus. It should be a blast.

September 2nd

Well, this is it. This is the game I've looked forward to all season. Quite honestly, I've been thinking about this game ever since the schedule came out last September. Tonight, three men who consider themselves Mets fans, as well as Brewers fans join me for the game. Steven Forst is from New York, and has been a Mets fan for a long, long time, but these days, follows the Brewers more closely, and will be rooting for the Brewers tonight. Demond Stewart lives in my hometown of Brown Deer, WI, is a Brewers fan, but tonight is donning Mets from neck to nuts. Jesus Maldonado-Reyes is also a Mets fan, but he will also be cheering for the Brewers tonight, as his father is a huge Brewers fan. I, of course, want to see a good, clean, well played ball game, much like the game I witnessed last July, when Geoff Jenkins beat the Mets in extras on a walk off homer. Jonathan Niese is making his Major League debut tonight for the Mets, and Manny Parra is pitching for the Brewers. As I'm sitting down with my pregame jumbo dog and Italian, I can't help but notice the Niese's birthday is October 27th, 1986. Any true Mets fan can tell you that was the night the Mets beat the Red Sox in Game Seven of the 1986 World Series. This is the kind of baseball trivia I live for.

Manny Parra looked very sharp in the top of the 1st, striking out Jose Reyes and Nick Evans, before getting David Wright to ground out to J.J. Hardy to end the inning. The Brewers started off with a bang tonight, as the first batter that Jonathan Niese would face in a big league game, Rickie Weeks, hit a towering home run to left field to give the Brewers the early lead. Niese would walk the next two batters, Hardy and Braun, and then settled down quite nicely, by getting Prince Fielder to ground out to first, and striking out Corey Hart and Mike Cameron.

Carlos Beltran led off the 2nd inning with a walk, and Carlos Delgado singled, as Beltran advanced to 3rd. Fernando Tatis would double, scoring Beltran, and Damion Easley drove in Delgado on a ground out to short, to give the Mets a 2-1 lead. The Brewers would go down quietly in the 2nd inning.

A J.J. Hardy fielding error and a single by David Wright set the stage for Carlos Beltran to hit a three run homer to left field to give the Mets a 5-1 lead in the 3rd. After getting the first two runners on in the 3rd, the Brewers were not able to capitalize, as Mike Cameron would fly out to shallow center field to end the inning.

The Mets were not able to score in the 4th, but the Brewers were able to bat around in their half of the 4th, scoring 4 times to tie the game at 5-5. The first five Brewers had base hits to start the inning, as Hall singled, Kendall and Parra each doubled, and Weeks and Hardy singled. My buddy Jesus is doing all kinds of celebratory dances, and Demond looks nervous. Later in the inning, Hardy would be thrown out at the plate, trying to score on a Corey Hart single, and Mike Cameron would strike out to end the 4th. Cameron would strand six runners on base in the first 4 innings.

Throughout the game, I asked the guys to name their all time favorite Mets and Brewers, asking each of them to give me five from each team. Including my picks, this is how the voting went. For the Mets, Dwight Gooden was the only player to receive 3 votes. Lenny Dykstra, Howard Johnson, Mike Piazza, John Franco, Keith Hernandez and Darryl Strawberry each received 2 votes, and David Cone, Carlos Beltran, Roberto Alomar, David Wright and Mookie Wilson each received 1 vote. For the Brewers, Robin Yount received votes from all 4 of us, Paul Molitor, Ben Oglivie, Cecil Cooper, Rollie Fingers and Ryan Braun each received 2 votes, and Juan Nieves, Ted Higuera, Gorman Thomas, Rob Deer, Prince Fielder and CC Sabathia each received 1 vote. No love for Doug Sisk or Joey Meyer?

The Mets would go down quietly in the 5th inning, and the Brewers would fail to score, despite once again getting 2 men on. Manny Parra's 2nd double of the night went to waste. Parra would face two men in the 6th before being lifted for Guillermo Mota. Mota would get Fernando Tatis to ground into a 5-4-3 double play, and got Damion Easley to ground out to 3rd to end the inning. Mota has pitched well as of late. The Brewers went down in order in the 6th.

In the 7th, 8th and 9th innings, neither team was able to get a runner into scoring position and I started to wonder if tonight's game would be like last year's contest, which went thirteen innings. I'm not sure about the other guys, but I'm in for the long haul. Daniel Murphy hit a pinch hit single to lead off the 10th

inning, with Salomon Torres now on to pitch for the Brewers. The super speedy Jose Reyes dropped down a bunt, and it was a beauty, as Jason Kendall's throw to 1st was wild, allowing Murphy to advance to 3rd. Endy Chavez, who was pinch hitting for Nick Evans, hit a fly ball to Corey Hart, which was deep enough to score Murphy, to give the Mets a 6-5 lead. Torres got out of the inning with no further damage by getting David Wright to ground into a 5-4-3 double play.

In the bottom of the 10th, Luis Ayala, the Mets' 7th pitcher of the night, came in to try to secure the win for New York. Mike Cameron struck out looking to lead off the inning. He would go 0 for 5 tonight, striking out three times and stranding six runners. Bill Hall flew out to Tatis for the 2nd out of the inning. Ned Yost called upon Brad Nelson to pinch hit for Jason Kendall, and at first I thought it was CC Sabathia grabbing a stick. Nelson is a big boy. The rookie would double down the right field line for his first big league hit, to keep the Brewers in the game. Gabe Kapler, who was pinch hitting for Torres, walked to extend the inning once again. Now it was up to Weeks, who already has 4 hits tonight, including the 1st inning big fly. The feeling I have watching this game is eerily similar to last year, when the Brewers came from behind to beat the Mets in extra frames. Weeks battled against Ayala, fouling off some really good pitches, but would strike out swinging to end the game. Jesus pointed out the smile on my face, and while it would have been great to see the Brewers take tonight's game, to set up a series deciding game tomorrow afternoon, I can't help but be happy that the Mets are beating good teams on the road. The Phillies won tonight, and the Cubs lost their 4th straight home game, so the Mets remain two in front of the Phillies, and the Brewers still trail the Cubs by 4.5 games.

I had as much fun tonight as I did last year. This isn't stressful at all. This is pure joy!

September 3rd

     With the Mets having taken the first two games of the series, I'd really like the Brewers to take today's game. If these teams are going to meet in the playoffs, it would be nice to know that the Brewers can hang with the Mets in a short series. I've said from day one that I don't want to see a sweep either way when these teams play each other. Unfortunately for me, and the many Milwaukee Brewers fans, Dave Bush did not get that memo. Bush allowed six runs in the top of the 1st, as he gave up a grand slam to Ryan Church, and a 2 run homer to Brian Schneider. I was at lunch at the time, so I didn't get to hear any of this. Joe gave me the news as I was coming back, and it seemed as if he wanted to punch me for not being completely upset.

     While the game was playing in the background, it was hard to follow what was going on, as this is our busiest time of the year at the credit union. I would hear updates on the score from time to time, but I didn't really have an idea what was going on in the game. During a brief down time, I heard Jim Powell call a J.J. Hardy homer to make it 6-2 Mets in the 7th inning, which means that Dave Bush eventually settled down. The Brewers bullpen gave up some late runs, and the final today would be 9-2 Mets. I got some pretty dirty looks from the people that knew of my love of the Mets. Look, as much as I like seeing the Mets go on the road, and sweep a great team, I never, under any circumstance, want to see the Brewers get swept in their own backyard. Hopefully, they can turn it around quickly against the San Diego Padres this weekend. They start a four game series at Miller Park tomorrow night.

     Philadelphia lost to Washington tonight, which gives the Mets a 3 game lead in the NL East. The Astros swept the Cubs at Wrigley Field, so the Brewers don't lose any ground to Chicago, and remain 4.5 games back. Had the Brewers swept the Mets, the Brewers would only be 1.5 games back of the Cubs, and the Mets would be tied with the Phillies atop the NL East. No Mets game tomorrow, as they open a huge series with the Phillies at Shea on Friday night.

September 4th

Tonight we said goodbye to our manager at the credit union, Hope Sterken, the only way the credit union knows how-delicious Applebee's. Hope and I were hired on the same day back in 2003, and while we were in training one day, I mistakenly called her Rose. Now, I had a fever of 102 that day, but that's no excuse. I have also been known to refer to Hope as "Shope Terkens" for a very childish reason not worth mentioning. Hope and a handful of people understand the story behind this, but as for the rest of you, it will have to remain a mystery.

While we were enjoying our appetizers and drinks, we had one TV with the Giants/Redskins game on, and another playing the Brewers/Padres. Eli Manning scored a rushing TD in the 1st quarter, marking the first points ever scored in "Son of Fugazzi", my bastard son scoring only fantasy football league debuting this season. Manning is my QB in that league, so I will carry a 6-0 lead into Sunday. The Giants won the game, 16-7.

The Brewers played a sloppy game tonight, losing to San Diego, 5-2. Jeff Suppan did not pitch well, which is a surprise, because of his 9-1 record in September since 2005. Rickie Weeks and Prince Fielder committed key errors, and the Brewers left 9 men on base tonight. Shawn Estes pitched well for the Padres, and I will always have a soft spot in my heart for Estes. Two years after Roger Clemens hit Mike Piazza in the head with a fastball, Estes retaliated by throwing a foot behind Clemens in a game, and then homering off Clemens later in that same game. That was a national game televised on FOX, and I remember every bit of it.

The loss tonight puts the Brewers five games back of the Cubs, heading into the weekend. While the Brewers will try to bounce back tomorrow night with CC on the hill, the Cubs will travel to Cincinnati for a three game series, in hopes of ending their five game losing streak.

September 5th

So Mike Schmidt wants to talk smack. In an e-mail that the Hall of Famer sent to Phillies manager Charlie Manuel, Schmidt said, "The Mets know you're better than they are. They remember last year." This message was posted on the clubhouse door prior to the Mets / Phillies game tonight, and Jimmy Rollins concurred, saying, "That part's true".

Tonight, Philadelphia was the better team, shutting out the Mets 3-0, behind a strong pitching performance by Brett Myers, who went eight innings, struck out 10 Mets, and only allowed three hits. Mike Pelfrey didn't give up an earned run until the 7th inning, when Greg Dobbs hit a two run homer to make it 3-0. The Phillies now trail the Mets by only two games.

Let's fast forward to the really predictable part of tonight's Brewers game against the Padres. Eric Gagne gave up a game tying home run to Brian Giles in the 8th inning. The home run by Giles blew a chance for CC Sabathia to go 10-0 with the Brewers. Sabathia pitched wonderfully once again, going seven innings, striking out nine, and only allowing one run on five hits. Thankfully, J.J. Hardy hit a walk off single in the bottom of the 11th to give the Brewers their first win on the homestand (1-4). The Cubs got smoked today, so the Brewers pull to within four games.

September 6th

Tonight, I made a new friend. His name is Jack Bryant, and he just turned celebrated his first birthday. I attended his birthoptionism this evening. For those of you scoring at home, that is birthday/adoption/baptism. The lasagna was wonderful, a Mike's Hard Lemonade or two were enjoyed, and everyone had a great time. Afterwards, I engaged in three games of tailgate toss, or as the kids call it, "bags". I am quite good at this game, and it

287

is quite addictive. So addictive, that I have to wear a patch to curb my cravings. The gum doesn't work.
The Mets were rained out tonight, and will play a day/night doubleheader tomorrow. Pedro will go in game one, and Johan will pitch in game two.

You could not ask for a better pitching matchup at Miller Park tonight than Ben Sheets vs Jake Peavy, pitting this year's NL All Star Game starter vs last year's NL Cy Young Award winner. And the game lived up to its billing. Prince Fielder hit an RBI double to left field in the 3rd inning, and that would be all the Brewers would need tonight. Sheets went the distance for his 5th complete game and 3rd shutout of the season. Incredibly, it was the first 1-0 complete game shutout win for the Brewers since 1992, when Jamie Navarro shutout the Boston Red Sox.

Tomorrow should be a lot of fun. The Brewers will try to take their 3rd straight against San Diego, and the NFL's first full weekend of games kicks off at noon. The plan is to hit Buffalo Wild Wings for the early games, come back home for the Browns game against Dallas, and head to Friday's for the Colts/Bears game, as well as Mets/Phillies. It will be a heavenly day of sports, and I will most likely gain about 20 pounds.

September 7th

This is one of my favorite days of the year.....the start of the NFL season. There are many questions entering the season. How will Aaron Rodgers respond to taking over as the starting QB in Green Bay? Does Brett Favre still have it, and how far can he take the J-E-T-S JETS JETS JETS? How will my Browns do in the AFC North? Can the Patriots rebound from the stunning Super Bowl upset and dominate once again? While those questions may not all be answered today, some of them may. We are at the Buffalo Wild Wings in Wauwatosa, and to my surprise, we have our pick of tables to choose from. It's 11:40am, and I thought the place would be packed already. I guess, with the Packers game scheduled for tomorrow night, it won't be as crazy as I anticipated. We do see a number of Favre Jets jerseys in the crowd. The original plan for Mike, Jeff, Amber and I was to order fifteen servings of wings, one with each sauce available on the menu, but that didn't happen. We did sample a number of them, but only ordered the Sweet BBQ, Spicy Garlic, Caribbean Jerk, Asian Zing and Medium flavors. I sampled the Mango Habanero, and nearly knocked Amber over trying to get to my complimentary water. WOW!

We enjoyed our wings as we watched the early games, all along watching for our respective fantasy players, and following our office pool picks. Favre threw a couple of TD's, and the Jets hung on to win his first game with New York. I have to admit, it felt strange seeing him as a Jet. I wish Favre well, but I won't root for him to make the playoffs. As soon as he's officially retired, for good, I will resume being a huge Favre fan. But for now, he is the enemy.

When we left the restaurant, the Mets and Brewers were both down 6-0 to the Phillies and Padres respectively, but the big difference was, the Mets had reached base in their game. Chris Young of the Padres was perfect threw 6 as we got to the car. As we arrived home, in time to see the kickoff of the Dallas/Cleveland game, the Mets game had just ended, with Philadelphia winning 6 to 2. The loss cuts the Mets lead to 1 game, with game three tonight. Chris Young carried his perfect game into the 8th inning, now leading 10-0, but Gabe Kapler hit a solo homer with two outs in the 8th to erase the perfect game, no-hitter and shutout on one pitch. The Brewers would not score again, and the final would be 10-1 Padres. The only good news for the Brewers was that the Cubs lost, so they lost no ground, and still trail them by just 4 games.

The Browns did not fair that well themselves this afternoon, losing 28-10 to the Dallas Cowboys. The big story in the NFL today was the Patriots losing Tom Brady for the season to a torn ACL and MCL. While you hate to see a player like Brady go down, I can name 31 other NFL franchises who think they have a slightly better chance of hoisting a Super Bowl trophy in February. Make that 30. The Rams looked terrible today. Three wins, tops, for them in 2008. You heard it here first.

      With all the football, and food consumption today, the main event for me was Mets/Phillies, the Sunday Night game on ESPN. We settled into the bar area at Friday's, and asked our server if we could get the baseball game on one of the big screens. We were granted our wish, as the Colts/Bears game was featured on most of the other screens. The Mets needed tonight's game to maintain an outright lead in the NL East. A loss would pull the Phillies even with the Mets, and give Philadelphia momentum heading into the last three weeks of the season. Tonight's pitching matchup was another great one this weekend, as Johan Santana squared off against fellow southpaw Cole Hamels. The Phillies were able to plate a run in the top of the first, but the Mets came right back and scored three times, with Carlos Delgado driving in two on a single to center field. After all the wings this afternoon, you'd think we wouldn't have had any room left for more tasty goodness, but Mike and I each ordered nachos, Jeff ordered a Cheesy Bacon Cheeseburger, which featured some sort of fried cheese patty on top of a bacon cheeseburger, and Amber ordered something foody and edible. I chased the nachos with some fries and blue cheese later in the evening, as the top button on my shorts officially popped off and hit the floor. I always say this, but never again, all this eating, at least not until next Sunday, for sure.

      Ryan Howard hit a solo HR in the 3rd to make it 3-2 Mets. Howard becomes the 1st Phillie in history to put up back to back to back 40 HR seasons. In the bottom of the 3rd, Carlos Delgado struck again, hitting a long solo HR to right field to make it 4-2 Mets. In the 5th inning, Delgado hit another solo HR off of Hamels, this one reaching the upper deck in right, to give the Mets a 5-2 lead. This guy was getting booed in early June, and now the faithful at Shea were chanting "MVP" as Delgado gave his curtain call following his colossal clout. Delgado became the 3rd Met this season to eclipse 100 RBI on the season (Wright, Beltran), and now has 33 homers on the season, to lead the team. Santana pitched great over 7 and 1/3 innings, and while Luis Ayala gave up one run in the 9th, no further damage was done, as Santana improved his record to 13-7 with the Mets 6-3 win tonight. Damn, did we need this one tonight. The lead is back up to two full games. No game tomorrow, before the Mets start a short two game series with Washington on Tuesday night.

With three weeks left in the season, the thought of a Mets / Brewers post season series is getting closer and closer to reality, but there is still a lot of baseball left. They have to treat the remaining three weeks like playoff games, and just play the game like they know they can. These are two very talented teams. Stay focused guys. Let's do this!

September 8th

I know it's a baseball book. I know it's a baseball book, but it has to be said. The Aaron Rodgers era is here! Rodgers looked great tonight, going 18-22 for 178 yards, throwing one TD and rushing for another. The Packers defeated the Vikings, 24-19 on Monday Night Football. The highlight of the night was Rodgers going up in the stands for a Lambeau Leap. Good for him, and good for the Packers fans who stand behind their new leader.

Game one of the Brewers' series with Cincinnati sure looked like it was going to go our way tonight, as the "good guys" took at 3-1 lead in the 2nd inning on the strength of Jason Kendall's 2nd homer of the season. J.J. Hardy added his 23rd home run of the season in the 5th inning to give the Brewers a 4-1 lead. Dave Bush pitched very well tonight, taking a 4-1 lead into the 8th inning, before giving up a solo HR to Joey Votto to make it 4-2. Bush would hand that 4-2 cushion to the usually reliable Salomon Torres, but tonight, Torres was awful, and there is no other way to put it. In the 9th, Torres walked 2 and gave up 4 hits, as three Cincinnati Reds crossed home plate, giving the Reds a 5-4 lead. Francisco Cordero got the Brewers in order in the 9th, after being greeted to 30,867 boos at Miller Park. Philadelphia beat Florida tonight, to pull within a game and a half of the Mets, and three games of the Brewers for the Wild Card. The Mets got some bad news tonight, as Billy Wagner was not only ruled out to come back this season, he will most likely miss all of next season as well. This is a huge blow to a bullpen that has struggled this year, and has been wildly overused. Guys like Brian Stokes and Luis Ayala will be asked to come up huge over the next three weeks, and hopefully beyond.

Thank you for the wonderful spread tonight, Amber. And Mike, don't think I forgot about you supplying the Dean's French Onion Dip and bag of Wavy Lays. That is clutch, my friend. Clutch!!

September 9th

Quick trivia, Brewers fans. What happened 16 years ago tonight? If you said Robin Yount singled to right field off of Jose Mesa of the Cleveland Indians for his 3000th career hit, you my friend are a true blue Brewers fan. I was at County Stadium that night, working as a vendor, and we all stopped selling while Yount was taking his cuts against Mesa. Right after he singled, I threw my arms up, I'm sure I teared up a bit, and turned around to give Tim Van Vooren a high five. He and John Anderson were covering the game for TV6 (which back then was the CBS affiliate, and is now FOX 6). It is still one of my favorite sports moments that I've seen live.

The game I saw tonight at Miller Park was not very fun to watch. The game just seemed to drag from the get go, and the Brewers trailed 4-1 heading into the bottom of the 7th. Ray Durham would hit a pinch hit, three run homer to tie the game, and while it did grab my attention, overall, this was not a well played game by either team. There were twelve walks allowed, four errors committed, and 20 men left on base throughout the game. Sixteen pitchers were used (eight for each team), as we sat through 4 hours and 21 minutes of the least enjoyable game I've seen all year. The Reds scored in the 11th, and Francisco Cordero made our hitters look like little leaguers in the bottom half of the 11th, to give the Reds a 5-4 win. Jamie, Pat and I did entertain ourselves, and others around us with our witty banter, and the jumbo dog I had before the game was phenomenal. The Italian was a little on the burnt side. I'm not gonna lie to you. The three of us shared some popcorn in the 8th inning. The walk back to Jamie's was rough, as the walk back always is after a loss, combined with the fact that I was wearing my "bank shoes". At least the Cubs lost again as well.

Now on to the good news! The Mets won a wild one at Shea tonight, beating the Nationals 10-8. The Mets slugged four home runs, including two more by Carlos Delgado, who now has 4 home runs and 7 RBI's in his last 8 at bats. Luis Ayala notched his 6th save since being named the closer, and the news gets better! The Phillies lost, so the Mets extend their lead to 2.5 games in the NL East.

I'm tired, but would you believe, still hungry? I'm going to attempt to down a "Volcano Taco" from Taco Bell. Hopefully, I come out of it alive.

September 10th

Today is my daughter's birthday, and I am very excited to see her. I haven't seen her in a week, as she and Heather spent the last week in Tennessee. I was able to take a half day today from work to spend the afternoon with her, and was thrilled to get to see her blow out her birthday candles and have some birthday cake. My heart overflowed with joy, seeing her so happy on her 3rd birthday. Earlier in the day, I took her to McDonald's for her favorite lunch, chicken and hot fries and she spent a good hour in the play area. Today was a very good day. I am very grateful for my beautiful daughter. Gracie, I love you so much. Thank you for the unsolicited kisses earlier. You're my angel.

The Brewers were able to salvage the final game in their series against Cincinnati this afternoon. Once again, CC Sabathia provided Milwaukee with a quality start, going seven innings, giving up three runs, and striking out eight Reds. He left trailing 3-1, but the Brewers were able to score one in the 7th, and two in the 8th to take the lead, 4-3. The bullpen was also great today, as Guillermo Mota pitched a scoreless 8th, and Salomon Torres redeemed himself by striking out the side in the 9th to record his 27th save of the year. The Cubs won, so their lead over Milwaukee remains 4.5 games.

The Mets won another wild one at Shea tonight, beating the Washington Nationals 13-10. When I left Port Washington, the Mets led 7-1, after scoring six runs in the bottom of the 3rd. But the Nationals scored one in the 4th, three in the 5th and two in the 6th to tie the game at 7-7. The Mets would score 4 runs in the bottom of the 7th, and it was, who else, Carlos Delgado's sacrifice fly that put the Mets ahead for good tonight. After allowing three runs to score in the top of the 8th, to make the score 11-10 Mets, David Wright hit his 28th home run of the season in the bottom of the 8th, to give the Mets the 13-10 lead that they held on to. Wright would go 4-4 with four runs scored and 3 RBI's tonight. Carlos Beltran went 3-5 with two runs scored and 2 RBI's and Fernando Tatis went 3-3 with two runs scored and 2 RBI's. Jose Reyes passed up Mookie Wilson for the all time lead in stolen bases in franchise history, and Luis Ayala recorded save # 7 in a Mets uniform. The Phillies were losers tonight against Florida, and the Mets lead in the NL East is now 3.5 games. Tonight is also the anniversary of the first night the Mets ever spent in first place, when they passed by the Cubs in 1969.

Life is beautiful tonight, as I day dream about post season baseball while I listen to Bon Iver, clutching my glove all the while. Tomorrow, the Mets are off, and the Brewers begin a huge four game series with Philadelphia. The Brewers have a four game lead on the Phillies, and don't look now, the Astros, for the NL

Wild Card. The Astros have won 14 of their last 15 games, and are making a run at being this year's Colorado Rockies. The way I see it, the Brewers simply have to take two of four of their games in Philadelphia if they want to feel good about heading into the last 2 weeks of the season.

September 11th

We will never forget.

Ben Sheets and the Brewers were not able to come up big in Philadelphia tonight, losing 6-3 at Citizens Bank Park. Sheets struggled early, and never really got in a good rhythm, as he gave up 5 runs over 6 innings, ending his streak of 20 scoreless innings pitched. Prince Fielder ended his homerless streak at 93 at bats, going deep for the 29th time this season, J.J. Hardy homered earlier in the game, but the Brewers were only able to collect six hits all night. Brad Lidge notched his 36th save in 36 chances to seal the victory for Philadelphia. The Phillies, as well as the Astros, who won again, find themselves only three back of the Brewers for the Wild Card. The Cubs won tonight in St Louis, so the Brewers are now 5.5 back of Chicago. Man, it would have been nice to take game one, now the pressure is on to take two of the next three games, with Sabathia scheduled to pitch game one in Chicago next week.

Taking a look around the rest of the league, the New York Metropolitans have a three game lead over the Phillies, with a four game advantage in the loss column. The Dodgers have won nine of ten, while the Diamondbacks have lost six straight, and the Dodgers find themselves up 3.5 games on the Snakes. I don't think any other National League team wants to face Arizona, with Webb, Haren and Johnson, but the Dodgers are playing solid right now, and they will not be a push over in the 1st round, if they indeed hang on in the NL West.

In the American League, Tampa Bay is holding on to their lead in the AL East, currently 2.5 games up on Boston. Toronto has passed up the Yankees for 3rd place, as they have won nine of their last ten games. The White Sox have a one game lead over the Twins with 16 left to play for each. The Angels wrapped up the AL West tonight, as Francisco Rodriguez, K-Rod, as it were, tied Bobby Thigpen's record for saves in a single season, with his 57th save of the year. And who owned Thigpen in 1990? Respect! Boston currently holds a 5.5 game lead over Minnesota for the AL Wild Card. It's looking like they'll be able to defend their title in October, barring a major collapse.

September 12th

It looks like Mother Nature has no interest in the book I'm writing, as every significant game to the Mets and Brewers run at the postseason was wiped out by rain. The Cubs entire series in Houston is in serious jeopardy of being cancelled because of Hurricane Ike. There is talk of that series resuming on Sunday, possibly at a neutral site, but no word as of yet. The Mets will play a doubleheader tomorrow at Shea against the Braves, and the Brewers will play tomorrow afternoon as scheduled, as part of FOX's national coverage, and then will finish their series with Philadelphia on Sunday with a day / night doubleheader.

With no games to follow, it looks like a night of coloring for Gracie and I. Put a little Charlie Brown on in the background, pop some delicious popcorn and you have one heck of a father / daughter night in the making. Now Lucy, if you'd just let ol' Charlie Brown kick that football one time, you'd make my daughter really happy. What do you say?

September 13th

    Today can really only be described as a "lazy day". The rain kept Gracie and I away from any parks, and we each took lengthy naps. Gracie fell asleep first, and as she slept, I tried to follow the Brewers game, but their play put me to sleep quickly, as the Phillies led 5-0 after two innings. I awoke to Tom Pippins, Jerry Augustine and Jen Lada telling me about the 7-3 loss on Brewers Blast. Pippins was adamant that Yost is gone if they don't make the playoffs, and they all wondered if Manny Parra is simply running out of gas, as he did not look good again today. Ryan Braun hit his 35th homer in a losing effort, as the Brewers' lead in the Wild Card race is now down to two games.

    In game one of the Mets' doubleheader with the Braves, Johan Santana carried a shutout into the 8th inning, as the Mets led 2-0. But the first two men the Braves sent to bat against Santana would reach base in the 8th, and they would both end up scoring on a two run single that Scott Schoeneweis gave up to Jeff Francoeur. Francouer later scored on an Omar Infante single given up by Brian Stokes, to give the Braves a 3-2 lead that they would not relinquish.

    The Mets would bounce back in a big way in game two, as Jonathan Niese pitched eight shutout innings while striking out seven Braves, as the Mets would go on to win, 5-0. Luis Ayala worked the ninth to seal the deal, and give New York an 83-64 record, and a 2.5 game lead on the Phillies. David Wright, Jose Reyes and Carlos Beltran all homered in the game as Wright's RBI total reached 111 for the season.

    It was learned today that Miller Park will be hosting two of the three games that were originally scheduled at Minute Maid Park between the Cubs and Astros this weekend. They will play tomorrow night at 7:05pm, then again at 1:05pm on Monday afternoon. I am not happy about this, nor are the Houston Astros. These are supposed to be home games for the Astros, and they have to travel to Milwaukee and host the Cubs, who you just know are going to fill Miller Park with obnoxious fans (sorry, Schewe. You're one of the good ones. And sorry to all the Cubs fans that I have alienated, but seriously, you're obnoxious, at times). I can't believe that Major League Baseball couldn't find another host city for these games. The way the Brewers have been playing in September (3-9 thus far), you almost want the Cubs to win, because the Astros are only 2.5 behind us, and it doesn't look like we're catching the Cubs.

SNL premiered tonight with Michael Phelps as host. It was not bad, but not great. Of course, Tina Fey played Sarah Palin. I think we all saw that coming. I'm excited for the upcoming season, as I always am.

September 14th

Are you kidding me? Talk about kicking someone when they're down. First, the Mets blow a 4-2 lead in the 9th, as Luis Ayala and Pedro Feliciano combine to give up 5 runs in 1/3 of an inning, as the Braves beat the Mets 7-4. David Wright hit two more home runs in a losing effort. So, OK, I'm down. Now, here's where all the kicking comes in. The Brewers also blew a lead today, as Dave Bush gave up a two run homer to Ryan Howard in the 6th inning to tie the game at 3-3, then the Phillies went on to score four runs in the 8th to win again, 7-3. Yost shuffled his lineup today, to give the team a spark, as Hart led off, Ray Durham hit 3rd, and Ryan Braun hit 5th. This seemed to work in the 1st, as Hart led the game off with a triple, and Ray Durham hit a two run homer shortly thereafter. But the Brewers could only muster 3 hits the rest of the way, one of them being a solo HR by Mike Cameron. Oh, wait...there's more. If this wasn't enough, between 7:00 and 10:30 tonight, the Brewers lost 6-1 in the second game of the doubleheader with Philadelphia, as the Phillies completed the four game sweep of the Brewers to pull even with them in the Wild Card race, the Browns looked awful in a 10-6 loss to the Steelers at home, and here's the clincher.......Carlos Zambrano threw a no-hitter against the Astros tonight, AT MILLER PARK, WITH 23,000 SCREAMING CUBS

298

FANS CELEBRATING IN OUR HOUSE !! God, it just made me sick to my stomach to think the 1st ever no-hitter thrown in Miller Park was thrown by Carlos Zambrano...in a Cubs/Astros game?!?! I have grown to hate the Cubs now! I don't know what would make me happier...seeing the Mets or Brewers win it all, or watching the Cubs choke once again. I just can't get the image out of my head! Mark it down. If the Mets and Brewers do play each other in the first round, BRING ON THE CUBS. I don't want them getting swept in the 1st round like last year. I want them to advance to the NLCS, and get so close, only to have one of my teams punch them in the mouth and advance to the World Series. Century Peat? Not on my watch...

September 15th

I thought Kevin was kidding when he told me. I actually laughed, but he never said, "I'm kidding", and he looked pretty serious. I still didn't believe it until I read it on espn.com. The Brewers fired Ned Yost today. TODAY! With twelve games left in the season! What the hell is going on here? Goddamn, I know it's a business, but come on! You're gonna go five seasons and 150 games into the 6th season with Yost as your guy, and you're gonna throw him under the bus with twelve games left? Look, I didn't like it when they fired Randolph in June, but at least by doing it then, it gives the team some time to gel under the new hire. There are twelve games left in the season! Players come and go, coaches come and go, owners come and go, but to make a change with twelve games left, really does prove that winning is the only thing that matters, at any cost. Yost should have been given the chance to win this thing, for Pete's sake. This team was a laughing stock when he and Melvin took over in 2003, and we are this close to getting to the postseason, and he won't get the chance to do it. Look, if we don't get to October, you fire him. I think we're all agreed on that. But to not even give him a chance to finish this is insulting. Don't talk to me about motivation! If these grown men need to be motivated, we need new players. If these guys need a "new voice" with 12 games left, then that is just sad. Look, I've been following sports long enough to know that if this works, and Dale Sveum gets this team to play better than they have thus far in September, and it leads to a postseason birth, then he and Melvin look like geniuses. And if they don't make the postseason, regardless of what the Brewers record is in the next 12 games, does that mean that Sveum failed? Part of the romance has been stripped from this story for me. I understand it when a team makes a change at midseason if a team is struggling, and when that team ends up making the postseason, or even a World Series, it's a great story. Hell, the 1982 Brewers fired their skipper early on, and ended up taking the '82 Series to seven games under the guidance of Harvey Kuenn. But this is absurd. It's Yost's fault that Braun/Fielder/Hart aren't producing in September? It's Yost's fault that Parra/Bush/Suppan can't hold leads in September? If you're gonna fire the guy, do it after the Boston sweep in May, but you can't get this far, and feel good about making a move with twelve games left. This is unheard of in the history of sports. This would be like if an NFL team was 9-6, and needed to win their last game to make the playoffs, and the head coach was fired because they were 9-4 two weeks ago. The baseball season is such a long season of ups and downs, and it's not like the Brewers are the only good NL team struggling these days. The Cubs have struggled, the Mets have struggled, the Diamondbacks have all but fallen out of contention, and the Cardinals are done. There's gotta be something that we don't know. Yes, we've been swept in four huge series this year, but we also have ten sweeps under our belt, and the last time I checked, we are 83-67, and tied for the NL Wild Card lead. I wonder if Joe Maddon will be fired from Tampa Bay for blowing their lead in the AL East. They lost to Boston tonight at home, 13-5. It looks like they'll need a "fresh perspective" for the next two weeks as well. What a joke. I guess there's a first for everything, and there's nothing that this season ticket holder can do about it, for now.

Now that I've put my two cents in, let's look at the remainder of the season. The Brewers sit atop the NL Wild Card standings with Philadelphia, while the Astros trail by 2.5 games. The Brewers have a new manager, Dale Sveum, and a new bench coach in Robin Yount (Ted Simmons was "reassigned"). This is the same Robin Yount who resigned after one year as bench coach after the 2006 season. We all love Robin Yount, don't get me wrong, but is this going to be a long term deal, or just a 12 game rental. Sveum brings a different demeanor to the dugout than Yost, as he is more laid back, and won't sweat the small stuff as much. I don't want people to think I want the Brewers to lose now that they've made a switch, I just don't see what difference it's going to make either way. Players have to perform. They get a lot of credit when they win, but don't shoulder enough blame when they lose. The next six games are on the road, as the Brewers start a three game series at Wrigley Field on Tuesday night, and will travel to Cincinnati this weekend for a three game series. They finish the season at home for six games, three with Pittsburgh and three more with the Cubs. The Phillies remaining schedule looks like this...three at Atlanta, three at Florida, then hosting the Braves for three and the Nationals for three. The schedule clearly favors the Phillies down the stretch.

The Mets, who came into tonight with a one game lead on the Phillies, have fourteen games left...four at Washington, three at Atlanta, four at home with the Cubs and three at home with Florida. Hopefully, the Cubs will have clinched the NL Central by the time they travel to Shea, and they can rest some starters, and the Mets can take advantage of the situation. Tonight, however, the Mets were not able to capitalize, as they dropped game one in Washington, 7-2. Pedro was not sharp, and we only collected 5 hits all night. Wright, Beltran and Delgado combined for an 0-11 night with 4 strikeouts and 6 men left on base. It was ugly, and now New York only holds a half game lead heading into tomorrow night.

Tonight, I am frustrated with the Mets, and disappointed in the Brewers. But I am a fan, regardless, and winning is the best medicine out there. It sure beats being a Seattle Mariners fan these days. I look forward to CC Sabathia pitching in the first game of a twelve game season against the Cubs at Wrigley Field. And the Mets still control their own destiny. Glass half full. Glass half full !

September 16th

It looks like Sveum is putting his stamp on things right away, as he is lifting Manny Parra from the rotation, and will move Dave Bush and Jeff Suppan up, making room for Seth McClung to start on Saturday night in Cincinnati. Sveum has also shuffled the lineup, putting veterans Mike Cameron and Ray Durham at the top of the order, and hitting J.J. Hardy 5th, and Corey Hart 6th. Ryan Braun has been moved back to the 3 hole.

Tonight's starting pitcher for the Crew, CC Sabathia, was looking to become only the 2nd major leaguer to ever win his first ten decisions with a team he was traded to mid-season. Sabathia uncharacteristically gave up a run in the 1st, and two in the 3rd, before setting down. Prince Fielder woke the team up a bit in the 6th, with a monstrous two run homer to make it 3-2 Cubs. Alfonso Soriano would homer in the bottom of the 7th to make it 4-2. Sabathia would go seven tonight, striking out five and walking none, but gave up four earned on nine hits. Fielder would hit another bomb in the 8th to make it 4-3, but the Cubs got a run right back to extend their lead to 5-3. In the top of the 9th, Ray Durham would hit his 2nd double of the night to score Alcides Escobar, making the score 5 to 4. Ryan Braun would reach on an infield single to extend the inning, setting the stage for Prince Fielder to come through once again. Coming into this at-bat, Fielder was 3-4 with a double and 2 HR, while driving in three runs. But in the 9th, Kerry Wood threw him a curve ball that buckled his knees, and the bat never left his shoulder, as the Cubs would take game one. It was a great game, but the win for the Cubs shrinks their magic number down to 4 games, and the Brewers find themselves in serious jeopardy to make the playoffs. The loss is the fifth in a row, and for the first time since mid-July, they are out of the Wild Card lead, with the Phillies winning tonight.

But it's not the Phillies that the Brewers trail in the Wild Card hunt anymore. It's the Mets, because they lost again in Washington, 1-0, and Philadelphia now leads the Mets by a half a game in the NL East, and the Mets lead the Brewers by a half a game in the Wild Card hunt. It's amazing to think that the Brewers led the Wild Card by 6.5 games less than two weeks ago, and now, they wouldn't even qualify for the playoffs if the season were over. What's even more amazing is how the Mets are letting a 58 win team bully them this late in the season. So now the emphasis has shifted from a possible Mets/Brewers playoff series to which team can back into a Wild Card berth. If the Astros pass them both up, I will have no choice but to have a seat, and share a laugh with the powers that be that have put me through this roller coaster ride for the second year in a row.

September 17th

I have two goals for tonight. The first is to witness the Brewers defeat the Cubs on ESPN, and the second is to channel my boy Tracy, and hit for the cycle; but not the sausage cycle. Tonight, I am going to attempt to hit for the TIZER CYCLE.

I am at Friday's tonight, and I've just spent the last 45 minutes putting the finishing touches on a presentation that I'm doing on campus tomorrow. Once the game starts, the Brewers will be my central focus (along with the food), as Dale Sveum tries to get his first win as a big league manager. The bar area is packed without 15-20 Brewers fans, and I have grabbed the table nearest to the giant HD on the wall.

As Jason Marquis is finishing up his warm up tosses, I put in an order for some boneless buffalo wings. I figure the wings would be the "double" of this particular cycle, because I plan on ordering fries later, which I figure is the "single". As I place my order, I can't help but notice how relaxed Sveum looks, standing in the dugout. One thing I noticed in his press conference on Monday was that he kept referring to the next six weeks, instead of saying the next twelve games, which tells me he has confidence in his ball club to go deep into October.

Mike Cameron got things under way tonight by hitting a hard single to left field. Cameron would steal 2nd before Ray Durham and Ryan Braun each drew a walk, setting up a bases loaded, nobody out situation Prince Fielder. Fielder wasted no time, hitting a towering double to right center on the first pitch he saw, which scored all three Brewers to give the Brewers a 3-0 lead coming out of the gate. The crowd went nuts. The next three batters (Hardy, Hart and Counsell) would go down quietly to end the inning. Ben Sheets looked great in the 1st inning, getting Alfonso Soriano to ground out weakly to Craig Counsell, and striking out Mike Fontenot and Derrick Lee.

The Brewers would go down in order in the 2nd, as the boneless wings were polished off, and the nachos were ordered. The nachos are definitely the "home run" of this cycle, for various reasons. They are the biggest appetizer in size, and the best tasting. As I'm placing the order for the nachos (no guacamole, of course), Aramis Ramirez went deep off Sheets to cut the Brewers' lead to 3-1. Sheets would retire the next three batters (Edmonds, DeRosa and Soto) pretty easily, as the game now heads into the 3rd.

Prince Fielder would draw a two out walk, and J.J. Hardy would follow that with a single to center, but Corey Hart grounded out to 3rd to end the inning, stranding two base runners. Coming back from commercial, I am disturbed at the sight of Mark DeFelice taking the hill for the Crew. Yet another Ben Sheets injury, I'm assuming (it would later be revealed as a forearm strain). DeFelice would set the Cubs down in order in the 3rd, and can I just take a moment here to give my compliments to the chef. These nachos are the best I've ever had at Friday's.

Jason Kendall would single with one out in the 4th, but the Brewers weren't able to capitalize. In the bottom of the 4th, DeFelice would walk Ramirez with two outs, and then give up a single to Jim Edmonds, sending Ramirez to 3rd, but he would get out of the inning, forcing Mark DeRosa to ground into a fielder's choice.

The Brewers' 5th inning looked very much like the 3rd inning, as Prince Fielder would come through with two outs, this time doubling to left center, and J.J. Hardy would once again single, but Fielder was unable to score. Corey Hart hit a lazy fly ball to right field, stranding two more base runners as the score remained 3-1 Brewers. Todd Coffey would pitch the 5th for the Brewers, and got out of the inning without giving up a run, despite walking Geovany Soto to lead off the inning.

The Brewers wasted another opportunity to add to their lead in the 6th, as Jason Kendall and Brad Nelson (pinch hitting for Coffey), each walked with one out, but Mike Cameron struck out swinging, and Ray Durham popped up to the catcher to end the inning. Carlos Villanueva took over for the Brewers in the 6th, and after he got Mike Fontenot on a called 3rd strike, and Derrick Lee to fly to center, he gave up a single to Aramis Ramirez, and then was pulled by Sveum in favor of Mitch Stetter. Jim Edmonds represented the tying run, but Stetter was able to get Edmonds to ground out to Durham to end the inning.

It's time for the fries and the jalapeno poppers. The fries are a very common order for me at Friday's, so that has to be the "single", and the poppers are new at Friday's, and they are cream cheese, instead of cheddar, so this is clearly the "triple". The Brewers would explode in the 7th, much to the delight of the fans watching with me at the restaurant. Ryan Braun was hit by a pitch to lead off the inning. Fielder would single, and J.J. Hardy would double home Braun, with Fielder stopping at 3rd. Corey Hart would step up once again with two men on base, but this time, he came through singling up the middle, scoring both Fielder and Hardy, to make it 6-1. Craig Counsell was hit by a pitch, and Jason Kendall laid down a great bunt to move Hart to 3rd, and Counsell to 2nd. Mike Lamb would be asked to hit for Mitch Stetter, and he hit a fly ball to left field, and Soriano would make a great throw home to nail Hart, for the inning ending double play. Eric Gagne would come in and work a 1-2-3 seventh inning for the Brewers, to hold the lead at 6-1.

The Phillies have just beaten the Braves, and the Mets have finally beaten the Nationals, after two big losses in Washington. The Mets hit four dingers tonight (Delgado, Reyes, and two for Beltran) in a 9-7 win. The Mets remain a half a game back of the Phillies. In the Brewers 8th inning, a one out Ray Durham single was stranded as Ryan Braun lined out to Ramirez, and Prince Fielder would pop up to Ramirez to end the inning. The Cubs would get two on in the bottom of the 8th, but could not score against Guillermo Mota, as Ramirez would hit into a 6-4 fielder's choice to end the inning. Despite leaving two poppers on the table, I am proclaiming that I have indeed hit for the TIZER CYCLE, since there were 9 poppers in the order, and I'm used to only ordering six, meaning I had one more than usual. If you want to put an asterisk by this record, that is up to you, but in my heart, I hit for the cycle, and I deserve to stand next to Mike Hegan, Charlie Moore, Robin Yount, Paul Molitor, Chad Moeller and Tracy Norrell (not to mention Jim Gantner...an inside joke between me and the boys).

The Brewers would go down in order in the top of the 9th, setting the stage for Salomon Torres to come on in the bottom of the 9th, in a non-save situation, to try to nail down Sveum's first W. Torres got Jim Edmonds to ground to Durham for the first out of the inning. Mark DeRosa singled to left and Geovany Soto also singled, sending DeRosa to 3rd with one out. Ryan Theriot hit a ground ball to Hardy, and it looked like it would be a 6-4-3 double play to end the game, however, Theriot beat the throw, and DeRosa scored to make it 6-2. Daryle Ward was asked to pinch hit, but grounded weakly to Durham to end the game. Cubs lose! Cubs lose! The Brewers stay within a half game of the Mets for the Wild Card lead. Congratulations to Dale Sveum, getting his first big league win as manager.

September 18th

Remember July 3rd? Off the top of your head, probably not, but I'll remind you. The Brewers had a 5-0 lead in the bottom of the 9th, at Arizona, only to lose 6-5. It was a Thursday afternoon game, much like today's game at Wrigley Field.

Let's just fast forward to the bottom of the 9th, and get this over with. Brewers are up 6-2, with two outs, and nobody on. Ramirez doubled. Edmonds singled, scoring Ramirez. DeRosa singled. Soto homered, to tie it. In the 12th, Derrick Lee broke an 0-5 for day by singling home the winning run. Not much more I can say.

Philadelphia completed their sweep of the Braves tonight; meaning the Brewers now trailed the Phillies by two games. A week ago today, the Brewers led the Phillies by four games, heading into their series.

The Mets took care of their own business tonight, scoring in each of the first five innings of tonight's game at Washington. They took a 7-0 lead into the 7th, as Johan Santana gave up his first run of the night on an Anderson Hernandez RBI double. The Nationals would score once again in the 8th, but that would be it, as the Mets earned a split in the four game series, winning 7-2. Brian Schneider hit two solo homers in his first two at bats, and Santana improved his record to 14-7, with an ERA of 2.65. The Mets remain just a half game back of the Phillies in the NL East. This weekend, it's off to Atlanta for three, before heading back to Shea for a 7 game home stand to finish the season. The Phillies will travel to Florida for three before ending their season with 6 at home.

September 19th

If I put out my own daily newspaper, tomorrow's headline would read, "METS TAKE OVER FIRST PLACE". That's because they won tonight in Atlanta, 9-5, after scoring 4 runs in the 8th inning and the Phillies got smoked, 14-8 in Florida. Daniel Murphy came up huge tonight, plating the go-ahead runs on a pinch-hit 2 run double, raising his average to .374 (albeit in just over 100 at bats).

The Brewers stunk from the bell, as Jeff Suppan gave up five runs before he retired a single batter. After only going two full innings, Manny Parra came in, and pitched even worse than Suppan, giving up five runs, and four homers, over four innings. Parra became the first reliever in the big leagues this season to surrender four home runs in the same game. The final from Cincinnati tonight was 11-2. The Brewers blew a great opportunity to pull within a game of the Phillies, as Dale Sveum falls to 1-3 as Brewers skipper. CC Sabathia is being moved up in the rotation, and will pitch tomorrow, because of Seth McClung being used yesterday in the twelve inning game at Wrigley. Hopefully Sabathia can carry this team on his shoulders, as the team has yet to lose a game that Sabathia has pitched in against teams not named "the Cubs". The Brewers are 12-0 vs. the league when Sabathia pitches, and 0-2 vs. the Cubs.

September 20th

The inevitable happened this afternoon, as the Cubs beat the Cardinals at Wrigley Field to wrap up the NL Central. This is good news for Brewers fans, and Mets fans alike, as the Cubs will not have much to play for in their last eight games of the season. This was the only good news that Brewers and Mets fans received today, as both teams lost this afternoon on the road. The Braves scored three in the 1st inning, and never looked back, as the Mets fell 4-2 at Turner Field. The Brewers took a 2-1 lead into the 6th at Cincinnati, but gave up three runs in the 6th, as the Reds hung on to win 4-3. It was CC Sabathia's second consecutive loss after winning his first nine decisions in a Brewers uniform. The Phillies won their game today, meaning the Mets fall back into 2nd place, a half game behind Philadelphia, and the Brewers are now 2.5 games behind the Mets for the NL Wild Card, and 3 games behind Philadelphia. Milwaukee also lost their coin flip with New York today, for the right to host a potential play-in game if they finish with identical records. The Brewers lost all four of their Wild Card scenario coin flips.

But today was a great day, because I got to play catch with my daughter outside. She throws a mean fastball, but needs to develop an out pitch. She's got good control, and knows when to throw one low and away.

September 21st

Are you ready for some multiple choice, kids? Who blew the game for the Mets today? Was it A) The bullpen, B) The bullpen, C) The bullpen, or D) The bullpen. I forgot to tell you, that there can be more than one right answer. The correct answers are A, B, C and D. But if you picked any of them, and not necessarily all of them, you know what, I'll give it to you anyway. But you should have concluded that all four were right, because they were the same answer. So I take it back. If you, for example, answered A, B and D, then something is wrong with you for leaving out C, again, because they were all the same. You think I'm bitter? The Mets could not hold on to a 4-2 lead in Atlanta, and lost today, 7-6. Philadelphia beat Florida, putting the Phillies a game and a half ahead of the Mets.

The Brewers avoided a sweep in Cincinnati today by defeating the Reds 8-1. Prince Fielder slugged his 33rd HR of the season, and Todd Coffey picked up his first win in a Brewers uniform. The Brewers find themselves just a game and a half behind the Mets for the Wild Card. Russell Branyan and Yovani Gallardo were activated from the DL today. Branyan will be used as a left handed option off the bench late in games, and I imagine that Gallardo will be used out of the bullpen, at least for now. I can't imagine that he is physically ready to start games, but could be a valuable addition to a bullpen that could use a fresh arm.

Shortly after the Brewers finished off the Reds today, Amber and I headed to Lambeau Field for the Sunday Night game between Dallas and Green Bay. There is really nothing in sports like seeing a game at Lambeau. Somehow, eight players from the Brewers (Sabathia, Sheets, Fielder, Weeks, Hall, Gwynn, Kapler and Rivera) were there by the time we got to the stadium at 6:30. They must have taken a flight from Cincinnati to the 50 yard line at Lambeau. And Jay-Z was in attendance as well. Who knows if Jessica Simpson was allowed in the building. It was great to hear the ovation for Aaron Rodgers, and it was a pretty decent game for a while. Dallas just proved to be the more talented team, beating the Packers 27-16. The attendance tonight set a regular season game record at Lambeau Field, and despite the outcome, we had a great time at the game. One particular highlight of the evening was finally, FINALLY finding a Mexican Restaurant to replace my love, Chi-Chi's. We ate at Margarita's in Green Bay, and it was the closest thing to Chi-Chi's I've had since they closed. There are still some Chi-Chi's locations opened, I believe in Germany somewhere, but I don't want to have to burn vacation time to fly to Germany for an hour of dinner. So, I've found a new baby!

September 22nd

The Yankees played their last game at Yankee Stadium last night, beating the Orioles, 7-3. I have yet to see any of the post game celebration, with the team gathering on and/or near the mound, with Derek Jeter leading the way, talking about what it's like to be a Yankee, and thanking the fans for their support, but I heard it was pretty neat. Hopefully, the Mets will be able to give their fans something neat to take away from their last game at Shea, and hopefully, it won't be this weekend. But the way they've been playing lately, Sunday might just be the last game at Shea. The Mets gave up 6 runs in the 4th to the Cubs, and were never able to recover, dropping tonight's game, 9-5. The Phillies beat Atlanta when they scored 4 runs in the bottom of the 8th to break a 2-2 tie, and the final would be 6-2. The Mets have gone from a half game lead on Friday night, to trailing the Phillies by 2.5 games this evening (Monday). The Brewers were off tonight, and will head into tomorrow's series opener with Pittsburgh a game behind the Mets in the NL Wild Card, and 3.5 games behind the Phillies. I mention this, because I'm still holding on to the idea that the Phillies are going to choke away the NL East to the Mets, and the Brewers will pass them up for the Wild Card. I guess anything can happen, but it's looking more and more each day like the NL Wild Card will be coming down to the Mets and Brewers, with Philly hanging on to the NL East crown. It's baseball. Anything *can* happen.

September 23rd

Do you remember the popular game show *The Joker's Wild*, back in the 70's and early 80's? Neither do I. I mean, I can't give too many specifics about it, as in, who hosted, who aired it, etc. But I do remember, vaguely, the part of the game where the audience would say, JOKER-JOKER-JOKER!!! I remember that being good for the contestant, and my Grandma's face would light up, as she was clearly happy for the person who hit this stroke of luck. But, as Amy Madigan said in *Field of Dreams*, "What does that got to do with baseball?" Nothing really, other than the fact that I screamed JOKER-JOKER-JOKER out loud in my parking lot, shortly after Prince Fielder hit a walk off home run against the Pittsburgh Pirates tonight. Why was I in my parking lot? Have a seat and stay awhile, and I'll tell you.

I was actually at the Brewers game tonight with my daughter, my sister and my niece. The Brewers scored two runs in the 1st, on what we originally thought was a two run inside the park HR by Ryan Braun. But as we continued to follow Braun as he rounded 3rd and headed home, we didn't see that an errant throw by Nate McLouth caused Braun to keep going, as it was ruled a triple and an error. It was McLouth's first error of the year, playing most of the season as Pittsburgh's everyday centerfielder. The Pirates would score three runs in the top of the 2nd to make it 3-2, and that would be it for the scoring for quite some time. In the 4th inning, I took Gracie out to play with the other kids, and we ended up spending close to 3 innings together, as I followed the game on one of the monitors. We ended up back in our seats in time for the 7th inning stretch, and we all sang "Take Me Out to the Ballgame" and "Roll out the Barrel" in unison. In the bottom of the 7th, Mike Cameron hit a two run double to give the Brewers a 4-3 lead, and we went nuts. But the reality was, we were all pretty tired, and Gracie was slowly nodding off. Gina had to get up for school the next morning, and I had to get up at 6:00 am. So we decided to leave after the Cameron double, hoping we would get to the cars in time to catch the ending. But before we could exit Miller Park, the Pirates took the lead right back, as Steve Pearce (I have no idea who he is), hit a two run HR off of Guillermo Mota. When we heard this, Jill and I were comfortable with our decision to leave, as we heard the stadium drowning in boos. Once I got to my car, it was confirmed that Philadelphia lost their game vs. Atlanta, 3-2. JOKER! Shortly after that, Bob Uecker gave the final from Shea Stadium. 6-2 Mets! JOKER!! Brewers fans are actually rooting for the Cubs in this series, but not I. Look, I'm not going to root for the Cubs over the Mets. Are you crazy? I root for my teams to win every game, and what ever happens happens. If Philadelphia continues to lose games, Mets fans and Brewers fans the world over will both be happy. Jason Kendall would tie the game with an RBI double in the bottom of the 8th, and as I was pulling into my parking lot at home, the Brewers were about to hit in the bottom of the 9th. Cameron and Durham went down quietly, and I decided that I would finish this inning in the car, then if we didn't score, quickly run inside to finish the game. But I wasn't going to miss anything, in case something great happened. Ryan Braun reached on an infield hit, and I sent my customary, "BRIZZLE FOSHIZZLE DIZZLE" text to Jill. Minutes later, Fielder hit the aforementioned walk off homer to end the game, as I threw up my arms in amazement. JOKER!!! I sat in my car for a few minutes after the Uecker call, yelled JOKER-JOKER-JOKER as I turned off the radio, then realized that I walked out on one of the biggest home runs in the last 25 years of Brewers baseball. I've been giving Greg Maternowski a hard time for years about leaving the game on Easter Sunday in 1987. Now I know what it feels like. Greg, you've been exonerated. I know that's a big word, Snoopy. It means you are now free from guilt or blame.

September 24th

Coming into tonight's games, the Mets trailed the Phillies by a game and a half in the NL East, and the Brewers trailed the Mets by a game for the Wild Card. Phil and I are at the game tonight, and I am stunned at the empty seats at Miller Park. There has to be 12,000 empty seats. Are people that jaded about the first part of this month's play, that they'd rather stay at home and watch "The New Adventures of Old Christine" and "Gary

Unmarried" then come out and see the Brewers make a push at the playoffs? All respect to Julia Louis-Dreyfus, but you're gonna stay home for Jay Mohr?

CC Sabathia is going tonight, once again on three days rest. Fellow left hander Paul Maholm opposes him. Sabathia pitched very well, but talk of a no-hitter tonight was grounded in the first inning. He was not scored upon until the 3rd, when right fielder Jason Michaels hit an RBI single to give the Pirates a 1-0 lead. The Brewers batted around in the bottom of the 4th, scoring three runs, and giving Sabathia all that he needed tonight. CC would go on to strike out eleven Pirates through seven innings. Eric Gagne worked a scoreless 8th, and Salomon Torres inherited a 4-1 lead in the 9th. Torres did give up a solo HR to Adam LaRoche to make it 4-2, but there would be no more damage, as the Brewers took game two against Pittsburgh.

The Braves hammered the Phillies tonight, 10-4, meaning that the Brewers are now within 1.5 games of the Phillies. A win by the Mets tonight would pull them within a half a game of Philadelphia, but a loss would drop the Mets to a dead heat with the Brewers for the NL Wild Card. With the Mets and Cubs tied at 1-1 in the bottom of the 3rd, Carlos Delgado hit a grand slam off Carlos Zambrano to make it 5-1 Mets. Of course, the fans at Miller Park, who have taken to cheering for the Cubs for the series against New York, did not like the update posted on the scoreboard. Out of respect to the fans sitting in my section, I was limited to simply nodding my head in approval. Speaking of my head, I was whacked in the head by an enthusiastic kindergarten teacher named Jenny Hartz during tonight's festivities. Of course she didn't mean it, she just got lost in her story telling, and after a full day of coloring and tying shoes, she has earned the right to let loose. I love the hair, Jenny! The "80's" owe you big time for reminding us how fun it was to listen to Adam Ant and watch Knots Landing.

Oliver Perez gave the four run lead right back, as the Cubs scored 4 in the 5th to tie the game at 5-5. The Cubs would score to make it 6-5 in the 7th, and the Mets blew a chance to tie it, or take the lead in the bottom of the 7th, as they had men on 1st and 3rd with nobody out, but failed to plate a run. The Mets were able to tie it in the bottom of the 8th, but once again stranded two runners to end the inning. Just as the Brewers game was ending, Daniel Murphy led off the bottom of the 9th with a triple. Surprisingly, the Cubs decided to pitch to David Wright, and Bob Howry struck him out swinging. After Wright struck out, they decided to walk Delgado and Beltran intentionally, to get to Ryan Church. We followed the game on my cell phone as we scurried towards T.G.I. Friday's to catch it in sweet HD. Church would hit into a fielder's choice, and Ramon Castro struck out on three pitches to end the inning. By the time we reached the restaurant, the Cubs had two outs and nobody on in the top of the 10th. Then, right before Freeway can approach me with his brand of shenanigans, Ryan Theriot singles, steals 2nd, Derrick Lee doubles him home, and Aramis Ramirez homers to give the Cubs a 9-6 lead. The crowd is naturally going crazy in Friday's, but Freeway is incensed. I wonder if he thinks the Cubs are playing the Brewers, because he can't stop yelling NO at the television. Could it be that Freeway is also a Mets fan like I am? If so, Michael, we have to go bowling.

Kerry Wood set the Mets down in order in the bottom of the 10th to end the game, and with four games left in the season, the Mets and Brewers are at a dead heat, both sitting at 87-71.

September 25th

As critical as I've been of Eric Gagne this season, literally from day one of him being a Brewer, I cannot argue with his character. Whenever he has blown a lead, or given up a big home run, he has never hesitated to take blame or admit that he's simply not getting it done on the mound. When asked if the boos bother him, Gagne has said that he acknowledges that the fans in Milwaukee are not booing the performer, rather the performance. Gagne did a great thing for the fans today. The idea came to him last night, after the Brewers beat the Pirates for the second straight night. Noticing the empty seats in the stands, Gagne decided to buy 5,000 tickets to tonight's game vs. Pittsburgh, and distributed them to fans for free, via the team's website. I was instantly moved by this gesture, and decided that I needed to be a part of the happenings tonight.

Yovani Gallardo, who was more or less written off back in May, is getting the start tonight, but it's not known how long he can go. The Pirates are countering with left hander Zach Duke, meaning that Rickie Weeks and Bill Hall will get starts tonight. I have secured a seat at field level, on the 3rd base side, and you better believe that I'll be following the Cubs/Mets game from Shea Stadium, which is being displayed on the monitor right behind the section that I'm in. The most common question I get, on a daily basis, "Who are you rooting for, the Mets or Brewers?", and I say, "And, not or".

Gallardo looked great tonight, going four innings, striking out seven, and only allowing a solo HR to Steve Pearce (again, no idea), and left with the game tied at 1-1. Eric Gagne would enter the game in the 7th, and was greeted to a nice ovation, and was able to complete the 7th without being scored upon, which the crowd also liked. As the Brewers were coming up in the bottom of the 7th, I started to make my way towards the monitor that was showing the Cubs/Mets game, while keeping an eye on the action here at Miller. Entering the 8th, the Cubs were up 6-4, as some guy named Micah Hoffpauir (as I'm triple checking to see if I'm spelling that right), has hit his first two major league home runs tonight to give the Cubs the lead. A couple of unlikely heroes helped the Mets tie the Cubs in the 8th, with Ramon Martinez singling in Carlos Beltran, and Robinson Cancel driving in Ryan Church, who's slide to avoid the tag of Chicago catcher Koyie Hill was something out of a baseball movie. The throw from right fielder Kosuke Fukudome was about five feet up the third base line, and beat Church to the plate, but Church some how avoided the tag, and had to crawl back to the plate after he passed it and tagged it with his right hand to tie the game. All the Brewers fans around me were upset, and it was so damn hard for me not to show my true emotions. I'm here at Miller, rooting for the Brewers to do their part, and I don't have the energy to explain to everyone around me that I have a vested interest in both the Mets and the Brewers. Now is not the time. I decide to stay near the monitor for the rest of the Mets game, as the Pirates and Brewers continue their pitching duel, now entering the top of the 9th, still 1-1. In the bottom of the 9th at Shea, Jose Reyes led off the inning with a single, and was able to steal 2nd after both Daniel Murphy and David Wright were unsuccessful in moving him over. The Cubs decided to walk Carlos Delgado intentionally to set up a force. There are around 30 Brewers fans watching the end of this game in anticipation of the Brewers possibly taking a full game lead in the Wild Card hunt tonight. But Carlos Beltran hits a frozen rope towards first, and Hoffpauir gets a glove on it, but the ball trickles down the right field line, as Reyes scores to give the Mets a very dramatic, come from behind 7-6 win. All the fans around me are disappointed in the finish, and I let my emotions get the best of me, and let out a "YES!" at the top of my lungs, but immediately put my head down and jogged back to my seat to avoid getting raped. As I got back, the Brewers were batting in the bottom of the 9th, but would go down 1-2-3, as the game would enter extra innings.

In the Pirates half of the 10th, Todd Coffey would come in to the game, and get Jack Wilson to ground to 3rd to start the inning. One down. Jason Michaels then reached on an infield single. On a hit and run, Freddy Sanchez grounded out to J.J. Hardy, with Michaels advancing to 2nd. Sveum would then go to his lefty, Mitch Stetter, to face Nate McLouth. McLouth would work the count in his favor, and get it to 3-1, but after swinging and missing on a huge cut to push the count to 3-2, he would go down looking to end the inning. A huge pop from the Miller Park faithful filled the air, as the Brewers entered the bottom of the 10th.

The Pirates called upon rookie right hander Jesse Chavez to pitch in the 10th. Rickie Weeks led off the inning by singling to right field. After a pickoff attempt, Chavez delivered home, with Jason Kendall laying down a great bunt to move Weeks over to 2nd, representing the winning run. It's good to see some of the "small ball" that Dale Sveum vowed to bring to this team in its playoff run. Ray Durham would pinch hit for Stetter, but was walked intentionally to set up the double play. Mike Cameron, who was 1-4 with two strikeouts thus far, would strike out swinging for the 2nd out of the inning. Sveum would go to his bench again, calling on Craig Counsell to hit for Bill Hall. Hall has accounted for the only run thus far for the Brewers, with an RBI double in the 3rd, but Sveum likes the matchup, and Counsell is a much better contact hitter than Hall. Counsell would draw a walk on five pitches, to set up Ryan Braun with the bases loaded, and two out. If you're a Brewers fan, you don't need to be reminded what happened next, but I'll tell ya...just to tell ya. Braun took a 2-2 pitch way out of Miller Park, almost clearing Bernie Brewer's slide in left field, for a walk off grand slam. It was Braun's first career grand slam, the first grand slam hit by Milwaukee this season, and maybe the greatest moment I've ever seen in person. With all due respect to Robin Yount's 3000th hit, I don't remember total strangers shaking me from behind, and high fiving an entire section on the way out. Can you imagine how much of an asshole I would have felt like had I left *this* game early, like we did on Tuesday? That was the first thing I was asked on Friday morning. Did you stay? I did, and I'll never forget it. It's what you dream of as a fan, and Braun could not have picked a bigger spot. With three games left, the Brewers season is very much alive! Bring on the Cubs!!!

September 26th

The Mets fan in me is very disappointed tonight, as the Phillies defeated the Nationals 8-4, after scoring seven times in the first two innings, and the Mets looked flat in losing to the Marlins, 6-1. As a result, the Mets find themselves two games back of Philadelphia with two to play.

The Brewers fan in me is proud of the way the Brewers have bounced back, after dropping 4 of 6 on the road to kick off the Sveum era, completing the sweep of the Pirates last night, and taking game one from the Cubs tonight, 5-1. Despite allowing nine Cubs to reach base in 5 innings pitched, Jeff Suppan only allowed one of them to score, when Jim Edmonds hit a solo homer in the top of the 2nd. Jason Kendall's two run double in the bottom half of the 2nd would tie the game. After Russell Branyan pinch hit for Suppan in the 5th, with the game still tied 1-1, Seth

McClung took over, and provided his best performance as a Brewer, when the team needed it the most. Corey Hart's 91st RBI of the season gave the Brewers the lead in the 6th, and Rickie Weeks' three run HR in the 7th gave the sold out crowd much to scream about. McClung would earn the victory by pitching the last four innings, only allowing one hit, and striking out six Cubs. The win puts the Brewers one game ahead of the Mets, with two games left, for the NL Wild Card. A Mets loss or Brewers win tomorrow assures that the Brewers will at least finished tied for the NL Wild Card lead.

I've had all year to think about how I'd feel if it came down to these two loves of mine, knowing that only one of them can move on. The feelings I'm having tonight are mixed. While I am extremely excited about the possibility of seeing the Brewers clinch tomorrow (ticket courtesy of my good friend, Mike Moser), I will be heartbroken if the Mets come up short for the 3rd straight year. It has been documented that I cried long and hard when Adam Wainwright struck out Carlos Beltran looking in 2006, and last year, when the Mets blew a seven game lead with seventeen to play, and still had a chance on the last day of the season, only to get crushed by Florida, I was numb for the rest of the day. This was the 3rd straight year that I predicted the Mets would win the World Series (and no, I don't make that prediction every year), and if they fall short of even making the playoffs again, I'll be hurt, especially in this last year at Shea Stadium. The answers to the questions I'm getting via text tonight still haven't changed. Who are you rooting for? I want the Mets to beat the Marlins tomorrow, and I want the Brewers to beat the Cubs.

September 27th

There were so many scenarios buzzing around in my head as I made my way to Miller Park for this afternoon's game. The Mets game with Florida was scheduled for noon, which meant, if the Mets were to fall to Florida, the Brewers would be playing for the right to go to the National League playoffs for the first time in 26 years. That would be a thrill of a lifetime, to see the Crew clinch, at home, and doing it against the Cubs would certainly add to the excitement. But, with the Mets still mathematically in the NL East race, I'm still holding on to any hope of the Mets winning their next two, Philadelphia losing their next two, the Brewers winning their next two, and the Mets and Phillies playing on Monday for the NL East crown. If Philadelphia wins either today or Sunday, the NL Wild Card will come down to the Mets or Brewers. There is still a chance that the Mets and Brewers face each other on Monday night for the play-in game.

Shortly before the first pitch at Miller Park, the capacity crowd in attendance, save one fan (me), was disappointed to see that the Mets had beaten the Marlins 2-0. Goddamn, I'm proud of them for coming through today. Considering the importance of this particular game, Johan Santana's performance today may go down as one of the most memorable in team history. Santana threw a three hitter, striking out nine batters, and only allowed one base runner to reach 3rd base all game. Unfortunately for the Mets, the Phillies were also winners today, as Philadelphia clinches their second consecutive NL East title.

With a win today, the Brewers can still clinch a tie for the Wild Card, basically guaranteeing that they will play beyond Sunday, whether it is at Shea Stadium on Monday night, or Citizens Bank Park on Wednesday afternoon. Ben Sheets took the ball today, coming off the 2 inning stint at Wrigley Field on September 17th, and he was opposed by Ted Lilly, who took a no-hitter into the 7th inning the last time he pitched at Miller Park...against the Astros. I'm still upset about that, as are the Houston Astros. Unfortunately, we very well may have witnessed the last pitch that Ben Sheets ever throws in a Milwaukee Brewers uniform, as he was pulled after 2 1/3 very ineffective innings, with clearly nothing on his fastball. He recorded seven outs, gave up five hits, and walked two, as he left down 4-0. And this was against a Cubs lineup that featured such names as Micah Hoffpauir, Daryle Ward, Henry Blanco, and Casey McGehee. There was no Derrick Lee, Aramis Ramirez, Geovany Soto or Mark DeRosa to contend with.

The bullpen for the Brewers looked great for the next 5 2/3 innings, as Mark DiFelice, Dave Bush and Manny Parra would hold the Cubs scoreless while only allowing two base runners. But that damn Ted Lilly was making us look bad all day, and carried yet another no-hitter into the 7th inning at Miller Park. If it wasn't for J.J. Hardy reaching on an error in the 2nd inning, he would have been perfect through 6 1/3. Ryan Braun broke up the no-hitter with a double, and Hardy would break up the shutout with an RBI single moments later. The Brewers could only put up one in the 7th, to make it 4-1, but for the first time all day, the crowd was really getting into the game.

The Cubs called upon Jason Marquis to pitch the 8th, and all hell broke loose. The inning started quietly enough, as Jason Kendall would ground out to third. Russell Branyan was asked to pinch hit for Manny Parra, and worked Marquis for a one out walk. Moser and I were surprised that Sveum didn't immediately send in for a pinch runner, but after Mike Cameron took strike one looking, Alcides Escobar came in to relieve Branyan. After Branyan walked, I couldn't help but think of Lee Mazzilli in Game Six, looking into the Mets dugout for a pinch runner after he reached on a single, pinch hitting for Jesse Orosco. Mike Cameron would single to center on the very next pitch as the tying run came up, in the form of Craig Counsell, pinch hitting for Bill Hall. Counsell came up huge, singling to right field to score Escobar and advance Cameron to 3rd. With the score now 4-2, and runners on the corners for Braun, the sell out crowd rose to their feet in unison, anticipating more of the magic they've seen since returning to Milwaukee on Tuesday. But Braun was hit by the first pitch he saw from Jason Marquis, which prompted Lou Piniella to call on Neal Cotts to face Prince Fielder with the bases loaded. You would figure that with Marquis walking Branyan and plunking Braun that Fielder would look at a pitch or two before offering, but Fielder swung at Cotts' first delivery, hitting a high pop-up to shallow left field. If I hate anything more than pop-ups, it's swinging at the 1st pitch, but Ronny Cedeno dropped the ball, allowing Cameron to score and everyone else to advance one base. It's now 4-3 Cubs, the bases are still loaded with one out, and J.J. Hardy is about to have the most important at-bat of his young career. Moser and I have lost our voices by now, everyone

320

is still standing and going bonkers. It's 1982, sans the moustaches and mullets.

After running the count to 1-1, Hardy hit a bouncer to 3rd basemen Casey McGehee, who threw to Henry Blanco at home to get Counsell, but Hardy would reach, as the bases remained loaded for Corey Hart. It's no secret that Hart has had a miserable September, but all of that would be forgotten if he came up huge here. He bounced to short to end the inning. The miserable September continues.

Salomon Torres would come on to pitch in the top of the 9th, in an effort to hold the Cubs scoreless, and give the Brewers a chance to win in the bottom of the 9th. Torres was awful, giving up a single to Ryan Theriot, a two run homer to Kosuke Fukudome, and a single to Ronny Cedeno before being lifted for Mitch Stetter. Torres simply has run out of gas, in my opinion. If the Brewers end up making the post season, I may end up on the post season roster to pitch a few innings, the way things are looking for our staff. The Cubs would end up scoring one more time, to make it 7-3, which totally deflated the team and the crowd. The Brewers went down quietly in the 9th against Kerry Wood, and wouldn't you know it, the Mets and Brewers are now tied atop the NL Wild Card standings, with one day of baseball left in the regular season.

Naturally, I'm disappointed that the Brewers could not pull out a win today. Mike and I are pretty quiet walking back to our cars, and there is only one scenario that I can think of that would be "storybook", at least for me. And that is, the Mets winning their last schedule game at Shea tomorrow afternoon, and the Brewers beating the Cubs to take the series, and force a one game playoff to determine the National League Wild Card. If that happens, I will be happy either way, knowing that both of my teams took care of business on the last day of the season. If both teams lose, they would still play each other Monday, but it wouldn't feel the same, knowing that each team would "back in" to the playoffs. If one team wins, and the other loses, I will be torn. I can't wait to see what happens.

September 28th

    Well, well, well. After the disappointing end to the 2007 season, and the long off season leading up to the 2008 season, it took every bit of this season's regular season schedule to show me truly where my heart lies. Unfortunately, there will not be a "Game 163" between the Mets and Brewers tomorrow night to determine the National League Wild Card. Any Mets or Brewers fans reading this now certainly will remember September 28th for a long, long time to come. Let me walk you through the roller coaster of emotions I felt today....

    I woke up this morning knowing a couple of things. First, the Mets would be hosting the Marlins this afternoon in the last scheduled game at Shea Stadium. I can't tell you how many great memories I have of watching games that were played there. There are far too many to mention here, for sure. Secondly, the Brewers are sending CC Sabathia to the mound in an attempt to assure the Brewers season is extended, if not for just one more day. I did not get much sleep last night.

    My sister, Jill, joined me for the games today. The Mets game was on SNY, and the Brewers were on FSN. Of course, Jill is pouring her heart out for the Brewers to win today, and is very quietly, out of respect to me, rooting for the Marlins to beat the Mets. While she is being very respectful, I can see her pumping her fist whenever a Met is retired (which is what she should do as a Brewers fan). The Mets and Marlins entered the 6th inning in a scoreless tie. The Marlins were able to get to Oliver Perez in the top of the 6th, scoring two runs and Joe Smith was able to put out the fire without any further damage. In the bottom of the 6th, Robinson Cancel was asked to pinch hit for Smith, and drew a walk. Jose Reyes was not able to capitalize, but Carlos Beltran hit a two run homer to tie the game. I jumped out of my seat, and it just felt like momentum would swing in the Mets favor. I barely sat the rest of the way. Within the next 40 minutes or so, I went through more ups and downs than most elevators do on any given day. In the top of the 8th inning at Shea, Scott Schoeneweis entered the game, and gave up a home run to pinch hitter Wes Helms to give the Marlins a 3-2 lead. My heart froze. Wes

Helms? Before I can even process what had just happened, the Mets called upon Luis Ayala to face Dan Uggla, and he homers as well, to make it 4-2. I am completely numb. I cannot believe this is happening again. Meanwhile, not ten minutes later, Ryan Braun hit a two run homer to give the Brewers a 3-1 lead over the Cubs in the bottom of the 8th inning. We had the game on the radio, as well as on TV, and I heard Bob Uecker's call just as the pitch was being delivered on TV, and I jumped up and screamed before we saw it unfold on color television. As the ball was deposited into the left field bleachers, Jill and I embraced, and it was an unbelievable moment, a moment that I will never forget, and in the back of my mind, all I can think about is that the Mets have six outs left to catch up to the Marlins. They did not score in the bottom of the 8th, and as the Mets and Marlins headed to the 9th, CC Sabathia took the hill in the top of the 9th for the Brewers, three outs away from giving the Brewers at least a share of the NL Wild Card.

Alfonso Soriano lined out to Ryan Braun in left field for out number one. Everyone in Miller Park is standing at this point, as are Jill and I. Ryan Theriot singles to center filed, bringing the tying run to the plate in the person of Derrick Lee. The tension is crazy. I'm trying my hardest not to think about the Mets, understanding clearly that it's been 26 years since the Brewers have made the post season, and that if I have to wait another 26 years, I will be 59 years old when it happens again. And as Lee bounced to Ray Durham, I can feel the hair on my arms stand straight up as J.J. Hardy took the toss from Durham and threw to Prince Fielder to complete the 4-6-3 double play to end the game and possibly clinch a playoff berth. Tears trickled down our faces as we saw Sabathia's emotional reaction to what had just happened. It was everything that I dreamed about. I felt like a kid on Christmas morning...but more like the kid who is wondering if there is possibly one more gift hidden behind the couch, just for me. And as the Brewers, who stayed on the field to watch the end of the Mets game on the centerfield scoreboard, along with 45,000 fans, witnessed Ryan Church line out to center field to end the game, it was then that I realized that there was no gift behind the couch for me this year. I only took a minute or so to reflect on the sudden end to the Mets season, and the end of an era at Shea

Stadium, before I realized that the Brewers are in the playoffs, and I better enjoy this.

I think the thing that I learned about myself today is that I really am a huge Mets fan. On the day the Brewers wrap up their first playoff berth in 26 years, it's bittersweet for me. About a month ago, I was asked by a friend which team I am deep down hoping makes the playoffs, and at first I said I didn't want to say, and that he'd find out next spring when the book comes out, but then thought for a moment, and explained that the Mets have the resources to be competitive every year, and they've been to the playoffs 5 times since I've been following them, and although this is the last year at Shea, it really would be neat to see this particular Brewers team win it all. That's all I said, but even as I said it, I'm not sure I was being completely honest with myself. It was a convenient answer to give to a Brewers fan, but as I sit hear tonight, as the Brewers prepare to face the Phillies next week, I can't help but wonder how the Mets would have fared against the Cubs in a short series. The truth of it is, after so many losing seasons that I've witnessed as a Brewers fan, I've realized that I don't need them to win for me to enjoy watching their games. Whether they are 54-108 or 90-72, my time spent at Miller Park is very much enjoyed. I go for the dogs. I go for the fresh air. I go with family, and I go with friends. Win or lose, I love going to Brewers games, and I want this team to do well. I love the Brewers, but I am a Mets fan. Witnessing the Mets win a World Series in 1986 got me hooked, and I want that again. Today isn't about me. Today's win is for Jill Buchholz, the Hohlweck family, Mike Moser, Jesus Maldonado-Reyes and his father, Michael "Freeway" McCarter, Mark "The Doorman" Simons, Audrey Kuenn, Tom Wopat and everybody else who loves this team with all their heart.

Afterword

It took the Brewers 26 years to return to the playoffs, and ironically, I didn't see a single pitch of their series with Philadelphia. Game one was a day game on a Wednesday, and we listened to it at work, but the game ended just before 5:00. Cole Hamels was dominant, and the Brewers were beaten 3-1. Game two started at 5:00 on Thursday the 2nd, which was my birthday. I had been planning for months to surprise my niece by taking her and Amber to Chicago for the Weezer concert, so we listened to the game in the car on the way down, and was disappointed to hear Shane Victorino hit a grand slam off CC Sabathia in the 2nd inning, as the Phillies would take game two, 5-2. Game three was in Milwaukee on Saturday night, but the games were exclusively shown on TBS, so we listened to the game on the radio, as the Brewers won their first playoff game since Game Five of the 1982 World Series, 4-1. Salomon Torres stranded the bases loaded with nobody out to slam the door in the 9th. Game four was scheduled for noon on Sunday, opposite the Packers game against Atlanta. Again, because of the game airing on TBS, we watched the Packers, and listened to the Brewers. The game was never close, as Jeff Suppan gave up 5 runs over 3 innings, and the Phillies beat the Brewers, 6-2 to advance to the NLCS. If there is any positive that came out of this year's playoffs, it's that the Dodgers swept the Cubs, and Chicago was the only team in this year's playoffs not to win a game. They were also swept last year in the first round. I'm sorry, Schewe. I'm confident they will make a run in 2108.

The Phillies continued their run by beating the Dodgers in the NLCS to advance to the World Series, and their opponent was the Tampa Bay Rays. The Rays beat the Chicago White Sox and Boston Red Sox en route to the World Series. The Phillies won the series in five games, in what I thought was a really well played series, interrupted by the first ever suspended game in World Series history. Game five started on Monday night, and was suspended with the score tied 2-2 in the 6th, and was completed on Wednesday night. The Phillies won 4-3. It was good to see Geoff Jenkins win a championship, after his Fred Jones like departure of Milwaukee last year.

The Mets extended Jerry Manuel for two years shortly after the season ended. They enter Citi Field next year with most of the team in tact from this year, probably looking for a corner outfielder and some starting pitching. They will be set at closer, as they inked Francisco Rodriguez to a three year contract. This is a huge get for the Mets, as the bullpen was clearly the weakness in 2008

The Brewers did not retain the services of Dale Sveum as manager, as they hired Ken Macha for the job he turned down in 2002, before the Brewers eventually hired Ned Yost. Bob Brenly and Willie Randolph were also interviewed, as Randolph has now been shunned three times by the Brewers since 2000. The Brewers eventually hired Randolph as the bench coach, and Dale Sveum took the job as Brewers hitting coach. I think it's a little strange that three of the men that interviewed for the manager's job will be on the same staff in 2009. Mike Maddux left the Brewers to take the job as pitching coach for the Texas Rangers, and Bill Castro was promoted from bullpen coach to pitching coach.

CC Sabathia did what most of us would do if we were in his boots. He signed the richest deal that a pitcher has ever received. 7 years, $161 million, to pitch with...the Yankees. Realistically, the Brewers never had a chance to sign him, unless Sabathia would be willing to take 70 cents on the dollar to stay. But as recent history as indicated, this signing does not guarantee anything for the Yankees. They will have the largest payroll, by far, in baseball, but they haven't won a championship since 2000. The Brewers were considered contenders coming into 2008 without Sabathia, and there is no reason why they can't compete again in 2009.

As for myself, 2008 was a very rewarding year, but at the same time, a very tough year. Heather and I separated right after

I started the process of writing this book, and while we both have moved on, divorce is never easy, especially with children involved. One thing we will always have in common is our love for our beautiful daughter, Gracie. Mommy and Daddy love you so much, sweetie.

Although I was not able to witness the Mets and Brewers play each other in the N.L.C.S., I *was* able to accomplish something that means a lot more to me. On October 11th, I finally got to have that catch with my dad.

Joey Buchholz is an employee of UW Credit Union in Milwaukee, Wisconsin. He lives with his girlfriend, Amber Kavaleris in Greenfield, Wisconsin, and when he's not clutching a baseball in his hand during a Mets or Brewers game, he is keeping up with his daughter, Gracie, and his niece, Gina.

If you love two teams like I do, I'd love to hear your stories! E-mail me at joeybuchholz.twoloves@gmail.com, and let's talk some baseball. Thank you for reading *Two Loves: The Story of a Baseball Polygamist.*